The World Heroin Market

THE WORLD HEROIN MARKET

Can Supply Be Cut?

Letizia Paoli
Victoria A. Greenfield
Peter Reuter

UNIVERSITY PRESS
2009

OXFORD
UNIVERSITY PRESS

Oxford University Press, Inc., publishes works that further
Oxford University's objective of excellence
in research, scholarship, and education.

Oxford New York
Auckland Cape Town Dar es Salaam Hong Kong Karachi
Kuala Lumpur Madrid Melbourne Mexico City Nairobi
New Delhi Shanghai Taipei Toronto

With offices in
Argentina Austria Brazil Chile Czech Republic France Greece
Guatemala Hungary Italy Japan Poland Portugal Singapore
South Korea Switzerland Thailand Turkey Ukraine Vietnam

Published by Oxford University Press, Inc.
198 Madison Avenue, New York, New York 10016

www.oup.com

Oxford is a registered trademark of Oxford University Press

Library of Congress Cataloging-in-Publication Data
Paoli, Letizia.
The world heroin market : can supply be cut? / Letizia Paoli,
Victoria Greenfield, Peter Reuter.
    p.   cm.
Includes bibliographical references and index.
ISBN 978-0-19-532299-6
1. Heroin abuse.   2. Drug abuse.   3. Drug traffic.   4. Drug control.
I. Greenfield, Victoria A., 1964–   II. Reuter, Peter, 1944–   III. Title.
HV5822.H4P36 2009
363.45—dc22   2008031121

9 8 7 6 5 4 3 2 1
Printed in the United States of America
on acid-free paper

For our children, four of whom came to us in the course of this project and one of whom went forth: for Maddalena, Isabella, and Leo; for Leila; and for Timothy, trying to do good in Afghanistan

Acknowledgments

The research project underlying this book received generous financial support from the U.K. Foreign and Commonwealth Office, the Netherlands Ministry of Justice and its Scientific Research and Documentation Centre (usually known under the Dutch acronym of WODC), and the Smith Richardson Foundation in the United States. We gratefully thank them. The Max Planck Institute for Foreign and International Criminal Law in Freiburg, where one of us, Letizia Paoli, was based up until late 2006, provided additional funding. We drew on a related project on drug markets and trafficking in Central Asia that benefited from the support of the RAND Center for Middle East Public Policy and the RAND Center for Russia and Eurasia. Victoria Greenfield and Peter Reuter were affiliated with the RAND Corporation during much of this research.

The work also profited from formal collaborations with international researchers who wrote reports for us on the markets in their respective countries on the basis of a common protocol. These researchers included (by country)

- *China*—Chen Xiaobo, Xie Hua, Yang Jinghong, and Zhou Tie, Institute of Public Security of the Chinese Ministry of Public Security
- *Colombia*—Sergio Uribe Ramirez and Carolina Navarrete Frías
- *India*—Dr. Molly Charles
- *Iran*—Dr. Fariborz Raisdana, University of Social Welfare and Rehabilitation Center; as well as Dr. Mohammad Ashouri and Dr. Mansour Rahmdel, Tehran University
- *Pakistan*—Dr. Ahmad Ali Khan, University of Peshawar

- *Tajikistan*—Vladimir Rakhmonov and Olga Muravljova, Analytical Center of the Tajikistan Drug Control Agency. In Tajikistan, a second research report was written by "Igor Khamonov," an experienced and high-ranking Tajik law enforcement officer, who carried out detailed field observations and interviews with more than 20 of his colleagues specifically for the study and has adopted a pseudonym for fear of retaliation.
- *Thailand*—Dr. Nualnoi Treerat, Nopparit Ananapibut, and Surasak Thamno, Chulalongkorn University
- *Turkey*—Dr. Sevil Atasoy and Dr. Neylan Ziyalar, Istanbul University
- *France*—Dr. Nacer Lalam, Institut des Hautes Etudes de la Sécurité Intérieure

Their collection of primary data greatly improved our understanding of the contemporary opiate market and we are thus very grateful for their support. In addition to the collaborators specifically recruited for this project, Emil Pain (Russian Center for Ethnopolitical Studies, Moscow) collected important data that are reflected in appendix C, which assesses Central Asia's trafficking revenues and its economic dependency on drug trafficking.

In the United States, we were helped by capable research assistance from Dr. Gustav Lindstrom (formerly, RAND Graduate School), who managed much of the development of data for the models in chapter 5, and from Alexa Briscoe (Department of Criminology, University of Maryland), who took on a major bibliographic responsibility at the end of the project. In Freiburg, Dr. Irina Rabkov provided invaluable assistance in managing the project on a daily basis, keeping contacts with our non-European collaborators, organizing three working conferences, and drafting the Tajikistan chapter. Michael Holland also provided competent and efficient support in literature and media search and review. We are grateful to all of them. Paoli would also like to thank the personnel of the Max Planck Institute Administration, who were always very efficient, reliable, and friendly in managing the financial flows of this complex project.

We also received advice, data, and logistic assistance from a project advisory board. This board was chaired by Dr. Hans-Jörg Albrecht (Director, Max Planck Institute for Foreign and International Criminal Law). Other members included (affiliations were at the time of advisory board participation)

- Christoph Berg, Head, GTZ Development-Oriented Drug Control Programme, Deutsche Gesellschaft für Technische Zusammenarbeit
- Christer Brannerud and Stephen Brown, Interpol
- Max-Peter Ratzel, Head, Division Organized and Common Crime, Bundeskriminalamt (Germany's Federal Criminal Police Office)
- Brian Lucas, Unit A4 (Drugs Coordination Unit), Directorate General Justice and Home Affairs, European Commission
- Dr. David Murray and Dr. Terry Zobeck, U.S. Office of National Drug Control Policy

• Dr. Marianne Van Ooyen, Scientific and Research Documentation Centre (WODC), Dutch Ministry of Justice

Collective thanks also go to all those around the world who found the time to answer our questions and discuss the dynamics of local or international opiate markets. Among our interviewees were police officers in several European countries (primarily Germany, Italy, the Netherlands, and the United Kingdom) as well as government officials and foreign liaison officers in India and Turkey. In particular, we thank

- Alexander Engert, Bundeskriminalamt (BKA, i.e., Germany's Federal Criminal Police Office), for his very friendly and committed support in retrieving interesting data and information, and introducing Paoli to other BKA officers
- Guido Beutler, the then-Bunderkriminalamt liaison officer in India, for his invaluable assistance in arranging meetings with Indian and foreign government officials during Paoli's research trip to Delhi
- Dott. Fabio Bernardi, head of the Milan Police Narcotic Squad until 2007, for sharing with Paoli his insightful analysis of drug trafficking patterns through northern Italy and giving her access to valuable police and judicial material
- Dr. Toon van der Heijden, National Police Agency, for providing data on heroin trafficking in the Netherlands
- Jim McColm, Her Majesty's Customs and Excise, for helping us better understand U.K. data on heroin purity and prices, for providing feedback on our modeling approach, and for facilitating meetings with other U.K. officials

The United Nations Office on Drugs and Crime provided indispensable data through the Research and Policy Analysis Section (special thanks to Sandeep Chawla and Thomas Pietschman) and field offices in Central Asia, India, Iran, and the Russian Federation.

We also received insightful comments from a number of other scholars and thank them all for their important contributions. Dr. Virginia Berridge (London School of Hygiene and Tropical Medicine) commented on an earlier version of chapter 2, which reviews the history of international drug control. Dr. Francisco Thoumi (Universidad del Rosario) commented on the Colombia chapter. Dr. Jonathan Caulkins (Carnegie-Mellon University) commented on chapter 4, which assesses the impact of the Taliban's 2000 cutback. David Mansfield shared his perspectives on Afghanistan's opium production. Dr. Kurtis Swope (U.S. Naval Academy) suggested important refinements in our discussion of market dynamics. Dr. Karen Thierfelder (U.S. Naval Academy) clarified enduring principles of international trade. Dr. Keith Crane (RAND Corporation) helped shape our analysis of the price data in chapter 4 and Central Asia's economic dependency in appendix C. Martin Jelsma (Transnational Institute, Amsterdam) shared his perspectives on the ongoing opium cutbacks in Burma and current attempts to reform United Nations drug conventions, and provided insightful comments on chapter 11.

We also thank the editors of *Addiction* and the *Journal of Drug Issues* for allowing us to include modified versions of articles that first appeared in their journals: *Addiction* published "India: The third largest illicit opium producer?" in early 2009 and the *Journal of Drug Issues* published "Tajikistan: The rise of a narco-state" in 2007.

Last, but not least, three anonymous reviewers—who later revealed themselves to be Dr. David T. Courtwright (University of North Florida), Dr. Francisco Thoumi (Universidad del Rosario), and Dr. William A. Byrd (World Bank)—gave precious suggestions for streamlining the final manuscript. Helpful comments in the final stage were also provided by James Cook (Oxford University Press) and Dr. Michael Tonry (University of Minnesota).

The authors are solely responsible for the views in this book.

Contents

PART III POLICY ANALYSIS AND IMPLICATIONS

The World Heroin Market

1

Introduction

Representatives of 13 countries laid the foundation for the international drug control regime 100 years ago in Shanghai, with the adoption of 9 resolutions on the control of opium. Nevertheless, the list of problems uniting the rich and poor still includes the flow of illegal drugs across national borders, causing crime, disease, and social distress throughout much of the world. Heroin, in particular, is a chronic problem, the result of the development of mass markets in the 1960s and '70s, made even more urgent by the emergence of acquired immune deficiency syndrome (AIDS) associated with injecting drug use in countries as varied as Russia, Thailand, and the United States.

During the past 50 years, leaders of many nations have denounced the drug traffic and resolved to suppress it through increasingly prohibitionist means. Many have emphasized the role of international controls and programs as central to that effort. In 1998, at the United Nations General Assembly Special Session (UNGASS, 1998: clause 19), leaders pledged jointly to develop strategies for "eliminating or significantly reducing the illicit cultivation of the coca bush, the cannabis plant and the opium poppy by the year 2008." Since then, world opium production has increased dramatically.[1]

However, this bad news masks the quite complex changes of the past decade. The world's two largest opium-producing countries, Afghanistan and Burma,[2] have experienced major upheavals. In less than 12 months from the start of the new century, the Taliban regime in Afghanistan achieved what most scholars and policy makers had thought to be impossible—namely, it cut Afghanistan's illicit opium production by more than 90% from peak levels, amounting to a 65% reduction in world production. Several years later, with the Taliban ousted, opium production in Afghanistan has returned to, and surpassed, previous record-breaking levels. The Taliban ban was harsh, effective, and short-lived. Over a somewhat longer period, straddling both the 20th and 21st centuries, a few insurgent groups dominating the northeastern part of Burma also took action by imposing similarly harsh and effective bans on opium production. As a result, Burma's production declined by about 80% and has not—yet—recovered.

Although implemented with authoritarian methods and causing great suffering among the local population, these unexpected events have garnered considerable attention in the international counternarcotics community. We recast that attention as a policy question: Can world heroin production and, more generally, opiate supply (including its international distribution) be reduced, and with what consequences?[3] The Taliban ban initially motivated our research, but the question is all the more relevant because the international drug control regime has focused largely on supply reduction since its inception at the start of the 20th century (see McAllister, 2000; chapter 2, this volume). However, an answer to this question requires an understanding of the nature of the world opiate market, which in turn requires a command of basic facts about the market and its operation.

Much of our research has sought to fill the need for basic facts. In effect, we take a step back: To answer the policy-relevant question, we first answer a series of more basic yet challenging questions about the market and its operation. How big is the market? How do market participants, including individuals, organizations, agencies, and entire nations, behave and interact? How does it respond to change? Is there really a singular "world opiate market" or do opiates flow through a series of segmented and largely unrelated production and distribution channels or networks?

Here we piece together a comprehensive portrait of the world opiate market, drawing together information from governmental and non-governmental sources, from conversations with policy makers and law enforcement officers, and from collaborations with researchers in several producing, trafficking, and consuming countries. We analyze current conditions, market trends, and the effects of particular events, including the Taliban ban, to improve our understanding of the nature and dynamics of the market. The ban was short-lived; nevertheless, we can learn from an assessment of how the market responded to the accompanying cutback. Just as the oil shocks of the 1970s provided valuable insight into the workings of the world energy market, so does the cutback provide insight into the workings of the world opiate market.

We do not abandon the well-honed models that social scientists have applied to other markets; rather, we use them as a frame of reference for our analysis. In some instances, the models offer simple and plausible explanations for what we observe in Afghanistan, Burma, India, Colombia, Tajikistan, and elsewhere, reminding us that not everything about this market is novel after all, and, in other instances, they leave us wanting. Comparisons of models and observations on events in producing, trafficking, and consuming nations reveal gaps between what we think we know about markets in general and what we see in this market in particular. To the extent possible, we attempt to fill the gaps, both empirically and theoretically. In doing so, we show the ways in which illegality affects supply and addiction affects demand, separately and jointly determining many of the distinctive features of the contemporary opiate market.

We also consider policy implications. Armed with a deeper understanding of the world opiate market and its operation, we return to the question of supply reduction. In answering this question, we pay close attention to the dependencies of producing and trafficking countries on the market and the potential effects of removing it.

Prior Research

Drug market research has been limited outside western countries and, even in the United States and Europe, it rarely has been carried out systematically.[4] Existing studies have made important contributions to our understanding of the global opiate market, but they do not provide an adequate base for international policy making.

Meyer and Parsinnen (1998), Trocki (1999), and Brook and Wakabayashi (2000), all of whom take a historical perspective, are among the few recent authors of comparative or systematic analyses of the international opiate industry. Meyer and Parsinnen (1998) produce a first history of the international drug trade. Anticipating one of our key findings, they show that illegal production and trafficking have tended to concentrate in weak states or regions characterized by warlordism. Trocki (1999) focuses primarily on the role of opium in trade prior to international regulation. Brook and Wakabayashi (2000) present a series of essays describing the effects of opium production, trafficking, and consumption on China, but tell an international story because of Britain and Japan's involvement.

Alfred McCoy's (1991) much-cited work provides a great deal of information and insight on heroin trafficking in Southeast Asia, but only about the pre-Afghanistan-dominated industry, even in the 2003 edition. He points to the recurring role of the Central Intelligence Agency (CIA) and other local government agencies in nurturing and protecting some of the largest opiate-trafficking enterprises in both Burma and Afghanistan. With *Les territoires de l'opium,* published in 2002, Pierre-Arnaud Chouvy (2002a) offers the first systematic comparison of conflicts and trades in the "Golden Triangle" and the "Golden Crescent,"[5] the two main opium-producing areas that are, today, centered around Afghanistan and Burma. His perspective, though, is that of a geographer, with less attention to the economics of the industry and few, if any, policy implications.

There are a small number of political studies of contemporary international drug markets and policies. For example, Paul Stares' *Global Habit*, published in 1996, provides a relatively brief survey of opiate and other drug consumption, production, and policy around the world. Stares (1996) views existing supply control policies pessimistically and argues that technological forces and the rapid growth of international trade in general, including freer borders, will inevitably lead to expansion of drug markets.

The United Nations Development Research Institute for Social Development also sponsored nine country studies in the mid 1990s and Tullis (1995) compares the main findings. Not all of the country studies were published and, apart from the study of Colombia by Thoumi (1995), the others are rarely referenced.[6]

Francisco Thoumi (2003) provides a comparative analysis of Latin American cocaine-producing countries that includes a brief discussion of heroin production in Colombia. Thoumi develops a theoretical model to account for the fact that so few nations produce illegal cocaine or heroin. He emphasizes the competitive advantage in illicit drug trafficking and production generated by high levels of corruption, low government legitimacy, high inequalities in income, and weak institutions. Although the primarily conceptual model has not been used for formal quantitative work, Thoumi (2003) is the first to point to the concentrated nature of illicit drug production among nations and to identify systematically the factors that might drive it.

Since 1994, the United Nations Drug Control Programme (UNDCP, now part of the United Nations Office on Drugs and Crime [UNODC]) has been collecting data on poppy cultivation in Afghanistan, including data on farm-gate prices and acreage, and has been publishing it in in-depth country reports. It has maintained this effort through periods of extraordinary political unrest—no mean achievement. Since 2002, the UNODC has also been collecting similar data from Burma, which has a growing region that is not under central government control. These data from Afghanistan and Burma are essential to the study of the global opiate trade.

The same organization has also published a number of studies of the Afghan trade, including several written by David Mansfield, a consultant working initially for the UNDCP and more recently for other international agencies. Since the mid 1990s, Mansfield has collected data on the characteristics of opium farmers and the determinants of planting decisions. For example, Mansfield (2002, 2006) reports on the uneven distribution of the returns from the opium trade and the implications of rural indebtedness. In 2003, the UNODC published a major report on the economic consequences of the opium trade for Afghanistan (UNODC, 2003c), providing a first systematic estimate of Afghanistan's earnings from production and trafficking, and demonstrating the nation's economic dependence on the drug trade.

The World Bank has also funded studies of the economic impact of the opiate trade on Afghanistan, notably by Ward and Byrd (2004). In 2006, the UNODC and the World Bank collaborated on a still more ambitious study of the many dimensions of the connection between the opiate industry and Afghanistan's development (Buddenberg and Byrd, 2006). The study includes new data and analyses, and the first formal model of the link between Afghanistan's macroeconomic performance and the drug trade.

The UNODC also publishes a now-annual review of global illicit drug markets, the *World Drug Report*, which assembles data on production, seizures, and consumption from national reports, UN-sponsored projects, and other sources. The compendiums are mostly descriptive, but they also include analytically oriented essays and methodological investigations. For example, the 2005 *World Drug Report* (UNODC, 2005d) features both a proposal for an international illicit drug index and the results of a model of global and regional drug consumption, expenditures, and income.

In summary, a range of historians, political scientists, economists, and international agencies—mostly UN agencies—have made important contributions to our understanding of the global opiate market. However, much remains to be done in systematically gathering, analyzing, and drawing policy-relevant conclusions from evidence across countries.

Data Collection and Model Development

Not surprisingly, shortcomings in available data on production, trafficking, and especially consumption have posed some of the greatest challenges to our research.[7] Some of the data are inherently weak, such as those on the prevalence of opiate use, and others simply do not exist, such as measures of the quantity consumed.

Thus, we cast a wider net and asked local researchers in China, Colombia, India, Iran, Pakistan, Tajikistan, Thailand, and Turkey to prepare detailed reports on market conditions, legal institutions, and the extent and effects of enforcement in their countries.[8] It is difficult to gather this information even in democratic nations with relatively open governments and sophisticated data collection systems. It is exceptionally difficult in nations that are closed, have weak data collection systems, or have little tradition of publishing policy-relevant data. Drug-related corruption creates still further obstacles in some countries. Nevertheless, the reports of our research collaborators have provided useful quantitative and qualitative data about important aspects of the world opiate market, and three of them—the reports on Colombia, India, and Tajikistan—provide bases for freestanding chapters in this book.

We conducted a more limited data collection in Europe. We gathered and analyzed many official, gray, and scientific sources, and we visited several drug-related policy-making, law enforcement, and academic institutions in Germany, Italy, the Netherlands, and the United Kingdom to collect data on the European opiate—largely heroin—markets. We gave priority to data on prevalence, addict consumption levels, and prices (all of which are necessary to produce estimates of consumption and expenditures), and to information on international trafficking patterns.

In addition to reviewing and collecting data, we developed empirical and theoretical models of market structure and participation. We use the models to fill some of the aforementioned gaps between what we think we know about markets in general and what we see in this market in particular. To the extent possible, we draw from the data to populate the models, be they in quantitative or qualitative terms.

We refer to our empirical model as a *flow model* of the world opiate market. The model is akin to an accounting framework, covering national and international transactions. We use it to compile and reconcile data on opiate production, seizures, and consumption, and to track opiate flows across countries and regions before, during, and after the Afghan opium cutback. The model imposes consistency on estimates of production, seizures, and consumption; enables quantitative comparisons of the pre- and postcutback periods; and facilitates estimation of the market's contributions to countries' gross domestic product (GDP). The general approach—of opiate flow and GDP estimation—also provides a basis for a detailed look at the economic implications of trafficking in Central Asia.

We refer to our theoretical model as a model of *varying illegality*. It addresses the role of governments in establishing the political, legal, and institutional environment in which growers, refiners, and traffickers operate. It pays special attention to differences in the degree of enforcement across countries and their implications for the configuration of the world opiate market (including the size, organization, and operating methods of illegal enterprises), and for society at large.

Major Findings

We believe that this book shows the importance of a fine-grained and comprehensive analysis of the world opiate market, even if our conclusions and policy prescriptions are not all novel. For example, this book is pessimistic about the long-term prospects for shrinking the global production of illegal opiates—a widely held view. Nonetheless, we think that our work offers a much sounder base for this conclusion than previously available and gives a better understanding of why production is concentrated in so very few countries. Our analysis also shows that lasting national or regional reductions in opiate production are possible even in societies that have become entrenched in cultivation, such as Thailand. These reductions require a long-term perspective, heavily weighing institution building and economic development, and sustained international support. However, squeezing the opiate industry in one location, such as Afghanistan or Burma, is likely to lead ultimately to a shift in production to another. The potential for industry relocation, the so-called *balloon effect,* suggests a need for careful consideration of the effects of policy—including the distribution and balance of effects—on both the location that sheds the industry and that which acquires it.

In addition to the possibility of national or regional reductions in production, this book identifies a small set of other policy opportunities and makes suggestions for leveraging them. In finding evidence of market segmentation, a characteristic that has attracted little attention in the past, our analysis suggests that consuming countries may benefit, at least temporarily, from carefully targeted supply-based interventions—specifically, interventions that target the particular source countries and distribution channels on which they most depend.

Furthermore, this book provides the first comparative analysis of national experiences in trying to control international trafficking. Trafficking tends to gravitate to those countries in close proximity to producing or consuming nations, even more so those with strong demographic or economic ties. We conclude that the most effective means of reducing trafficking locally may be an effective intervention against production or consumption in neighboring countries or regions.

Our research is also the first to analyze systematically the effects of differences in the stringency of the enforcement of global production and trafficking prohibitions on the organization of the market, the behavior of its participants, and society at large. Strict national enforcement of prohibitions on opiate production and trafficking may eventually reduce the drug-related violence, corruption, and instability associated with opiate production and trafficking; however, we also find that strict enforcement cannot occur in isolation, nor can a country expect to make an abrupt shift from laxity to stringency without negative consequences. It is not a question of political will alone, but, as in the case of lasting local reductions in opiate production, largely the result of long-term economic development and political institution building. Moreover, for countries that have become accustomed to little or no enforcement of prohibitions, even a gradual shift toward strict enforcement may entail a worsening of drug-related corruption, violence, and instability in the interim.

This book also provides new descriptive and analytical insights on a number of more specific points. India's involvement in illicit opiate production through large-scale diversion from licit production places the country among the world's largest illicit producers. In less than a decade, Tajikistan has become a key transit country for Afghan opiates and has taken its place among the nations most economically dependent on the drug trade, possibly rivaling Afghanistan. Through analysis of the development of Colombia's heroin industry and use of the international flow model, we find that the United States still likely imports a good deal of heroin from Asia, notwithstanding official claims to the contrary. The examples of Tajikistan, Colombia, and others, such as Russia and Central Asia, also show that changes for the worse can occur with tremendous rapidity and magnitude, rarely matched by changes for the better. Moreover, inventories appear to cushion the effects of market interventions and "shocks," as they did during and after the Taliban-induced opium cutback in 2001.

Lastly, this book provides the first integrated analysis of the development of the world opiate market and international efforts to control it. We are able to connect the development of the market and the control regime to larger sociopolitical, economic, and technological developments, and to single out the influences of major geopolitical events. Examples include World War I, in the case of the ratification of the 1912 Opium Convention, and, in the case of the expansion of the opiate industry in Afghanistan, the overthrow of the Shah of Iran and the Soviet Union's invasion of Afghanistan in 1979. Yet we also show that single individuals or decisions taken by slim majorities occasionally have contributed to major policy turns in the control regime.

Our historical analysis further demonstrates how much both the world opiate market and international and domestic drug control policies have changed since the early 20th century. Recognition of this change—and of the very limited possibilities of successful global reductions in opiate production and supply under the current international control regime—have led us to consider some unorthodox approaches to supply control in our final chapter.

Book Outline

This book proceeds in three parts. The first part sets out basic facts. It reviews the historical development of the world opiate market, including the international policy regime that surrounds it (chapter 2); characterizes the contemporary market in terms of its major producers, traffickers, and consumers (chapter 3); explores the dynamics of the market, as evident in its response to the Afghan opium cutback (chapter 4); and presents a unified model of international opiate flows (chapter 5). Three appendixes relate to this first part. Appendix A provides a brief overview of contemporary legal opium production. Appendix B reviews the difficulties of estimating the average consumption of opiate users and explains how we have developed a default rate for the annual consumption of the typical non-U.S. user. Appendix C applies the general principles of the flow model to an assessment of production, trafficking, and drug-related income in Central Asia.

The second part explores market conditions in Afghanistan, Burma, India, Colombia, and Tajikistan in greater detail, with the help of local researchers in the latter three countries (chapters 6–9). The fourth appendix, D, provides information on five other countries—Albania, Kosovo, Mexico, Pakistan, and Turkey—that are important in our analysis of the market and the effects of illegality.

The third and final part of this book includes a theoretical model of effective illegality that helps to explain the role of government in determining each country's mode of participation (chapter 10). In combination with the earlier chapters, it also suggests opportunities and challenges for policy makers. We conclude with a synthesis of our findings and a discussion of policy implications (chapter 11).

This is undeniably a long and complex book, with a considerable variety of materials and analyses. Thus, we provide readers with a few suggestions on how to approach it. Chapter 2 is a historical review; it provides context for our policy analysis. Chapters 3, 4, and 5 are the analytical heart of the book; they address key characteristics, recent trends, and important events, such as the Taliban ban. The chapters of part II, "Country Studies," may be especially interesting for regional or national scholars, or for drug market experts. Part III is important for all readers: Chapter 10 is a foundational chapter whereas chapter 11 presents our policy analysis.

Part I

The Development, Composition, and Behavior of the World Opiate Market

2

The Past as Prologue

The Development of the World Opiate Market and the Rise of the International Control Regime

Introduction

Opium, derived from the opium poppy, *Papaver somniferum,* has been consumed medicinally, recreationally, and sometimes habitually throughout many centuries. In broad terms, the market has evolved from a set of predominantly regional and legal markets for opium, centered in Asia, to a predominantly global and illegal market for opium and its derivatives—morphine and heroin—still centered in Asia but with a broad geographic spread. The evolutionary path has not been smooth. Indeed, the market has grown, ebbed, reemerged, and transformed itself in response to changing social perspectives on opiate use, technology, economic and political development, and, at least in part, to the development of international and national control regimes.

This chapter explores the period of growth of the opiate market in the 19th century, the decline that occurred during the first half of the 20th century, and the reemergence and transformation that occurred during the latter part of the 20th century. It focuses especially on the development and impact of international and, to a lesser extent, domestic controls, and draws insight whenever possible for contemporary policy makers.

Until the late 19th century, the limited range of opiates that were technologically available were legal almost everywhere and were subject to little or no regulation. A variety of factors led to a change in the perception of opiates and the rise of an international control regime at the beginning of the 20th century, including concerns about the large and growing Chinese opium market and the spread of natural and semisynthetic opium derivatives—particularly morphine and heroin—in the West, but also western developments in medical practice and organization, technological progress, changes in commercial interests, revised political calculations, and pressures from social reform movements and cultural anxieties. Both the changed perception and the new regime, in turn, contributed to the formation of national regulations and prohibitions.

The extent to which the onset of controls, regulations, and prohibitions can be credited with the market's ebb is debatable, but both demand and supply did decline markedly before finding new life in present-day illegal mass markets and widespread distribution networks. If policy played a part in the decline, then it is certainly worth exploring whether it might do so again, notwithstanding the many important differences in market conditions.[1] This exploration is also justified by the international drug control regime's persistent focus on supply reduction (McAllister, 2000) and by the UNODC's recent claims of success in containing the drug problem through a network of international and domestic drug controls (UNODC, 2006:7–8, 31–33). Despite these claims it is, in our view, also worth considering the eventual role of policy in the regrowth and transformation of the market in the latter third of the 20th century.

Production and Consumption, 1800–1909

Opiate production and consumption at the start of this period were largely regional phenomena, concentrated in a handful of Asian countries. In the last two decades of the 19th century, the market for opiates began to expand beyond Asia to include the United States and western Europe, which became the main seat for the production and consumption of the new opiate derivatives—namely, morphine and heroin.

Production

Throughout the 19th and early 20th centuries, India was the principal exporter of opium in Asia. Famously, the British fought two "Opium Wars" with China (1839–1842 and 1856–1858) to open up that nation to opium exports from India and balance its own imports of tea and textiles (Beeching, 1975). India also was the dominant source for Indonesia and other East Asian countries during the 19th century; imports from India were licensed by government monopolies in these various countries. From 1858 to 1947, taxes on opium production and export accounted for about one seventh of the revenue of the British authorities ruling India (Owen, 1934). The colonial administration was heavily involved in the regulation of production, determining the size and location of fields (Trocki, 1999:110). Foreign exports and the growing Chinese market in particular accounted for most of India's production, although a substantial quantity also went to "opium eating" in India itself.

Responding to a budding internal demand, China also became a major opiate producer during the second half of the 19th century. According to Newman (1995), in 1879 (the peak year for China's imports from India), China already produced two thirds of its domestic consumption; by the turn of the 20th century, the share was even larger.

Iran entered the market as a secondary producer around 1890. At this time, it was selling mostly to other countries and, to the extent that China continued to import, was seen as a potentially important competitor for India. In 1904, Iran produced about 560 metric tons of opium, of which 160 metric tons were consumed domestically. The industry was important for Iran's trade; even in 1889, opium was estimated to be the largest source of export revenues for Iran (Hansen, 2001). Nevertheless, total production (<1,000 tons) was small relative to the estimated Chinese market, some tens of thousands of tons, or even relative to India's exports to China, which amounted to thousands of tons until 1910 (Newman, 1995:770).

Turkey was the principal supplier to the European market during the 19th century. Even Britain, despite having India as its colony, imported almost exclusively from Turkey (Berridge, 1999:3–10). According to the data provided to the International Opium Commission, which met in Shanghai in 1909, Turkey produced 477 tons of opium in 1906—roughly the same amount as Iran (McCoy, 1991:495). Other minor producers included French Indochina,[2] Siam (today's Thailand), and Korea (Jennings, 1997:32).

In Britain, opium was sold by wholesale pharmacists in a wide variety of pills and medicines. Before the advent of the Pharmacy Act in 1868, opium preparations could be bought freely in pharmacies, street markets, pubs, and local shops. In the 1850s, between 16,000 and 26,000 people were engaged in selling them (Berridge, 1999:21–37).

Two of opium's most important derivative products—morphine and heroin—first came to marketplace during the 19th century. The German pharmacist Friedrich Wilhelm Adam Sertürner isolated morphine in 1803. Commercial production began when Heinrich Emanuel Merck, founder of the pharmaceutical dynasty, undertook it in 1827 (de Ridder, 2000:23–24). However, production and use grew substantially throughout the western world only after the development (in 1853) and spread of the hypodermic needle—a relatively effective mode of delivering doses of morphine.[3]

As morphine consumption spread and its addictive consequences became better known, pharmaceutical companies struggled to synthesize opiates with the same analgesic effects as morphine but none of its addictive ones. Diacetylmorphine was first synthesized in 1874. Under the trademark of "heroin," this was produced in large quantities and marketed by Bayer & Co from 1898 onward (de Ridder, 2000:66; more generally, see 33–66).[4] Heroin was an immediate commercial success. Between 1902 and 1913, Bayer sold between 700 kilograms and 1 metric ton of pure heroin yearly. More than half was exported to the United States. Russia, Britain, and Germany itself accounted for 5% to 7% each. In 1902, heroin sales constituted about 5% of Bayer's pharmaceutical turnover and heroin ranked eighth amongst the firm's drugs in terms of value (de Ridder, 2000:73–74). Bayer was not alone in producing and selling heroin. As the synthesis of diacetylmorphine was not patented, many other companies in Germany and other countries sold drugs containing it. Thirteen diacetylmorphine-based products were available in Germany and at least 18 others were available internationally (de Ridder, 2000:75–77).

Consumption

China dominated 19th-century consumption both in terms of the number of users and the amount consumed. Chinese opium smoking began as an off-shoot of tobacco smoking, introduced during the early 17th century. Later, about 1760, the Chinese discovered how to prepare opium so that they could smoke it without tobacco. Smoking was initially a pastime of the wealthy. By the 1830s, it began to spread among the middle and lower classes and, by the late 19th century, among the peasantry itself (Courtwright, 2001b:31). From the Qing dynasty's first opium suppression edict in 1729 up until the end of the Second Opium War in 1858, opium trade was formally illegal; however, prohibition, poorly enforced, did not prevent its rapid spread (Zhou, 1999:12–18; see also Bello, 2005).

Newman (1995) estimates that total opium consumption in China in 1879 amounted to about 25,000 tons.[5] To give a sense of the magnitude, the 25,000-ton figure is more than twice the figure for early 21st-century global consumption of opiates, including both legal (for pharmaceuticals) and illegal, for a population barely 5% as large.[6] By 1906, according to the same source, total consumption in China had almost doubled, reaching the extraordinary figure of more than 48,000 tons.

Opium filled many roles in China. It served as a medical product, a recreational item, an addiction soother, a badge of social distinction, and a symbol of elite culture (Dikötter, Laamann, and Zhou, 2004:46; see also Zheng, 2005). A remarkably high percentage of China's population consumed opium, but only infrequently. For example, Newman (1995:786–788) comes to the conclusion that, as of 1906, about 60% of the adult men in China and 40% of adult women smoked approximately 15 grams of opium a year for festive purposes. Even the number of "light users" (smoking about 1.5 grams every 3 days) was about 37.8 million (about 20% of adult men and 8% of adult women). Assuming that dependence began somewhere in the lowest category of daily use, Newman (1995) concludes that about 16 million Chinese (6% of the adult population) were drug dependent, although he stresses that addiction from recreational smoking would have been substantially less.[7]

Newman (1995) and a whole generation of new historians believe that most users, including many regular users, were still able to lead normal lives and suffered no negative consequences from their opium use. As Dikötter et al. (2004:3) put it, "in most cases habitual opium use did not have significant harmful effects on either health or longevity: moderate smoking could even be beneficial, since it was a remarkable panacea in the fight against a wide range of ailments before the advent of modern medications" (see also Zhen, 2005).[8]

China was not the only large Asian nation with a substantial opium-using population in the 19th and early 20th centuries. Indochina, India (then including modern-day Pakistan and Bangladesh and, from 1824 onward, increasingly larger portions of Burma), Indonesia, Iran, Malaya, the Philippines, and Thailand also had substantial numbers of users. In most of these countries, opium was largely ingested, drunk, or, more rarely, smoked in moderate amounts for recreational or medical reasons without any loss of control. The Royal Commission on Opium set up by the British government in 1892, for example, concluded that opium use in India did not cause "any extensive moral or physical degradation: the habit is generally practised in moderation, and…when so practised injurious effects are not apparent" (quoted in Dikötter et al., 2004:103; see also Richards, 2002).

Each nation (or its colonial master, in most cases) wrestled with different methods of regulating opium consumption domestically, usually to gather government revenues, but later, in some cases, to try to cut consumption. For example, the Dutch were the first to establish an opium monopoly on Java already in the 18th century, auctioning "opium farms" or franchises to the highest bidder, usually a consortium of influential Chinese who then primarily sold the drugs among their people (Rush, 1991; Van Ours, 1995). During the early 19th century, similar arrangements were adopted by most colonial governments throughout Southeast Asia. In 1881, however, the French administration in Saigon established the Opium Régie, a direct state marketing monopoly that showed far greater efficiency and profitability. During the following decades, the new model spread to the Netherlands Indies, British Burma, and Malaya and Siam. Ostensibly presented as a drug control measure, the new monopolies remained central to colonial finances until World War II. From 1905 to 1906, for example, according to the data provided to the International Opium Commission in Shanghai, opium sales provided 16% of taxes for French Indochina, 16% for the Netherlands Indies, 20% for Siam, and 53% for British Malaya (McCoy, 1991:90–93, 100–101).

Although Asia accounted for most of the global opiate consumption during the late 19th century, the West also engaged in use, but increasingly involving more refined versions of opium. The experiences of the United States and Great Britain have been well documented.

The United States developed a serious opiate problem in the late 19th century (Musto, 1987). Opium had been available earlier, but the spread of morphine during the second half of the 19th century greatly increased opiate consumption. Other opiates were available in low-potency liquid preparations, such as laudanum (an opium tincture) or patent medicines, which could be bought freely in any store or by post until 1906. Dependence spread initially through medical prescription, at a time when opiate addiction was little understood; it affected all classes. According to Courtwright (1982:9), the rate of opiate addiction reached a maximum of 4.6 per 1,000 in the 1890s—almost 50% higher than the contemporary rate of chronic users (slightly more than 3 per 1,000) (Office of National Drug Control Policy [ONDCP], 2001).[9]

Courtwright (1982) also shows convincingly that by the turn of the century—that is, 15 years before the passage of the Harrison Act—opiate addiction in the United States began to decline. "The major reason for the rise, as well as the fall, in the rate of opiate addiction," he writes, "was the prevailing medical practice of the day" (Courtwright, 1982:2). As much as physicians inadvertently promoted opiate spread in the 1870s and 1880s, their changing practice led to a decline of opium and morphine addicts from the late 1880s onward. From the 1870s onward, there was also a pattern of non-medical consumption in the United States—mainly, opium smoking within Chinese ethnic communities and among members of the white underworld. Gradually, morphine and, later, heroin supplanted opium smoking, and heroin became the underworld drug of choice (Courtwright, 1982:3).[10]

In Britain, opium was widely used up to the early 20th century by members of all social classes, although it carried different connotations in literary circles (Thomas de Quincey and Samuel Taylor Coleridge) than in working-class homes. For the latter in particular, it was the cornerstone of self-medication. No estimate of the prevalence of opiate use in late-19th-century Britain has ever been produced. However, Virginia Berridge (1999:34) estimates that the amount consumed varied from 600 to 1,600 grams per 1,000 population from 1827 to 1860 (see also Sweet, 2001:23–28), amounts that can be considered roughly equivalent to the current U.S. heroin consumption per capita.

As in the United States, opiate consumption expanded up until about the turn of the 20th century, thanks also to the spread of morphine, and then began to decline even before the passage of any restrictive legislation. In evidence, the overall narcotics mortality rate dropped from 6.6 per million population in 1897 to 4.2 per million in 1901 and 2.9 per million in 1913. By the outbreak of World War I, opium use had become largely a problem of the lower social classes. Nevertheless, a small middle-class population of morphine addicts, the great majority of whom had started their habits through medical prescription, also emerged. In addition, a few artistic and mystic groups smoked opium and cannabis (Berridge, 1984). Heroin appears to have accounted for a much smaller share of opiate use in Britain than in the United States (Berridge, 1999; see also Parsinnen, 1983).

In France, too, opium was an essential ingredient of self-medication. In contrast to England, opium smoking became popular toward the end of the 19th century, first among colonial administrators returning from Asia and later mainly among naval officers. Opium houses appeared in all the major French cities and became a feature of the Belle Epoque in Paris, catering to various social classes (de Liederkerke, 2001:184–197). In Germany, opium consumption primarily resulted from self-medication, and physicians' prescriptions to wounded soldiers (during the 1866 and 1870–1871 wars) and persons affected by chronic sicknesses (Scheerer, 1981:51–53). Up until 1901, opium itself and a variety of opiate-containing medicines could be bought freely in pharmacies. Unlike France, non-medical opiate use was very limited and largely restricted to the intellectuals and the upper classes up until World War I (Schreier, 2003:11–12).

Development and Impact of the International Drug Control Regime, 1909–1945

A global control regime emerged in the early part of the 20th century. Internationally agreed rules and related domestic legislation aimed to ensure the medical and scientific availability of opiates while suppressing other use. Striking a balance between these two goals has bedeviled efforts to evolve a workable international drug control policy since the early 20th century (Bruun, Pan, and Rexed, 1975). Although the early initiatives focused on regulation, the tone and provisions of later treaties became increasingly prohibitionist, mainly at the insistence of the United States.

Why the Policy Shift?

The creation of an international control regime for opiate and other psychoactive drugs has been described as "one of history's great about-faces, however slowly and imperfectly executed" (Courtwright, 2001b:167). This shift took place despite the limited harms produced by much of the opiate use at the turn of the 20th century, and the financial and non-financial gains drawn by western elites from the opium trade. A strong social and political movement began to crystallize in different parts of the world, pushing for the regulation of the opiate trade and use and, increasingly, the suppression of its non-medical sale and use. A variety of concerns and interests within and among nations intersected to foster changes in public perceptions of opium and its derivatives at the same time as the expansion of formal medical care and the introduction of new medicines made opium less central to medical practice.

First, whereas opium use had limited harmful effects for the majority of Asian users, opium derivatives turned out to be highly addictive and to produce serious negative consequences for their abusers in western countries. A growing fear of opiates and morphine addiction developed during the late 19th century, particularly in the United States, that manifested itself in the adoption of antimorphine laws by various U.S. states during the 1890s (Musto, 1987:4–6). In Asia too, much opium consumption had limited negative consequences, but the harm it inflicted upon the minority of heavy users was real and visible. Although the images of the emaciated and depraved opium addicts popularized by many Protestant and Catholic missionaries did not reflect the typical reality of opium use (Dikötter et al., 2004:96–101), some addicts were reduced by opium addiction to a piteous state. Even if only heavy opium users had addiction problems, according to Newman's calculations

(1995) these still afflicted 4.8 million people at the beginning of the 20th century.

Second, the concerns about opium and its derivatives were exploited for professional, political, and racist reasons. In most western countries, the second half of the 19th century saw the rise of the medical profession, and the newly created medical and pharmacist associations sought moral authority and legal power by presenting opium as a dangerous poison that they alone were qualified to administer in controlled dosages. Opiate addicts were increasingly portrayed as sick people, victims of a chemical dependence that only the medical professional was entitled to cure (Musto, 1987:10–21; Berridge, 1999:193–194; Dikötter et al., 2004:95, 104).

The "narcophobic discourse" (Dikötter et al., 2004:2) also served domestic and foreign political purposes in a number of countries. The early U.S. initiatives were dictated by moral concerns and by political and economic interests. From 1906 onward, U.S. diplomacy began campaigning for international drug control initiatives in China. It was eager to end the profitable opium trade dominated by the colonial powers and to curry favor with the Chinese, thereby improving Sino-American economic relations (Musto, 1987:24–35). In China, Han officials and Confucian scholars increasingly used opium prohibition as a tool to regain political and moral authority. They presented opium as a marker of backwardness, the principal cause of China's "racial" decline, and the epitome of imperialist power, particularly after China's defeat by Japan in 1894 to 1895 (e.g., Zhou, 1999:18–25).

Just as opium was portrayed in China as a poison used by foreigners to destroy the "race," in western countries its demonization was used for the racist discrimination against the Chinese. Opium smoking, primarily associated with Chinese immigrants, was especially stigmatized. It was portrayed as a means through which the Chinese would undermine western, and specifically American, society. In the United States, opium prepared for smoking, although milder and less addictive than morphine, was the first narcotic banned by federal legislation as early as 1909, whereas no restriction other than a tariff was placed on other forms of opium or its derivatives before 1915 (Ahmad, 2007). Australia and Japan acted similarly. The latter's government prohibited opium smoking as early as 1868, additionally threatening Chinese residents with deportation should they indulge (Manderson, 1987; Wakabayashi, 2000:66–70).

Lastly, as Courtwright (2001b:173–179) points out, the rise of the international drug control regime must be understood in the overall perspective of industrialization, which also changed attitudes vis-à-vis alcohol. Users and abusers of psychoactive drugs were much less disruptive in traditional cultures with undisciplined pastimes and work settings: "As the social environment changed, becoming more rationalized, bureaucratized and mechanized, the distribution of cheap intoxicants became more troublesome and divisive" (Courtwright, 2001b:178). In premodern settings, the consumption of drugs suited western elites' interests; it helped the subjugation of colonized peoples and, in the case of stimulants, the exploitation of unskilled workers. However, the same drugs in a growing number of industrial contexts rendered the new proletarians' work worse than useless. Thus, industrialization created influential groups for whom unregulated commerce in intoxicating drugs was not profitable, and these groups constituted a powerful support to those that opposed opiate consumption and trade on moral grounds.

International Controls

The International Opium Commission, which convened in Shanghai in 1909 at the insistence of the United States, represents the cornerstone of the contemporary drug control regime. Involving 13 nations, the conference had no authority to approve a binding document; rather, it adopted nine resolutions. A number dealt exclusively with the Chinese opium problem, but one, which was addressed to all governments, called for the "gradual suppression" of opium smoking; other forms of opium consumption were not mentioned. It stated that the use of opium for other-than-medical purposes was held "by almost every participating country" to be "a matter for prohibition or for careful regulation" (International Opium Commission, 1910:96). This represented a compromise between the views of the U.S. and British governments, the latter of which was still anxious to protect the Indian–Chinese opium trade (Lowes, 1966:121–175; Bruun et al., 1975:11).

Three years later, 12 countries met at The Hague to draft a treaty. The result of their efforts, known as the first International Opium Convention or as the Hague Convention of 1912, entailed weak provisions; it left the interpretation of control to the individual governments and called on domestic, rather than international, regulation for production and distribution (Bruun et al., 1975:12). The convention required parties to "take measures for the gradual and effective suppression of the manufacture of, internal trade in, and use of prepared opium, with due regard to the varying circumstances of each country concerned" (International Opium Convention, 1912), unless such laws were already in place. It did not, however, restrict the production of raw opium, but only the right to sell opium to nations that had prohibited its import (McAllister, 2000:33–34). Even weaker were the requirements set for opiates and cocaine, which were added at the request of the British government and despite the opposition of Germany, which was the leading country in the synthetic drug production at the time. Article 10 of the convention merely called on parties "to use their best endeavours" to control all persons producing or selling morphine, cocaine, and their derivatives.

Nonetheless, the Hague decision that the use of morphine and cocaine, and opium as well be confined "to medical and legitimate purposes" was crucial. Thanks to British and German maneuvering, the first International Opium Convention also transformed the far eastern emphasis of the Shanghai conference into a full-scale international system (Berridge, 1984:19). At the insistence of Germany, which aimed at postponing controls, it was agreed that the convention should have universal signature before going into effect. Because of this peculiar ratification procedure, the convention might never have entered into force had the British government not made its ratification a condition of the Treaty of Versailles that ended World War I in 1919 (McAllister, 2000:36–37).

The establishment of the League of Nations in 1919 provided the international community with a centralized body for the administration of drug control. In 1920, the League set up the Advisory Committee on Traffic in Opium and Other Dangerous Drugs, the forerunner of the UN Commission on Narcotic Drugs (CND). However, enforcement of the 1912 convention remained ineffective because the European countries with a leading role in the advisory committee had no interest in tight controls. They were the main opiate manufacturers and ran opium monopolies in their Asian colonies (Bruun et al., 1975:13).

Although the United States did not join the League of Nations, its influence in international drug control matters remained strong. Pushing for concrete limitations on opium production, the United States pressured the League to convene a new conference. Between November 1924 and February 1925 two back-to-back conferences were held in Geneva and two separate treaties were concluded, which for the first time established some transnational controls over a wider range of drugs. The second Geneva Convention, known as the International Opium Convention of 1925, also set up a new body, the Permanent Central Opium Board (PCOB), which had to monitor an import certification system to limit the amount of drugs each country could legally import (McAllister, 2000:57–78; Senate of Canada Special Committee on Illegal Drugs, 2002:446–447).

This import control system turned out to be only partially effective and the League of Nations convened another conference in 1931. The result of that conference was the so-called 1931 Limitation Convention. It limited the manufacture of opiates and other drugs to the amounts necessary to meet medical and scientific needs. Countries were required to provide estimates of need, and the newly established Drug Supervisory Board would monitor them. Nevertheless, the effectiveness of the convention was seriously undermined by several loopholes for manufacturing states and by Article 26, which absolved states of any responsibility under the Convention for their colonies (McAllister, 2000:108–109; Senate of Canada Special Committee on Illegal Drugs, 2002:447–448).

To deal with the growing illicit trafficking, an additional treaty was drawn up in 1936 in Geneva at the initiative of the International Police Commission, predecessor to Interpol. The treaty called on parties to use their national criminal law systems to punish "severely," "particularly by imprisonment or other penalties of deprivation of liberty," any act directly related to drug trafficking (Taylor, 1969:288–298).

The first phase of development of the international drug control regime was almost exclusively supply oriented and aimed at reducing the production and distribution of manufactured drugs through careful monitoring and trade regulations. During this phase, the focus shifted from a paternalistic effort to reduce opium smoking in China to controls on the manufacture of opium derivatives and cocaine, the drugs most consumed in the developed countries. The controls on drug manufacturing were included in the 1925 and 1931 treaties despite the opposition of countries with strong pharmaceutical industries, such as the Netherlands, Germany, and Switzerland. Only with the 1936 convention did illicit drug traffic become the key concern of an international treaty (Carstairs, 2005). Almost paradoxically, despite the supply-side bias, none of the early treaties entailed any binding provision to limit the production of opium itself. Article 1 of the Hague Convention of 1912 merely required parties to "enact effective laws or regulations for the control of the production and distribution of raw opium," and this minimalist approach, primarily at the insistence of colonial powers, held up in later treaties. According to Block (1989:317), the focus on manufacturing was also a consequence of the fact that the League had little control over the world's opium harvest. Four of the major opium-producing countries in the world—namely, China,[11] Iran, Russia, and Turkey—had not signed any of the early drug control conventions.

Impact of International Controls

Among the most tangible products of the bodies set up by the early international drug control treaties are the data on drug production, medical demand, and transactions that they collected from governments. This information sheds some light on the impact of the early international drug control system on opiate markets and, specifically, documents the rise of illicit channels of distribution and production.

On the basis of governmental estimates, the PCOB concluded in 1931 that legitimate morphine demand during the 6-year period 1925 to 1930 had been about 195 tons. Member states reported to the PCOB that more than 266 tons of morphine had been produced during the same time frame. The difference between the two figures, 71 tons in aggregate or nearly 12 tons per year, can be considered a minimum estimate of the quantities of morphine and its derivatives that entered the illicit market out of legitimate production channels. With an estimated legitimate demand of 12 tons in 1925 to 1929, the discrepancy for heroin was proportionally even larger, as the world production during the same time period was 32.5 tons (de Ridder, 2000:136–138). Together, the figures suggest a total of about 16 tons of illicitly marketed morphine and heroin annually, amounting to about 0.008 grams per person globally compared with an estimate for 2004 of about 275 to 350 tons and about 0.04 to 0.05 grams per person.[12]

During the 1920s and early 1930s, several legitimate pharmaceutical companies were involved in illicit deals. Some companies, including the leading firms of the day, were pinpointed by the League, which scrutinized the import and export certificates introduced by the second Geneva Convention. In 1925, for example, the Swiss firm Sandoz exported more than 1,300 kilos of morphine to a Japanese firm that had no record of the transaction (Block, 1989:320). More than 6 tons of heroin were also smuggled by the French firm Roessler in the Far East between 1926 and 1929 (de Ridder, 2000:140). Drugs were not just sent to Asia. The League of Nations also documented many cases of diversion and smuggling within Europe with Swiss, French, Dutch, and German companies involved (e.g., Block, 1989:318–320; Meyer and Parssinen, 1998:25–36).

The League of Nations was quite effective in using the power of adverse publicity, a common tactic in other international forums.[13] Despite its limited means, the League managed to convince large pharmaceutical companies to reduce diversion and cut heroin production drastically.[14] As far as heroin was concerned, the League's efforts were also helped by changing perceptions of the drug. After World War I, heroin was progressively stigmatized, denied any therapeutic value, and increasingly associated with the criminal underworld. As a result, legitimate pharmaceutical companies had less and less interest in being linked to heroin. Whereas world heroin production oscillated between 3.7 tons and 9 tons yearly during the late 1920s, by 1932 it had sunk to less than 1 ton, and by 1948 it was reduced to 60 kilograms yearly (de Ridder, 2000:128–129).

Coupled with the criminal law restrictions enforced by national governments, the League's successful tactic of adverse publicity also transformed the market. In the early 1920s, the illicit trade in narcotics depended to a large extent on diverting legally manufactured drugs. Underworld members were typically located at the bottom of the drug-manufacturing and marketing system. In combination with manufacturers and numerous middlemen and retail outlets, they diverted a portion of the product to non-medical consumers. By the beginning of World War II, professional criminals were almost alone at the beginning of the process, owning clandestine factories around the world (Block, 1989; Meyer and Parssinen, 1998). The market for opiates thus began to resemble today's.

Rise and Impact of National Controls, 1906–1945

The 1912 International Opium Convention marks the first instance in drug control in which an international agreement impelled national legislation. Some countries, however, had already passed restrictive measures on opiates even before 1912.

National Controls in the United States and Europe

Most western nations passed restrictive legislation in the years after the first International Opium Convention. In the United States, for example, the convention itself became a tool for antiopium advocates, who claimed that a federal law was necessary for the United States to fulfill its obligations. In 1916, the U.S. Supreme Court ruled that this was not so, but by then the Harrison Narcotic Act of 1914 had become the first federal drug control law in the United States (Musto, 1987:128–130). Under the Harrison Act, anyone selling drugs had to be licensed, buy a tax stamp, and keep records of all sales, ostensibly for tax purposes. The U.S. Treasury Department was responsible for enforcing the statute.

Although the Harrison Act was initially designed to "medicalize" opiate and cocaine by restricting their prescription to physicians, it soon became the central legislation for prohibition. The Treasury Department, backed by the Supreme Court in a key decision of 1919 (*Webb et al. v. United States,* 249 U.S. 96 [1919]) rejected the argument that addict maintenance constituted legitimate medical practice (Musto, 1987:131–132). Following another Supreme Court decision of 1922, the more frequent prosecution of physicians and pharmacists prescribing or selling opiates, and the increasingly negative perception of opiates in the medical profession and the general public, legal supplies of opiates and other drugs fell sharply (Courtwright, 1982:113–147).

The supposed drug emergency of World War I provided the main impetus for stringent regulation in Britain. In 1916, the Home Office issued regulation 40B under the Defence of the Realm Act, making it an offense for anyone except medical practitioners, pharmacists, and veterinarians to possess, sell, or give cocaine, or raw or powdered opium. This wartime regulation became broader legislation (the Dangerous Drugs Act) in 1920, which included medical opium and morphine as well. By the mid 1920s, however, the medical profession and the Ministry of Health prevailed in their view of addiction as a disease requiring treatment, not a vice demanding punishment. With the report of the Rolleston Committee in 1926, the so-called "British System" was born, which allowed a doctor to prescribe a drug, including heroin if necessary, for a patient already addicted (Berridge, 1984, 2005).

Other European nations, including France, Germany, and the Netherlands, also passed restrictive legislation on opiates during or after World War I. In 1916, France passed "one of the most draconian" (Charras, 1998:15–16) narcotic statutes in Europe. This did not prevent its chemical firms from playing a major role in opiate production and smuggling during the 1920s (Block, 1989). In contrast, the Netherlands' statute was less stringent. The Netherlands Opium Act of 1919 also prohibited the manufacture, sale, processing, transport, and supplying of opiates and cocaine, but it prescribed relatively mild penalties: a maximum of 3 months of imprisonment or a fine. Moreover, under a license system, Dutch companies were allowed to continue to produce heroin and cocaine. Up until the late 1930s, the Netherlands remained the principal cocaine producer and one of the main heroin producers (de Kort and Korf, 1992).

Germany passed three decrees in 1916, 1918, and mid 1920 to regulate the trade in opiates. It ratified the Hague Convention only in late 1920, when it was forced to do so by the Treaty of Versailles. As in the Netherlands, production of opiates could be licensed for medical purposes, and addicts could be maintained by doctors either with opium or with a variety of opium-containing medicines not controlled by the law. Several loopholes in the 1920 acts and the spread of non-medical use of opiates and cocaine among small circles of bohemians especially in Berlin led to a new, more restrictive and wider ranging statute—the Opium Act of 1929—which redirected lawmakers' attention from regulating legal production to fighting addiction (Scheerer, 1981:39–67; Schreier, 2003:14–16).

National Controls in Asia

China, the main producer and consumer of opium during the late 19th century, began an antiopium campaign even before the International Opium Commission in Shanghai in 1909. In 1906, the Qing imperial court issued a second edict of opium suppression: Each year, for the next 9 years, domestic opium production had to be cut by one ninth. The British government was a signatory to this effort because there were to be parallel declines in both imports from India and domestic production. The measures adopted for consumption included shutting down all opium dens within 6 months, registering addicts, issuing purchasing licenses, and requiring younger addicts to undergo detoxification therapy (Zhou, 1999:25–32).[15]

The early Chinese republican governments continued the restrictive policy, but the rise of warlords and decline of a functioning central government after about 1915 effectively ended the effort. Taxation of opium production and distribution became a major source of revenue for individual warlords, and many of them encouraged opium use (Walker, 1991). Both the Nationalists and the Communists also profited from the opium trade and its taxation. As Alan Baumler puts it (quoted in Zheng, 2005:191), the Chinese administration of Chiang Kai-Shek "attempted, with considerable success, to profit both politically and economically from control of the opium trade and avoid the loss of legitimacy that came with involvement in the trade." After passing a series of suppression laws between 1929 and 1934, the Kuomintang launched a 6-year plan to discourage consumption and to control distribution through a state monopoly in 1935. The Communists also profited from opium in that they confiscated huge amounts of it and traded it for supplies, and even encouraged its cultivation and trade in Yan'an during the 1930s and 1940s to finance the growing Red Army. Although not yet thoroughly researched, the Communists' involvement in the opium economy seems to be so extensive that, according to Zheng (2005:198), they, too, should be considered an "opium regime" before 1949.

Interestingly, the adoption of restrictive legislation in Britain and other European countries was, in the 1920s and 1930s, rarely accompanied by a restriction on opium production or the abolition of opium distribution monopolies in the colonies. The colonial powers continued to supply their

Asian colonies with Indian opium, generating substantial revenues. League of Nations data show that in the mid 1920s, the number of estimated opium smokers in the main 11 Asian colonies of European powers totaled more than a million (Meyer and Parssinen, 1998:74–75).

Britain, one of the moving forces for international prohibition, had a second and comparably important role at this time as the governing power for India. There were considerable pressures to restrict exports from India to maintain Britain's leadership role in the international control regime. A powerful domestic antiopium movement was active in the press and parliament, whereas externally the United States actively criticized the British position. However, the colonial administration in India fought hard against a policy that would deprive it of an important source of revenue (Goto-Shabata, 2002). Finally, in 1924, the British government committed itself to reducing Indian production by about 10% annually. Production in India declined, but exports were still substantial up until World War II. Even in the late 1930s, the Straits Administration of the Colonial Office (covering Malaya and Singapore) derived about one sixth of its total revenues from the distribution of Indian-produced opium (down from one third during the late 1920s). Production in India also continued to serve a substantial, albeit declining, domestic market (Pakyntein, 1958).

The Japanese opium control regime imposed on Formosa (Taiwan) in 1897, 2 years after Japan seized control of the island, also became increasingly restrictive after World War I. Although sharply prohibitionist in the home country, the Japanese administration initially assumed that the widespread use of opium in Taiwan made prohibition unfeasible. It set out to register all addicted smokers, who would receive a maximum daily total; this would cut off supplies to non-smokers, who could not purchase opium at licensed centers. The Japanese also took control of the supply of opium to licensed smoking dens through the Medicine Manufacturing Bureau, which processed imported opium into the smoking form. Initially, the efforts to reduce consumption remained limited and the monopoly was an important source of revenue for the colonial administration, accounting for one fifth of the total during the early days. During the 1920s, though, distribution policies became increasingly stringent, with negative consequences for the colony's finances. By 1930, opium revenues had declined to 3.7% of the total (Jennings, 1997:18–28).

Not all colonial powers made efforts to restrict consumption. For example, the French administration for Indochina maintained a network of 2,500 opium dens and retail stores, with about 100,000 "addicts"[16] until the end of World War II. This contributed 15% of the administration's revenues. Even Thailand, not under the control of any colonial power, ran a government-controlled distribution system until the late 1950s. According to the data provided to the League of Nations, throughout Southeast Asia, government-run opium monopolies still supplied more than half a million opium smokers as of 1930 (McCoy, 1991:90).

As early as 1910, Iran passed the Opium Limitation Act, which imposed taxes on opium transactions to be progressively increased during the next 7 years, but was largely unable to implement the provisions (MacCallum, 1928:7; Hansen, 2001:98–99). After World War I, the new government of Reza Shah refused to sign the international drug control agreements or to participate in the import/export certification system (McAllister, 2000:117). Domestically, the regime experimented in the 1920s and 1930s with various ways of regulating the trade to maximize its revenues and to keep smuggling to a minimum. It was now dealing with a predominantly domestic market. Raw opium production peaked in 1936 at 1,346 metric tons, of which barely 10% was exported (Hansen, 2001).

Impact of National Controls

It is not easy to single out and assess the impact of the restrictive legislation adopted, because legislative changes toward drug prohibition largely reflected changes in the very perception of opiates. David Courtwright (1982) has shown, for example, that the decline in opiate supply engendered in the United States by the passage of the Harrison Act in 1914 did not foster, but was preceded and accompanied by, the decline in demand. As mentioned earlier, opiate consumption had been falling in the United States before 1914, reflecting state-level restrictions, changes in the beliefs of medical practitioners about the dangers of opiates; and growing public concerns about the spread of non-medical addiction that involved younger and poorer males (Speaker, 2001). The declines in opiate consumption continued after the Harrison Act, but cannot be attributed to it, because the Act merely codified ongoing social trends. According to Courtwright (1982:33–34), there could be no more than 210,000 addicts, or slightly less than 2 per 1,000, in 1920 and their real number was probably lower than that. Although non-medical heroin use among poor underworld white males grew progressively at the expense of medical addiction, this did not disappear at once, because a few clinics offering maintenance treatment remained opened up until 1924, some practitioners continued prescribing morphine and other opiates long after that, and a gray market of pure drugs persisted as an alternative to the black market of adulterated heroin (Courtwright, Joseph, and Des Jarlais, 1989:8–13).

In Great Britain, too, the adoption of restrictive legislation was preceded and accompanied by a sharp decline in opiate consumption. Only a few hundred addicts were registered in any year through 1925 to 1965, and there was no indication of a substantial illicit market.[17] Unlike the United States, possibly as a result of the aforementioned "British System," there was no expansion of heroin use among low-class, young males. Up until the 1960s, the typical British opiate addict was likely to be female, middle age or elderly, and from the middle classes; a substantial minority were themselves doctors or health professionals (Spear, 2005; Strang and Gossop, 2005).

As in the United States and Great Britain, in China, too, the first years of implementation of the 1906 edict on opium were accompanied, to almost universal surprise, by substantial reductions in both consumption and production.[18] This decline, however, must be seen in the overall changing perception of opium, which was increasingly stigmatized and seen politically as an instrument of foreign oppression. Moreover, as Newman (1995:790) suggests, one has to consider the actual patterns of opium use in assessing the achievement of the late Qing campaign: "if we appreciate that most opium smokers were light or occasional consumers, it is not difficult to understand that they would have given up when the practice was made to seem unfashionable, leaving only the genuine addicts to smoke on in secret, using black market supplies."

This assessment of China's opium consumption decline is reinforced by the parallel decrease in opium consumption in Indonesia, where the Dutch Opium Régie kept on distributing opium until Indonesia's occupation by the Japanese Army. Despite the lack of radical legislative changes, perception also changed in Indonesia, as opium began to be seen as old-fashioned, if not uncivilized, first among the elite and increasingly among the population at large. Only after World War I did the colonial administration subject opium smokers to some license requirements. These combined forces succeeded. It has been estimated that in the 1880s, 1 Javanese in 20 used opium; by 1928, the ratio was 1 in 600 (Rush, 1985; see also Chandra, 2000).

Formosa's experience shows most clearly that, although tangled by conflict of interests, government monopolies could eventually reform themselves and curb opium consumption. In 1900, 170,000 addicts were registered, representing 6.3% of the Taiwanese population. Thirty years later, the number was less than 25,000. Even though a market had emerged outside the licensed system, particularly in rural areas, there seemed little doubt that the number of opium smokers in Formosa had declined greatly (Jennings, 1997:19).

Even if they cannot be seen as the driving force of opiate consumption declines, the growing state restrictions had tangible impacts on opiate users' behavior, quality of life and legal status, as well as on the type of drugs used and the method of administration. Certainly, not all impacts were for the better. In the United States, for example, historical evidence from the 1920s and '30s supports the contention that the antimaintenance policy increased the amount of crime among opiate users (Courtwright, 1982:145–146). Heroin use also spread as a result of the new restrictive laws, because dealers and their customers came to appreciate its black-market virtues. For dealers, heroin's main advantages included its potency, its compactness, and the ease of its adulteration, thus potentially multiplying their profits. Users were happy to buy heroin because it was much cheaper than morphine, but stronger and faster acting when administered in a comparable manner. In addition, heroin could be injected or sniffed, with the latter method appealing to new or potential users who were afraid of needles (Courtwright, 1982:107–110).

Antimaintenance laws also fostered the spread of subcutaneous or even intravenous injection of heroin. As purity decreased, many addicts resorted to the most drastic and direct route of administration to derive maximum satisfaction from increasingly diluted drugs. In its turn, the drift to the needle caused sepsis most frequently, but also hepatitis, endocarditis, emboli, tetanus, overdose, and early death.

A similar pattern can be observed in China. There, too, the prohibitionist legislation enacted first in 1906 accelerated and broadened the use of opium in a variety of new applications, in particular as powders and as tinctures. It also introduced consumers to opium derivatives, such as morphine and heroin, because they had many practical advantages. Sold in pills or powder, they were convenient to transport, cheaper than opium, odorless, and thus almost undetectable in police searches, and easy to use, because they did not require the complicated paraphernalia and time-consuming rituals of opium smoking (Dikötter et al., 2004:146).

Loopholes in China's prohibitionist drug policies also favored the shift to morphine and heroin, as opium was outlawed in 1906, whereas morphine and heroin remained on sale openly until World War I (Dikötter et al., 2004:174). Consumption of heroin pills spread to such an extent that according to contemporary observers, by 1922 "it exceeded smoking of opium itself" (Dikötter et al., 2004:163). As in other contexts, prohibitionist policies also promoted the spread of injecting drug use, which in China encountered few cultural obstacles given the widespread use of needles (Dikötter et al., 2004:171–191). And, as in other parts of the world, the spread of injecting drug use also had negative, sometimes lethal, side effects.

Moreover, as a result of a series of short-lasting but harsh antiopium campaigns, drug-related crime surged. In 1931, for example, the use and sale of opium emerged as the most common criminal offenses, representing 27,000 out of the 70,000 reported convictions throughout the country (Dikötter et al., 2004:126–130). Tens of thousands of otherwise law-abiding opium smokers were confined to overcrowded cells, and many of them died in disproportionate numbers of epidemics, whereas those deemed beyond any hope of redemption were simply executed. In just 2 years, 1935 and 1936, almost 2,000 drug offenders were executed (Dikötter et al., 2004:143).

Coupled with international controls, prohibitionist domestic legislation also provoked the development of illegal markets for opiates in many countries and offered the most unscrupulous members of the underclass a new set of illegal commodities to sell. In the United States, the illegal distribution of opiates was primarily undertaken by criminals belonging to different national, ethnic, and other minorities, such as Chinese, Jewish, and Italian (Courtwright et al.,1989:99–100, 178–206; Meyer and Parssinen, 1998:236–266).

As legitimate pharmaceutical companies gradually stopped supplying illegal distributors, new producers sprang up. For a few years in the late 1920s, Turkey and Bulgaria became the preferred site of semilegal and clandestine factories set up by European legitimate entrepreneurs-turned-traffickers. By the mid 1930s, however, the bulk of opiate production had moved to Asia and, above all, to China, which also remained the main opium producer (Block,

1989). Thanks to the complacency of local government authorities—including the colonial powers ruling the international concessions in Shanghai and Japan, which occupied Manchuria in 1931 and larger portions of China from 1937 onward—large, modern factories, occasionally employing as many as 2,000 to 3,000 workers, produced enormous quantities of heroin and morphine. Many of these factories were owned by high-ranking officials and local potentates. During the 1930s in Shanghai, they were mostly run by powerful and extremely well-connected gangster groups, which had formed a virtual cartel (Meyer and Parsinnen, 1988:141–171; McCoy, 1991:262–269).[19]

Downslide and Upswing, 1945–1970, and a Brief Coda

A general decline in opiate consumption and the almost complete breakdown of the webs of international trade characterize the first two decades after World War II. With few exceptions, the remaining markets were serviced by opium and heroin largely produced nearby. The downslide turned into an upswing from the late 1960s onward, when the heroin demand began to expand considerably, first in the United States and then in Europe and several Asian countries, and the current global market began to take shape. The second half of the 20th century also saw the consolidation of the international drug control regime, with three conventions establishing contemporary policy makers' framework of action.

National Controls and National Markets

For global opiate problems, the most significant event immediately after World War II was the rise to power of the Communist Party in China, which brought with it an effectively enforceable aversion to opiates. The elimination of opium consumption and production in China, then still by far the largest market in the world, was part of a general movement by the new Communist-led regime to end traditional ways that were seen as barriers to creating a well-functioning Marxist society. The opium suppression campaign reached its peak during the second half of 1952, when more than 80,000 drug traffickers were arrested, more than 30,000 were sent to prison (many for life), and at least 880 were sentenced to death. Users were forcefully rehabilitated either at home or in treatment facilities run by the government, with the exception of the elderly and the sick, who could be granted an extension. The opium suppression campaign was supported by a massive propaganda campaign that, although not relying on official media, involved more than 750,000 mass anti-drug rallies and hundreds of public trials (Zhou, 1999 and 2000).

Without downplaying the achievement of the Communists' antidrug crusade, Dikötter et al. (2004:208–209) convincingly argue that medical and social variables were at least as important as the political factors in the long-term decline of narcotic culture in China. Penicillin began to be sold in the

1940s as the first antibiotic capable of treating a whole range of diseases that had been previously managed with opiates. The social status of opium was already on the decline in the 1930s. By then, social elites had begun to consider opium smoking morally reprehensible and old-fashioned, and began to praise abstinence instead. As in Java (Rush, 1985), tobacco smoking progressively superseded opium smoking.

In other parts of Asia, too, legislative changes were promoted and reinforced by the changed perception of opium and the new availability of medical alternatives. Britain eventually prohibited opium consumption in its Asian colonies (apart from India) in 1943, while they were occupied by Japan. Right after the war, the government of the newly independent Indonesia abolished the Opium Régie operated by the Dutch colonial administration and also by the Japanese occupation authorities. The French colonial administration ended the legal distribution of opium in Indochina in 1950, during the war against nationalists. Thailand, which had not followed through on its 1946 promise to end the opium monopoly by 1951, did finally terminate the regime in 1959 (McCoy, 1991:179–193). The effects of these measures on consumption were mixed. Although hard to document, the disappearance of opium from Indonesia is not a contested historical phenomenon. In other contexts, such as Laos and Thailand, the demand for opium declined but did not disappear, and was increasingly satisfied with opium illicitly produced in the northern part of those countries and in Burma's Shan State.

The story for Iran is more complicated. As a result of mounting pressure from domestic and foreign sources, the Iranian government forbade opium poppy cultivation, use, and sales in 1946. Nevertheless, the reduction in oil revenues during the early 1950s, when Britain cut off exports after nationalization of Anglo-Iranian Oil, led to a resurgence of legal, taxed production, providing 20% of national government revenue during that period (Hansen, 2001:108–109). In 1955, the government imposed anew a complete ban on opium production and consumption (Saleh, 1956). At the end of 3 years of prohibition, the Health Minister wrote that the problem was reduced by two thirds and now involved imported rather than locally produced opium (Radji, 1959). However, the prohibition on consumption was not consistently enforced, so that Iran remained a large market for illicit opiates.[20] By 1968, the illegal market was so large that the government reintroduced legal production, which continued until the creation of the Islamic Republic of Iran in 1979 (Booth, 1998:253–254). Iran may have constituted the single largest market in the world in the 1960s.

World War II interrupted supplies to the small and declining illicit opiate market that had persisted up until 1940 in the United States and to the even smaller ones in Europe. By the end of the conflict, "heroin and other illicit drugs had receded from national consciousness" (Courtwright, 2001a:148). Starting in 1947, the United States experienced a small, brief heroin epidemic, but this remained concentrated in a handful of big cities (New York, Chicago, Los Angeles, and Detroit), affecting almost exclusively black and Hispanic minorities.[21] Heroin was initially diverted from Italian pharmaceutical manufacturers. From the early 1950s onward, this Italian source was supplanted by the product of the Marseille heroin labs (the so-called *French Connection*), with the raw material coming from Turkey or Lebanon (Courtwright, 2001a:148–156; see also McCoy, 1991:46–70). Extremely harsh legislation was passed in 1951 and 1956, when the death penalty was introduced at the federal level for adults convicted of selling heroin to those younger than 18 years of age. As seen 40 years earlier with the Harrison Act, though, the number of new cases of addiction began to fall even before the passage of the first act, as heroin purity declined and the long-term effects of heroin addiction scared new recruits (Courtwright, 2001a:156–157).

Western markets remained very modest until the late 1960s. In 1969, filings with the United Nations showed a total of 65,000 heroin abusers in the United States, 2,700 in Canada, 1,400 in Great Britain, and 100 in France (Bayer and Ghodse, 1999). Although hardly the most authoritative numbers, they probably are indicative that the problem was small at the time. By that date, however, heroin use had started to go up again in the United States and the United Kingdom, whereas heroin became available again in "continental" Europe between 1971 and 1973 (Paoli, 2000:25–26, 83–84).[22]

In the United States, in particular, the second postwar heroin epidemic was already in full swing by 1969, creating the bulk of the contemporary addict population. The first wave of this epidemic again involved primarily young blacks and Hispanics. From 1969 onward, these marginalized ethnic minorities were joined by two highly untraditional groups: white suburbanites and Vietnam soldiers, the latter having got used to smoking the very pure heroin produced in the triborder region of Burma, Thailand, and Laos. According to Courtwright (2001a), by the early 1970s, heroin addiction in the United States had passed the half million mark, possibly coming close to the rate of 3 per 1,000 (by comparison, the maximum rate in the 1890s is estimated by Courtwright himself at 4.6 per 1,000 [2001a:165–170]; see also Hughes and Rieche, 1995).

By 1971, Americans listed heroin addiction as the nation's third most pressing problem, after Vietnam and the economy. In response to the growing heroin problems and the social damages and fears it caused, in 1971 U.S. President Richard Nixon declared a "war on drugs."[23] On the supply side, through diplomatic pressures and an economic aid package for Turkey, the U.S. administration was able to engender a heroin shortage in 1972 and 1973 (Courtwright, 2001a:171). Turkey was then a major licit opium producer and, thanks to large leakages, a major supplier of the illicit market as well. By signing a bilateral agreement with the United States, the Turkish government first committed itself to step out of opium production altogether. Although the ban was reversed a few years afterward, Turkey shifted from licit opium to poppy straw production and, thanks to this new harvest method, was able to stop opiate leakages into the illicit market effectively by the mid 1970s (Lamour and Lamberti, 1974; UNODCCP, 2000:2, 29). On American streets, however, Turkish heroin was soon replaced by Mexican. This substitution made clear to the U.S. administration that, to control the drug supply, multilateral action was needed, and so it turned again to tightening the international drug control regime.

Consolidation of the International Drug Control Regime

After World War II, the drug control bodies and functions of the League of Nations were transferred to the newly formed United Nations. The UN Economic and Social Council took over primary responsibility through its CND. Under the CND, the Division of Narcotic Drugs was charged with the preparatory work for the conferences. Despite opposition by the United States and Canada, the World Health Organization (WHO) was also officially involved in drug control matters. Through its Drug Dependence Expert Committee, the WHO became responsible for deciding which substances had to be regulated (Senate of Canada Special Committee on Illegal Drugs, 2002:449–450).

The first substantive treaty concluded after World War II was the 1953 Opium Protocol, which contained the most stringent drug control provisions yet embodied in international law. The agreement extended to raw opium the reporting provisions placed on manufactured drugs in the 1931 treaty. Upon signing, producer states committed themselves to provide UN bodies with estimates concerning the amount of opium planted, harvested, consumed domestically, exported, and stockpiled, and they allowed UN bodies to make inquiries into discrepancies, conducting inspections and imposing embargoes. In exchange for accepting such burdens, the seven producer states named in the agreement received a monopoly on licit sales (McAllister, 2000:179–184).[24] Interestingly, among them, neither Afghanistan nor Burma, the two largest contemporary illicit producers, were mentioned.

Even before entering into force, the 1953 Opium Protocol was superseded, along with eight other treaties, by the Single Convention on Narcotic Drugs, which was opened for signature in March 1961. This treaty, which constitutes a pillar of the contemporary drug control regime, did not merely synthesize older treaties, it also extended the scope of control to other drugs (e.g., cannabis and coca leaf) and was the most prohibitionist document yet concluded, although it was not as stringent as the United States and a few other western states would have wished. The Single Convention maintained the principal foundation of the preceding treaties, setting up the International Narcotics Control Board (INCB), which took the place of two previous UN agencies.[25] It also retained the concept of schedules of control first introduced in the 1931 treaty, but expanded the number of schedules from two to four. Heroin and opium were placed in the most restrictive schedule, Schedule I, together with cocaine and cannabis. Heroin and cannabis were also inserted in Schedule IV, which contains the most dangerous substances of very limited medical or therapeutic value (United Nations, 1972).[26]

The convention also built on the trend of requiring parties to develop increasingly punitive criminal legislation. Subject to their constitutional limitations, parties were to adopt distinct criminal offenses and punish them by imprisonment if the offenses were considered serious for each of the all basic drug-related activities carried out in contravention of the Single Convention (Article 36) (United Nations, 1972:18).[27] Furthermore, the granting of extradition was described as "desirable" (Senate of Canada Special Committee on Illegal Drugs, 2002:454). The Convention's emphasis on prohibition was reflected in the minimal attention paid to drug abuse problems. Only one article (Article 38) was devoted to "treatment of drug addicts," and this merely required parties to "give special attention to the provision of facilities for the medical treatment, care and rehabilitation of drug addicts" (Senate of Canada Special Committee on Illegal Drugs, 2002:455).[28]

In 1971, the Convention on Psychotropic Substances, which does not concern opiates, was opened for signature.[29] One year later, at the insistence of the Nixon administration, a protocol was adopted to revise the Single Convention and strengthen the INCB's control powers over licit and illicit opium production, and illicit drug trafficking. Additionally, the treaty called on states to pursue rehabilitation and treatment as an alternative to incarceration (Senate of Canada Special Committee on Illegal Drugs, 2002:461–462). Despite these changes, the system still focused on eliminating excess supplies of narcotics (McAllister, 2000:236).

In 1971, the UN Fund for Drug Abuse Control (UNFDAC) was also launched with an initial $2 million donation from the United States. Although initially seen as a U.S.-led entity, the predecessor of the UNDCP and of the contemporary UNODC gradually became an accepted mechanism of distribution and coordination of western aid to developing countries. Largely dependent on rich countries' donations, the UNFDAC and its successor agencies expended the majority of their resources on crop substitution, law enforcement, and technical assistance to national drug control agencies. However, from the 1980s onward, they have pursued (at least rhetorically) a more balanced approach between demand and supply reduction (McAllister, 2000:236–238, 242–243).

The traditional focus on the supply side also inspired the UN Convention against Illicit Trafficking of Narcotic Drugs and Psychotropic Substances, which was opened for signature in December 1988. As the Senate of Canada Special Committee on Illegal Drugs (2002:463) puts it, the new treaty "is essentially an instrument of international criminal law." Its aim is to harmonize criminal legislation and enforcement activities worldwide with a view to curbing illicit drug trafficking through criminalization and punishment. The cornerstone of the 1988 Convention is Article 3, "Offenses and Sanctions." Here the treaty requires criminalization of the full range of activities associated with consumption, production, and trafficking, spelled out in minute detail and including, for the first time, precursors as well. It also requires nations to confiscate proceeds from drug offenses and establish formal mechanisms for helping each other in criminal investigation and prosecution (United Nations, 1988:3–11).

Despite the focus on trafficking, the 1988 Convention is influenced by the growing attention to demand issues. Almost paradoxically, though, this attention translates into a thorough criminalization of drug users. Article 3(2) of the 1988 treaty explicitly requires each party, subject to its constitutional principles and the basic concepts of its legal system, to establish as a criminal offense the possession, purchase, or cultivation of narcotic drugs or psychotropic substances for personal consumption (United Nations, 1988:3).

A Brief Coda for 1970–2000

We conclude this section with a brief coda for the period 1970 to 2000, bridging this chapter on history with the next on the present-day market. Although the golden era of 1945 to 1965 was one of declining and even low use, the remainder of the 20th century saw a rebound in consumption and the emergence of an entirely new phenomenon: illegal mass markets in heroin and widespread, international distribution networks. Mass markets developed in countries on all continents except Africa. European nations emerged again as major consumers, along with the United States, Australia, and others. Paralleling trends in the general economy, which witnessed an extraordinary growth in international trade in the 1970s, the opiate market became a more truly international, possibly even global, market (see chapter 3).

From the early 1960s onward, production gradually shifted to Southeast Asia, which previously accounted for just a small share of world production. The so-called Golden Triangle (Burma, Thailand, and Laos) became the dominant source; McCoy (1991) estimates that it accounted for two thirds of world production in 1970. Although all these countries had some population groups with long histories of opium consumption, they had not been large-scale producers. Afghanistan, also a minor producer in earlier times,[30] became the most important producer outside the Golden Triangle, with some opium poppy cultivation and even more opiate processing spilling over into Pakistan.

During the last quarter of the 20th century, some major illicit producer countries gradually dropped out of the international market or became very minor producers, possibly the result of both policy changes and increasing wealth. As already mentioned, Turkey did so during the early 1970s; Pakistan and Thailand followed suit in the 1990s, although Pakistan has resumed production more recently. Illicit production became increasingly concentrated in two Asian nations—Afghanistan and Burma—but it has continued in other countries, such as Laos, Mexico, and, through diversion from legal production, India. One new producing country entered the market in the 1990s—Colombia—but its production has recently declined. With the exceptions of Laos and India, each of these countries produces largely for export.[31]

The market also underwent changes in the nature of production. At one time, production consisted largely of cultivation and, to a lesser extent, refining into smoking opium in the producer countries. However, with an increased global demand for heroin, refining into morphine and heroin, which can bring far greater financial reward to producing countries, gained in importance. Countries that had once focused on cultivation became increasingly involved in these latter stages of refining.

Concluding Remarks

Over the past two centuries, the opiate market has experienced major changes and upheavals, including a substantial ebb in consumption from the early 20th century to the 1960s. Although conditions for policy interventions are much different now from what they were at the start of the 20th century, the fact that the market is not static and has already once undergone a lasting phase of decline may encourage modest optimism for the roles of policy intervention in the future.

The historical evidence also suggests that changes in policies, some stemming from international agreements, especially the first and second International Opium Conventions of 1912 and 1925, played a part in the major reductions in opium consumption that occurred during the first half of 20th century. Historical evidence, however, also clearly shows that changes in societal and, specifically, physicians' perceptions of opiates played the greater part (as clearly exemplified by the experiences of China, the United Kingdom, and the United States).

To the extent that policies played a part in the early reductions, a key element in their success was the fact that opium markets were tightly controlled and, in some cases, even directly organized by national governments or colonial administrations. Thus, policy makers had effective—or potentially effective—leverage in the opiate market, after they decided to restrict distribution and consumption. The relatively few private producers of opium derivatives were all large pharmaceutical companies, which were vulnerable to adverse publicity. For them, it was, in the long run, not worth producing morphine and heroin in violation of international conventions and national laws, although the pharmaceutical companies aggressively lobbied against their adoption and some were involved in smuggling cases in the 1920s.

Another important difference between then and now is that during the early 20th century there was no world illicit distribution system. The early efforts made to develop it during the 1920s and 1930s were disrupted by World War II. The remaining illegal markets developed on a local, sometimes national, basis. Up until the late 1960s, after the gradual exit of national governments, colonial authorities, and large-scale pharmaceutical companies from the supply side of the market, there were no powerful connecting links between the segmented local markets. Domestic Asian markets were largely supplied with opium diverted from licit production (India, Turkey, and, intermittently, Iran) or from illicit production in the countries themselves (Laos, Thailand, and again Iran) or in neighboring ones (increasingly Afghanistan and Burma). With the partial exception of the United States, western countries remained, up until the 1960s, largely cut off from illegal opium-producing areas. Despite the mythology surrounding it, even the famous French Connection was responsible for relatively small heroin flows into the U.S. market.

The consolidation and expansion of the control regime in the 1960s, '70s, and '80s, to include prohibition against consumption, did not prevent renewed expansion of opiate consumption or the tendency toward mass markets and widespread distribution networks. Nor does the adoption of the more stringent policies appear to have caused them. Nevertheless, the enactment of restrictive legislation was not without effects on consumption. It engendered, first of all, a shift from opium to heroin, which is much more practical as an illegal drug; it fostered the spread of injecting drug use; and, in prohibitionist regimes, it prevented users from seeking medical help.

Moreover, we believe that prohibition of opiate production and trade affects the structure and functioning of the market. Contemporary suppliers are much less sophisticated and stable than the big players of the early 20th century—a notable consequence of the international drug control regime (see chapter 10). The relative disorganization of suppliers has both advantages and disadvantages. Few producers or traffickers have enough means and authority to challenge the control system; however, the illicit opiate production and distribution chain is today hardly governable.

Let us now briefly summarize what we have learned about international and domestic drug control efforts. Increasing control and prohibition of opiates reflected cultural biases of western societies and governments. Other psychoactive drugs, and tobacco and alcohol in particular, have not been subject to any comparable international control regime, because their use and production were widespread and accepted in at least some key western nations; and they enjoyed, at least since the early 20th century, more substantive corporate backing and fiscal influence than opiates (colonies excluded) ever did (Courtwright, 2001b). Historical evidence also shows that domestic policy reactions depend very much on who the users are. In several western countries and in Japan, the first restrictive provisions targeted opium smoking, because this was primarily a Chinese migrant behavior. Courtwright (2001a) has also shown that increasingly prohibitionist policies were adopted in the United States whenever opiate consumption was primarily associated with the underworld and/or ethnic minorities.

The development of the international drug control regime and the parallel domestic legislation have neither been a linear process, nor have they always been purely prohibitionist. The international drug control regime has, since it began, had a definite supply-side focus, which has been only partially moderated since the 1980s by increased international attention to demand reduction programs.

The fact that the international drug control regime initially lacked a clear prohibitionist rationale is one reason that historical evidence provides insight to the advantages, drawbacks, and risks of differing policy options. During the course of the past century, one finds an extraordinary variety of policies, ranging from an almost complete absence of regulation to almost complete prohibition. We discuss some options for supply-oriented policy at the end of the book (chapter 11).

3

The Contemporary Market

Introduction

This chapter presents an overview of the contemporary world opiate market and supply–control programs. It provides both a static portrait—a "snapshot"—of the market and insight to its dynamics. We consider both sides of the market—supply and demand—because, as is true of all markets, be they for illicit or licit products, one side cannot exist meaningfully without the other.[1] As a practical matter, there would be no opiate production and trafficking without consumption, and no opiate consumption without production and trafficking. Moreover, actual patterns of production, trafficking, and consumption ultimately depend on interactions between the two sides. If, for example, the costs of production and trafficking increase, the simultaneous and sequential responses of producers, traffickers, and consumers to the changes in costs will determine the new levels of production, trafficking, and consumption, and the prices of opiates along the supply chain. Only by considering both sides of the market can we fully assess the potential effects of efforts to reduce the world supply of opiates.

One feature of notable interest in this market is the relative concentration of global supply vis-à-vis demand. Only a small number of countries produces opiates or engages in transshipment whereas many countries, particularly in Asia, but also in North America, Europe, and Oceania, which includes Australia and New Zealand, report large numbers of consumers.

Another noteworthy feature is the market's apparent *segmentation*. Producers in one specific country or region serve consumers in another via a small number of particular routes. They face higher costs in supplying new regions, at least initially and sometimes indefinitely. Traffickers rely heavily on "relational capital"[2] ; shifting from one route to another or servicing a new market may require that they establish new connections or build new networks. Moreover, underlying differences in operating costs, ranging from the most ordinary, such as those associated with basic transportation, to the least ordinary, such as those associated with the risks of doing business illegally, may provide little incentive to implement change. In this as in other markets, neighbors may trade among themselves simply because transportation costs are lower, but also because the odds of seizure, arrest, and punishment are lower.[3]

Segmentation has important implications for market adjustments and outcomes. For example, if buyers in western Europe depend on sellers in Afghanistan, a "shock" to the market, like a drought or the Taliban ban, may elicit more serious initial disruptions in western Europe than would otherwise occur in a globally integrated market. We explore four sources of evidence of segmentation in this and later chapters: first, data on opiate prices and seizures, which we discuss in this chapter; second, the response of the market to the Taliban ban (chapter 4); third, evidence of conditions that might give rise to segmentation, including the reliance on relationships that arises from illegality and enforcement (chapter 10); and fourth, official opinions (chapter 5). In this last category most U.S. government officials suggest that Colombia and Mexico provide opiates to the United States, largely meeting its needs, and that Asia provides opiates to itself, Europe, Australia, and other major consumers. Our analysis of the evidence suggests that this segmentation occurs, but is not absolute.

Current Conditions and Market Trends

This section presents data on production and then moves through the market to trafficking and consumption. All of the data are weak—this is, after all, an illicit market spanning multiple countries and regions—but the data on production have a more systematic and scientific basis than those on consumption, which in turn are stronger than those on trafficking.

Notwithstanding the shortcomings of the data, some basic facts emerge. Afghanistan and Burma lead in production, and neighboring countries such as Iran, Pakistan, and Tajikistan lead in cross-border trafficking. Some of these nations are very poor and none is rich. Consumption is diffuse, having spread through North America, especially the United States, and Europe during the late 20th century, but Asia still dominates in terms of volume, if not retail revenues. Some of the West's leading consumer countries are quite wealthy and they account for more of the market's retail revenues. The relative concentration of supply—producers and traffickers in a few countries supply consumers in many countries—suggests that suppliers could have a market advantage, but we find little evidence of advantage in our analysis.

Producing Countries

When assessing producer countries, the big picture is clear, but the specifics are sometimes blurry. Although the data on production are the strongest, substantial uncertainties remain with regard to the amount of land under cultivation and the amount of opiates that the land produces.

Using different measurement methods, the United Nations and the United States sometimes arrive at markedly different estimates of the area under cultivation.[4] For example, the United States (U.S. Department of State, Bureau of International Narcotics and Law Enforcement Affairs, 2006:23) reported 51,500 and 64,510 hectares under cultivation in Afghanistan in 1999 and 2000, respectively, suggesting a substantial increase; by comparison, the United Nations (UNODC, 2006:57) reported 90,583 and 82,171 hectares for the same years, respectively, suggesting a substantial decrease. The differences in the U.S. and United Nations estimates for Afghan cultivation in 2004 are even more dramatic: The United States reported 206,700 hectares and the United Nations reported 131,000 hectares.

Extrapolating from the amount of land under cultivation to the amount of opiate production requires estimates of the opium content of poppies and the efficiency of the laboratories that process the opium gum or latex into morphine or heroin; both are known to vary across and within countries and over time. They have been the subject of considerable debate, and occasionally the U.S. government, which produces regular estimates in its annual *International Narcotics Control Strategy Report* (INCSR), has announced major changes in its estimates resulting from revisions in its assumptions about yields—specifically, the amount of opium, morphine, or heroin that can be obtained from each hectare of poppies—in particular countries.[5] Until recently, the UNODC universally applied a 10-to-1 rule of thumb conversion rate for opium to heroin; it now reports potential heroin production for Afghanistan on the basis of annual survey data, but the differences are slight. The implied conversion rates for 2004, 2005, and 2006, were 9.77, 9.76, and 10.99, respectively (UNODC, 2007a:40).

Uncertainties notwithstanding, the data suggest a clear pattern of production across countries (table 3.1). Afghanistan and, to a lesser extent, Burma effectively "own" world opium production, with a fringe of second- and third-tier producers contributing very little. Together, Afghanistan and Burma accounted for about 97% of world production in 2006, amounting to 6,415 out of 6,610 metric tons, based on estimates from the UNODC (2007a:40).[6] These two countries have ranked first or second every year since 1988, when systematic estimation first began. Even in 2001, when the Taliban cut Afghanistan's production by more than 90%, Afghanistan was still the world's second largest opium producer. However, in the years postdating the cutback, Afghanistan has consolidated its lead. Afghanistan's share of the total was 92% in 2006. Its share appears to be rising both because of increases in production in Afghanistan and declines elsewhere. Burma's opium production, although

Table 3.1
Potential world opium and heroin production, 1988–2006.

	1988	1989	1990	1991	1992	1993	1994	1995	1996	1997	1998	1999	2000	2001	2002	2003	2004	2005	2006
Potential opium production (in metric tons, dry weight)																			
Southwest Asia																			
Afghanistan	1,120	1,200	1,570	1,980	1,970	2,330	3,416	2,335	2,248	2,804	2,693	4,565	3,276	185	3,400	3,600	4,200	4,100	6,100
Pakistan	130	149	150	160	181	161	128	112	24	24	26	9	8	5	5	52	40	36	39
Subtotal	1,250	1,349	1,720	2,140	2,151	2,491	3,544	2,447	2,272	2,828	2,719	4,574	3,284	190	3,405	3,652	4,240	4,136	6,139
Southeast Asia																			
Laos	267	278	202	196	127	169	120	128	140	147	124	124	167	134	112	120	43	14	20
Burma	1,125	1,544	1,621	1,728	1,660	1,791	1,583	1,664	1,760	1,676	1,303	895	1,087	1,097	828	810	370	312	315
Thailand	17	31	20	23	14	17	3	2	5	4	8	8	6	6	9	*	*	*	*
Vietnam	60	70	90	85	61	21	15	9	9	2	2	2	*	*	*	*	*	*	*
Subtotal	1,469	1,923	1,933	2,032	1,862	1,998	1,721	1,803	1,914	1,829	1,437	1,029	1,260	1,237	949	930	413	326	335
Latin America																			
Colombia				16	90	68	205	71	67	90	100	88	88	80	76	76	56	28	14
Mexico	67	66	62	41	40	49	60	53	54	46	60	43	21	91	58	101	73	71	n/a
Subtotal	67	66	62	57	130	117	265	124	121	136	160	131	109	171	134	177	129	99	85
Other																			
Combined	8	57	45	45		4	90	78	48	30	30	30	38	32	32	24	68	59	51
Grand total	2,794	3,395	3,760	4,274	4,143	4,610	5,620	4,452	4,355	4,823	4,346	5,764	4,691	1,630	4,520	4,783	4,850	4,620	6,610
Potential heroin production (in metric tons)																			
Grand total	279	340	376	427	414	461	562	445	436	482	435	576	469	163	452	478	495	472	606

Note: *Included in "other" category. Through 2003, the UNODC applied a 10:1 ratio of opium to morphine or heroin to establish potential heroin production for all countries. Beginning in 2004, it reported potential production for Afghanistan on the basis of annual survey data, but the differences are modest. As have other UN reports, the UNODC (2007a) contains revised estimates of past production; e.g., the UNODC (2006:57) reported Pakistani production as 70 metric tons and 61 metric tons for 2004 and 2005, respectively, and Mexican production as 71, 47, 84, and 69 metric tons for 2001, 2002, 2003, and 2005, respectively.
Source: UNODC (2007a:40) for 1990–2006 production statistics, and UNODCCP (2002c:47) and UNODCCP (2001:60) for earlier years.

44

still substantial, has declined markedly since 2001, largely reflecting political decisions by the ruling autonomous regional irredentist authorities, such as the United Wa State Army (UWSA), to ban production and exit the market.

As table 3.1 shows, second-tier opium producers include Colombia, Laos,[7] Mexico, and Pakistan. Production in Colombia and Laos has declined during recent years, but is still substantial; production in Pakistan fell to near nothing during the late 1990s, but has since reemerged on par with other second-tier producers. Pakistan's experience suggests that a nation can reverse course on a seemingly long-term market exit strategy. Moreover, Colombia's entry in the early to mid 1990s demonstrates the potential for growth and reconfiguration in the market. At one time, the vast majority of U.S. consumption originated in Southeast Asia and Mexico; now, with Colombia's entry, Latin America's role has expanded.[8] A sustained reduction in Colombian production could result in yet another reconfiguration. Note that we do not include diversion from India's licit production in these estimates because neither the United Nations nor the United States accounts for it in their production estimates, but in later chapters we find that India probably ranks among the second-tier illicit producers. Thailand and Vietnam comprise the third tier; once major producers, they now are almost insignificant.

The price of opium at the farm gate varies greatly across countries and over time. For example, according to the UNODC, farmers in Afghanistan received an average of $283 per kilogram in 2003, whereas their counterparts in Burma received $130 (UNODC, 2004:68). The average harvest price in Afghanistan has generally declined since 2003, falling to $125 per kilogram in 2006, whereas the average price in Burma has generally increased, reaching $230 per kilogram during the same year (UNODC, 2007a:195, 212).[9] The relative price changes are directionally consistent with reported changes in production in both countries. For 2004, the UNODC reports that the price of opium latex in Colombia was $164 per kilogram and that about 24 kilos of latex were needed to produce 1 kilogram of heroin, generating an opium equivalent farm-gate price of almost $400 per kilogram (UNODC, 2006:232).[10] For 2006, it reports an average latex price of $237 per kilogram, suggesting an opium equivalent price of $565 per kilogram (UNODC, 2007a:205).

The cross-country differences in farm-gate prices are conceptually consistent with market segmentation and may provide evidence to support it. Cross-country price differences for agricultural and other commodities typically stem from differences in costs of production.[11] In this case, they also stem from differences in the risks of eradication, seizure, or arrest and punishment associated with production. The higher the risks in a given location, the higher the effective costs of production. However, absent capacity constraints, these differences can persist only if there are barriers to trade—or entry—or offsetting differences in costs elsewhere in the supply chain, such as those involved in bringing the opiates to market.[12] In the opiate industry the need for relational capital poses a potential barrier to entry for traffickers and the costs of trafficking, including basic transportation costs and, as in production, the risks of seizure or arrest and punishment, may differ across supply routes.[13] After accounting for all the costs along the opiate supply chain, it may be economically feasible for seemingly higher cost producers in one county, like Colombia, to produce for the U.S. market, even if it is not feasible to produce for the European market, simply because it is cheaper to smuggle to the United States from Colombia than from Afghanistan. Similarly, it may be economically feasible for producers in a seemingly low-cost country like Afghanistan to produce for the European market, but not for the U.S. market.

Trafficking Countries

Opiate transshipments also involve a relatively small number of nations. For Afghanistan's opiates, large quantities flow through four of its neighbors: Iran, Pakistan, Tajikistan, and, to a much lesser extent, Turkmenistan. Little seems to flow through either China or Uzbekistan. The border between China and Afghanistan is small and inhospitable, even for drug smugglers.[14] The border with Uzbekistan is longer, but the government of Uzbekistan has made it difficult enough to penetrate that the more porous border with Tajikistan attracts much of Central Asian traffic. We address Tajikistan's role as an opiate-trafficking nation, which took shape over less than a decade, in chapter 9 and appendix C. Turkey is also a major trafficking country because western European-destined heroin exits Iran through Turkey.

Golden Triangle opiates, such as those originating in Burma, have been transshipped traditionally through Thailand and, since the late 1980s, also through China to a number of distant markets, including Australia, Canada, and western Europe. The borders between Burma and its neighbors are not densely settled and, with their thick jungles, they are hard to police. However, the decline in production in Burma is likely to render Thailand and China less important as trafficking nations.

Knowledge about trafficking volumes and routes derives from the barest of indirect statistical evidence. Almost the only available quantitative indicator is drug seizures, but these data require careful interpretation.[15] Seizures can be driven by production, local consumption, and transshipment. Nations with large seizures that are neither producers nor major consumers are, by default, likely to be nations involved in trafficking to other countries. The relatively large amounts seized in Turkey and Tajikistan illustrate this reasoning. It is also a one-sided indicator; some trafficking nations, either as a result of corruption or limited enforcement effort, may have few seizures. The figures for Russia illustrate this problem. Although it constitutes one of the three largest markets for heroin and serves as a major transshipment country, Russia seized barely 1 metric ton of heroin annually until 2003.[16] In addition, the annual series for most countries are quite noisy, because a few large seizures can substantially affect the total. Historical data for Germany help to illustrate this point. For example, in 1992, German heroin seizures totaled 1,438 kilograms. In 1993, that figure fell by

Table 3.2

Selected nations' average 2003 to 2005 opiate seizures (in metric tons unless otherwise stated).

	Opium*	Heroin[†]	Total	Share
Iran	16.77	15.49	32.26	0.27
Pakistan	0.49	27.74	28.23	0.24
Tajikistan	0.19	4.25	4.44	0.04
Afghanistan	4.03	4.15	8.18	0.07
Subtotal	21.48	51.63	73.11	0.62
Russia	0.19	3.95	4.14	0.03
Turkey	0.02	9.34	9.36	0.08
China	0.13	9.82	9.95	0.08
Other countries	1.08	20.93	22.01	0.19
Total seizures	22.90	95.67	118.57	1.00

Note: *In pure heroin equivalent units, assuming a conversion ratio of 10 units of opium to 1 unit of heroin or morphine. †As reported (in street purity, without adjustments), including morphine when data on morphine seizures are available.

Source: Authors' calculations base on UNODC (2007a:53–54, b:n.p.).

almost 25% to 1,095 kilograms; it rose by nearly 50% the following year to 1,590 kilograms and then it fell by more than one third to 995 kilograms in 1995 (BKA, 2001:112). Throughout a number of years, however, the seizure data may suggest patterns and routes of trafficking.

Table 3.2 lists the countries with the largest seizures of opiates (i.e., heroin, morphine, and opium) in 2005 and provides figures on their average annual seizures for 2003 to 2005. We measure opiate seizures in heroin equivalent units, using a rule of thumb of 10 units of opium per 1 unit of heroin or morphine. We do not adjust for any differences in purity along the supply chain (see appendix B). The far right column in table 3.2 presents each country's share of global seizures.

Total seizures during 2003 to 2005 averaged about 25% of potential production, and well more than half the opiates seized came from countries that border Afghanistan and from Afghanistan itself. Iran, Pakistan, Tajikistan, and Afghanistan together accounted for more than 60% of global opiate seizures; together, they accounted for nearly all the opium seizures.

Because the purity of opiates tends to decline as they move through the supply chain, any purity adjustment would be likely to reinforce the conclusion that most seizures occur in a small number of Asian nations. We might also conclude that these countries are deeply involved in trafficking because most, if not all, do not produce or consume enough opiates to account independently for the reported levels of seizures.[17] The results of the data analysis in chapter 5 reinforce these conclusions.

The seizure data, which trace distinct and sometimes complex patterns of distribution, also suggest market segmentation. In a manner that is stable over a number of years, opiates appear to flow through specific channels to particular destinations: From Afghanistan through Pakistan, Iran, and Turkey, on to western Europe; from Afghanistan through Central Asia, especially Tajikistan, to Russia and other eastern European countries; from Burma through Thailand and China, on to Australia, Canada, and western Europe. Data on the chemical composition of seizures, such as those from the U.S. Heroin Signature Program, provide further evidence (Abt Associates, 1999). For the United States, a large fraction of seized opiates now originates in Latin America, specifically Mexico and Colombia, although at least some still originates in Asia.[18] Here too, however, the data may suffer biases. For example, it may be that interdictors tend to pick up a larger fraction of heroin flowing from Latin America compared with that coming from Asia because the Asia-originating shipment sizes are smaller and less easily detected. Nevertheless, it seems clear that a Latin American production capacity has emerged largely for the purpose of serving U.S. consumers, even if it cannot meet the entire U.S. demand.

Consuming Countries

In its *World Drug Reports*,[19] the UNODC publishes estimates of the annual prevalence of illicit opiate and other drug use that are reported to the UNODC by national governments.[20] Yet, with the exception of the United States and more recently a few other industrialized nations,[21] most countries have not developed the necessary capability to collect such information. Thus, the UNODC prevalence reports suffer from the absence of data in many countries, from differences in estimation methodologies across countries, and also from the biases that governments bring to their reports of prevalence. Some governments seek to exaggerate their drug problems, perhaps in the hope of attracting international aid, whereas others seek to minimize the appearance of their problems.[22]

Opiates are considered to be the biggest "problem drug" in the world in that they result in the greatest demand for treatment; opiates account for almost two thirds of all treatment demand in Asia and 60% in Europe (UNODC, 2006:74). Moreover, heroin injection is a principal vector for the spread of human immunodeficiency virus (HIV) in a number of countries, including Thailand and the United States. Ranked by the estimated number of "users," opiates would rank third among illegal drugs. Nearly 16 million people, about 0.4% of the world's adult population, use opiates; a roughly similar number, about 13 million, use cocaine. By comparison, more than 160 million people use marijuana and almost 35 million people use amphetamine-type stimulants (ATS), including Ecstasy. Most opiate users, about 11 million people, use heroin; of the remainder, those that use opium tend to reside in Asia, oftentimes in or in close proximity to producing countries. However, in

Russia and some other eastern European countries, including Poland and the Ukraine, a substantial number of so-called heroin users still use a less potent and domestically produced liquid extract of poppy straw, known as *compote*. We address the different modes of consumption in more detail later in this chapter.

Table 3.3 reports prevalence figures for opiates, both in terms of percentage of population and number of persons, for major regions and nations. National governments report the percentage of population figures to the UNODC and may include both dependent and casual or occasional users. In theory, the prevalence rates could consist mostly of casual or occasional users, but the evidence, albeit limited, suggests that the majority of heroin users in rich countries are dependent users who consume frequently.[23] Anecdotally, this also appears to be true for heroin users in developing nations. We have less evidence of the extent of dependence among opium users.

Table 3.3
Prevalence estimates for opiate use in recent years (percent of population and number of persons age 15–64).

	Percent of Population	No. of Persons	Share
Europe	0.7	4,030,000	0.254
West and Central Europe	0.6	1,565,000	0.099
Southeast Europe	0.2	180,000	0.011
Eastern Europe	1.6	2,285,000	0.144
Russian Federation	2.0	2,000,000*	0.126
Americas	0.4	2,280,000	0.144
South America	0.3	980,000	0.062
North America	0.5	1,300,000	0.082
United States	0.6	1,200,000*	0.076
Asia	0.3	8,530,000	0.539
India	0.4	2,800,000*	0.177
China	0.2	1,900,000*	0.120
Iran	2.8	1,300,000*	0.082
Pakistan	0.8	750,000*	0.047
Oceania	0.4	90,000	0.006
Africa	0.2	910,000	0.057
Total	0.4	15,840,000	1.000

Note: *The estimate for the number of persons age 15 to 64 is from the CIA (2006). The prevalence rates in this table, as reported by the UNODC (2006), are not greatly different from those found in the UNODC (2007a). The only differences are in the rates for Pakistan (0.7) and for western and Central Europe (0.5).

Source: Authors' calculations based on UNODC (2006:75–80, 383–384), reporting the most recent estimates for each country; and the CIA (2006:n.p.).

As shown in table 3.3, the bulk of opiate users are in developing nations, largely in Asia, which accounts for more than half of all users. Even though China has a low estimated prevalence rate, the UNODC figures show that it has more opiate users than all but one or two other nations, simply because of its huge population. (China recently increased its reported prevalence rate from 0.1% to 0.2%, resulting in an apparent doubling of opiate users, but more likely reflecting a change in data collection or measurement practices.) India, with a moderate estimated prevalence rate, has by far the largest number of opiate users for the same reason. In most of western Europe and the United States, the rates are moderately high, but there has been little growth since the mid 1990s.[24] In contrast, Central Asia and eastern Europe have seen sharp increases in opiate use in recent years (Ponce, 2002; Roston, 2002). By the beginning of the 21st century, for example, the prevalence rate of opiate use had shot up to 2.3% in Kyrgyzstan, 2.1% in Russia, 1.7% in Latvia, 1.3% in Kazakhstan, and 1.2% in Estonia (UNODC, 2004:390–391). However, the prevalence rates for Russia and other eastern European countries may significantly overstate the use of opium, heroin, and morphine, and their participation in the world market, because the rates likely include a large number of compote users. More generally, we note that the prevalence rates for Russia—and Iran—are high relative to those for other countries and result in extraordinarily large numbers of users. These numbers have appeared regularly in UNODC and other publications, but we repeat them with skepticism.[25]

These data indicate numbers of opiate users, but estimates of national consumption require information on quantities. Unfortunately, however, there are almost no data on the average quantities that typical users consume in each country (see appendix B). This reflects the fact that users, be they addicts or otherwise, can report only how much they spend on drugs, such as heroin, or how frequently they inject, but cannot report how much of the active drug they purchase; purity is variable and cannot be observed directly. There is some evidence to suggest that U.S. heroin addicts, faced with higher real prices, even relative to incomes and purchasing power, consume less pure heroin per annum than their counterparts in Europe and elsewhere. On the basis of that evidence, we estimate that the average U.S. user consumes about 15 grams of pure heroin each year and that users in other countries consume about 30 grams.[26] (See appendix B for a discussion of the available evidence and the basis for our calculations.) We refer to the 30-gram estimate as a "default" estimate for non-U.S. consumption and use it in later chapters for various benchmark calculations.

Calculations based on this approach strongly suggest that countries in Asia account for a substantial majority of all opiate consumption in tonnage if not revenue. (This result on tonnage does not depend on the lower U.S. estimate.[27]) On the basis of the 15- and 30-gram estimates, 1.2 million U.S. users and 14.6 million users in other countries would consume about 457 metric tons of pure heroin, amounting to about 75% of total production in 2006, before subtracting seizures.

How Much Revenue Does the Market Generate—and For Whom?

Opiates generate revenue all along the supply chain, starting with the farmers who plant the opium poppies and ending with retail-level traffickers or "dealers." Gross estimates of revenues by market level are typically largest at the retail level and smallest at the farm level, but all are subject to conjecture and debate, and those at the retail level are subject to some of the most visible controversy (Reuter and Greenfield, 2001).

Chapter 2 of the UNODC's 2005 *World Drug Report* (UNODC, 2005d) contains the most recent systematic effort to produce a comprehensive set of estimates; the UNODC model uses 2002 and 2003 data from a prior UNODC report. For illicit drugs as a whole, the UNODC estimates a total of almost $322 billion in retail sales, $94 billion in wholesale revenues, and almost $13 billion in producer sales (UNODC, 2005d:127). Retail opiate sales, mostly heroin, amount to almost $65 billion. Of this $65 billion, Europe accounts for $37 billion (or 56%), Asia accounts for $14.4 billion (or 22%), and North America accounts for $8.9 billion (or 14%) (UNODC, 2005d:134). Oceania, Africa, and South America account for the remainder. Were we to update the figure found in Reuter and Greenfield (2001), we would arrive at a slightly lower figure for total retail opiate sales, but still well into the tens of billions of dollars.

Retail expenditures are dominated by rich-country consumers, simply because retail prices are so much higher in those nations. For example, at roughly similar purities, the retail price of a gram of heroin in Tajikistan in the year 2003 ranged from $1.30 to $2.60 compared to about $116 in the United States (UNODC, 2005d, 345–347; UNODC, 2006:365–367). In Thailand, a relatively successful developing nation, the estimated annual expenditure for a heroin addict in the mid 1990s was approximately $1,150, compared with $30,000 in Italy (UNDCP, 1997:269–280, 303–310).

However, the prices received by growers and traffickers in producing countries are not generally dependent on the final destination. A shift of consumption of Afghanistan-originating heroin from Europe to China has little significance to Afghan producers or traffickers in terms of the revenue they receive. Hence, it is approximately true that the consumers in the developing world, principally in Asia, account for most of the earnings of opium producers and source–country traffickers, because they account for most of the volume of opiate consumption.

Afghanistan can expect to see only a small fraction of the retail value that its opium ultimately generates. As a general rule, revenues from illicit drug production are tiny relative to the total revenues generated by retail sales, and opium is no exception. For all illicit drugs, the UNODC (2005d) figures suggest an average of about 4%; for opiates alone, the share seems to be even lower. In contrast to the total retail figure of almost $65 billion, of which Afghan farmers might have been responsible for almost $50 billion based on their share of total opium production in 2003, the UNODC (2005d:181) estimates that Afghan farmers' revenues for 2003 were only about $1 billion.[28] The United Nations figures indicate that Afghan opium farmers received about 2% of Afghan-originating retail revenues. Even with a more conservative estimate of total retail revenues, the farmers' share is likely to be less than the 4% average for all drugs. Afghanistan's traffickers, especially those at the border, may have fared slightly better because the export value of Afghan opium was about $2.3 billion or almost 5% of the retail value of the opium and its derivatives (UNODC, 2005d:181).

The data also speak to the accrual of value added along the opiate supply chain and across national borders. Accrual rates tend to be lowest in the vicinity of the point of origin (i.e., the farm gate and local markets), and highest across national borders and, eventually, in retail markets. In sharp contrast to licit agriculturally based products, markups may be enormous as opiates transit from one country to another, even more so as they enter western nations (Reuter and Greenfield, 2001:166–169). The foregoing data support this claim. In 2003, the total export value of Afghan opium was more than twice the farm-gate value ($2.3 billion compared with $1 billion).[29] The final retail value of the opium, largely converted to heroin, was an order of magnitude greater than the export value (almost $50 billion compared with $2.3 billion). Opiates generate far more income outside producing countries than in them.[30]

Processing, which most typically occurs after opium leaves the farm gate, may account for some of the increase in value added as the opiates move along the supply chain. In conventional agricultural markets, processing can add substantially to the value of agricultural commodities, depending partly on the extent of processing and related capital and labor requirements. For example, in the United States, processing accounted for about 45% of the retail value of sugar, 14% of the retail value of pork, and only 6% of the retail value of beef in the 1990s (Elitzak, 1999:36, 40). In the opiate market, we generally observe heroin selling at prices in excess of the opium equivalent, but have some difficulty calculating the value added in processing because of differences in purity. The capital and labor requirements for heroin processing are modest; however, we conjecture that the gains are large enough to help explain the increasing tendency to convert opium to heroin in Afghanistan. Perhaps ironically, economists typically regard processing— of ordinary, legal goods—as a sign of economic advancement in developing countries.

The distribution of risk along the supply chain may also be an important factor, perhaps the most important factor, in explaining the accrual patterns, notably the very large jumps in value added that occur in cross-border transit. The business of trade across countries may be significantly riskier than trading within countries, particularly within known producing countries. Reuter and Greenfield (2001) address the basis for the distribution of value added along the supply chain in greater detail, including the potential roles of illegality and risk. We offer additional evidence in appendix C, on Central Asian incomes, and continue our discussion in chapter 10, which focuses on the roles of illegality, enforcement, and risk.

Properties of Supply and Demand

We begin with a discussion of opiate production. Notwithstanding its formal illegality in major producing nations, such as Afghanistan and Burma, UNODC observers, aid workers, and others have had the opportunity to study poppy cultivation and opium production much as they might study other agricultural commodities and agriculturally based products. (Appendix A provides supplemental information on production in legal settings.) For the most part, we focus more on the mechanics of production, and how they would affect the supply of opiates, and less on trafficking, illegality, and risk, which we address in greater detail in later chapters, such as chapter 10. Next we turn to demand, considering both the epidemic nature of demand creation and consumers' responses to changes in market conditions.

Properties of Supply

Opiates are agriculturally based commodities, subject to the same types of biological and physical considerations as other agriculturally based commodities.[31] They must be grown, harvested, processed, and distributed.[32] Farmers, mostly family farmers with small plots of land, plant the opium poppy, *Papaver somniferum,* from seed for each harvest. When it reaches maturity, they extract opium from the caplet that forms at the base of the flower. Extraction requires a large amount of labor over a relatively short period of time; farmers may employ a combination of family and hired labor.[33] Ultimately, refiners convert much of the opium to heroin of varying grades through a series of simple chemical processes. As it transits the supply chain, the heroin may then undergo dilution to varying degrees of purity.[34]

The poppy that gives rise to opium is captive to conditions of seasonality, rainfall, soil quality, and so forth, but it can tolerate a range of conditions, which can be found in Afghanistan, Burma, Laos, Colombia, Mexico, and elsewhere, with or without human intervention.[35] The plant is not equally productive in each setting, in that it may yield less opium per poppy plant or per hectare, but it can be sufficiently productive to make economic sense as a part of a country or region's agricultural landscape. For example, the UNODC (2006:55–56) reports Afghan yields of 39 kilograms of opium per hectare compared with Burmese yields of only 5.4 to 13.4 kilograms per hectare.

Constraints of Nature and Growing Cycles

Notwithstanding the tolerance of the opium poppy, nature imposes certain limits on production.[36] There may be some "give" around the edges of each season (e.g., a farmer may be able to plant a little later than usual, possibly in exchange for a loss of yield), but seasonality still poses a real constraint. Moreover, once farmers within a particular region have made their planting decisions and the time to plant is truly over, little can be done to change— especially to augment—the outcome. Farmers might, for example, consider hiring more labor for a more thorough harvest, but they cannot add more seed to the ground. However, if market conditions were to deteriorate, they could choose to hire no one and abandon their harvests partly or entirely. Apart from the potential for some amount of abandonment, the planting decisions of one moment largely determine the harvests of another; together they form a growing cycle.

The Afghan growing cycle typically spans 2 calendar years. Planting begins in the autumn of one calendar year and harvests commence the following spring in the next calendar year. Later plantings yield later harvests, depending on the location and climate. For example, in the north of Afghanistan, planting can occur in February or March (UNDCP, 2001a:10, note 9), so that the growing cycle does not span 2 calendar years. Thus, during the typical Afghan growing cycle, the planting decisions that farmers make in the autumn of one calendar year largely determine the size of the harvest the following spring in the next calendar year. Important factors beyond each farmer's control include weather conditions, although, in the case of rainfall, irrigation can restore some amount of control to the individual farmer.[37] Although planting usually begins the year preceding the harvest, both cultivation and production statistics are generally attributed to the year in which the harvest takes place.

In Burma, the growing cycle also spans 2 calendar years. Farmers typically grow opium poppy in the winter season—roughly September through February—in the Shan State, which accounts for the vast majority of Burma's remaining production (UNODC and Central Committee for Drug Abuse Control, 2005:18).[38] During the past few years, though, some farmers have prolonged the growing season by using multistage cropping to avoid eradication (UNODC, 2007a:212). The UNODC, Central Committee for Drug Abuse Control, Lao National Commission for Drug Control and Supervision, and Office of the Narcotics Control Board (2007:73) also report that, for the same reason, growing has been observed increasingly in the summer monsoon season—July through September—primarily in South Shan.

Setting aside the possibilities of off-cycle or multiseason plantings, it seems likely that most Afghan and Burmese farmers have been making their planting decisions contemporaneously or nearly contemporaneously. As such, it seems unlikely that Burmese farmers would have much chance to respond, at least in the same growing season, to changes in Afghan production, and vice versa. By the time farmers in Afghanistan or Burma learn of the planting decisions of farmers in the other country, they are probably locked into and constrained by their own planting decisions. Absent more definitive information about actual harvests, the farmers in either country might be hesitant to commit to a new allocation of resources.

Moreover, it also seems unlikely that farmers within or across countries are coordinating their activities or behaving strategically, in the sense that they are attempting to manipulate prices through decisions about how much they produce. Although we may refer to Afghanistan and Burma as if they were two discrete producers, they are not. In reality they are two countries, each with hundreds of thousands of actual producers—households of farmers.[39] Except to the extent that their respective state or quasi-state authorities can enact and enforce policy to effect strategic-like behavior, or traffickers are sufficiently well organized to exert similar pressures, we would have no reason to expect anything but competition at the level of individual farmers or households of farmers. Although some have argued that the Taliban ban is a prime example of policy-induced market manipulation, we have seen no comparable events in Afghanistan in more recent years, nor, as we discuss in the following chapter, do we have strong evidence that the ban was intended to manipulate prices.[40] And, although traffickers may have more sway than farmers, we lack compelling evidence of any significant control over production. Indeed, reports of increases in opium production in Afghanistan after the ban strongly suggest the opposite—a free-for-all.

Short- and Long-Run Supply Responses

Taken together, these depictions of natural requirements, growing cycles, and farmers' behavior suggest important temporal distinctions in the supply's responses to changes in market conditions. Using common economic vocabulary, supply tends to be "inelastic" or relatively unresponsive in the short run (i.e., within a growing season), and, depending on the potential for expansion within and across regions, it may be "elastic" or responsive in the long run.[41] Market conditions might change dramatically within a growing season, but farmers are usually ill-positioned to respond until the next or an even later growing season. The length of the delay would depend on the form of the change and the nature of the response. If, for example, market conditions were to improve, farmers who already grow opium poppies could choose to grow more, either by producing less of something else or by acquiring more land. In addition, farmers—or prospective farmers—who do not already grow opium poppies could choose to enter the market. Farmers who already grow opium poppies might be better poised to respond than new entrants: Current growers would need to line up additional resources, possibly including land and labor, but new entrants would also need to learn the "ins and outs" of the business.

Given that Afghanistan's farmers currently devote less than 3% of the country's cultivated land to opium growing (Mansfield, 2006:48) and that rural labor is seriously underemployed, it is plausible that production within Afghanistan could expand dramatically in the future. The recent explosion in Afghan production would seem to confirm that ample land and labor exist for expansion.

Temporal distinctions between short- and long-run supply responses are in no way unique to opium poppies. They are so well recognized in major commodity markets that a standard undergraduate microeconomic text book includes a discussion of a particularly relevant example involving the weather in Brazil and the price of coffee in New York (Pindyck and Rubinfeld, 2005:45–46). When Brazil, a dominant coffee producer, experiences a freeze or drought, the price of coffee tends to increase sharply, but the rise in price is usually short-lived.

Opium prices also can be expected to increase sharply in the short run in the face of a supply-reducing market shock, such as a drought or the Taliban ban, with lags in the responses of producers in other regions reinforcing the effect. Producers with later planting seasons, such as those in the north of Afghanistan, might have an opportunity to step in, if they know of the ban—in fact, there was an initial northward expansion in Afghanistan in 2001—but others would not. The short-run effects of the shock would be exacerbated if the market were highly segmented (e.g., if Burmese, Laotian, Mexican, or Colombian producers lacked the contacts and conduits to service Afghanistan's "ordinary" customers). Over time, however, production could expand in other regions. Whether it would expand into currently low- or non-producing areas would depend on a combination of conditions, such as the availability of land and labor, the suitability of climate, and the extent of enforcement against growing and trafficking (on the latter factor, see chapter 10). If other regions also have ample land and labor, suitable climates, and tolerable risks, the cost of opium might increase only modestly with relocation.[42]

The growth in production in Afghanistan, the apparent reemergence of production in Pakistan, the entry of Colombia as a major producer during the first half of the 1990s, and the reductions in production in Burma and, even more recently, in Laos and Colombia all demonstrate the possibility of movement into and out of the market, further implying that supply can and will eventually respond to shocks.

Nevertheless, even in the very short run, there are ways in which the market can respond and adjust to changes in market conditions.

In this, as in many or most other agricultural markets, storage offers a means of cushioning the blow of a market shock. Once harvested, opium can be and often is stored. Although bulky and reportedly malodorous, opium tends to retain its essential characteristics over reasonably long periods of time; it has a very respectable shelf life, which permits storage over several years (Pain, 2006:87). Farmers in Afghanistan have been known to hold stores of opium in lieu of reliable currency (Pain, 2006). With some non-negligible amount of storage, we can expect prices to increase less in response to droughts or bans. However, prices would also take longer to return to earlier, lower levels while farmers and others replenished their stocks. Storage may also occur at other points in the supply chain. As risk builds along the supply chain, the potential costs of holding inventory will increase, but even if traffickers hold only a very small fraction of their throughput, the cumulative effects could be substantial. The results of the flow model, which are presented in chapter 5, suggest that the amount of opiates in storage at the time of the ban were more than just substantial; they may have been large enough to meet the world's demand in a typical year.

Lastly, the effect of a supply-reducing market shock would also depend on the behavior of consumers. The less able—or willing—they are to adjust their consumption in response to the shock, the greater the increase in prices.

Properties of Demand

We turn now to the demand side of the market, first considering the epidemic nature of demand creation and then consumers' responses to changes in market conditions.

Drug Epidemics and Demand Creation

The concept of "epidemic" is often used to describe the initial and usually precipitous but limited phase of illicit drug demand creation and, particularly, the sudden expansion of heroin demand in a variety of contexts from the 1960s onward. The notion of a drug use epidemic captures the fact that drug use is a learned behavior, transmitted from one person to another. Contrary to the popular image of the entrepreneurial drug pusher who hooks new addicts through aggressive salesmanship, it is now clear that almost all first experiences are the result of being offered the drug by a friend. Drug use thus spreads much like a communicable disease; users are "contagious," and some of those with whom they come into contact become "infected" (e.g., Coomber, 2006).

During an epidemic, rates of initiation (akin to infection) increase sharply as new and highly contagious users of a drug initiate friends and peers (Hunt and Chambers, 1976; Rydell and Everingham, 1994). Most of those who try heroin are able to desist without treatment or intervention, but addiction has turned out to be a long-lived and sometimes lethal condition for many (Hser, Hoffman, Grella, and Anglin, 2001). At the end of an epidemic, initiation into drug use declines rapidly as the susceptible population shrinks, both because there are fewer non-users and because some non-users have developed "immunity," the result of better knowledge of the negative effects of a drug. At least with heroin, cocaine, and crack, long-term addicts are not particularly contagious. They are more socially isolated than new users and, knowing the pitfalls of prolonged use, may not want to expose others. Moreover, they usually present an unappealing picture of the consequences of addiction; they are more likely to retard than accelerate initiation.

The United States has experienced three major drug epidemics since 1965, each of which has left a legacy of users with long-term problems. The first epidemic involved heroin and developed with rapid initiation in the late 1960s, primarily in a few big cities, and heavily in inner city minority communities. The experiences of a large number of American soldiers in Vietnam also contributed (Courtwright, 2001a:165–170; chapter 2, this volume). By 1975, the number of new heroin initiates had dropped significantly (Kozel and Adams, 1986), perhaps because the negative consequences of regular heroin use had become so conspicuous in those communities. Rocheleau and Boyum have also found evidence of much higher initiation rates during the early 1970s than in the following two decades (ONDCP, 1994). The second and third major drug epidemics in the United States involved powder cocaine and crack cocaine, respectively.

Many other countries have seen the same pattern of sharp increases in the rate of initiation into heroin use and then comparably sharp declines in initiation, leaving a relatively stable population of long-term, dependent heroin users. Western Europe, Germany, Italy, and the Netherlands experienced heroin epidemics during the early 1970s; Spain experienced its epidemic at the end of the Franco era in the late 1970s. The Swiss epidemic occurred primarily during 1985 to 1995 (Nordt and Stohler, 2006). Russia has just begun to emerge from its epidemic, which occurred during the late 1990s (Paoli, 2001). The population of heroin users in Russia grew rapidly during the late 1990s, but the growth appears to have abated and the population may be leveling off. At least four countries in Central Asia—Kazakhstan, Kyrgyzstan, Tajikistan, and Uzbekistan—experienced a similar epidemic during the late 1990s.

The epidemics have varied in both their length and severity and—notwithstanding the visibility of a few public figures—the resulting addicted populations have been primarily of low socioeconomic status (see, for example, Parker, Bury, and Egginton, 1998).[43]

In most western nations, the drug is injected, but the Netherlands has long had a large fraction of heroin users who smoke heroin or "chase the dragon" (Strang, Griffiths, and Gossop, 1997).[44] This may reflect the initial prominence of Asian heroin users who brought the habit of smoking from their home culture, but it is a pattern not found in most of the western world. In Poland, the Ukraine, and many parts of Russia, the principal form of the drug until the mid 1990s was a locally originating and less potent compote. Heroin first became widely available in the former Warsaw Pact bloc in the mid 1990s, spreading rapidly from urban to rural areas, but compote use still occurs.[45] The former bloc countries of Central Asia have also become enmeshed in heroin consumption, partly as a consequence of geography; they are positioned between the world's largest producer, Afghanistan, and a now formidable consumer, Russia.

For most of the rest of Asia, the data are too sparse to allow a statistical description of the spread of heroin dependence over time, although the general impression is that increases have also happened rapidly. Description is complicated by the prior existence of opium users in some countries. It is impossible to determine how many of Thailand's heroin addicts in 2000 were former opium addicts, but the overlap may be modest. The Thai opium users were mostly in villages and were older, whereas the initial heroin users were mostly in urban areas and younger.

However, opium use likely remains significant in much of Asia. According to the UNODC (2006:75), 64% of opiate users in Asia are heroin users. The remaining 36% could include both opium and synthetic users. And, in some key Asian countries, such as India and Iran, opium users still constitute the majority of the opiate-using population. (For India, refer to chapter 7.) In Iran, according to estimates of the drug control headquarters (Cultural Research Bureau, 2001:79–80), heroin and morphine users represent less than a fourth of opiate users. In the late 1990s, they estimated 200,000 heroin addicts and 150,000 recreational users compared with 900,000 opium and *shiray*[46] addicts, and 650,000 recreational users.[47]

For better or worse, after an epidemic has unfolded in a given market, formal models of drug-use epidemics (e.g., Caulkins, Behrens, Knoll, Tragler, and Zuba [2004], which assesses relationships among epidemics, the population of frequent drug users, and various policy instruments) and other available evidence suggest stability.

For "worse," there appear to be no instances of a democratic nation with a major heroin problem that has managed to cut the number of regular users sharply within a decade, either through application of penalties or encouragement of treatment, even when a large share of the eligible population has access to and is served by treatment services (Reuter and Pollack, 2006). Consider the Netherlands, committed to the provision of treatment for anyone in need. It provided treatment to an average of 15,000 heroin users annually throughout the 1990s (about 50% of the heroin-dependent population). Yet in 2001, the estimated number of heroin-dependent persons was 28,000 to 30,000—essentially unchanged from the 1993 estimate.[48]

For "better," a second and much more encouraging set of observations emerges from a survey of estimates of heroin dependence in western Europe and the United States.[49] During the past decade, large declines in the purity-adjusted price of heroin have been observed in many nations that have been through an epidemic. Yet these declines—or the underlying changes in market conditions that induced them—have not generated new epidemics in these nations.[50] The bad reputation of a drug seems to serve as a durable but not eternal barrier to high rates of initiation. Current heroin users may choose to consume additional heroin per annum[51] and some former users could return to the market if prices decrease or purity improves, but new epidemics do not blossom in these markets simply because drugs become less costly.[52]

The epidemiological models and evidence help us to trace the path of demand creation for heroin and possibly other opiates. First, demand grows rapidly and a market takes shape; second, rates of initiation taper off as the market saturates or "matures"; and third, the market enters a period of relative stability in which demand is unlikely to grow rapidly again until the effects of the initial epidemic have been forgotten.[53] As a corollary, global demand is unlikely to grow substantially absent the onset of a new epidemic in a new market, as in Russia and parts of Central Asia. Nevertheless, it is also the case that demand is unlikely to decrease rapidly in a mature market. Attrition may occur over a period of many years, often involving death of users, and some users may enter treatment, but reductions in demand will not occur dramatically or quickly.[54] Indeed, after demand has matured, attrition may be the surest path to reductions in the number of users and, ultimately, in aggregate consumption.[55] Thus, we can treat mature markets, which now account for the majority of all major opiate markets, as being stable, although not necessarily unchangeable.

Consumer Responses to Changes in Market Conditions

An epidemic may begin because heroin becomes available in a market in which it was not previously available (e.g., along a new trafficking route, as it did in Central Asia in the mid to late 1990s) and encounters a waiting latent demand. As the epidemic unfolds, demand expands as a function of existing demand; use begets use. Economists describe this type of expansion as a "bandwagon" or "fad" effect. However, a key difference between a drug-use epidemic and a standard fad is non-reversibility. When an ordinary fad ends and products like mood rings and hula hoops fall out of favor, demand may collapse. In the case of a heroin epidemic, addiction prevents a dramatic decline in demand. Throughout its expansionary period, demand for the drug is relatively elastic or responsive to changes in market conditions; after stabilizing, it becomes less responsive, but not necessarily non-responsive. Given that most major markets are now mature or nearing maturity, the extent of that responsiveness will be a key determinant of the ultimate effects of most policy measures.

This observation raises an important empirical question: Just how responsive are consumers in a mature market to changes in market conditions? For many years it was widely assumed that addiction created a "fixed" demand. The notion was that addicts require a certain amount of drug to continue their habit and could not cut usage in response to an increase in price. Nevertheless, for some addicts, a price increase may lead them to treatment, which could cut (although not necessarily end) their consumption.

A very small number of quantitative studies have tried to evaluate the responsiveness of heroin consumers to changes in prices (for a review, see Bretteville-Jensen, 2006). They have estimated the elasticity of demand with respect to retail price, and have found values close to –1, suggesting that a 1% increase in the price of heroin in a nation would reduce consumption by about 1% (Manski, Pepper, and Petrie, 2001:46). In general, an estimate less than –1 (e.g., –1.5 or –2) is considered "elastic," and an estimate greater than –1 (e.g., –0.5 or –0.25) is considered "inelastic." Although we have found no specific study on the economics of contemporary opium demand, it seems plausible to assume that the demand for opium might be more elastic than for heroin, given the lower addictive potential of opium. This conjecture finds possible support in the sharp decline in opium consumption registered in China after the 1906 to 1911 and 1950 to 1953 waves of repression (see chapter 2).

The price elasticity estimates for heroin are roughly in line with the U.S. average for non-food commodities and for some food products, including butter and other dairy, beef, and vegetables (U.S Department of Agriculture, Economic Research Service, 2008: www.ers.usda.gov/Data/Elasticities/). However, the estimates for heroin indicate considerably more price responsiveness than the estimates for a number of less substitutable food items and also for the potentially analogous category of beverages and tobacco. These price elasticity estimates suggest that heroin consumers are modestly responsive to changes in market conditions.

In the long run, during which new users can enter the market (although likely at lower rates than during an initial epidemic) and existing users can exit the market, either through attrition or treatment, demand may be more responsive. In the very long run, here defined as sufficiently long for society's collective awareness of the initial epidemic and its ill effects to fade, a new epidemic may unfold (Musto, 1987).

Estimates of the price elasticity of demand provide insight to the ways in which consumers might respond to changes in market conditions, showing that consumers *can* respond to changes in market conditions, but it is also important to consider the nature of the change. Market conditions may change for any number of reasons: Production costs may increase because land or labor becomes more expensive; penalties against users may increase, resulting in higher than expected consumption costs; interdictors may force traffickers to establish new, costlier routes; or, in the extreme (at least theoretically), some supply may simply vanish, with no replacement in sight.[56]

If, in the extreme, the heroin is just not available, users must adjust their total consumption in an amount equal to the reduction in supply. Over time, new production may fill the gap left by the missing heroin, but in the short run, consumers, as a group, must bear the full extent of the shock with an equal reduction in consumption. Prices must adjust sufficiently to induce consumption at the new level of availability. The extent of the price increase will depend solely on the responsiveness or elasticity of demand. The less responsive the consumers are to the change in market conditions, the greater the price change.

If we accept the foregoing estimate of demand elasticity, roughly –1, and further assume constant elasticity, we would expect the price to increase by 10% for a 10% reduction in quantity, 20% for a 20% reduction, and so forth. (In this market, we would need to look for changes in the purity-adjusted price of heroin; product dilution is a common means of implicitly effecting price changes.) Were demand more inelastic (closer to "fixed"), the price increases would be greater.

If, instead, heroin is available, but production, trafficking, or consumption costs increase, then a combination of producer, trafficker, and consumer responses will jointly determine the market outcome. As long as each side can adjust its behavior, both sides will absorb some of the burden of the cost increase, but the side that is less responsive—or more locked in to its behavior—will generally absorb more of it. In general, and given what we know about the price elasticity of demand for heroin, we would still expect to see prices increase and quantities decrease, but by less than they did in the case in which heroin was not available.

In practice, however, tough enforcement against sellers has not often shown any great success in driving down the numbers of heroin users, suggesting either that the policy measures are not affecting availability or costs, or that reductions in the number of users cannot be detected in the available data.

In the United States, where policy has emphasized enforcement against selling rather than treatment and prevention, heroin has not become less available or more expensive (Boyum and Reuter, 2005), but we cannot isolate the effects of this policy.[57] The number of addicts is estimated to have declined by about one third from 1988 to 2000 (ONDCP, 2001), the only years for which consistent estimates are available, but the decline appears to reflect the natural evolution of an epidemic. Sweden, which by a number of measures has both an aggressive enforcement regime and generous treatment services, has also been unable to decrease the number of heroin users through policy [Olsson, Adamsson-Wahren, Byqvist, 2001; REITOX (Sweden), 2005].

By contrast, an unanticipated and substantial decrease in heroin availability in Australia, referred to as the *Australian heroin drought,* which started at the end of 2000 and lasted for some years, may represent the rare instance of an enforcement success, to the extent that the shortage was, truly, a result of enforcement (Degenhardt, Reuter, Collins, and Hall, 2005).[58] However, the experience of Australia is fundamentally different from that of the United States and Sweden, in that it more closely approximated the extreme case of non-availability. There seems to have been a reduction in the capacity of the importing system that simply reduced the amount of heroin able to enter the country, perhaps facilitated by Australia's geographic status: Australia is a remote island, albeit a very large island, with limited points of entry.[59]

Taking the example of the Taliban ban, in which inventory may have served as an alternate but costlier source of supply, we might expect to observe less success than in the case of a complete Australian-like *drought*, but still more success than in the U.S. or Swedish examples. In 2001, global output decreased by about 65%; in a fully integrated (i.e., unsegmented) market, we would expect to see consumption fall by less than 65% and prices increase by less than 65%, but how much less would depend in part on the amount of inventory available to enter the market and replace output. In a segmented market, we might expect to see a larger increase in prices in those regions served by Afghan producers than in other regions. Indeed for some regions, the short-run response might be almost as extreme as in the case of the Australian-like *drought* and, in other regions, almost imperceptible. Chapter 4 explores the actual consequences of the Taliban ban in relation to these expectations.

In summary, heroin users—and possibly other opiate users—can and will adjust their consumption in response to changes in market conditions. However, it is the combined actions and sometimes inactions of producers, traffickers, and consumers that jointly determine the market outcome. If producers and traffickers have nothing to offer the market, then the result hinges on consumer behavior; if production or trafficking costs increase, but producers and traffickers can still make some heroin available, then both sides of the market will have an opportunity to adjust. All else being equal, the more willing and able consumers are to adjust their consumption, the less we would expect to see prices increase, whether opiates simply vanish or become costlier. Over the long term, we expect the demand for opiates, like the supply of opiates, to be more adjustable.

The apparent inefficacy of enforcement efforts in nations with long-standing addict populations (i.e., in mature markets such as the United States and Sweden) is not a general refutation of enforcement efforts. To the extent that such efforts actually reduce the availability of opiates or raise their costs, they may have marginal effects on consumption in mature markets and they may have more substantial effects in less mature or newly burgeoning markets. Our observations find support in formal models (e.g., Tragler, Caulkins, and Feichtinger, 2001), which suggest that enforcement will have its greatest effects during the early stages of an epidemic rather than the later stages. And an extreme event, such as the so-called Australian heroin *drought* or a cutback comparable with that of the Taliban era, may, by necessity, result in a reduction in consumption that could have even more lasting effects.

Supply Control Policies

Apart from the outright bans of the Taliban regime and Burmese quasi-state authorities, three principal types of programs have been used to reduce or disrupt supply in source countries: eradication, alternative development,[60] and in-country enforcement against traffickers and refiners. The first two, eradication and alternative development, might also be viewed as special cases of a larger category of programs that seek to eliminate production. Another set of control programs, largely relying on interdiction against traffickers, targets drug smuggling across international borders. We briefly introduce the vocabulary, intent, and use of these programs in the contemporary market.

Eradication

Eradication, through aerial spraying or ground-based operations, aims to reduce the amount of drugs available for shipment to consumers and to increase the costs of producing those drugs or otherwise discourage farmers from growing them. The immediate targets, peasant farmers, are often among the poorest of a country's citizens, even when growing opium poppy or other illicit crops. Eradication may be "forced," in which case farmers have no voice in the destruction of their plants and crops, or it may be "voluntary," in which case farmers typically obtain some financial compensation for that destruction. Occasionally, a government implements a mixed program; farmers must either allow or undertake the eradication—it is not optional—but they receive some financial compensation for the loss. Programs to prevent farmers from planting, such as those implemented in Nangarhar province in eastern Afghanistan in 2004 and 2005 (Mansfield, 2006), may be included within the broad category of eradication even though no eradication takes place.

Few producing countries use aerial eradication, which is believed by many observers to cause environmental damage.[61] Mexico and Colombia, neither of which is a traditional drug producer, have been most willing to allow spraying, but it is illegal in Bolivia and Peru. In a few other nations, such as Bolivia and, more recently and relevantly, Afghanistan, the government has allowed manual eradication, which is very labor intensive and less likely to have major environmental effects (see chapter 6).

There is little evidence that eradication—forced or otherwise—has been effective in recent years, notwithstanding reports of large areas of eradication and occasional claims of success.[62] Postdating the far more extreme Taliban ban, the Karzai administration launched a voluntary eradication program in April 2002 with the support of the British government. However, this initiative did not work, in part, because the compensation rate was too low relative to the market price of opium. Since 2004, a much wider forced eradication program has been launched by the Afghan government, mainly at the pressure of the United States (see chapter 6). Bolivian authorities, too, with the help of U.S. funding, have implemented similar schemes with similarly disappointing results in Bolivia in the 1990s (Riley, 1996). Plan Dignidad, an effort at total eradication by the Bolivian government in the late 1990s, did accomplish substantial reductions for some years, but it was accompanied by extensive development efforts as well, and the story has multiple interpretations (Reuter, 2006)

Eradication has had one possible success story in modern times: the Mexican eradication program of the mid to late 1970s, which targeted opium and marijuana (Reuter and Ronfelt, 1992:93, 106–108). A drug industry that had operated fairly openly in a compact area, with large and unprotected fields, took approximately 5 years to adjust to spraying. Production subsequently became more dispersed and growing fields were smaller and more frequently hidden in remote locations. Good data are lacking, but farm-gate prices may have been substantially higher as a result. By the mid 1980s, Mexico's drug exports had begun to rebound, but for several years there had been a substantial reduction in availability in the United States, particularly in western regions, where Mexican supply dominated heroin markets. However, Reuter and Ronfelt (1992:93) suggest that some of the apparent success of the program may have been related to an extended drought and other poor growing conditions. In any case, given the current dispersion of opium poppy cultivation throughout Afghanistan, there seems to be little chance of repeating the Mexican experience under current conditions.

Alternative Development

Alternative development aims to encourage farmers that grow illicit crops to switch to other, legitimate income-earning activities, by making the other activities, be they agricultural or non-agricultural, more financially attractive. Typical agricultural strategies include introducing new crops and more productive strains of traditional crops, improving transportation for getting the crops to market, and various marketing and subsidy schemes (for a review, see Thoumi, 2003).

Alternative development, almost always funded by western donors, is more politically attractive than eradication, at least in-country, because it provides new resources for marginalized farmers. Nevertheless, there are numerous obstacles to successful implementation. For example, it requires a credible long-term commitment; otherwise, farmers will not be willing to shift to new crops or occupations. Political instability may foster skepticism: Afghan farmers understandably may doubt the Afghan government's ability to ensure a dependable market and reliable transportation infrastructure for shipments of produce from the Helmand Valley.[63]

There are a few instances of well-executed local crop substitution programs, in which farmers in a small area have been persuaded to move from illicit to legitimate crops.[64] However, it does not appear that these programs, in isolation, have had far-reaching effects. A recent report by the Independent Evaluation Unit of the UNODC (2005c) reached a pessimistic conclusion:

There is little empirical evidence that the rural development components of AD [Alternative Development] on their own reduce the amount of drug crops cultivated. Agriculture, economic and social interventions are not seen to overcome the incentive pressure exerted by the market conditions of the illicit drug trade. Where reduction in drug cropping occurs it seems that other factors, including general economic growth, policing, etc., can be identified as contributors to the change that takes place. (p. 9)

Thailand, which has taken a more comprehensive approach to eliminating opium production, including not just crop substitution, but other forms of development assistance and community empowerment, appears to have had a higher degree of success (see chapter 11). It is, however, difficult to separate out the effects of the growing wealth of Thailand in general.

In-Country Enforcement

In-country enforcement against refiners and traffickers aims to disrupt the market and, at least temporarily, reduce supply or raise supply-side costs by targeting refineries, stocks, and business dealings. It may be more politically attractive than eradication in that it does not affect farmers directly, but it may be less attractive if refiners or traffickers enjoy ties to government officials or provide substantial employment.

Intermittent crackdowns on refineries or storage facilities have limited potential because neither requires much fixed investment (e.g., in equipment or buildings), and both can be replaced cheaply and rapidly. Substantial improvements in domestic enforcement may be more effective in the long term, because they may yield tangible increases in drug entrepreneurs' risks and thus increase their costs of doing business (see chapter 10). In this arena, western donors most frequently fund programs to train investigators, strengthen the judiciary, and improve extradition procedures. Evidence from Afghanistan (see chapter 6) and Latin America suggests that long-term success requires a wider, albeit more challenging, process of institution building.

Interdiction

Lastly, another set of programs aims to disrupt the market and at least reduce temporarily supply or increase supply-side costs by targeting international trafficking and smuggling operations. Most large seizures are made through interdiction (e.g., as heroin or cocaine is moving toward or across an international border). As shown in this and later chapters, opiate seizures account yearly for a substantial share of total production. Most seizures occur in Asia, close to the production centers (Afghanistan and Burma) and to some of the largest consumer populations (China, Iran, and Pakistan). That interdiction has some effect on the world opiate market can be deduced from the vast markups in opiate prices as the drugs transit from one country to another, most visibly as they enter western nations. Unfortunately, we have little concrete or consistent evidence on the relationship between interdiction and either availability or pricing.[65]

Concluding Remarks

Despite the apparent asymmetry of supply and demand—specifically, the small number of producing and trafficking nations versus the large number of consuming nations—we find little evidence of market control or power except possibly in the past actions of the Taliban and, to a much lesser extent, among some present-day traffickers. Although only a few nations are involved in production and trafficking, those nations are the sum of their largely uncoordinated parts, consisting of hundreds of thousands of households and individuals that produce, and a smaller number of sometimes family-based networks that traffic. Barriers to entry in trafficking—arising from the need for relational capital—may confer a modicum of market power, but persistently low and declining prices in the United States and other major markets suggest little ultimate leverage.

The evidence is more supportive of market segmentation, at least in the short run. Differences in farm-gate prices of opium across Afghanistan, Burma, and Colombia may be indicative of segmentation. The data on seizures, which trace distinct patterns of distribution along particular routes (e.g., from Afghanistan through Pakistan, Iran, and Turkey to western Europe), also suggest market segmentation. Other data on the chemical composition of seizures provide further evidence. The chemical signature of seizures in the United States suggests that a large but uncertain fraction of the heroin entering the U.S. market now originates in Latin America.

Market segmentation, as noted at the outset, has important implications for market adjustments and outcomes. Consumers who are highly dependent on flows from particular countries, via particular routes—such as western Europeans supplied by Afghanistan and U.S. consumers supplied by Latin America—may be more susceptible to disruptions in production or trafficking than might otherwise be the case.

However, the recent experience of several countries, such as Afghanistan, Burma, Pakistan, Colombia, Tajikistan and other Central Asian republics, and Russia, demonstrates that the market is not unchanging and can, over a period of time (occasionally even a few years, as in the case of Colombia's entry into the market in the 1990s) reconfigure itself. Their collective experience suggests that other countries might still enter the market, with varying degrees of speed, whether in opiate production, trafficking, or consumption. Their experience also suggests that change for the worse most typically occurs more rapidly than change for the better. We address each of these observations in more detail in chapter 11.

This chapter addressed market dynamics in often theoretical or hypothetical terms; in contrast, the following chapter takes a more empirical stance, by providing a detailed discussion of the market's actual response to the Taliban ban and the accompanying cutback in opium growing. As a natural extension of this chapter, it explores observed changes in the price and purity of opiates throughout the market as outcomes of interactions between supply and demand. It also continues to explore the issues of market power and segmentation, specifically in relation to the apparent effect of the ban. This analysis creates a bridge to chapter 5, which presents a comprehensive model of the world opiate market and charts the immediate aftereffects of the ban, using data from the United Nations and other public sources.

4

Did the Taliban's Ban Really Matter?

Introduction

The prior discussion of the properties of supply and demand provides a market-based framework for anticipating and evaluating the effects of the Taliban ban of 2000 to 2001. We can also use information about the response of the market to the ban, which constitutes a large disturbance or "shock"—in effect, a natural experiment like the oil shocks of the 1970s—to update and revise our view of the workings of the market.

The sudden and unanticipated cutback in Afghanistan's opium production in 2001 initially appeared to be the shot that was not heard around the world. In the immediate aftermath, there was no discernible supply response among current producers. For example, farmers in Burma did not increase cultivation, nor did any new producers enter the market other than those in the north of Afghanistan. Moreover, there was little indication of substantial decline in consumption. Only a few regional markets close to Afghanistan saw price increases. Instead, as shown in the following pages, it appears that there was sufficient inventory of opium and heroin in the pipeline to mute the effects of the supply shock and that much of the inventory did enter the market.

However, a longer term analysis yields a notably different picture. The effects of the cutback persisted long after the fall of the Taliban in late 2001. Opium prices in Afghanistan peaked just prior to September 11, 2001, and then dropped sharply, before beginning a second ascent that continued, with fluctuations, though early to mid 2003. After 2003, prices trended downward.

Correspondingly, there are signs that in western Europe the consequences were first felt only in 2002 and 2003. Inventory depletion and rebuilding may help to explain the observed changes in prices.[1]

The Ban, the Cutback, and the Aftermath

Starting in July 2000, Afghanistan's opium poppy growers began to experience the dangers inherent in operating under a relatively effective quasi-state authority unbound by the rule of law. In September 1999, the Taliban had issued a decree ordering all such farmers to reduce their cultivation by one third. According to the UNDCP, this decree was not effectively implemented; the actual decline in the area under cultivation amounted only to 10% (UNDCP, 2001b:8).[2] In July 2000, however, Mullah Muhammad Umar, the Taliban's supreme leader, issued another decree imposing a total ban on opium cultivation in the country. This ban was imposed just prior to what would have been the planting season for the 2001 crop year in all but the north of the country. To the surprise of most, the ban was effectively enforced for more than a year. As a result, opium production in Afghanistan decreased by 94% in 2001, returning to the low levels recorded two decades earlier (UNDCP, 2001b:8).

The ban was enforced principally by the threat of punishment, the close local monitoring and forced eradication of any continued poppy farming, and the public punishment of transgressors, which gave credibility to the threat. Local community leaders were held accountable for the poppy cultivation of local farmers, giving them a clear incentive to implement the enforcement effort (Farrell and Thorne, 2005). To achieve the astonishing reduction, the Taliban also negotiated with and provided hefty subsidies to major tribes (Major Donors Mission, 2001). To make the ban more palatable, moreover, the Taliban did not attempt to ban processing or trafficking of existing stocks, which was a major source of revenue for the wealthier and more influential strata of the population, and the taxation of which had become an important source of revenue for their infant state apparatus as well. As a result, between 2000 and 2001, seizures of trafficked opiates in the countries neighboring Afghanistan decreased only by 40%, almost certainly indicating continued trafficking of accumulated stocks.

The motivation for the ban remains a matter of controversy. Some U.S. officials argue that the goal of the ban was to increase the value of existing stocks, either held by the government or held by groups that the Taliban wished to benefit; bumper crops in the previous years had led to low opium prices.[3] Others suggest the regime's desire to gain legitimacy in the eyes of the international community, as an act of diplomacy to encourage inflows of foreign assistance if not capital (e.g., Felbab-Brown, 2006).[4] The additional claim of a religious doctrinal basis for the ban, which would not rule out either market manipulation or diplomatic action, was undercut by the Taliban's willingness to allow continued sale from stocks. However, the Taliban's decision making was so opaque and arbitrary that no one can claim any base for choosing among the alternatives.

According to many observers (e.g., Rubin, 2004; Thoumi, 2005; Felbab-Brown, 2006; Mansfield, 2006), it is highly improbable that the Taliban could have sustained the ban in the following years without the financial support of the international community, which they were unlikely to receive. The political legitimacy of the Taliban was also threatened, because the ban encountered widespread popular resistance. Despite its shortness, the ban had very real consequences for the thousands of peasant families that had become dependent on poppy cultivation for their livelihoods. In fact, not only did their major source of cash income suddenly disappear, but most poor peasants also fell into a deep financial trap. As was a common practice in Afghan agriculture, they had accepted advance payments before planting; but, under the ban, they could not repay them. The heavy debt of the peasantry, which the Taliban chose not to cancel, was an important contributing factor in the immediate resurgence of opium cultivation after the start of the U.S.-led bombing campaign in November 2001 and the subsequent fall of the Taliban regime (Mansfield, 2004b; Rubin, 2004:4).

The Afghan Interim Administration that succeeded the Taliban instituted new opiate prohibitions on January 17, 2002. These prohibitions went well beyond the Taliban's decree, to include not just opium poppy cultivation, but also processing and trafficking. The efforts to translate these provisions into practice and the unplanned consequences of such efforts are reviewed in chapter 6. Here it suffices to say that, by any objective measure, the policies of the new Afghan government failed. Opium production immediately resumed at preban levels. A total of 3,400 and 3,600 metric tons of opium were produced in 2002 and 2003, respectively, and production has been trending upward since then to a record-breaking harvest of 6,100 metric tons in 2006 (UNODC, 2006:57; 2007a:40, 195). Moreover, production that had traditionally been concentrated in a few provinces in the south and east of Afghanistan is now broadly distributed across the nation (Mansfield, 2006).

The Market Response

Not surprisingly, given the enactment of the ban just before the 2001 planting season and the brevity of the cutback itself, there is little evidence of an immediate supply response outside of Afghanistan. Only growers in the north of Afghanistan, outside the Taliban's reach, were well positioned to both learn of, and act on, the ban.

There was an immediate and prolonged effect on prices in Afghanistan; however, we have more difficulty drawing information from the data for other countries. In general, they tend to suggest a somewhat delayed response, possibly mitigated by inventory, market segmentation, and the paucity of reliable information.

Opium Production

Production in the north of Afghanistan increased, but no other major producing country increased land under poppy cultivation or in any other way substantially raised production in 2001. Production in Burma was roughly on par with the previous year;[5] Laos and Colombia, two of the three second-tier producers, witnessed substantial reductions in percentage terms.[6] The data for Mexico are too weak to provide useful indicators. No new producers outside Afghanistan entered the market. For example, there was no shift across the border into Tajikistan, a potential production source, or into other Central Asian republics.

The timing of the cutback, likely exacerbated by the fact that information travels poorly and unreliably in this business, offered almost no opportunity for a short-run response. Growers in other nations did not know that there would be a deficit. There was initially widespread skepticism that the Taliban were serious in imposing the ban or that it had the capacity to do so. The ban promulgated in 1999 had not been implemented. Although, as discussed later, local markets in Afghanistan and Iran reacted promptly—and perhaps overreacted—with large price increases, it was not until an official international delegation reported in March 2001 that there was acceptance outside of the region that 2001 Afghan opium production would fall substantially (UNODC, 2002:16).

Given the timing of growing cycles, most opium growers outside the Taliban's reach could not take immediate action. By the time those in Burma and elsewhere knew that the ban was real, it was too late for them to do anything in the 2000–2001 growing cycle, other than possibly add labor to the harvest, because, for the most part, they were already locked into their planting decisions. Indeed, by the time they *really* knew about the ban, many or most had already completed their harvests.

The only clear exception to be found was among farmers in the north of Afghanistan—those under the control of the Northern Alliance. They benefited from a later planting season and relatively good information about the ban. In response, they expanded their previously minor plantings, although they still provided less than 10% of what Afghanistan had produced in earlier years.[7]

And then, before anyone outside Afghanistan had time to act, the ban was over. The ban was rescinded by the Taliban themselves by mid September 2001 at the start of the 2001–2002 growing cycle (Caryl, 2001). During the turmoil that followed the American-led bombing campaign and the fall of the Taliban regime, production resumed in provinces with a historical record of production and in other areas as well. The resulting near-record harvests of 2002 reflect the reaction of farmers to unprecedentedly high prices. Among those factors, the strength of the rebound in production may also reflect the need of Afghan farmers to draw down the debt they had accumulated during the ban year.

Prices in Afghanistan

Figure 4.1 provides data on opium prices (collected by the UNODC) in Afghanistan for August 1997 through April 2006. Note that the prices are reported in current U.S. dollars. This removes the difference between Afghanistan and U.S. inflation, but still includes U.S. inflation rates, which were modest during the period.

The farm-gate price of opium in Afghanistan rose very sharply after the imposition of the ban. The average price for Nangarhar and Qandahar ranged from $34 to $87 per kilogram between August 1997 and July 2000; it rose to more than $550 per kilogram in August 2001, and reached $675 per kilogram in early September 2001.[8] The price plunged shortly after the September 11th terrorist attacks and remained relatively low at the outset of the Allied military operations, but returned to its earlier highs over a 12- to 18-month period. It reached $576 per kilogram in January 2003. Regarding the plunge, Byrd and Jonglez (2006:120) suggest that traders sold off stocks, fearing that they would be destroyed, but other possible reasons include speculation and the virtual absence of a functioning market during a period of extreme turmoil.[9] After January 2003, the price then began a fairly steady descent. By July 2004, the average price had fallen to $119 per kilogram, about 80% below the pre-September 11 peak. It then rose again in late 2004 and early 2005, peaking at

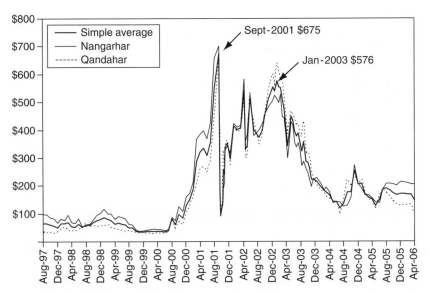

Figure 4.1 Monthly and weekly farm-gate opium prices.
Note: Price per kilogram, dry weight; current U.S. dollars.
Source: UNODC (2006) and Pietschmann (personal communications on various dates).

about $250 per kilogram in November 2004. As of April 2006, the UNODC reported an average price of $146 per kilogram, almost twice as high as the highest average price during the preban period. The 2007 edition of the *World Drug Report* reports an average harvest price of $125 per kilogram, suggesting a continuation in the decline.

In general, the data confirm expectations regarding a potentially sharp initial price increase, albeit with fluctuations around September 11, 2001, that may have delayed the peak, and an elongated return to lower levels; however, two points bear noting. First, the increase may have been sharper than warranted, given potentially large inventories and the prospect of an eventual supply response in other regions, not to mention the strong possibilities that (1) the ban would collapse and (2) consumers would adjust their consumption in the meantime. Such "overshooting" is not uncommon in commodity and other markets, especially in those experiencing imperfect information or exchange rate realignments.[10] Both phenomena (i.e., imperfect information and exchange rate realignments) were prevalent in Afghanistan at the time.[11]

Second, prices have decreased since 2001 to 2003, but they have not yet returned to prior levels, even with the more recent burgeoning of Afghan production. This is true even if one takes account of inflation.[12]

Regarding the initial increase, it is possible that, at the local level, the market seriously miscalculated the extent of inventories along the supply chain and, having grown accustomed to segmentation, did not account for potential extraregional responses. As previously noted, reliable information on which to base such calculations does not flow freely in this market. Moreover, traders may have assumed a highly unresponsive demand. Prices rose by about 675% from their preban peak, whereas local production fell by more than 90% and global production decreased by about 65%. The relative changes in prices and quantities suggest a much lower price elasticity of demand than most studies report (Manski, Pepper, and Petrie, 2001).

However, other factors may tie both points together. Four economically important events occurred after the Taliban ban: (1) the Afghan exchange rate fluctuated, in a transitory appreciation; (2) Afghan wage rates rose; (3) Russia and other former Soviet republics substantially increased their consumption; and (4) Burma substantially reduced its production.[13] As a consequence of the first event, some of the price movements, including some of the increases, may appear to have been more dramatic than they really were. As a consequence of the second, third, and fourth events, prices may not fall to prior levels. Even so, given land and labor availability in Afghanistan—less than 3% of Afghanistan's cultivated land grows opium (Mansfield, 2006:48) and, notwithstanding the rise in wages, rural labor is still underemployed—it seems likely that, in the long run, farm-gate prices will not be very different from those encountered during other periods of peak production. Figures 4.2 and 4.3 show the movement in exchange rates and compare local farm-gate opium prices denominated in Afghan and in U.S. dollars.

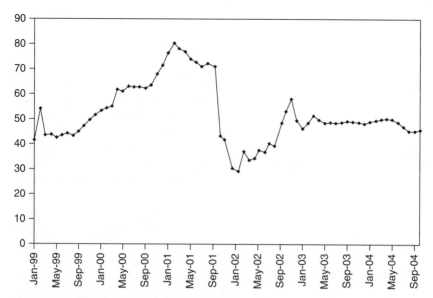

Figure 4.2 Afghani per U.S. dollar, 1999–2004.
Source: International Monetary Fund ([IMF] 2003) for IMF exchange rates from January 1999 to August 2003; and data from direct communication with IMF for other months.

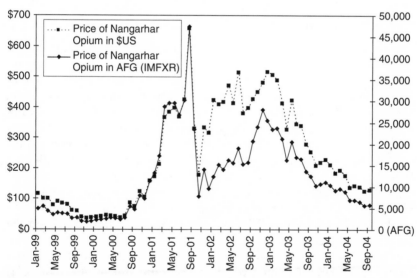

Figure 4.3 Farm-gate opium prices in U.S. and local currency, 1999–2004.
Note: Price per kilogram, dry weight. An analysis of farm-gate opium prices for Qandahar shows similar patterns, but less pronounced differences in prices denominated in local and U.S. currencies.
Source: UNODC (2006) and personal communications for farm-gate opium prices denominated in U.S. dollars; International Monetary Fund ([IMF] 2003) for IMF exchange rates from January 1999 to August 2003; and data from direct communication with IMF for other months.

Lastly, it is hard to be precise about average prices for Afghanistan during the period after the ban because of rapid and difficult-to-measure changes in the composition of production across provinces. The UNODC reports simple averages for Nangarhar and Qandahar, which dominated production at the time, and that may be the best one can do in the face of this uncertainty. However, for more recent years, the introduction of new growing areas and the decline of an old one (Nangarhar) substantially complicate the price analysis. For example, in April 2006, the average price across Nangarhar and Qandahar was $146 per kilogram, largely supported by a price in Nangarhar of $204 per kilogram. Because production in Nangarhar has dropped precipitously and now accounts for only a small fraction of Afghan output, the average may give too much weight to local, Nangarhar conditions. By comparison, the price of opium was only $88 per kilogram in Qandahar, not so far from preban levels.

Data are also available on opium prices received by traffickers within Afghanistan, also referred to as *traders*. Their margin is variable but consistently small. For example, in May 2005 in Helmand, the trader margin was $5 to $6 per kilogram, compared with the farmer price of $150, or about 3% to 4% (Pain, 2006:90).[14] Unfortunately, there is no price series for Afghanistan-origin heroin (as opposed to opium), which has grown in importance in recent years. It appears that Afghanistan is processing an increasing share of its own opium.

Prices in Neighboring Markets

The persistence of high opium prices in Afghanistan even after the bumper crop of 2002 and the drawn-out period of decline suggest that downstream prices may also have responded to the cutback with lags and carryover. Iran and Tajikistan, two of the three major markets neighboring Afghanistan, both reported large increases in prices,[15] but the quality of price data from both nations is low. There is no regular reporting of purity from Tajikistan and there may have been substantial shifts in purity during the past 5 years, as noted by our research collaborators (Drug Control Agency of Tajikistan [DCA], 2004; Khamonov, 2005). Similarly, national figures are averages for areas with very different prices and thus may appear to change just because of a shift in the distribution of transactions or a change in the location of observations. When available, we use local data to avoid shifts in the weighting of specific areas.

Table 4.1 provides data from Fariborn Raisdana's report on Iran (2004). The price of opium, which still accounts for most Iranian opiate consumption, increased very sharply in 2001, peaked in 2002, and remained quite high in 2003. Only during the first quarter of 2004 did it fall back to preban levels.[16] Thus, the price of opium in Iran followed a path that, in its shape, is not unlike that of the farm-gate price in Afghanistan. Heroin prices in Iran did not increase as sharply in 2001, as indicated by the decline in the ratio of heroin to opium prices (see the right column of table 4.1).[17]

Table 4.1
Prices per Kilogram of Opium and Heroin in Iran 1992-2004.

Year	Opium	Heroin	Heroin/Opium
1992	1,660,000	4,350,000	2.6
1993	1,580,000	4,250,000	2.7
1994	1,460,000	4,150,000	2.8
1995	1,740,000	5,800,000	3.3
1996	2,500,000	10,000,000	4.0
1997	3,000,000	13,500,000	4.5
1998	3,200,000	15,650,000	4.9
1999	3,650,000	18,500,000	5.1
2000	5,750,000	20,900,000	3.6
2001	10,750,000	24,500,000	2.3
2002	11,950,000	30,000,000	2.5
2003	10,750,000	27,000,000	2.5
2004 est	7,800,000	21,000,000	2.7

Notes: Prices in current rials; 2004 estimate based on first quarter data.
Source: National Drug Control Reports of Drug Control Headquarters (as reported by Raisdana, 2004).

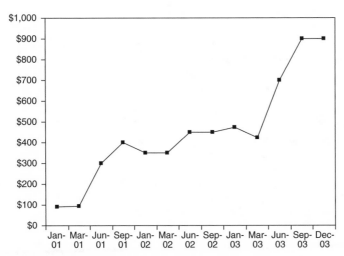

Figure 4.4 Raw opium prices in Tajikistan, 2001–2003.
Note: Prices per kilogram in U.S. dollars.
Source: DCA (2004).

Data on real prices from 1989 through September 2002, which take account of inflation in Tehran, show a somewhat less consistent picture. Real prices of opium declined substantially prior to 1996 and rose thereafter in an alternating pattern, consisting of modest falls and somewhat larger increases. One particular decrease occurred in September 2001, possibly mirroring the fall in opium prices in Afghanistan, and another in September 2002, with no obvious explanation (Raisdana, 2004).[18]

Data reported by our Tajikistan research collaborators (DCA, 2004; Khamonov, 2005) show somewhat similar price patterns in that market. Figure 4.4 shows a large increase in price in 2001, relatively stable prices in 2002, and another very large increase in mid 2003.

Prices and Purity Downstream

Turkey is the major transshipment country to the richer markets in the West. Sevil Atasoy (2004) and her research collaborators at the Forensic Sciences Institute in Istanbul collected retrospective data on wholesale prices from officials and dealers for 1996 through 2003; quarterly purity data were available from a laboratory testing program. The results are summarized in figure 4.5.

The purity data are stronger and tell a story consistent with a tightening market (fig. 4.5).[19] Purity fell steadily from the second quarter of 2000 (just before the Taliban imposed the ban on opium growing) to the third quarter of 2003 (the most recent quarter for which data were available). The decline was substantial—from 52% to 36%. However, even this latter figure was above levels recorded for the first two quarters of 1999. It is unclear why purity would begin to decline before the announcement of the ban, at a time when Afghan opium growers were producing at record and near-record levels, but the

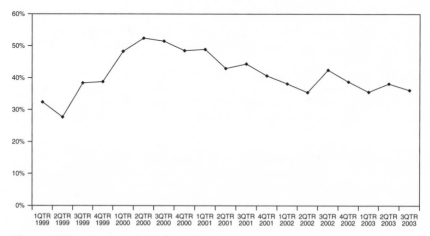

Figure 4.5 Heroin purity in Turkey, 1999–2003.
Source: Atasoy (2004).

appearance of a decline during the second quarter may not be large enough to bear significance and may simply be "noise" in the data. The increase in purity up to that point is directionally consistent with a run-up in production; the decline in purity after that point is directionally consistent with a cutback and a subsequent period of inventory accumulation. Less explicable is the fact that purity remained at a somewhat higher level in late 2003 than in early 1999.

The wholesale price data, without adjustment for purity, are ambiguous (fig. 4.6). The estimated maximum price for both no. 3 and no. 4 heroin[20] rose, but the minimum price for no. 3 fell and was stable for no. 4. However, with purity adjustment, the story is unambiguous; wholesale heroin prices rose through mid 2002 and then either stabilized or continued to rise.

In western Europe there was evidence of a decline in purity in some countries. Street prices generally did not change, but the decline in purity means that the effective price (price per pure gram) rose in those countries. Assuming that demand in western Europe is not perfectly inelastic, as we have previously argued, the increase in effective price would have occurred in tandem with a decline in aggregate consumption.

Specifically, in the United Kingdom, purity declined from 54% to 29% between the first quarter of 2001 and the third quarter of 2003, but this is hard to distinguish from other large purity fluctuations that have been observed since 1999.[21] Figure 4.7 presents purity data for the United Kingdom from 1999 to 2003.[22] During this period, the street price was reported to be stable. This would indicate a 50% increase in the per-pure-gram price at the retail

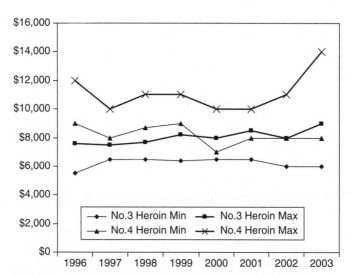

Figure 4.6 Heroin wholesale prices in Turkey, 1996–2003.
Note: Price per kilogram in U.S. dollars.
Source: Atasoy (2004).

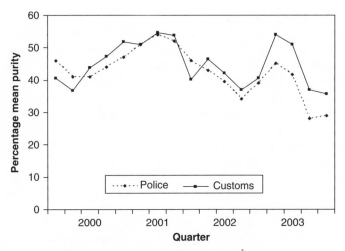

Figure 4.7 Purity of heroin seizures in the United Kingdom, 1999–2003.
Note: Mean purity of police and customs seizures in percentage terms.
Source: H.M. Custom and Excise data provided by Jim McColm (personal communication).

level between 1st quarter 2001 and 3rd quarter 2003. For a demand elasticity of about –1.0, it would imply an equivalent decrease in consumption.

German wholesale purity data show substantial change during 2001 through 2004.[23] The average purity of seizures of larger than 1 kilogram declined from more than 45% in 2001 to less than 10% in 2003, and then increased to almost 50% in 2004. During this same period, the purity of smaller lots seized remained relatively stable, with purity levels for retail doses ranging between 10% and 12% (Bundeskriminalamt [BKA], 2005b:40). The wholesale price (not purity adjusted) was constant during the same period (BKA, 2005b:46).

Data from Spain show minimal change in price at any of three levels of the market (retail, gram, or kilogram) between 2000 and 2003. Purity also did not change at either the retail or the gram levels. However, purity of heroin kilograms declined from 64% to 49% between 2000 and 2003 (Observatorio Español sobre Drogas, 2005:172). For France, both price and purity declined in 2001, the most recent year for which our collaborator, Nacer Lalam (2004), provided data. Data at individual city levels shows so much cross-city variation in price that it is difficult to determine whether the reported decline is real or the result of a shift in the mix of cities represented.

Norway has better data than many larger nations.[24] For 2002, there was a marked drop in purity (from 48% to 33%) and a much smaller decline in prices for heroin (from $153 per gram to $125 per gram), implying an increase in effective price. At the same time, the number of drug-related deaths (the vast majority of which involve heroin) declined sharply (from 338 deaths to 210 deaths), whereas policy interventions remained unchanged. There was a further drop in purity in 2003 (to 26%) and decline in drug deaths. These changes suggest that the market tightened and that heroin consumption dropped. For 2004 and 2005, price and purity were roughly constant; drug-related deaths showed no trend.

The western European data are more numerous and better documented than those available from nations earlier in the chain. However, they are still weak in almost all dimensions. They support the hypothesis that, in 2002 and probably 2003, there was a perceptible tightening of heroin supplies in western Europe.

Regions Supplied by Other Producers

We hypothesize that prices will increase less, and less rapidly, in regions typically supplied by producers other than Afghanistan because of market segmentation. Likely examples include the United States, China, Thailand, and Australia. Latin American producers account for a substantial, if uncertain, share of U.S. consumption; Burma supplies China and Thailand, two countries for which research collaborators provided new studies, and Australia, for which many studies of recent events are available (e.g., (Degenhardt et al., 2005). Burma may no longer produce enough to account for all heroin consumption in these three countries, but it may have at the time of the Taliban ban.

The available evidence supports our hypothesis. In China, neither official data nor the new data gathered by our research collaborators (Institute of Public Security, Chinese, Ministry of Public Security, 2004) yielded any indication of market tightening after the ban. The data were collected retrospectively—meaning, in 2004, addicts were questioned about their perceptions of changes during the past 3 years. This was the only way that data could be gathered, but it is inherently a weak design, particularly for a population (heroin addicts) that has poor recall. Unfortunately, officials were unable to provide additional insights on the matter. This lack of information is a weak indicator that any disturbance was too small to be registered or remembered.

For Thailand, our research collaborators Nualnoi Treerat, Nopparit Ananapibut, and Surasak Thamno (2004) report that there was no response in 2001 and 2002 in heroin prices. On the Thai–Burma border, the wholesale price of heroin ranged from $6,050 to $7,600 per kilogram in 2000; by 2002, it was reported to range from $3,800 to $5,950 per kilogram. The situation was complicated in 2003 by a general domestic crackdown on drug dealers. The crackdown generated immediate, large increases in the retail price of heroin, but is clearly distinguishable from other international market events; no data are available for import prices after 2002.

In Australia, which had a medium-size market (about 80,000 addicts) supplied almost exclusively from Burma, prices also increased sharply in early 2001 in an event frequently referred to earlier as a heroin *drought*. In New South Wales, Weatherburn, Jones, Freeman, and Makkai (2003; 86) report that "the average cost of a half gram has risen by 35%, from $138 to $186. The average cost of a gram has risen 75%, from $218 to $381." However, that increase seems to have been for reasons specific to Australia's smuggling routes and not because of events in Afghanistan (Degenhart et al., 2005). A recent analysis has suggested that there was a similar decline in Canada (Wood, Stoltz, Li, Monaner, and Kerr, 2006), but there are questions about the timing of the Canadian change that make it seem unrelated to changes in international markets (Caulkins and Reuter, 2006).

The United States accounts for a small share of the world's total consumption, but has engendered the development of its own niche producers—Colombia and Mexico—although there is controversy regarding just how much of the U.S. market they account for (Drug Availability Steering Group, 2002; see also our discussion in chapter 5, this volume). Colombia and Mexico supply no heroin to any other rich-country market, despite Colombia being the principal source of cocaine for western Europe. The Afghan cutback cannot be detected in U.S. wholesale price series for heroin; there is no interruption to the decline that began in 1991.

Figure 4.8 shows the continued decline for three levels of the U.S. market: retail (seizure amount < 1 gram), low-level wholesale (amount from 1–10 grams), and high-level wholesale (amount > 10 grams). It also lends further weight to the claim that the supply side is not leveraging its position.

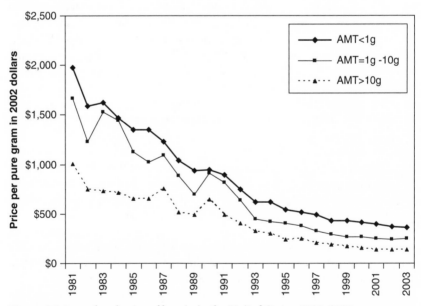

Figure 4.8 Annual real price of heroin in the United States, 1981–2003.
Note: AMT (amount) refers to the total weight of purchase.
Source: ONDCP (2004).

Concluding Remarks

A reasonable interpretation of the admittedly flawed evidence is that, with hiccups and delays, the cutback did indeed cause disruptions in many markets dependent on Afghanistan for heroin. In particular, changes in purity in the wholesale market in Turkey starting in 2001 and then some European markets starting in 2002 are consistent with hypothesis that heroin became less available. Given the frailties of the data, it is remarkable that we were able to uncover these changes. They could easily have been subsumed in the "noise" of the data sets.

The elongated decline in Afghan farm-level prices from their peak in 2003 and their subsequent "failure" to fall to preban levels initially reflected a combination of inventory buildup,[25] demand growth in Russia and elsewhere, reductions in production in Burma, and possibly more general economic phenomena, including increases in Afghan wages, after the events of 2001. Although there is no direct evidence on inventories, it is plausible that the need to rebuild after the run-down in 2001 increased effective demand at the farm-gate level and beyond. The decline in prices, starting in mid 2003, is further consistent with that story. The apparent excess of production over consumption during the postban era, modest during the early years and most striking since 2006, has been such that inventory may be rising closer to desired levels.

Moreover, we have fairly direct evidence of substantial inventories in Afghanistan or just across its borders in 2000 and 2001. The sum of seizures in 2001 in Iran, Tajikistan, and Pakistan, the three neighbors of Afghanistan that traditionally have accounted for most of the region's seizures, was below the 2000 levels but in heroin equivalents by only about 40%, whereas production fell by more than 90%. Only inventory could account for these seizures.[26]

There has also been an expansion in global heroin demand since the late 1990s because of the emergence of the large Russian market and those in other former Soviet republics. In addition, the decline in production in Burma, reflecting political decisions by authorities in growing areas, may have increased demand for Afghanistan-origin opium; China and India are both potential sources of such demand. However, the price effect in Afghanistan will ultimately depend on the responsiveness of the long-run supply curve for opium. Given the aforementioned availability of agricultural land and rural labor in Afghanistan, it is plausible that the curve is very elastic, suggesting that the new equilibrium price may not be much higher than that of the late 1990s. The general decline in farm-gate prices since mid 2003 is consistent with the hypothesis that the system is moving to equilibrium with higher production in Afghanistan than in the late 1990s, but with prices not greatly different from those of that era.

This analysis also suggests short-run market segmentation, as discussed in chapter 3. The very dramatic events in Afghanistan certainly had no detectable effect in the large U.S. market and appear not to have influenced China or

Thailand, two major destinations for Burma's production. The sharp decline in Australian heroin availability in early 2001 is so different in timing from that in any other downstream market that it cannot plausibly be attributed to the Afghan cutback, but rather to Australia-specific events.

We assume that the eventual price increases in downstream markets occurred in tandem with reductions in consumption, but we do not have indicators that can support this assumption reliably and clearly. Existing estimates of heroin-using populations in Europe are very imprecise—a change of 10% would fall within the typical ranges of those estimates. Data on overdose deaths and hospital emergency department admissions are available on an annual basis, but are very difficult to interpret (MacCoun and Reuter, 2001). Data for most European countries in the period 2001 to 2003 show decreases in heroin related mortality (European Monitoring Centre on Drugs and Drug Addiction [EMCDDA], 2007:84–85), but often with idiosyncratic explanations, such as the continuing increase in the availability of a substitute pharmaceutical in France (Emmanelli and Desenclos, 2005).

Nevertheless, assuming that consumption did decline, our analysis suggests that production interruptions, even if not sustained for long, can make a difference in affected markets. Note, though, that the cutback achieved by the Taliban is far more than can be plausibly projected as possible in a short time period for any intervention compatible with a democratic regime. To reduce global production by more than 60% within 1 year is not a realistic goal, so the response to the 2001 cutback probably represents an upper bound of what might be achieved by a short-term production intervention. However, a smaller cutback in a year when stocks are lower could generate more interruption.[27]

On the other hand, by highlighting the role of inventory in market adjustments, the analysis also suggests that the effects of a cutback that is even moderately longer than that achieved by the Taliban might be greater, depending largely on the responses of current and potential producers in other regions. The global distribution system was able to run down stocks during a 12-month period and largely meet demand, perhaps reflecting the bumper crops and inventory accumulation specific to the late 1990s. A second year might have produced a sharper increase in prices in both regional and downstream markets, although it may also have afforded opportunity to other producers in other regions to increase their output or enter the market anew.

In general, this analysis of the Taliban ban and opium cutback serves to reinforce our more theoretical discussion of the properties of supply and demand in chapter 3, and rests comfortably with our exploration of current conditions and market trends. We find evidence of (1) short-run supply rigidity and consequent price increases, (2) the potential for expansion in other regions. and (3) the cushioning effects of inventory. We also find evidence of market segmentation in the response to the ban. However, segmentation is not absolute. Over time, the market can reconfigure itself with new patterns of production and trafficking. Thus, it seems quite reasonable to refer to a *world market* for opiates.

5

Keeping Track of Opiate Flows

Introduction

To understand the world opiate market better and to assess the immediate effects of the Taliban ban and the associated Afghan opium cutback, we constructed an accounting framework, or *flow model,* that covers domestic and international transactions. We use the framework to compile and reconcile data on opiate cultivation and production, seizures, and consumption, and to track opiate flows across countries and regions.[1] It imposes consistency on estimates of production, seizures, and consumption, and enables quantitative comparisons of market activities in the periods preceding, during, and immediately after the ban and cutback. In so doing, the model provides further insight into the behavior of the world opiate market, including implications for opiate inventories and supply routes.

In this chapter we briefly describe the model and report three basic findings:

1. Asia dominates not just production, but also consumption and seizure of opiates.
2. It is likely that total world production exceeded consumption and seizures during the late 1990s and that inventory accumulated. The interruption in 2001 depleted that inventory and, in 2002 and 2003, although seizures grew rapidly, there was modest replenishment of the inventory. This, as already mentioned in chapter 4, may have cushioned the effects of the Taliban ban and opium cutback, and may partly account for the slow decline in postban farm-gate opium prices.

3. Tracking opiate flows provides insight to trafficking routes and market relationships. The estimates of production, seizures, and regional consumption in Latin America show exports much lower than estimates of U.S. consumption and seizures for the years 2001 and 2002. Thus, it is likely that the United States imports a substantial share of its heroin from Asia, contrary to official statements. Postban data also indicate the increased importance of Central Asian trafficking routes and suggest that new routes may be opening up to serve Chinese consumers from Afghanistan rather than the traditional source, Burma.

An Outline of the Approach

The framework consists of a series of linked spreadsheets, containing primarily official, open source data on poppy cultivation and on opiate production, seizures, and consumption. Most of the data are reported as annual statistics at the national level, with the important exception of the data on consumption, which we discuss later. The first spreadsheet contains data on poppy cultivation and opiate production; the second contains data on opiate seizures; the third and fourth contain data and calculations related to opiate consumption, from which we derive consumption estimates; the fifth, which we refer to as the *final compilation spreadsheet,* combines data and results from the first four; the sixth and seventh summarize the data for countries, regions, and the world; and the eighth tracks opiate flows across countries and regions.

We completed the data collection for this chapter in 2004, during the formative stages of our research, and note important recent changes in market conditions in the text and footnotes. We consider the data in three parts: (1) for 1996 to 2000, the period leading up to the Taliban ban and the associated cutback; (2) for 2001, the year in which the cutback occurred; and (3) for 2002 to 2003, the 2 years immediately after the cutback.[2] For the most part, our data cover the entire period of analysis: 1996 to 2003. However, we note two important exceptions: First, the seizure data for 2003 were not available at the time of our data collection;[3] second, the consumption data yield approximate estimates for the late 1990s and early 2000s, but they do not yield specific estimates for individual years. We address related computational and analytical challenges as they arise.

The data enable comparisons of production, seizures, and consumption across periods, and establish a basis for measuring the effects of the Taliban ban and the associated cutback. Thus, the framework provides a means to assess quantitatively the consequences of those events in Afghanistan—amounting to a supply shock—on the world opiate market. In addition, we also demonstrate another application of the framework in appendix C, in which we incorporate price data to estimate the income from opiate trafficking in Tajikistan and the rest of Central Asia.

Ideally, the framework would allow us to track opiate flows from cultivation to consumption, as shown in figure 5.1, with detailed information about opium cultivation and production, heroin and morphine manufacture, and opium, morphine, and heroin storage, transshipment, and consumption. However, we have only partial information on cultivation, production, seizures, and consumption, and almost no information on manufacturing, storage, and transshipments. In fact, what little information we have on manufacturing, storage, and transshipments largely derives from the partial information on cultivation, production, seizure, and consumption. The elements in bold type in figure 5.1 indicate data availability.

Given the significant data limitations, our approach proceeds as follows. First, we compile the available data on cultivation, production, seizures, and consumption. With regard to consumption, there are few direct estimates of national consumption; thus, we use United Nations prevalence rates, along with World Bank population estimates and our own estimates of average per-user consumption to calculate national consumption levels and, eventually, regional and global consumption levels. Second, we attempt to reconcile the data in aggregate and, to a lesser extent, regionally. That is, we compare the total production, seizures, and consumption estimates over a period of several years to determine whether the numbers line up and, if not, what might be the cause. Third, we use the data to track flows of opiates from cultivation to consumption.

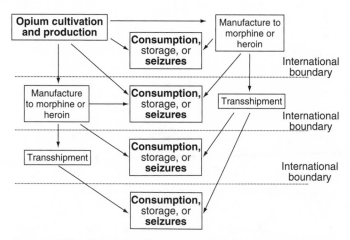

Figure 5.1 Tracking opiate flows from cultivation to consumption.

Data Compilation

We present and compile data on cultivation, production, seizures, and consumption in five of the eight spreadsheets. Each contains data by year, if available, and country.

Cultivation and Production

In the first spreadsheet, we compile United Nations and other data on illicit opium cultivation and production for each source country, as shown in table 5.1.

For the most part, the production data come from the United Nations' 2001 and 2002 *Global Illicit Drug Trends* reports (UNODCCP, 2001, 2002c) and

Table 5.1
Description of cultivation and production data.

Region/Country	Data Coverage	Data Sources
Southwest Asia		
Afghanistan	1988–2003	UNODCCP, 2001, 2002c; UNODC, 2004
Pakistan	1988–2003	UNODCCP, 2001, 2002c; UNODC, 2004
Southeast Asia		
Laos	1988–2003	UNODCCP, 2001, 2002c; UNODC, 2004
Burma	1988–2003	UNODCCP, 2001, 2002c; UNODC, 2004
Thailand	1988–2002	UNODCCP, 2001, 2002c; UNODC, 2004
Vietnam	1988–1999	UNODCCP, 2001, 2002c; UNODC, 2004
South Asia		
India	1996–2003	India country profile and INCSR
Other Asian countries	1988–2003	UNODCCP, 2001, 2002c; UNODC, 2004
Latin America		
Colombia	1991–2003	UNODCCP, 2001, 2002c; UNODC, 2004
Mexico	1990–2003	UNODC, 2004

Note: "India country profile" refers to the UNODC ROSA (2003), *India Country Profile* for 2003; and "INCSR" refers to the U.S. Department of State, Bureau of International Narcotics and Law Enforcement Affairs (2003), *International Narcotics Control Strategy Report* for 2002. The cultivation data are reported in hectares of potentially harvestable land, net of eradication. The UNODC (2004) includes the data for Vietnam and Thailand as of 2000 and 2003, respectively, in the category "Other Countries"; the UNODCCP (2001, 2002c) previously referred to this category as "Other Asian Countries." Although we do not use the data preceding 1996 for preban comparisons, we include the earlier data in the spreadsheet to establish broader market trends.

the statistical component of the 2004 *World Drug Report* (UNODC, 2004). For Mexico, the United Nations itself has derived production data from U.S. government surveys. For India, we derive our own estimates of illegally diverted production from estimates of licit production found in the United Nations' 2003 *India Country Profile* (UNODC ROSA, 2003), using diversion rates reported in the U.S. Department of State's 2002 INCSR (U.S. Department of State, Bureau of International Narcotics and Law Enforcement Affairs, 2003). According to the U.S. State Department, Bureau of International Narcotics and Law Enforcement Affairs (2003:VII-13). "Indian officials and drug enforcement officials have speculated in estimating that 10 to 30 percent of the crop is diverted." We have adopted the lower bound (i.e., the 10% diversion rate) as a conservative assumption,[4] but we investigate the implications of choosing other rates, including the upper bound.

Figure 5.2 illustrates the effect of the dramatic decline in Afghanistan's opiate production on its share of world production in 2001, the year of the ban-induced cutback, and its resurgence in 2002 and 2003. As of 2003, production in Afghanistan was approaching, but had not yet reached its record preban level of 1999.[5] Nevertheless, as shown in table 5.2, Afghanistan's opiate production level in 2003 was well above its 1996 to 2000 average. In contrast, production in Burma had fallen—and still remains—below 1996 to 2000 production (see chapters 3 and 6). In later calculations, we convert the estimates in table 5.2 to pure heroin equivalent units, applying a standard conversion ratio of 10 units of opium for every 1 unit of heroin or morphine.

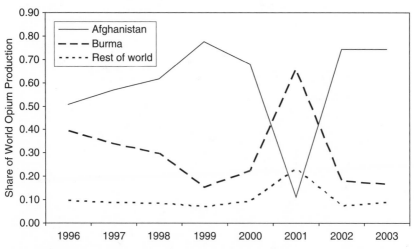

Figure 5.2 Shares of world illicit opium production.
Source: Authors' calculations based on UNODCCP, 2002c; UNODC ROSA, 2003; U.S. Department of State, Bureau of International Narcotics and Law Enforcement Affairs, 2003; UNODC, 2004.

Table 5.2
Illicit Opium production (in metric tons).

	1996	1997	1998	1999	2000	2001	2002	2003	1996–2000 (average)
Southwest Asia									
Afghanistan	2,248	2,804	2,693	4,565	3,276	185	3,400	3,600	3,117
Pakistan	24	24	26	9	8	5	5	52	18
Total Southwest Asia	2,272	2,828	2,719	4,574	3,284	190	3,405	3,652	3,135
Southeast Asia									
Laos	140	147	124	124	167	134	112	120	140
Burma	1,760	1,676	1,303	895	1,087	1,097	828	810	1,344
Thailand	5	4	8	8	6	6	9	—	6
Vietnam	9	2	2	2	—	—	—	—	4
Total Southeast Asia	1,914	1,829	1,437	1,029	1,260	1,237	949	930	1,495
South Asia									
India	85	99	26	108	133	73	79	79	90
Total South Asia	85	99	26	108	133	73	79	79	90
Other Asian countries	48	30	30	30	38	40	40	50	35
Total Asia	4,319	4,786	4,212	5,741	4,715	1,540	4,473	4,711	4,755
Latin America									
Colombia	67	90	100	88	88	58	50	50	87

Table 5.2
(continued)

	1996	1997	1998	1999	2000	2001	2002	2003	1996–2000 (average)
Latin America									
Mexico	54	46	60	43	21	71	47	84	45
Total Latin America	121	136	160	131	109	129	97	134	131
Total world opium production	4,440	4,922	4,372	5,872	4,824	1,669	4,570	4,845	4,887

Note: For Vietnam, the "1996–2000 average" is actually a 4-year average for 1996 to 1999. The estimate of illicit production for India assumes a 10% diversion rate. Table 3.1 in this volume presents updated estimates for Colombia and Mexico; it also presents updated estimates for the re-defined category of other countries.

Source: Authors' calculations based on UNODCCP, 2002c; UNODC ROSA, 2003; U.S. Department of State, Bureau of International Narcotics and Law Enforcement Affairs, 2003; UNODC, 2004.

On the basis of these production estimates, India generally ranks fourth among the world's illicit opiate producers, with Afghanistan, Burma, and Laos in the lead. By comparison, had we adopted the 30% diversion rate for India's contribution to the illicit market, India would have ranked third, well ahead of Laos.[6]

Seizures

In the second spreadsheet, we compile United Nations data on opium, morphine, and heroin seizures for more than 150 countries in 15 geographic subregions (North America, South America, Central America, Caribbean, Transcaucasia, Central Asia, East and Southeast Asia, Middle East and Southwest Asia, South Asia, North and East Africa, Southern Africa, West and Central Africa, Central and eastern Europe, western Europe, and Oceania) and five aggregate regions (the Americas, Asia, Africa, Europe, and Oceania).

For comparative purposes, we convert the seizures to heroin equivalent units using a ratio of 10 units of opium to 1 unit of morphine or heroin. Absent a purity adjustment factor, we may be giving too much weight to downstream seizures (e.g., those taking place in western Europe or North America), where more dilution likely occurs. Moreover, we do not account for the possibility that some seizures may reenter the global market, for example, as a result of corruption in drug enforcement agencies.[7]

Figure 5.3 reports the data for 1996 to 2002. It shows the distribution of seizures before, during, and after the cutback across the five aggregate regions (the Americas, Asia, Africa, Europe, and Oceania), one subregion (Central Asia), and select countries.

Figure 5.3 shows substantial declines in Asia's share of world seizures in 2001 and 2002, primarily as a result of declines in seizures in Iran.

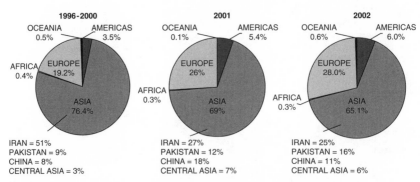

Figure 5.3 Shares of world opiate seizures by region, 1996–2002.
Note: Shares for 1996 to 2000 are production-weighted 5-year averages.
Source: Authors' calculations based on UNODCCP, 2002c; UNODC, 2004.

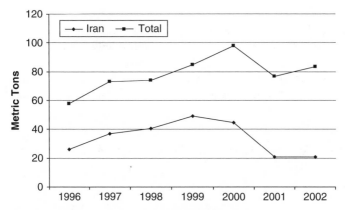

Figure 5.4 Opiate seizures worldwide and in Iran.
Note: Opiates are measured in heroin equivalent units, without adjustments for
purity, using a ratio of 10 units of opium to 1 unit of morphine or heroin.
Source: Authors' calculations based on UNODCCP, 2002c; UNODC, 2004.

Figure 5.4 shows the absolute declines in both world and Iranian seizures,
with Iranian seizures declining to levels just below those of the mid 1990s.

However, opiate seizures in some other major transshipping countries in
Asia—and elsewhere—have not followed Iran's lead. Figure 5.5 shows a spike
in seizures in China in 2001 and the continuation of an upward trend in seizures in Central Asia. In contrast with the sustained decline in seizures in Iran
in 2002, seizures in neighboring Pakistan and Turkey appeared to rebound
and surpass earlier levels.

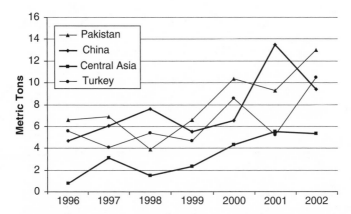

Figure 5.5 Opiate seizures in selected major transshipping countries.
Note: Opiates are measured in heroin equivalent units, without adjustments for
purity, using a ratio of 10 units of opium to 1 unit of morphine or heroin.
Source: Authors' calculations based on UNODCCP, 2002c; UNODC, 2004.

A closer look at the data for each country also reveals underlying changes in the composition of seizures (see table 5.3). For example, although Turkey's total opiate seizures rebounded after the ban, the composition of the total in 2002 differed markedly from the composition of the total in 2000, with morphine and heroin reversing positions. In 2000, Turkey's reported morphine and heroin seizures amounted to 2.5 and 6.1

Table 5.3
Seizure data for selected major transshipping countries (in metric tons).

	1996	1997	1998	1999	2000	2001	2002
Iran							
Opium	15.0	16.2	15.4	20.4	17.9	8.1	7.3
Morphine	10.4	18.9	22.3	22.8	20.8	8.7	9.5
Heroin	0.8	2.0	2.9	6.0	6.2	4.0	4.0
Total	*26.2*	*37.2*	*40.6*	*49.2*	*44.9*	*20.8*	*20.8*
Pakistan							
Opium	0.7	0.7	0.5	1.6	0.9	0.5	0.3
Morphine	0.0	0.0	0.0	0.0	0.0	1.8	6.8
Heroin	5.9	6.2	3.4	5.0	9.5	6.9	5.9
Total	*6.6*	*6.9*	*3.9*	*6.6*	*10.4*	*9.3*	*13.0*
China							
Opium	0.2	0.2	0.1	0.1	0.2	0.3	0.1
Morphine	0.2	0.4	0.1	0.0	0.0	0.0	0.0
Heroin	4.3	5.5	7.4	5.4	6.3	13.2	9.3
Total	*4.7*	*6.0*	*7.6*	*5.5*	*6.5*	*13.5*	*9.4*
Central Asia							
Opium	0.7	1.0	0.5	0.9	1.1	0.4	0.3
Morphine	0.0	0.0	0.0	0.0	0.0	0.0	0.0
Heroin	0.1	2.1	1.0	1.4	3.2	5.1	5.1
Total	*0.8*	*3.1*	*1.5*	*2.3*	*4.3*	*5.5*	*5.4*
Turkey							
Opium	0.0	0.0	0.0	0.0	0.0	0.0	0.0
Morphine	1.2	0.6	0.8	1.0	2.5	0.8	7.9
Heroin	4.4	3.5	4.7	3.6	6.1	4.4	2.6
Total	*5.6*	*4.1*	*5.4*	*4.6*	*8.6*	*5.2*	*10.5*
Totals for selected countries							
Opium	16.6	18.2	16.6	23.2	20.1	9.4	8.0
Morphine	11.8	19.9	23.2	23.8	23.2	11.3	24.3
Heroin	15.5	19.3	19.3	21.3	31.3	33.6	26.7
Total	*43.9*	*57.3*	*59.1*	*68.3*	*74.6*	*54.3*	*59.0*

Note: Opiates are measured in heroin equivalent units, without adjustments for purity, using a ratio of 10 units of opium to 1 unit of morphine or heroin; e.g., in 1996, Iran seized 150 metric tons of opium, equivalent to 15 metric tons of heroin or morphine.
Source: Authors' calculations based on UNODCCP, 2002c; UNODC, 2004.

metric tons, respectively; in 2002, the comparative figures were 7.9 and 2.6 metric tons. We also see a substantial increase in morphine seizures in Pakistan in 2002.

The sustained decline in Iranian seizures and the increased role of morphine seizures in both Pakistan and Turkey merit further consideration. Very speculatively, these phenomena could relate to the ban, through its effects on inventories and shipping patterns. For example, were opiates, especially morphine, stored in Pakistan and Turkey, but not in Iran, then after the ban those countries might draw down their inventories to satisfy market demand and potentially risk greater than usual seizures. Unfortunately, we lack specific evidence to test this hypothesis.

Consumption

In the third and fourth spreadsheets, we compile United Nations data on the prevalence of opiate abuse in about 100 countries and combine them with quantity and population estimates to calculate the amount of opiate consumption by country and for 15 regions. For each country and region, we produce one annual consumption estimate for 1996 to 2000 and another for 2001 to 2003. We do not produce year-by-year estimates because the data are too imprecise to support them. For example, in many instances the United Nations attributes a reported prevalence rate to a time frame, such as the late 1990s. In truth, it might be more accurate to describe the first estimate as one for the late 1990s and the second as one for the early 2000s. The two consumption spreadsheets are more complex than the production and seizure spreadsheets because the data require more manipulation.

We calculate opiate consumption, as shown in figure 5.6, for each of the 100 or so countries for which the United Nations reports the prevalence rate (i.e., the share of opiate users, most typically expressed in terms of the adult population, either older than 15 years of age or between the ages of 15 and 64).[8]

For the 1996 to 2000 estimates, we use prevalence rates from the United Nations' 2002 *Global Illicit Drug Trends* report (UNODCCP, 2002c); for the 2001 to 2003 estimates, we use prevalence rates from the United Nations' 2004 *World Drug Report* (UNODC, 2004). The prevalence rates in the earlier volume refer to adults age 15 years and older and, in the later volume, adults between the ages of 15 and 64. Thus, for 1996 to 2000, we multiply each country's prevalence rate by an estimate of its population age 15 years and older and, for 2001 to 2003, we multiply by an estimate of its population between the ages of 15 and 64. We use population estimates from the World Bank's 2002 and 2004 *World Development Indicators* (World Bank, 2002; World Bank, 2004b).

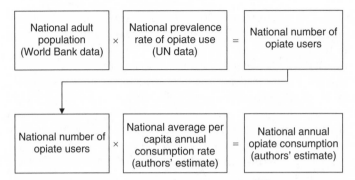

Figure 5.6 Calculating national, regional, and world opiate consumption. The model's spreadsheets sum consumption over countries to calculate regional and world opiate consumption in pure heroin equivalent units.

By and large, the prevalence rates in the United Nations' 2002 volume (UNODCCP, 2002c) characterize behaviors in the late 1990s. Although some of the prevalence rates in the United Nations' 2004 volume (UNODC, 2004) also characterize behaviors in the late 1990s, many or most have been updated to reflect behaviors in the early 2000s. As noted in chapter 3 and appendix B, the prevalence rates may include both dependent and casual or occasional users, but research suggests that dependent users likely make up the majority. Moreover, the rates include opium and morphine users, who may consume larger quantities by weight because their consumption methods (such as smoking, in the case of opium) are less efficient.

Absent national consumption estimates, we follow the approach outlined in appendix B, which makes use of U.S. and other evidence, and adopt a "default" rate for annual consumption outside the United States—an average, expressed per user in pure heroin equivalent grams. The ONDCP (2001) reports that U.S. heroin addicts consume roughly 15 grams of pure heroin per year, or about 50 milligrams per day when actively using, which we assume to be about 300 days per year, allowing for sickness, a few days in a local jail or treatment program, and other short-lived breaks in use. We use this rate for U.S. consumption. For our non-U.S. default rate, we further assume that opiate users in other countries consume twice as much per capita as those in the United States (i.e., 30 grams of pure heroin per user per year), largely reflecting the lower effective prices of opiates outside the United States.[9]

Tables 5.4 and 5.5 provide results for selected top-ranked opiate-consuming countries for 1996 to 2000 and 2001 to 2003. The calculations are indicative, not definitive; we intend them to provide a starting point for debate.

The differences in the consumption estimates for 1996 to 2000 and 2001 to 2003 arise partly from changes in behaviors and partly from

Table 5.4
Opiate consumption data and calculations for 1996 to 2000.

	Population Age 15+ (millions)	Prevalence Rate (%)	No. of Opiate Users (millions)	Consumption Rate (grams/year)	Opiate Consumption (metric tons)
India	676	0.40	2.70	30	81.1
Iran	40	2.80	1.12	30	33.5
China	949	0.10	0.95	30	28.5
Pakistan	75	0.90	0.68	30	20.3
United States	220	0.50	1.10	15	16.5
Russia	120	0.45	0.54	30	16.1
United Kingdom	48	0.60	0.29	30	8.7
Burma	32	0.90	0.29	30	8.6
Thailand	44	0.60	0.27	30	8.0
Bangladesh	80	0.30	0.24	30	7.2
Italy	39	0.60	0.23	30	7.0
Subtotal	2,340	NA	8.41	NA	235.6
Other	1,486	NA	2.72	NA	81.6
Total	3,825	NA	11.13	NA	317.2

Note: Opiates are measured in pure heroin equivalent units, using a ratio of 10 units of opium to 1 unit of morphine or heroin. We do not include poppy straw (compote) consumption and we have adjusted Russia's prevalence rate downward to eliminate poppy straw (compote) from the estimate. The population, prevalence, and consumption estimates for Pakistan and Italy are for adults age 15 to 64.
Source: Authors' calculations based on UNODCCP, 2002c; World Bank, 2002; UNODC, 2004; World Bank, 2004b.

changes in methodologies. With regard to behaviors, the United Nations notes a substantial increase in heroin abuse in Russia;[10] it also notes a substantial increase in heroin abuse in Indonesia. Russia's annual consumption increases from 16.1 metric tons for 1996 to 2000 to 31.9 metric tons for 2001 to 2003, and Indonesia becomes a top consumer. For other countries, like China and India, apparent changes in national consumption derive from the shift to a narrower population range (i.e., 15–64 years) and from other methodological changes.

In addition to the uncertainties already noted, we find that the calculations are highly sensitive to changes in prevalence and consumption parameters, which are especially important for heavily populated countries like China and India. For example, were the prevalence rate for India reduced as one of our collaborators (Charles, 2004) has suggested (e.g., to 0.2%), the national total would drop to about 41 metric tons annually for 1996 to 2000 and

Table 5.5
Opiate consumption data and calculations for 2001 to 2003.

	Population Age 15–64 (millions)	Prevalence Rate (percent)	No. of Opiate Users (millions)	Consumption Rate (grams/year)	Opiate Consumption (metric tons)
India	652	0.40	2.61	30	78.3
Iran	42	2.80	1.18	30	35.4
Russia	101	1.05	1.06	30	31.9
China	878	0.10	0.88	30	26.4
Pakistan	81	0.90	0.73	30	21.9
United States	191	0.60	1.15	15	17.2
Indonesia	138	0.20	0.28	30	8.3
United Kingdom	39	0.70	0.27	30	8.2
Italy	39	0.70	0.27	30	8.1
Bangladesh	82	0.30	0.25	30	7.4
Thailand	43	0.50	0.22	30	6.5
Burma	31	0.70	0.22	30	6.5
Subtotal	2,319	NA	9.11	NA	256.0
Other	1,238	NA	3.10	NA	93.1
Total	3,557	NA	12.21	NA	349.1

Note: Opiates are measured in pure heroin equivalent units, using a ratio of 10 units of opium to 1 unit of morphine or heroin. We do not include poppy straw (compote) consumption and we have adjusted Russia's prevalence rate downward to eliminate poppy straw (compote) from the estimate. *Source*: Authors' calculations based on UNODCCP, 2002c; World Bank, 2002; UNODC, 2004; World Bank, 2004b.

39 metric tons annually for 2001 to 2003. Conversely, were China's prevalence rate increased to 0.2%,[11] its annual consumption estimate would rise to about 57 metric tons for 1996 to 2000 and about 53 metric tons for 2001 to 2003.[12]

Figure 5.7 shows the distribution of global opiate consumption across the Americas, Asia, Africa, Europe, and Oceania for 1996 to 2000.

Figure 5.8 shows the distribution of global opiate consumption across the Americas, Asia, Africa, Europe, and Oceania for 2001 to 2003.

Despite Russia's, hence the Central and eastern European region's, increasing share of world opiate consumption, Asia remains the world's leading consumer, by tonnage.[13]

Data Summary

Absent the seizure data for 2003, figure 5.9 considers Asia's role in the market before, during, and after the cutback, but ending in 2002. Despite the drop in Afghanistan's production in 2001 and the decline in Iran's seizures in 2001

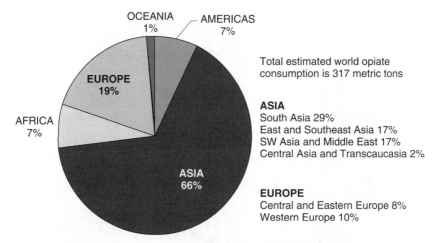

Figure 5.7 Shares of world opiate consumption by region, 1996–2000.
Source: Authors' calculations based on UNODCCP, 2002c; World Bank, 2002;
UNODC, 2004; World Bank, 2004b.

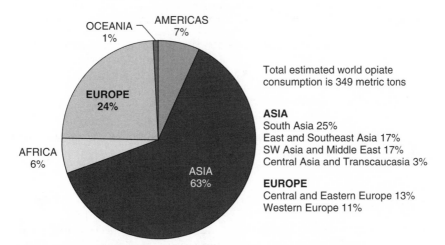

Figure 5.8 Shares of world opiate consumption by region, 2001–2003.
Source: Authors' calculations based on UNODCCP, 2002c; World Bank, 2002;
UNODC, 2004; World Bank, 2004b.

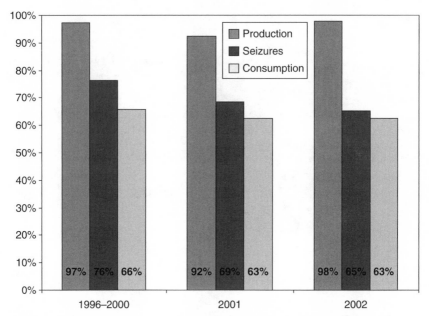

Figure 5.9 Asia's share of opiate consumption, seizures, and production.
Note: The consumption estimates for 1996 to 2000 are based on data for the late 1990s,
and those for 2001 and 2002 are based on data for the early 2000s. We do not have separate
estimates for 2001 and 2002.
Source: Authors' calculations based on UNODCCP, 2002c; World Bank, 2002; UNODC, 2004;
World Bank, 2004b; UNODC ROSA, 2003; U.S. Department of State, Bureau of International
Narcotics and Law Enforcement Affairs, 2003.

and 2002, Asia has held its position as the world's leading producer, confiscator, and consumer of opiates. Arguably, the diminution in Asia's role in 2001
is barely perceptible, except in the seizure data.

Data Reconciliation

We use the data summaries in the sixth and seventh spreadsheets to attempt to
reconcile the estimates of opiate production, seizures, and consumption. At the
most aggregate possible level (i.e., the world), reconciliation requires little or no
information about shipping routes and practices. That is, we can add an estimate of world seizures and an estimate of world consumption, and compare the
gross figure—world disappearance—to an estimate of world production without immediate concern for the routes and methods by which the opiates reach
their final destinations. Although, to the extent that the numbers do not add
up, information about storage or transit may help to explain discrepancies. As
shown in figure 5.10, the estimates of world opiate production typically exceed
estimates of world "disappearance" (consumptions and seizures, combined).

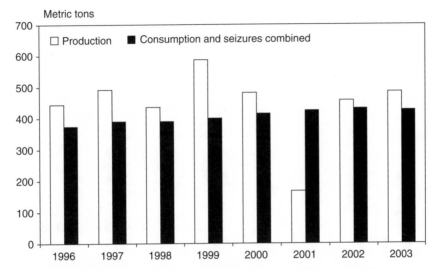

Figure 5.10 World production estimates typically exceed "disappearance" estimates.

Note: Disappearance refers to the total of consumption and seizures. Absent United Nations seizure data for 2003, we estimate seizures for 2003 as 16% of total world production, based on the 1996 to 2000 average.

Source: Authors' calculations based on UNODCCP, 2002c; World Bank, 2002; UNODC, 2004; World Bank, 2004b; UNODC ROSA, 2003; U.S. Department of State, Bureau of International Narcotics and Law Enforcement Affairs, 2003.

A closer look at the underlying numbers (table 5.6) shows that the combined production "surpluses"—the amounts of opiates left over after accounting for seizures and consumption—during the 5 years preceding the 2001 cutback offset or more than offset the "deficit" in the year during which production fell. Moreover, in 2002 and 2003, the production surpluses appear to be growing and approaching the 1996 to 2000 average.[14] With surpluses ranging from 5% to 32% of production in the years around the cutback (figure 5.11), it may be that we are systematically underestimating consumption or overstating production,[15] but the figures may also suggest a role for storage in explaining the market phenomenon in 2001 and in the years immediately after the cutback.

At the national or regional level, data reconciliation typically requires much more detailed information. For example, to reconcile production, seizure, and consumption estimates across and within Afghanistan and Central Asia requires an understanding of how much heroin enters Central Asia from Afghanistan and how much continues on to other destinations. Not surprisingly, this type of information often is unavailable. Absent hard data about shipping routes and practices, we make certain baseline assumptions. We discuss these issues in more detail later, in the context of tracking.

Table 5.6
Production surpluses and deficits for 1996 to 2003 (in metric tons unless otherwise stated).

	1996–2000 Total	1999–2000 Total	2001	2002	2003	1996–2000 Average
Consumption	1,584	634	349	349	349	317
Seizures	388	183	77	84	78	78
Total disappearance	1,972	816	425	432	426	394
Production	2,443	1070	167	457	485	489
Surplus	471	253	NA	25	58	94
Deficit	NA	NA	259	NA	NA	NA
Seizures as share of						
Production	0.16	0.17	0.46	0.18	0.16	0.16
Consumption	0.24	0.29	0.22	0.24	0.22	0.24
Surplus/deficit as share of						
Production	0.19	0.24	1.55	0.05	0.12	0.19
Consumption	0.30	0.40	0.74	0.07	0.17	0.30

Note: NA, not applicable. Absent United Nations seizure data for 2003, we estimate seizures for 2003 as 16% of the total world production, based on the 1996 to 2000 average.
Source: Authors' calculations based on UNODCCP, 2002c; World Bank, 2002; UNODC, 2004; World Bank, 2004b; UNODC ROSA, 2003; U.S. Department of State, Bureau of International Narcotics and Law Enforcement Affairs, 2003.

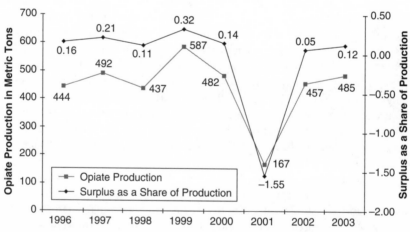

Figure 5.11 Opiate production and opiate surpluses as a share of production.
Note: Absent United Nations seizure data for 2003, we estimate seizures for 2003 as 16% of total world production, based on the 1996 to 2000 average.
Source: Authors' calculations based on UNODCCP, 2002c; World Bank, 2002; UNODC, 2004; World Bank, 2004b; UNODC ROSA, 2003; U.S. Department of State, Bureau of International Narcotics and Law Enforcement Affairs, 2003.

Trafficking Routes and Opiate Flows

Tracking occurs in the eighth and final spreadsheet. In that spreadsheet, we draw data from the final compilation sheet and combine it with information about possible cross-border trafficking routes to map out opiate flows. In particular, as shown in figure 5.12, the spreadsheet tracks flows of opiates via three broad categories of routes.[16]

To illustrate the approach, we turn to the "Americas Routes" in figure 5.12, which are relatively self-contained. To start, we assume that the regional supply chain begins with Colombia and Mexico, and that all consumption and seizures in Latin America originate in one of these two countries. Opiates do not flow into Latin America from other regions. Furthermore, we assume that any opiates that Latin America does not consume or seize flow onward to the United States.[17]

We track opiate flows as follows:

1. Begin with production in Colombia and Mexico.
2. Subtract the amount of opiates that are either consumed or seized in Latin America, including Colombia and Mexico.
3. Assign the remainder (i.e., the amount available for export) to the United States, where it is either consumed or seized.
4. Assign the difference—the gap—between the amount that the United States imports from Latin America and the amount that it consumes and seizes to other, presumably Asian, sources.

Table 5.7 shows the implementation of the approach for 1996 to 2000, 2001, and 2002. It does not show calculations for 2003 because the United Nations had not yet published the seizure data for that year when this research was completed.[18] However, the combined 2003 production figure for Colombia

Americas Routes

Colombia, Mexico ⟶ Latin America ⟶ United States

Southwest Asia Originating Routes

Afghanistan ⟶ Central Asia ⟶ Russia ⟶ Europe (except Russia and Turkey)

Afghanistan, Pakistan ⟶ Iran ⟶ Turkey, Transcaucasia ⟶ Europe (except Russia and Turkey), United States

Afghanistan, Pakistan ⟶ India

Southeast Asia Originating Routes

Burma, Laos ⟶ China, Hong Kong ⟶ Oceania, Indonesia, Europe (except Russia and Turkey), United States

Burma, Laos ⟶ Thailand ⟶ Oceania, Indonesia, Europe (except Russia and Turkey), United States

Burma, Laos ⟶ India, Bangladesh

Figure 5.12 Major transshipping routes.

and Mexico is somewhat higher, which, all else being equal, would tend to indicate a somewhat larger share of U.S. consumption originating in Latin America in 2003 than during previous years.[19]

Given uncertainties regarding the purity of seizures and the possibility of market reentry, we present alternative calculations in table 5.8, setting seizures to zero.

Even in this simple case, the data suggest important linkages across international trade routes and markets. During 1996 to 2000, and 2001 and 2002, Colombia and Mexico appear to have accounted for a large share of U.S. imports, but not the vast majority, implying that the United States would have imported significant quantities of opiates from other—presumably Asian—sources. During 1996 to 2000, the United States would have imported about 55% of its opiates from other sources

Table 5.7
Tracking opiate production, seizures, and consumption in the Americas (in metric tons).

	1996–2000 Average	2001	2002
Latin America			
Production			
Colombia	8.7	5.8	5.0
Mexico	4.5	7.1	4.7
Total production	13.1	12.9	9.7
Seizures	(1.1)	(2.1)	(2.2)
Consumption	(4.0)	(4.6)	(4.6)
Amount available for export to the United States	8.1	6.2	2.8
United States			
Seizures	1.5	2.0	2.8
Consumption	16.5	17.2	17.2
Required imports	18.1	19.2	20.0
Amount of U.S. imports from Latin America	(8.1)	(6.2)	(2.8)
Amount of U.S. imports from other sources	10.0	13.1	17.2

Note: We define Latin America as including South America, Central America, the Caribbean, and Mexico, but production within Latin America is limited to Colombia and Mexico. We apply heroin-only prevalence rates to Latin American consumption to avoid inclusion of synthetic opiates. As a consequence, the rates tend to be lower than those appearing in the United Nations' *Global Illicit Drug Trends* and *World Drug Report* volumes (the UNODC provided us with the heroin-only rates). We define "required" U.S. imports as the sum of U.S. seizures and U.S. consumption. Parentheses indicate subtraction.
Source: Authors' calculations based on UNODCCP, 2002c; World Bank, 2002; UNODC, 2004; World Bank, 2004b.

if including seizures (data in table 5.7), and about 45% if not (data in table 5.8). It would have imported 68% and 86% of its consumption from other sources in 2001 and 2002, respectively, if including seizures; and 52% and 70% if not.[20]

We apply the same general approach, albeit more complicated and requiring additional assumptions, to Southwest- and Southeast Asian-originating routes, including routes to Europe and the United States. For example, for the Afghanistan-originating route through Central Asia, we assume that all shipments to and through Central Asia originate in Afghanistan; opiates do

Table 5.8
Tracking opiate production and consumption in the Americas (in metric tons).

	1996–2000 Average without Seizures	2001 without Seizures	2002 without Seizures
Latin America			
Production			
Colombia	8.7	5.8	5.0
Mexico	4.5	7.1	4.7
Total production	13.1	12.9	9.7
Seizures	(0)	(0)	(0)
Consumption	(4.0)	(4.6)	(4.6)
Amount available for export to the United States	9.1	8.3	5.1
United States			
Seizures	0	0	0
Consumption	16.5	17.2	17.2
Required imports	16.5	17.2	17.2
Amount of U.S. imports from Latin America	(9.1)	(8.3)	(5.1)
Amount of U.S. imports from other sources	7.4	8.9	12.1

Note: We define Latin America as including South America, Central America, the Caribbean, and Mexico, but production within Latin America is limited to Colombia and Mexico. As in table 5.7, we apply heroin-only prevalence rates to Latin American consumption. We define "required" U.S. imports as the sum of U.S. seizures and U.S. consumption, but set seizures to zero. Parentheses indicate subtraction.
Source: Authors' calculations based on UNODCCP, 2002c; World Bank, 2002; UNODC, 2004; World Bank, 2004b.

not flow into Central Asia from Burma, Laos, or Latin America. Furthermore, we assume that any opiates that Central Asia does not consume or seize flow onward to Russia and that all opiates flowing into or through Russia arrive via Central Asia. Finally, we assume that a share (25%) of the rest of Europe's consumption and seizures transit through Russia.[21]

By applying these kinds of allocation rules to each of the trafficking routes, we can begin to establish where shortfalls might have occurred in 2001 or where routes may have shifted over time. For example, as production in Burma has declined, we find evidence that new Afghanistan-originating routes may have developed to service Burma's former customers, possibly including those in China. In particular, if we hold our allocation rules constant over time, we find that customers initially served by Southeast Asian-originating routes eventually experience shortfalls, suggesting—if our initial allocations are reasonable—that those customers must be receiving more of their opiates from Southwest Asian-originating routes.[22] These results, along with our findings on seizures and consumption (e.g., the increases in Central Asian and Chinese seizures, and the rise in consumption in Russia), suggest that supply routes may be shifting, with an expansion through Central Asia and possibly eastward.

In addition, with information about farm-level, border, and retail prices, we can extend the approach to estimate the value of opiate-related transactions along these routes, and their contributions to national and regional incomes. Appendix C, "Central Asia: Trafficking Revenues and Economic Dependency," illustrates the extension. It tracks opiate flows into or through Central Asia to each of the region's major end markets, including Russia, the rest of Europe, and Central Asia itself. Using price data along each route, it estimates the region's opiate trafficking income in terms of its potential contribution to GDP.

Concluding Remarks

The creation of the flow model has enabled us to develop a more complete understanding of the world opiate market and has demonstrated Asia's dominance as an opiate producer, confiscator, and consumer. However, our efforts to reconcile and evaluate estimates of production, seizures, and consumption suggest the importance of continuing the process of primary data collection, especially in China, India, and other populous nations, but also in other nations playing significant roles as producers, traffickers, or consumers. For example, plausible changes in assumptions about prevalence rates in populous nations like China and India have dramatic effects on estimates of flows.

To the extent possible, we have used information gathered by our research collaborators to better inform our assessments of consumption—and production and seizures—but many uncertainties remain. Beyond issues of prevalence and consumption, we also face the challenge of uncertainty regarding the "true" rate of illegal diversion in India. Here, too, potentially reasonable differences in assumptions about rates can bring about significant changes in estimation results. For example, shifting from a low-end estimate, based on a 10% diversion rate, to a midrange estimate, using a 20% diversion rate, would add about 80 metric tons of illicit opium into the market. India's illicit total would then be large enough to cover about 20% of its own consumption, an amount roughly equivalent to U.S. consumption. Chapter 7 considers other plausible alternatives for calculating illegal diversion.

Nevertheless, the model generates results of importance to the policy analysis. It strongly suggests the presence of significant stores of opiates immediately preceding the ban, a rapid draw-down in the year of the cutback, and the possibility of stock accumulation shortly after the cutback. It also suggests a shift in supply routes, with some expansion through Central Asia and eastward.

Part II

Country Studies

6

Afghanistan and Burma

The Two Dominant Producers

Introduction

As shown in chapters 3 and 5, two nations—Afghanistan and Burma—have dominated the illicit cultivation of opium poppy at least since the 1980s when systematic data collection began. Although their individual market shares have changed during the past 20-odd years, jointly they have been responsible for 70% to 95% of the world's opium supply. Their dominance has become more pronounced since the mid 1990s, when their combined market share first exceeded 90%. Only in 2001 has that share fallen below 90%, but Afghanistan now accounts for the overwhelming majority of production. In the following pages we explain why and how Afghanistan and Burma have become the two dominant producers, singling out the lack of government control and the parallel rise of quasi-state authorities as key promoting factors of the opiate industry in both countries.[1]

In Search of an Explanation

Francisco Thoumi (2003) contrasts the distribution of illicit drug production across nations with that for legitimate agricultural products. Whereas many countries can and do produce coffee, many countries can but don't produce opium. For example, poppies can grow in parts of Europe, large portions of Africa and Asia, parts of North America, the tropical highlands of South America, and other parts of the southern hemisphere. Still, very few countries grow poppies and, indeed, the bulk of opium illicit production occurs in only two countries: Afghanistan and Burma.

Although no precise estimate exists, the same two nations also account for a consistent and increasing share of world heroin production, opium's main illegal derivative. According to the UNODC, for example, Afghanistan's laboratories converted by 2007 90% of the country's opium into heroin and morphine (Agence France Presse [AFP], 2007). Again, this development has taken place despite the fact that morphine and heroin can be refined almost anywhere. Opium processing is, in fact, an archetypal footloose industry. It requires very little capital and few labor skills, the needed technologies are fairly simple and well-known, and the chemical inputs used are common and all have possible substitutes (Thoumi, 2003:53).

Afghanistan's and Burma's current hegemonic position in illicit opiate production is only marginally rooted in history. Although opium poppies were cultivated in both countries since at least the 19th century, neither Afghanistan nor Burma was a major opium producer before World War II. In contrast to India, Iran, and other parts of Asia, opium poppy was not a traditional crop in Afghanistan. It was not cultivated in most parts of the country until the 1990s. Unlike many other countries in the region, Afghanistan did not have an opium culture. Only in some parts of the country, primarily in Badakhshan in the north, could one speak of an opium tradition, but even there it did not predate the late 18th century (UNODC, 2003c:87–88).[2]

In Burma, poppy cultivation spread from Yunnan in the mid-19th century. The small state of Kokang in the northeastern Shan State was primarily affected. This formally belonged to China up until 1896 and was well connected to the large Chinese opium market through established tea trade routes and its substantial ethnic Chinese population. From Kokang, production spread to the Wa area, which is situated southeast of Kokang and was, until the 1930s, considered untamed, and to Shan areas in the Kengtung region, just north of Siam (present-day Thailand) (Renard, 1996:13–43). Kokang as well as the Wa and Kentung regions remained the key opium-producing bastions until contemporary times. However, Burmese opium production in the late 19th century was still limited; it was estimated at about 30 tons per year before World War II, only becoming more substantial in the 1950s. (Lintner, 2000:4; chapter 2, this volume).

History alone, thus, does not suffice to explain the long held dominance of Afghanistan and Burma. This must be seen as the result of the interplay of several factors and relatively recent historical events, which have embedded opium cultivation and trade in the daily lives of millions of people and have turned the illegal opium industry into a significant element of the two countries' economies. Given that opiate production is an industry, albeit an illegal one, some of these factors are—unsurprisingly—economic. Both Afghanistan and Burma are poor nations with sufficient land for production and relatively low-cost labor, a potential source of advantage in the production of low-technology agricultural items such as opiates. Abundant land and low-cost labor are not unique to the two nations; they are traits that these nations share with many other Third World countries, although Afghanistan, among the world's 10 poorest counties, may have an even greater advantage in producing opium than others.

The Lack of Government Control

The key explanatory factors lie in the two countries' institutions and in the way they affect the opium industry. A formidable competitive advantage results from the reluctance and/or inability of the two countries' governments to act aggressively against growers and early-stage traffickers and refiners. Since gaining independence from the British—an event which took place in 1919 in the case of Afghanistan[3] and in 1948 in the case of Burma—both countries have been led, if at all, by a variety of ineffective, and usually corrupt central governments, which have mostly lacked popular legitimacy. Despite occasionally applying brutal and indiscriminate violence against political opponents, these regimes have consistently been unable to impose their authority—much less the international bans on opium—in large areas of the territory in which they are formally sovereign.[4] On the contrary, the governments ruling Afghanistan and Burma have frequently been—both at a personal and an institutional level—permeable to drug interests and money.

In Afghanistan's recent history there was a 20-year-long period during which there was no effective central government, which was initiated by the Soviet Union's invasion of the country in 1979. After 10 years of devastating civil war, the USSR was forced to withdraw by the anti-Communist mujahedin, who were primarily supplied and trained by the United States, Saudi Arabia, and Pakistan (Laber and Rubin, 1988). Fighting continued among the various mujahidin factions, giving rise to a state of warlordism and anarchy:

> [W]hen the Soviet Union withdrew and then dissolved and the
> United States disengaged, Afghanistan was left with no legitimate
> state, no national leadership, multiple armed groups in every locality,
> a devastated economy and a people dispersed throughout the region,
> indeed the world. (Rubin, 2003:x)

During the mid 1990s, by establishing a common authority, collecting weapons, and guaranteeing peace and security, the Taliban presented themselves as an Islamic solution to the problems of a failed state.[5] However, the Taliban continued to behave as a quasi-state authority, uninterested in providing the services of a full-fledged state throughout their dominion, which covered most of Afghanistan during the late 1990s and lasted until late 2001.

The stateless period of Afghanistan's history was put to an end, at least formally, by the constitution of a new democratic government under the leadership of Hamid Karzai in late 2001. This government has taken a firm official stance against opiate production, trade and consumption. One of the first acts of the Afghan Interim Administration in early 2002 was to prohibit all these activities. However, despite having been endowed with popular legitimacy in nationwide elections in October 2004, the Karzai administration has only formal authority over large parts of the country and it is still forced to share power with local warlords. In the south and the east, moreover, the Taliban have recovered terrain and spread insecurity and terror. As in the past, both the warlords and the resurgent Taliban "tax" and, in some cases, are directly involved in opium production and opiate trade. The worrying novelty is that some of the most prominent warlords have been incorporated into the official power structures and even entrusted with drug control tasks.

In Burma, too, the bulk of opiate production and trade have always taken place in what is today known as the Shan State (the northeastern part of Burma), over which the control of the central government has always been most tenuous. Unlike the rest of Burma, the Shan States, as they were known before 1959, were never fully subject to British rule. From 1886 until the country's independence in 1948, the 30-or-so Shan principalities in northeastern Burma were merely British protectorates. Neither the British colonial administration nor the Japanese invaders during World War II nor even the postcolonial Burmese administrations were ever able to exercise full sovereignty over the Shan States, particularly in the regions east of the Salween river, known as Kokang and Wa, where much of opium poppy cultivation has been concentrated since the 19th century.[6]

Because neither the British colonial rulers nor the Burmese independent governments, at least up until the beginning of the 21st century, ever made concerted efforts to stop opium production and trade in the Shan States, opium was long a licit commodity there, with its status just shifting from full to de facto legality. Indeed, from 1962 onward, successive military regimes ended up franchising the opium trade and its taxation to several quasi-state authorities, including government-sponsored militias and allied insurgent groups, in exchange for fighting other rebels. Other quasi-state authorities fighting the Burmese government have also made opium the principal source of their funding.

The Strength of Premodern Ties

Another institutional factor favoring Afghanistan and Burma's dominant position in the illicit opiate industry is the persistent strength of family, ethnic, and tribal identities. According to a pattern typical of all premodern societies, the primary loyalty of most people in both countries is still directed to the family, tribe, and/or ethnic group, whereas the central government is seen as a distant and unhelpful, if not openly hostile, entity. The strength of these premodern ties is both an effect and a cause of the weakness of Afghan and Burmese central governments. Ethnic segmentation has produced endemic conflict in Burma since the late 1940s (Smith, 1991; Kramer, 2005), and in Afghanistan it has been a major factor in prolonging the civil war ignited by the Soviet invasion in 1979 and in making the process of state reconstruction more difficult since 2001 (Rubin, 2003).

In both countries, tribal, ethnic, and local ties have been important facilitators of the opiate trade.[7] Ethnic Chinese networks have been in charge of much of the opium (and, later, opiate) trade in northeastern Burma since the mid-19th century, and many of the most successful traffickers still today have Chinese origins (Renard, 1996; Lintner, 2002). Likewise, a few tribes located on both sides of the Afghan–Pakistani border, such as the Pashtun Shinwari, have run a considerable part of the cross-border opiate trade since the 1970s, largely unbothered by the arbitrary borders set by British authorities in the 19th century (UNDCP, 1998b; see also Khan, Shah, Asad, Amjad, Shahzad, 2000; Khan, 2004). Collective identities and clan ties of several Persian-speaking (the so-called "Tajik") ethnic groups also straddle the Tajik-Afghan border on the river Panj (Centlivres and Centlivres-Demont, 1998). Since the early 1990s, they have greatly facilitated the formation and consolidation of a new smuggling route for Afghan heroin through Tajikistan (see chapter 9).

International Developments...

In addition to the economic and institutional factors mentioned, Afghanistan and Burma's current predominance in the world illicit opiate industry is also the result of international and domestic evolutionary processes. In both countries, illicit opium cultivation was strongly enhanced by the success of neighboring nations, which had been major opium producers, in curbing the cultivation of poppies. Burma's opium industry, for example, profited from the eradication conducted forcefully but effectively by the Chinese communist regime during the 1950s (see Renard, 1996:55; chapter 2, this volume) and, to a lesser extent, also from Thailand's progressive reduction of domestic production from the 1960s onward (Renard, 2001).

The first, significant wave of expansion in Afghanistan's opium production was likewise recorded after the promulgation and effective enforcement of opium bans by three other countries of the so-called Golden Crescent. During the early 1970s, under the pressure of the United States, Turkey was able to curb the previously extensive leakage from its licit opium production (see chapter 2). After the Islamic Revolution of 1979, Iran also effectively banned opium production. However, its efforts to curb demand were less successful: this created strong incentives for supply increases from Afghanistan (Haq, 1996; Raisdana and Nakhjavani, 2002). After the prohibition of production, sale, and consumption of all drugs in 1979, Pakistan's opium production also came under increasing control during the 1980s. At the same time, the demand for opiates continued to grow and was fed primarily with Afghan products (UNDCP, 1994; Khan, 2004).

A few non-opiate-related international events also forcefully fostered the development of the illicit opium industry in the two countries. The Soviet invasion of Afghanistan in 1979 has also already been mentioned; a comparable earlier event in Burma was the Nationalist Chinese Kuomintang (KMT)'s invasion of parts of the Shan State in the early 1950s (discussed later).

...and Domestic Ones: The Advantages of Opium
Poppy Cultivation...

Domestic developments affecting the socioeconomic, cultural, and political realms have also fostered the expansion of the illicit opium industry in both Afghanistan and Burma. Civil war and—especially in Burma—disastrous experiments with a socialist-type centralized economy have greatly slowed down the economic and social development of the two countries, thus increasing the attractiveness of employment in the illegal opium industry and the latter's relative importance in the domestic economy.

In the case of Afghanistan, one can speak of a virtual reversal of development. By 1991, Afghanistan GDP per capita had sunk to the third lowest in the world. Ten years afterward, it was still listed as the second poorest country by the United Nations Development Programme (UNDP) in the human poverty index ranking of the 90 developing countries, and 70% of its population was considered undernourished (UNDP, 2002b:151). Today, Afghanistan ranks at the bottom of all measures of human well-being; illicit activities have become key elements of its people's survival strategies (International Monetary Fund [IMF], 2003:14–18; Asian Development Bank, UN Assistance Mission to Afghanistan, UNDP, and World Bank Group, 2004:3–4).

Compared with Afghanistan, Burma fares better, as it ranked 131st out of 175 countries in the Human Development Index of 2003. Despite being a very resource-rich country, however, Burma has been largely cut off from the rapid growth that has occurred in neighboring countries. The situation is all the more dire in the Shan State. This is home to a number of ethnic minorities and has been devastated since the 1950s by a variety of ethnic, ideological, and opportunistic insurgencies, and by mass retaliation campaigns of the Burmese military.

In the devastated economies of Afghanistan and Burma's northeastern provinces, opium has become the main source of cash incomes for a significant proportion of the local population. This has happened although opium does not necessarily grant the farmers larger profits than legitimate crops. Even in Afghanistan, except for the post-Taliban ban period, there are a range of crops including apricots, apples, black cumin, and melons that can generate higher apparent returns than opium poppy (Mansfield, 2002; UNODC, 2003c). Nonetheless, opium fills some of the farmers' basic needs, playing "a multifunctional role in the livelihood strategies of the poor" (Mansfield, 2002:12).

First, a poppy crop presents technical advantages. It grows even in areas where there is no artificial irrigation, such as in Burma's hills. It is relatively weather resistant with a short growing season. The early harvest frees resources to harvest other crops later and makes it possible, even in semitropical areas, to plant a second crop of other plants. Second, an opium crop is particularly attractive for farmers supporting a large household in relation to the size of their land holdings, because it is extremely labor intensive. As the opportunity cost of family labor is minimal, opium poppy is perceived to be profitable.

Third, opium is easy to store, because it is not perishable, and it has a ready market, with buyers usually collecting the product at the farm gate. In contrast, marketing of legitimate high-value crops such as vegetables can often be problematic given their perishable nature and the absence or inadequacy of the transportation infrastructure. As we noted in chapter 3, opium may also serve as a store of value in the absence of a safe and reliable banking system. Fourth, opium is the only crop against which farmers in Afghanistan (and to a lesser extent in Burma as well) can easily obtain credit, albeit at usurious rates under a system of future contracts known as *salaam* in Afghanistan (UNDCP, 1999a; Mansfield, 2001b; IMF, 2003:40). Fifth, opium is compact enough to be hidden and transported easily, which are important advantages in a climate of anarchy, and the poppies in the field cannot be stolen easily because it would be too laborious for warlords' troops to harvest them (Cowell, 2005:16–17).

More generally, as a rapid monetization of the economy took place from the 1960s onward in Burma and in Afghanistan from 1979 onward, opium became the main local means of satisfying the tremendous incentives for cash-producing activities that were thus created (Rubin, 2000; Cowell, 2005). For an increasing number of farmers, the only possible way to acquire cash in sufficient quantities was to produce opium.

In cultural terms, the growing size of the illicit opium industry and the persistent lack of prohibition enforcement have effectively legitimated opium cultivation and trade. These have progressively become routine economic activities, to which little or no stigma is attached and for which crime is an artificial label. In Afghanistan, even the traditionally cautious, if not openly critical, stance of Islam vis-à-vis opium cultivation, trade, and consumption has been largely offset, with persisting restrictions concerning exclusively heroin (UNDCP, 1998b; Macdonald, 2005:95).[8] As a result, for several decades, up until the late 1990s at least, the initial stages of the world illicit opium industry were considered de facto legitimate activities by both the people directly involved in them and the population of the main producing areas.

...and the Rise of Quasi-State Authorities

At the political level, the power vacuum left by central government has been filled by a variety of quasi-state authorities, such as the warlords fighting the Soviet invaders and then the Taliban themselves in Afghanistan, as well as the KMT, and numerous rebel and government-sponsored militias in the Shan State. Although their aims were at least initially political, quasi-state authorities have long fostered, profited from, and, in some cases, even organized opium production and trade.

In neither country have opium cultivation and trade ever been exclusively controlled by quasi-state authorities. Whereas opium growing has traditionally been left to poverty-stricken but formally independent farmers, the commercialization of opium has always been at least partially run by local classes of merchants trading opium along with a variety of other commodities. Nonetheless, with their mixture of political and economic power, the quasi-state authorities have been the main engine of the growth of the opium industry in both Afghanistan and Burma. Even when they have merely preyed on the other participants in the opium industry, they have indirectly fostered its growth by leaving farmers and merchants no other choice but to raise their output. In most cases, moreover, quasi-state authorities have played a more positive role, either by providing effective security in exchange for their "protection" fees or by themselves taking the lead in some crucial phases of the two countries' opium industries.

As already mentioned, the consolidation of quasi-state authorities has also strongly contributed to the perpetuation of the central government's weakness and low legitimacy and, more generally, of an institutional setting favorable to opium production. In both countries the power of quasi-state authorities is such that the central governments have been forced to come to terms with them (and in post-Taliban Afghanistan, even to co-opt some of their leaders into the official ruling elite) and to accept de facto their involvement in the illicit opium industry.[9]

Afghanistan: From Quasi-State Authorities to Protectors within the State?

Since 1979, the year of the Soviet Union's invasion, Afghanistan has seen a 30-fold expansion of its potential opium production: from an estimated 200 metric tons in 1980 to 4,500 metric tons in 1999 and then to an astonishing 6,100 metric tons in 2006. Afghanistan's share of world opium production has grown steadily and rapidly since 1980s, when it was 19%; this proportion grew to 52% in 1995, the year prior to the Taliban's takeover, and rose to 79% in 1999 and then to 92% in 2006 (UNODC, 2003c:89, 2007a:195; chapter 3, this volume). According to UNODC calculations, the total potential income produced by opium-related activities in Afghanistan, measured in terms of the export value of opium to neighboring countries, would correspond to roughly half or more of the country's legitimate GDP in almost every year from 2002 to 2006 (UNODC and Government of Afghanistan, Counter Narcotics Directorate, 2004:1; UNODC, 2006:212, 2007a:195).[10] This means that Afghanistan is now very heavily dependent on the illicit drug trade.

Producers

In 2003, the number of households involved in opium cultivation was estimated for the first time by the UNODC at 264,000 (UNODC and Government of Afghanistan, Counter Narcotics Directorate, 2003:8). By 2005, that number had grown to 309,000 (UNODC 2006:212). Considering that the average household consists of six to seven people, opium poppy cultivation nowadays directly supports the livelihood of about two million people, or about 9% of the total population of Afghanistan (UNODC, 2006:211). The number of itinerant workers who work on poppy cultivation is not included in this figure; it was estimated at about 480,000 persons in the late 1990s, but it now likely to be higher (UNODC and Government of Afghanistan, Counter Narcotics Directorate, 2004:5).[11]

The gross opium income of farmers was estimated by the UNODC (2003c:8, 63) at about $150 million per year for 1994 to 2000, ranging from a minimum of $110 to a maximum of $250 million. As opium prices increased dramatically after the 2000 Taliban ban and remained high when production resumed, farmers' income levels were much higher at the beginning of the 21st century than in the 1990s. For 2003, the total farm-gate value of Afghanistan's opium was assessed at around $1 billion, a figure equivalent to about 22% of the country's GDP, which was then about $4.6 billion (UNODC and Government of Afghanistan, Counter Narcotics Directorate, 2003:8; UNODC, 2005d:181). Through a combination of falling prices and rising GDP, the total farm-gate value of Afghanistan's opium has since declined both in absolute terms and relative to legitimate market activity. In 2005, the farm-gate value fell to $560 million, a figure equivalent to about 11% of the country's 2005 GDP, which was about $5.2 billion (UNODC, 2005b:2, 2006:211). In 2006, the farm-gate value of opium increased to $760 million, but still amounted to about 11% of the country's GDP, which was about $6.7 billion (UNODC, 2007a:195).

Originally concentrated in the south and eastern part of the country, opium poppy cultivation has spread rapidly since the beginning of the new century. In 1994, the first year the UN survey was conducted, opium poppy was reported in eight provinces. By 2006, opium had spread to 28 of all 34 provinces (UNODC, 2007a:195) (fig. 6.1). Nevertheless, opium remains a relatively minor crop in term of relative cultivation levels, accounting for only around 3% of total national agricultural land. Nearly half of the 364 districts of Afghanistan still report no opium poppy cultivation, and the intensity of cultivation by district can range from very small to as much as 70% to 80% of the agricultural land in a district (Mansfield, 2006).

This scattered spread mirrors the great diversity in the socioeconomic groups involved in opium poppy in Afghanistan, the assets at their disposal, and access to markets. Consequently, there is great disparity in the revenues that they accrue from its cultivation. Some households can earn significant returns on opium poppy by utilizing the inequitable land tenure system, providing advance payments on the crop, and selling their opium long after the harvesting season. However, for the majority of households in Afghanistan, opium poppy is a means of survival, providing access to land, credit, and an important source of off-farm income for those households with insufficient land to satisfy their basic needs (Mansfield, 2001b, 2002). Even the by-products

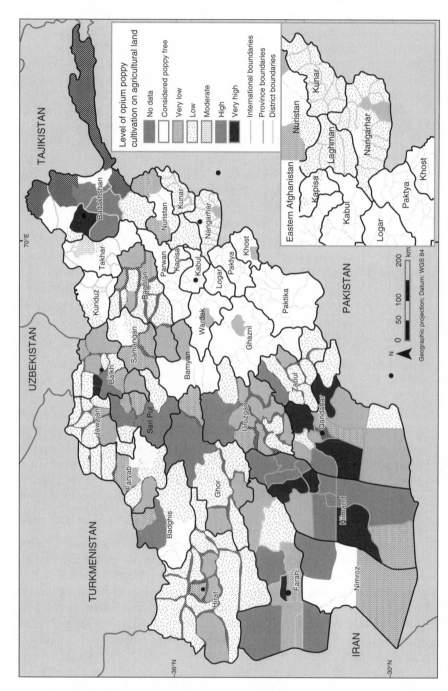

Figure 6.1 Opium poppy cultivation in Afghanistan in 2005 (at the district level).
Source: UNODC (2006).

of opium poppy, including seeds, capsules and, above all, stalks, are found to have a high use value (UNDCP, 1998a:32).

This diversity in household characteristics, assets, and access to markets leads to a diverse pattern of dependence on the opium economy and has engendered different responses to the attempts to eliminate opium poppy cultivation locally pursued by the Karzai administration since 2003. This diversity of responses was well shown by David Mansfield (2006) in his evaluation of the efforts to eliminate opium poppy cultivation between 2003 and 2005 in Nangarhar, the traditional stronghold of poppy cultivation in eastern Afghanistan. On the one hand, households that are smaller, have a higher ratio of able-bodied workers to total household size, own significant land, have other assets like livestock, and are located in areas with a favorable climate, good irrigation, and access to commodity and labor markets were able to diversify and stay out of opium cultivation for 2 years in a row up to 2006. On the other hand, households with limited human capital, small or no landholdings, and few other assets, and located in areas with poor irrigation and infrastructure, and distant from commodity and labor markets adopted coping strategies in response to the ban that ended up increasing their long-term dependency on opium. These households were likely to have returned en masse to opium cultivation by 2006.

Traffickers and Protectors

According to UNODC estimates (2003c:129), there are approximately 15,000 people participating in the concentric trafficking circles that funnel opiates out of Afghanistan. At the outer rim, there are the itinerant traffickers, the most numerous group that buys from farmers and encourages them to produce by providing advice and incentives such as credit. With relatively small average turnover, many of these traffickers trade opium on a limited seasonal basis during the main period of production, dealing perhaps with 10 to 15 kilograms per month (Pain, 2006). Fieldwork studies carried out in 1998 and in 2005 (UNDCP, 1998b; Pain, 2006) show that small traffickers are either small shopkeepers selling cloth or essential commodities, government servants, or teachers. The two studies also concur in showing that markups appear to be modest close to the farm gate, in the range of 7% to 10% between farmers and small traffickers (Pain, 2006:101).[12]

Closer to the center of trafficking are middle-level traffickers, who are mostly shop owners who are often involved in selling imported goods, such as motorbikes. Much as small traffickers, their business is also quite seasonal. According to Pain (2006), middle-level traffickers may be dealing with 50 to 100 kilograms of opium per month. Up to 2000, middle-level traffickers operated openly from their shops in regional bazaars. Since then, reflecting the official antidrug stance of the Karzai administration, their business has become much more secretive (Shaw, 2006).[13]

At the center of the opium trade are large-scale specialist traffickers who buy opium throughout the year and organize shipping to border areas or directly abroad, sometimes amounting to several tons. Today, this core consists of a relatively small number of traffickers, who own land and are as a rule quite wealthy, so much so that many of them have gone on Hajj (that is, on pilgrimage to the Mecca) (Pain, 2006; Shaw, 2006). Profit margins for this category of traffickers are much higher and have increased considerably since the late 1990s. In the late 1990s, traffickers in southern Afghanistan shipping dry opium to the border regions could earn profits, net of transportation costs, of around 12% expressed in terms of farm-gate prices, or up to 50%, if they exported the opium across the border (UNDCP, 1998b as reported in UNODC, 2003c:130). According to Pain's fieldwork (2006:101, 90) in the same region, margins might have been as high as 50% and 100% as of mid 2005, respectively.

A relatively new figure in the Afghan opium industry is that of the heroin refiner. Up until the mid 1990s, in fact, there were few heroin processing laboratories in the country, and most opium was processed into morphine or heroin in Pakistan—particularly in the North West Frontier Province (UNDCP, 1994; Haq, 1996; Asad and Harris, 2003). Since the mid 1990s, laboratories have been established in the border regions of most opium poppy-growing areas (i.e., in eastern, southern, and northern Afghanistan). Most of these are small- to medium-size labs: they produce, on average, 10 kilograms of brown heroin per day, and are usually active only for the 4 to 5 months after the opium harvest. Classified information also suggests that there are large morphine/heroin laboratories in southern, eastern, and northern Afghanistan capable of producing up to 150 kilograms of morphine base a day (UNODC, 2003c:132–140).

Since the outbreak of the civil war after the Soviet invasion in 1979, many self-styled "protectors" have extorted protection money from opiate producers and traders. Most of these protectors consist of the several quasi-state authorities that have at different moments claimed portions of Afghanistan's territory, although since 2002 some of the protectors also come from the ranks of the local and central government. In exchange for protection money, some protectors have provided some real services to opium producers and traffickers, whereas others have not. With varying intensity and success, some protectors have also become directly involved in the opiate production and trade. Their impact upon the opiate drug industry has thus varied, with some protectors being largely dysfunctional and others playing a more benign role for the industry itself. We review their role in the following three sections.

The Mujahedin

During the 1980s, the anti-Soviet mujahedin controlled much of the countryside and used this asset not only to tax local farmers and extort tolls from traders at hundreds of checkpoints along the major road routes, but also to engage in opium cultivation and opiate manufacturing and trade themselves. In 1989, a report written by a Russian lieutenant colonel based in Afghanistan attributed to the seven major mujahedin groups "an annual production of opium...of over 800 tons" (quoted in Felbab-Brown, 2006:130; see also Shaw, 2006). Although the Russian figures may be exaggerated, there is no doubt that various mujahedin groups became increasingly enmeshed in Afghanistan's opiate industry.

Some of the commanders directly involved in the commercialization of opium merely continued family traditions. One prime example of this first group is Ismatullah Muslin, who belonged to the chiefly family of a tribe engaged for several generations in raiding and smuggling activities in the area between Qandahar and the Pakistan border. As early as 1979, Muslin led his tribe into the resistance against the Soviet invaders and, even after his defection to the regime in 1984, continued to conduct smuggling operations of opium, heroin and a variety of other licit and illicit goods in the area between Qandahar and Quetta (Rubin, 2003:158–159).

Other commanders got into the opiate trade after gaining smuggling skills and revenues with the import and unauthorized resale of the weapons supplied to them by the CIA and its Pakistani counterpart, the Directorate of Inter-Services Intelligence (usually known as ISI). As Jonathan Goodhand (2005:198) notes, in the mid 1980s "there was an arms pipeline going in and a drug pipeline coming out of Afghanistan." The weapon trade, in fact, provided a logistics system that was ideally suited for the trade in drugs. It operated under military control and involved a large network of trucks running loaded with weapons to the Afghani border and empty coming back, which could thus be filled easily with opiate shipments (Rashid, 2001:120–217; Rubin, 2003:198).

In the main poppy-growing areas in the east and south of the country, a third group of mujahedin specialized in the organization and protection of opium cultivation. In the Helmand Valley, for example, Mullah Nasim Akhundzada, an Islamic scholar affiliated with one of Afghanistan's traditionalist–nationalist parties, the Harakat, became a powerful warlord by organizing opium poppy cultivation in the Helmand province, which had by then become the largest poppy-growing area of the country. Thanks to his ruthlessness and the profits from the opium trade, Akhundzada developed a brief local dictatorship in this area, which had been detribalized as a result of the Helmand Valley dam and irrigation scheme. In an interview published in 1989, he claimed to have established hospitals, clinics, and 40 *madrasas* (i.e., Islamic schools) (Rubin, 2003:245).

Since the mid 1980s, a fourth group of mujahedin became increasingly involved in the manufacturing of morphine and heroin along with a variety of non-political syndicates and tribal leaders. Among these there were, for example, members of Hizb-i Islami, the most disciplined and radical of Afghanistan's Islamist parties, which was led by Gulbuddin Hikmatyar. Despite this involvement in the drug trade, Hikmatyar remained the ISI's chief protégé and the recipient of more than half of the CIA's assistance to the Afghan resistance (Haq, 1996; Griffin, 2003:123–127, 145).

The revenues the mujahedin extracted from opium production and trade became even more important when the Soviet withdrawal in February 1989 reduced both military pressure and external aid. By the early 1990s, opium rivaled the smuggling of legitimate goods into neighboring countries and, in northern Afghanistan, the gem trade, as the main source of income for the mujahedin.

The most systematic exploitation of the whole opium industry was briefly achieved immediately after the retreat of the Soviet army by Akhundzada in the Helmand Valley. Along with his political duties as deputy defense minister of the Islamic Interim Government of Afghanistan, in 1989 Akhundzada established centralized control over opium production, setting production quotas on farmers and imposing draconian penalties on those who did not fulfill them. Although Akhundzada sold much of the opium to representatives of the six main local refineries, he also had a direct interest in the cross-border trade into Pakistan and Iran, which granted the highest returns. This centralized planning and coordination of the whole opium production process did not last very long. Akhundzada was murdered in 1990 after he accepted an offer from the U.S. ambassador to Pakistan to stop opium cultivation in return for $2 million. The killing was probably organized by drug traffickers, including high-ranking members of Hizb-i Islami, who had counted on continued high levels of production of raw opium from Akhundzada (Rubin, 2003:263–264).

The mujahedin's overall impact on Afghanistan's opium economy was mixed. By extracting extortionate rents, the commanders constituted a major impediment to the free interplay of market forces in the case of opium as of all other commodities. By organizing opium cultivation and export, they also positively contributed to this illegal industry, fostering its further development. With their unified roles of entrepreneurs and military chiefs, the mujahedin enjoyed considerable advantages in comparison with other entrepreneurs, because they could easily protect their own opium stocks and shipments, and occasionally even succeeded in establishing local oligopolies, as Akhundzada did in the Helmand Valley. All in all, though, the negative effects likely exceeded the positive ones. True, the mujahedin never tried to prohibit or even to restrict opium production or trade, and they depended heavily on these formally illicit activities for buying weapons, rewarding their associates, and strengthening their legitimacy with the local population. However, few of them were productively engaged in the opium industry as entrepreneurs, and none was able to exercise quasi-governmental functions, by providing lasting enforcement for contracts other than their own.

Most commanders hindered any type of economic enterprise, because they extracted exorbitant tributes from traders and travelers at omnipresent checkpoints. According to UNDP estimates, Afghanistan's overall GDP declined by almost 60% between 1979 and 1992 (UNODC, 2003c:90). This decline was not exclusively caused by the predation by commanders, but there are no doubts that their predation imposed heavy costs on commerce and prevented the consolidation of any order. It was indeed the primary need of security that prompted the ascent of the Taliban from 1994 onward and favored the acceptance of their despotic and ultraconservative regime among many strata of the Afghan population.

The Taliban

The Taliban captured Qandahar and Helmand, the southern opium-producing region, in fall 1994. They took Herat a year later, and in September 1996 they conquered Jalalabad and the eastern opium-producing region just before occupying Kabul. As already mentioned in chapter 4, until 1999 the Taliban made no real effort to prohibit opium cultivation and trade, and indeed they profited extensively from these activities, despite ambiguities on the matter in Islamic law.

The Taliban never became as directly involved in the opium industry as had most mujahedin. However, they systematically taxed opium cultivation and, to a lesser extent, trade, so much so that this taxation most probably constituted their second largest source of revenue after the taxation of the flourishing smuggling economy.[14] According to the UNODCCP (Sub-Office in Tajikistan 2000:5), the overall income extracted by the Taliban from the opium industry ranged between $10 and $30 million per year, collected at different points in the market and benefiting different parties. The total did not find its way into a common Taliban reserve. Growers paid the Islamic tithe (*ushr*) at the farm gate on opium and other produces, mostly in kind. At least in the south, the Taliban also levied *zakat* of 20% on traffickers in opium and opium derivatives (UNDCP, 1998b:6).[15] Additionally, individual commanders and provincial governors imposed their own taxes to keep their coffers full and their soldiers fed. Some of them also became substantial dealers in opium or used their relatives to act as middlemen (Rashid, 2001:118; UNODC, 2003c:92).

The Taliban's main political opponent, the Northern Alliance led by Ahmad Shah Massoud, also profited from the drug trade, though the northeastern part of the country it controlled produced only 3% of Afghanistan opium before the Taliban's ban. Commanders levied *ushr* on opium farmers, and at least some local authorities taxed opium traffickers as well (Rubin, 2003:xxv).

Up until the Taliban's first publicized restrictions on opium cultivation in September 1999, neither the Taliban nor their opponents regarded opium growing and trading as criminal activities. Opium was openly sold in most bazaars of the two main producing regions in the south and east of the country (UNDCP, 1998b). Opium being a legitimate commodity, its trade did not diverge from that of other commodities, it was largely unrestrained by the so-called *constraints of illegality* (Reuter, 1983; chapter 10, this volume), and it reflected the characteristics of the local institutional settings. In the eastern region, the opium trade had become fairly centralized as a result of the influx of about 40 large-scale opium traffickers in Ghani Khel, who largely belonged to the local dominant tribe, the Pashtun Shinwari. According to the UNDCP (1998b:2), this tribe had not only traditionally cultivated poppies and traded opium, but also through its links with the Afridi Pashtuns on the other side of the Afghan–Pakistan border had developed "a virtual monopoly on the processing and the final transportation of heroin into Pakistan." The expression *monopoly* should be understood here in a loose, non-technical sense, because neither tribe constituted a single economic entity. It seems likely, however, that the large-scale opium traffickers belonging to the Shinwari played a pivotal role in wholesale opium trade in eastern Afghanistan. In the south, in contrast, the market was more decentralized, as opium was bought and sold in a number of the region's bazaars and there were fewer large-scale traffickers. The decentralized pattern of opium trade in the southern region also reflected local tribal patterns and, in particular, the lack of a dominant tribe. In the south, in fact, numerous Baloch tribes were involved in cross-border opium trade both into Pakistan and Iran (UNDCP, 1998b:2).[16]

Although the Taliban did not impede the opium trade in any way, increased the security of persons and goods along the major routes of the country, and even made some efforts to regulate the drug industry (e.g., UNDCP, 1998b:2; Rashid, 2001:120), their law enforcement and judicial systems were not sophisticated enough to provide security of contracts and property rights to the participants in the opium industry. Traffickers interviewed in a 1998 UNDCP (1998b) field study in southern and eastern Afghanistan thus reported they still had to pay for their own security guards, resorted sparingly to the opium credit system, and had to be very cautious in transporting opium directly to the border with Pakistan, Iran, and Turkmenistan. The Taliban, in fact, guaranteed neither a police to protect properties from thieves nor a court to appeal for redress of injury, and the traffickers had to enforce contracts themselves with direct resort to violence.[17]

As discussed fully in chapter 10, until the point of the opium ban of 2000, the Taliban constituted, in the illegal opiate industry, the closest example of a governing body supportive of an illegal activity. Yet, they were unable to fill the oversight and governance roles that are today expected from a full-fledged state.

The State, State Providers of Protection, and Their Rivals

With the establishment of the Afghan Interim Administration (AIA) in 2001, the "state" reemerged as an actor in the Afghan opiate industry after a break of more than 20 years. Admittedly, this "state" also lacks some of the standard oversight and governance capabilities associated with central authorities.

As already mentioned, one of the first acts of the AIA was the issuance of a decree that banned the opium poppy cultivation, heroin production, and drug use on January 17, 2002. Despite this early ban and other decrees that followed, culminating in the adoption of a counternarcotics strategy in 2003, until that year no serious effort had been made to curb the opium industry. As Vanda Felbab-Brown (2007b:2) put it, "until 2003 [it was] essentially laissez-faire." The de facto tolerance of the opium industry was primarily the result of the priorities set by the international community, which emphasized more immediate military objectives, such as the dispersion of the Taliban remnants and the arrest of Al-Qaida operatives, and Bin Laden in particular, and the economic and political consolidation of the ravaged country. Even before the installment of the AIA, U.S. troops forged alliances with warlords who provided ground forces in the battle against the Taliban. Some of those allies are suspected of being among Afghanistan's biggest drug traffickers controlling networks that include producers, criminal gangs and, more recently, even members of the counternarcotics police force (Griffin, 2001; TNI, 2005:6).

Up until late 2004, moreover, the United Kingdom, which was given the lead in international drug control efforts in Afghanistan, took an approach in which repressive actions were aimed at the level of heroin processing and trafficking. Despite a limited compensated eradication scheme in early 2002, emphasis was on creating alternative livelihoods for farmers, a gradual and long-term approach grounded in a realization of the extraordinary significance of the opium industry for the country's overall economy.

It was only during 2004 that priorities shifted as a result of increased U.S. pressures. Uncompensated manual eradication on a large scale was planned and, on a much smaller scale, implemented (TNI, 2005). The area eradicated corresponded respectively to 5% and 8% of the area under poppy cultivation in 2005 and 2006 (UNODC, 2007a:195). The most striking successes were achieved in the Nangarhar province, where farmers were prevented from planting opium, and production was thus slashed by 90% in 2005 (Mansfield, 2006). Since 2004, increased in-country enforcement has also been undertaken. By 2005, for example, Afghanistan's share of the world's opiate seizures had grown from 2% in 2002 to 15% (UNODC, 2007a:47).

These first, apparent drug control successes have come at a heavy price. As the promises of alternative development did not materialize in time, a considerable portion of the affected households have been devastated by eradication (including cultivation suppression). Unable to repay their debts, many farmers in Nangarhar fell into a form of serf labor, growing poppy on their creditor's land, were forced to sell their very young daughters, or to flee into Pakistan (Felbab-Brown, 2006:143–144; Mansfield, 2006). It is not accidental that, in 2006, cultivation in Nangarhar rebounded by 346%, although remaining far from the levels reached at the beginning of the century (Felbab-Brown, 2007b).

The political costs incurred by the local and provincial governors and the national government in implementing eradication have also been very significant. Unsurprisingly, the eradication teams have often been met with violent resistance from the peasants. As a consequence, the Afghan Central

Poppy Eradication Forces largely failed to meet their eradication targets in 2005 (Blanchard, 2006:12–13, 32). If continued and expanded, eradication has the potential to alienate the local population from the local and national government, and from the local tribal elites that agree to it.

Predictably, in a country with a nascent and struggling state apparatus, the governmental bodies in charge of both eradication and interdiction have been susceptible to corruption. Mansfield's assessment (2006:69) of the Nangarhar eradication experiment came to the conclusion that "eradication has typically targeted the 'needy,' not the 'greedy'"—that is, those households that were so poor and peripheral they lacked powerful connections and could not pay protection money (see also Anderson, 2007). Likewise, different pieces of recent empirical research in Afghanistan consistently show that traffickers at all levels are nowadays forced to pay protection to police officers—on an ad hoc or systematic basis—to operate (Mansfield, 2006; Pain, 2006; Shaw, 2006). These studies also show that interdiction has been perverted to benefit local police at the expense of small traffickers. In Helmand, for example, many small traffickers interviewed by Pain (2006:92) reported higher risks of being targeted by the police, who allegedly confiscated their opiates to sell them to the bigger traffickers. In Helmand, as elsewhere, high-level political, police, and military appointees also reportedly distort law enforcement activities to protect traffickers of their own tribes (Felbab-Brown, 2006; Pain, 2006:92; Anderson, 2007).

A process of consolidation of the opiate industry may be taking place, giving rise to major drug-trafficking enterprises with very good connections to various levels in the government. In a recent UNODC–World Bank publication, Shaw (2006:200) goes as far as to claim that the Afghan opiate industry has transformed itself since 2004 into "pyramids of protection and patronage," at the apex of which there is an elite of about 25 to 30 key traffickers, who have important political connections and are primarily located in the south of the country. These key traffickers allegedly control the wholesale traffic in opiates, by supervising the processing of heroin, regulating the market through the stocks they hold, and even excluding unconnected individuals from engaging in large-scale trafficking. Although Shaw's claims may go too far, circumstantial evidence from a number of sources does suggest a process of consolidation. Whereas there are no barriers to entry at the lower levels, several scholars (e.g., Pain, 2006; Felbab-Brown, 2007b; Rubin and Sherman, 2008) indicate that wholesale transactions are conducted largely by traffickers who enjoy high-level protection among police forces and politicians, and many less connected traffickers have been effectively excluded from wholesaling.

Despite the lack of hard evidence, there is also unanimity in academic studies, policy, and media reports, and the occasional candid analyses of Afghan officers and foreign diplomats that many key traffickers have either become politicians or are tightly linked with former warlords-turned-politicians who now occupy key political positions in the provinces and governments.[18] In contrast to the past, these former warlords have now publicly distanced themselves from drug trafficking; however, at the very least, they still receive benefits from it in exchange for the political protection they provide. The point was clearly made in late 2004 by Mirwais Yasini, who was then head of the Afghan Counter-Narcotics Directorate: "There are warlords involved, high government officials, police commanders, governors are involved. We have to reform our judicial system and put big culprits behind bars, otherwise going after poor farmers we will fill our prisons but still the drug business will be going on" (AFP, 2004).[19]

It is also widely acknowledged in academic and other reports that the main locus of interaction between state institutions and criminal interests is currently the Ministry of the Interior, which since 2002 has directed counter-narcotics enforcement activities under the leadership of the Deputy Minister of Interior for Counternarcotics, General Mohammed Daud.[20] The Ministry of Interior has, so to say, inherited this function from the Ministry of Defense, which in 2002 and 2003 demilitarized, financially supported, and to the extent possible integrated members of armed groups in the Afghan National Army (ANA). Whereas the Ministry of Defense has been reformed, the Ministry of the Interior has not and has remained highly vulnerable to corruption (Buddenberg and Byrd, 2006; Shaw, 2006). Provincial and national politicians now rival in conditioning the appointment of police officers at the national and local levels, and in determining the target and scale of law enforcement interventions.

Lastly, eradication and interdiction have provided financial means and political legitimacy to armed groups, ranging from the resurgent Taliban in the south to the many smaller militias throughout the country, which offer protection to peasants and traffickers. According to the UNODC and Afghan officials, some armed groups impose informal taxes and checkpoint fees on farmers, traffickers, and opiate-processing laboratories within their areas of control, receiving cash or payment in opium (UNODC and Government of Afghanistan, Counter Narcotics Directorate, 2004:65–66; see also Zeller, 2002). Especially in the south, many opiate traffickers allegedly fund the Taliban in an effort to frighten away North Atlantic Treaty Organization (NATO) soldiers, government representatives, and eradication teams from the main poppy-growing areas (Moreau and Yousafzai, 2003). Some Taliban and even Al Qaeda operatives are also allegedly directly involved in the drug trade (Blanchard, 2006:15–17). Although no precise estimates exist, 30% to 50% of the current revenues of the Taliban purportedly come—directly or indirectly—from the opiate trade (Felbab-Brown, 2007b). Crucially, law enforcement interventions also provide political legitimacy to such groups, at the same time that they critically undermine the motivation of the local population to provide intelligence on the Taliban to ANA and NATO. Thanks to these assets, the Taliban have made a comeback since 2005. They are now the de facto authority in large portions of the south and eastern provinces, and have since 2007 spread their violence to parts of the north as well (Anderson, 2007).

The weakening of quasi-state authorities and the reemergence of the state in Afghanistan have done little to weaken the illegal opiate industry and have instead promoted a process of consolidation within it. As a result, a powerful criminal "underworld" may be forming, linked through bribes and patronage ties to high-ranking state representatives operating in the "upperworld" (Shaw, 2006). This corrupt "upperworld" has probably become, since 2004, the main provider of protection for opium producers and traffickers. Its power, though, and the very process of state building are challenged by quasi-state authorities that also profit from the protection of, and even direct involvement in, the booming Afghan opium industry.

Burma: A Succession of Quasi-State Authorities

Despite the lack of exact statistics, Burma was likely the main illicit producer of opiates for about three decades from 1960 to 1990. Since then, it has progressively lost its share of the world's illicit opiate market to Afghanistan (see table 3.1). However, Burma, which has substantially lower opium poppy yields than Afghanistan, maintained its unenviable primacy in terms of hectares under poppy cultivation up to the beginning of the 21st century. Only in 2003 was Burma's opium poppy acreage for the first time surpassed by Afghanistan's (UNODC, 2006:209).

Being a much larger and comparatively richer country, Burma is economically less affected than Afghanistan by its illicit opiate industry, which is primarily concentrated in the northeastern Shan State. The farm-gate value of Burmese opium production was estimated in 2004 by the UNODC in US$87 million, corresponding to roughly 1% of Burma's GDP (UNODC and Central Committee for Drug Abuse Control, 2004:19–20). There are no systematic estimates for Burma on its trafficking and processing income, which is probably much larger.[21]

Even more devastating have been the political consequences of the drug industry, with insurgency and counterinsurgency being largely drug funded in the Shan State since the 1950s. The role of quasi-state authorities, sometimes operating on the Burmese government's behalf, has been so crucial for the development of the Burmese illicit drug industry that this can be read as a succession of quasi-state authorities.

The Kuomintang

The KMT was the main engine prompting the development of Burma's opium industry from the 1950s up until the 1970s. Initially, the KMT forces primarily extracted taxes from the opium farmers and traffickers under their sphere of influence but, starting in the early 1960s, their leaders organized an overwhelming portion of the wholesale trade of opium from the poppy-growing areas in the northern Shan States to the Thai border. According to Alfred McCoy (1991:348–349), who relied on a leaked CIA report, around 1970 the KMT armies controlled about 90% of Burma's opium trade. Given the presence of a multiplicity of other traffickers, this estimate is most probably exaggerated: according to Adrian Cowell (2005:10), for example, "the KMT's role was very close to that of a trading and travel service for independent merchant adventurers." However, by providing such services with an efficiency and on a scale never seen before, the KMT remained—for three decades—a key actor in the Burmese opium industry.

After the victory of Mao Zedong's communists in 1949, hundreds of defeated KMT forces from the Yunnan province crossed over into Shan territory in northeastern Burma. By the end of 1953, at least 12,000 KMT soldiers were stationed there, trying to retake China from the communists. Weakened by the assassination of its designated leader and his closest associates in 1947, ethnic rivalries, and army mutinies, the newly independent Burma had no means to defeat the KMT, which received plenty of weapons, supplies, and technical support from the Nationalist Chinese headquarters in Taiwan and its covert allies, most notably the United States and Thailand. From late 1952 onward, the KMT became the only effective government authority in the territories between the Salween River and the Chinese border (Kokang, Wa, and Kengtung states), extracting taxes and customs duties (McCoy, 1991:162–178; Lintner, 2002:236–238).

Unsurprisingly, because the territories conquered by the KMT were Burma's major opium-producing regions, a significant part of KMT revenues came from the taxation of opium producers and traffickers. In fact, the KMT required that every hill-people farmer pay a heavy annual opium tax, and thus fostered a rapid increase in local opium production (McCoy, 1991:173). In addition to levying taxes, the KMT centralized the wholesale transportation of opium into Thailand, where most of it was shipped primarily by mule but occasionally by train or aircraft. As most of their munitions and supplies were carried overland from Thailand, the KMT mule caravans found it convenient to haul opium on the outgoing trip to Chiang Mai, a Thai city close to the Burmese border (McCoy, 1991:173). In Chiang Mai, the KMT long enjoyed the full protection of Thai authorities, including that of the commander of the Thai police. Opium production, trade, and consumption remained legal in Thailand until 1959 (Lintner, 2002:242–244).

After the repatriation of some troops to Taiwan in 1961 and the collapse of the last garrison in Burma in mid 1962, the remaining KMT forces were moved across the Mekong River into Thailand. There, with the full knowledge and consent of the Thai government, the KMT established two new bases on the mountains just a few miles from the Burmese border. These became the headquarters of the KMT Third and Fifth armies, which consisted of about 1,400 and 1,800 men, and were commanded by General Ly Wen-huang and General Tuan Shi-wen, respectively (McCoy, 1991:352). After Taiwan cut back financial support, generals Ly and Tuan were forced to rely primarily on the opium traffic to finance their military operations.[22]

The forced move to Thailand did not hamper the KMT's involvement in the Golden Triangle's opium trade. With an auxiliary of ethnic Chinese traders, the KMT was able to gain the upper hand in the local opium trade in northern Thailand (McCoy, 1991:351–352). Most of the KMT's revenues, however, kept on flowing from the transportation, sale and, increasingly, processing of Burmese opium (McCoy, 1991:353–354) (for more detail on the operation of the enterprises, see chapter 10, this volume).

The KMT's involvement in the Burmese opium trade was enhanced by the fact that most of the itinerant merchants were also, as in Thailand, Chinese—the so-called Panthays or Yunnanese Muslims, who are termed *Hui* in China and *Haw* in northern Thailand. These were—and still are—respectable, local businessmen who lived quite openly in government-controlled market towns and were usually the owners of ordinary trading houses. Since the 19th century, Chinese merchants had exploited their well-developed network of settlements and contacts all over the region for the opium trade. In the opium-growing areas of Burma, Chinese traders sent their agents to the hills to purchase opium, and then either sold it directly to the KMT brokers or relied on the protection of the KMT (or, more rarely, of other armed bands) to transport the drug to the Thai or Laos borders (Lintner, 2002).

By the early 1970s, the two KMT generals' purchasing network covered most of the Shan State, and their caravans transported the largest chunk of Burma's opium exports into northern Thailand (Kamm, 1971). The caravans did not transport only the KMT's opium. According to Cowell (2005:7–8), more than half the opium on any convoy was owned by independent traffickers or Shan rebel groups, who traveled with the KMT troops for protection. Some KMT high-level military officials also traded on their own account under the protection of the two KMT generals. In addition to the revenues of their own opium sales, the two generals thus extracted a protection fee from the independent traffickers as well as "custom duties" on every kilo of opium entering Thailand (McCoy, 1991:354–355).

With time, the processing of opium also became another source of income for the KMT generals and their staff. By the early 1960s, large quantities of morphine and low-grade no. 3 heroin were produced by the KMT and other smugglers in Burma and northern Thailand. In late 1969, opium refineries in the Burma–Thailand–Laos triborder region, newly staffed by expert chemists from Hong Kong, began to produce high-grade no. 4 heroin as well. In the processing stage, the KMT never held a dominant position, and opium refineries were also run by other traffickers, such as Shan rebel armies and Burmese government militias (discussed later), as well as some of the KMT clients, including the powerful general Ouane Rattikone, the former commander-in-chief of the Royal Laotian Army (Belair, 1971).

The development of the KMT's hegemony on the Golden Triangle's opium trade could not have been possible without the benevolent tolerance and support of Thai military and political authorities.[23] These attitudes changed only after a new democratic government was installed in Thailand in the early 1980s. In 1984, the new government carried out a crackdown on the remnants of the KMT, whose hegemonic position in the opiate industry had already been weakened by Burmese competitors (McCoy, 1991:432–433).

The Insurgent Groups

Starting in the early 1960s, the growing number of Shan rebel armies also became interested in opium production and trade. The first such groups began to form out of the existing feudal machinery in the late 1950s, despite the Shan princes' initial commitment to the strengthening of a federal, democratic Burma. After the coup staged by General Ne Win in 1962, rebellion flared anew in the Shan State and additional rebel armies emerged (Cowell, 2005). In the Shan State, there was only one local commodity that could finance the rebels' cause: opium. Although the actual trade remained in the hands of well-connected, ethnic Chinese businessmen and the KMT, the rebels controlled the countryside where the poppies were grown and were thus able to tax the farmers and, less systematically, the merchants or their envoys as well who came to buy from the farmers. Although on a much smaller scale than the KMT, a few rebel groups also profited from the transportation and smuggling of their opium into Thailand and Laos.[24]

Opium farmers and traffickers were also regularly taxed by the Communist Party of Burma (CPB), which from the early 1970s onward exercised firm control over the Kokang and Wa regions. The control of this area along the Chinese frontier, which measured more than 20,000 square kilometers, was gained thanks to financial and military support from China. A troop of 15,000 to 20,000 heavily armed soldiers, largely composed of local hill-people recruits commanded by Burmese communist ideologues, guarded this de facto buffer state between Burma and China (Lintner, 2002:255–256; Treerat et al., 2004:7–8).

Despite the taxation of opium production and trade, the CPB did not have to depend on the drug trade as long as the Chinese government provided generous support. In the 1970s, it even made some efforts to enforce crop substitution programs (Smith, 1991:314–315; Cowell, 2005:7–8). At the end of that decade, however, the old Maoist policy of supporting revolutionary movements in the region was suddenly abandoned under Deng Xiaoping's new leadership, and the CPB suffered badly as a result. It began to engage more frequently in opium trafficking and processing, but it never succeeded in threatening the much larger businesses run by the KMT first and, then by Khun Sa (discussed later). It was only the CPB's successors that, in the 1990s, were able to challenge successfully this long-held supremacy (McCoy, 1991:424–434).

The Government Militias and the Warlords

Since the outbreak of ethnic conflict during the early 1960s, the Burmese army has proved to be incapable of overcoming the innumerable rebel armies active in the Shan State and in other parts of the country. To fight the insurgents, in 1963, General Ne Win thus authorized the establishment of "home guard" units, the so-called *Ka Kwe Ye* (KKY; the actual meaning in Burmese is "defense"). These units were given the right to use all government-controlled roads and towns in the Shan State for opium trafficking in exchange for fighting the rebels. By allowing them to trade in opium, the Burmese government hoped that the KKY militias would be self-supporting. There was hardly any money in the state coffers in Rangoon to support a sustained counterinsurgency campaign (Smith, 1991:95–96; Cowell, 2005:5–6).

In addition to trading in their own opium, the KKY units were often hired by traffickers to convey drugs to the Thai border. The KKY commanders usually carried their opium to the market town of Tachilek, near the border junction between Burma, Laos, and Thailand. There, the revenues of the opium trade were used to finance the purchase of the consumer goods that the commanders and the traffickers took back as return cargo in their lorry and mule caravans. To implement General Ne Win's "Burmese Way to Socialism," in fact, by the mid 1960s all large, private companies and banks had been nationalized, small-scale firms had been heavily regulated, and a vibrant black economy had developed to fill the resulting economic vacuum. Within a few years, most of the consumer goods available in Burma were smuggled from neighboring countries, primarily Thailand. In northeastern Burma, the smuggling and retail sale of consumer goods were largely taken over by opium traffickers—the same trucks and mules used to bring opium to the Thai border were loaded with Thai goods and commodities, which were then sold at high prices in the Shan State. As the Burmese *kyat* became worthless for trading with other countries, opium—and increasingly heroin—became the preferred medium of exchange. As Chao Tzang Yawnghwe, son of the Shan leader and Burma's first president Sao Shwe Thaike, recalled, "Rather than creating socialism, the Burmese Way to Socialism in effect delivered the economy into the hands of the opium traffickers. As such, opium became the only viable crop and medium of exchange" (quoted in Lintner, 2000:9; see also Chao, 2005).

Burmese government troops not only cooperated with the KKYs in the battlefields against the rebels, but occasionally also provided security for the KKYs' opium convoys. The garrison town of Tang-yan, strategically located among the main opium-growing areas in the northern Shan State, developed into one of the most important centers for the opium trade (Lintner, 2000:10).

Thanks to the opium revenues, several KKY commanders accumulated considerable economic and military power in just a few years, and used it to set up their own armies and to start rewarding careers as independent drug lords. The most prominent were Lo Hsing-han, a Kokang Chinese who was the chief of the Kokang KKY, and Khun Sa, half-Chinese/half-Shan, who headed the KKY unit next to the garrison town of Tang-yan (Kramer, 2005).

Lo was famously branded as the "kingpin of the heroin traffic" by U.S. law enforcement agencies, when the Nixon administration launched the first war on drugs during the early 1970s (McCoy, 1991:426). Although there is certainly some exaggeration in that statement, Lo's drug-trafficking enterprise was one of the largest in the early 1970s, as he sent 20 to 40 tons of opium yearly to the Thai border (McCoy, 1991:308; Wren, 1998). When the Burmese government disbanded the KKY system in 1973, Lo briefly joined a Shan nationalist coalition fighting for independence from Burma, until he was arrested in Thailand and deported to Burma. A court in Rangoon sentenced him to death for "insurrection against the state," but the execution was not carried out and Lo was released during a general amnesty in 1980—to become one of Burma's most prominent businessmen in the 1990s, with interests in the hotel industry, transport, road construction, timber, gems, and the import and export of various legal commodities (Emerson, 1998; Lintner, 2002:262–263).

In 1967, Khun Sa used the money and military resources gained as KKY commander to challenge openly General Ly's dominion over the Golden Triangle's drug trade. Although Khun Sa eventually lost this confrontation and spent 6 years in prison (until 1976), soon afterward he was able to acquire a very prominent position in Burma's opiate industry (McCoy, 1999). He first settled his new army and heroin refineries in northern Thailand, where he enjoyed the protection of prominent friends, including General Kriangsak, Thailand's prime minister from 1977 to 1980. According to the U.S. House of Representatives Select Committee on Narcotics Abuse and Control (1977:55–58), in 1977 Khun Sa's Shan United Army hauled 70 tons of raw opium in 12 caravans averaging 116 mules and 335 armed guards each.

During the early 1980s Khun Sa resettled in Homong, just across the Burmese border, which remained his headquarters for the next 14 years. With the tacit consent of the Burmese Army, his 3,000 troops occupied a 250-kilometer-wide area of strategic trafficking territory along the Thai–Burma border, where he set up numerous refineries of his own and claimed protection taxes from independent traffickers and processing labs. In 1987, the U.S. DEA Bangkok office estimated that Khun Sa's refineries processed 80% of the Golden Triangle's heroin (Gooi, 1986; McCoy, 1999:311). Although this estimate cannot be independently verified, it is true that Khun Sa had emerged as the key broker between the poppy-growing areas controlled by the communists and Thailand, because the communists could not trade opium directly to a Thailand that was capitalist (Cowell, 2005:13). In an interview with *Newsweek* in 1989 (Liu, 1989), Khun Sa claimed an annual income of US$200 million from heroin processing and trade.

With these heroin profits, Khun Sa transformed his warlord militia into the Mong Tai Army, a force of 20,000 heavily armed men, and used it to take control of the Shan nationalist cause. In 1993 he had himself elected leader of the Shan State National Congress and transformed his headquarters in Homong into the capital of a secessionist state. However, by doing so, Khun Sa lost the long-term backing of the Burmese government and inevitably became the prime target of its attacks. He also progressively lost control of the growing flows of opiates being smuggled from the Wa and Kokang poppy cultivation areas into China (Cowell, 2005). After several bloody clashes with the Burmese army and the UWSA (which was promised control by the government of any territory it managed to occupy in the southern Shan State [discussed later]), Khun Sa surrendered to the central government in early 1996. He was given immunity from prosecution and, much as his predecessor, Lo Hsing-han, was allowed to invest drug money in a range of legal and semilegal economic activities (Emerson, 1998; McCoy, 1999). Khun Sa died in 2007.

The United Wa State Army, Other Contemporary Quasi-State Authorities, and the Burmese State

In spring 1989, the hill-people rank-and-file of the CPB, led by indigenous military commanders, mutinied against the party's ageing, mostly Burmese, political leadership. While the old leaders and their families escaped to China, the former CPB split along ethnic lines in three main quasi-state authorities, which have since been main players in the Burmese opiate industry.

The biggest splinter group was the United Wa State Army and Party (respectively known as UWSA and UWSP—for reasons of simplicity we refer to both of them by using the more common acronym of UWSA), which comprised the bulk of the CPB's fighting force (8,000–10,000 men at the time of the mutiny, expanding to 15,000 in the following years [Milsom, 2005]).[25] Although its main settlement was in the Wa region (now officially known as Special Region No. 2), the UWSA also incorporated a small, southern nationalist faction, the Wa National Army (WNA), based in the so-called Southern Command Area close to the Thai border. This southern faction has long been dominated by three ethnic Chinese brothers, the Wei, who have decade-long experience in opiate trade, as they were involved first in the KMT smuggling ring and then in Khun Sa's Mong Tai Army. Wei Hsueh-kang, in particular, is considered today to be the most notorious heroin and amphetamine trafficker of the Golden Triangle (U.S. Department of Justice, 2005). The second relevant splinter group was the Myanmar National Democratic Alliance Army (MNDAA), which occupied Kokang. The third main ex-CPB grouping is the Eastern Shan State Army (ESSA), which controls the Special Region No. 4, where the borders of Burma, China, and Laos meet (DEA, 2002a; Altsean-Burma, 2004:68–77).

The State Law and Order and Restoration Council (SLORC), the new military junta that had assumed power in Rangoon in September 1988, hurried to negotiate with the main splinter groups of the CPB. The SLORC's main goal was to prevent their alliance with other ethnic rebels and with the urban dissidents who had led the demonstrations for democracy in August and September 1988. Within a few months, ceasefire agreements were struck between Burma's military government and the main former CPB forces thanks to the mediation of Lo Hsing-han.[26] On the Burmese side, the negotiations were personally carried out by Major-General Khin Nyunt, the chief of Burma's military intelligence, who later became the country's prime minister before being arrested on corruption charges in October 2004. In exchange for promises not to attack government forces and to sever ties with other rebel groups, the CPB mutineers were granted permission to engage in any business, including, almost inevitably, opiate production and trafficking (Davis and Hawke, 1998; Altsean-Burma, 2004:50–51). Together with the Taliban's Afghanistan, the areas controlled by the UWSA and the two other CPB splinter groups became the only regions of the world in which an opiate industry for non-medical purposes was de facto fully legalized.

Initially, Burma's opium production boomed under the three ex-CPB quasi-state authorities. According to UN data, the opium harvest grew by 60% between 1988 and 1993 (see table 3.1). During the same span of time, a string of new, large heroin refineries were set up near the main growing areas in Kokang, the Wa region, and the area surrounding the town of Möng La, Special Region No. 4, east of Kengtung (Lintner, 2002:263, 272–274). At least up until the beginning of the 21st century, the refineries were run both by the militia commanders and by independent traffickers, who were obliged to pay a "protection" tax to the militias.

The militia commanders as well as the independent traffickers located in the regions controlled by the CPB splinter groups have also profited from the legalization of cross-border trade with China, which was decided by the Burmese junta in 1988. Since then, increasing shares of the opium and heroin produced in the Shan State are exported into China to serve the growing Chinese market and to be smuggled further in other countries. According to some estimates, 60% to 80% of Burmese heroin now exits the country through China (Chouvy, 2002b; Institute of Public Security, 2004).

During the 1990s, the Burmese illegal drug industry also diversified. Paralleling the rapid expansion of their use in all Southeast Asia, a phenomenal increase in the production of methamphetamines (or ATS) was recorded. Burma today rivals China in being the largest producer of these "new" drugs, with much of its production taking place in the Shan State (DEA, 2003a; UNODC, 2005d:100; U.S. Department of State, Bureau of International Narcotics and Law Enforcement Affairs, 2005).

Except for the Möng La area, neither the opiate industry nor that of the ATS has ever been fully controlled by any CPB splinter group. Although many militia commanders, and possibly even the leaders, dealt with drugs, a large portion of the trade has always been in the hands of many independent, primarily Chinese, enterprises (Lintner, 2002:273–274; Kramer, 2005:46–47). Up until the turn of the century, however, the cadres of the UWSA and other militias were frequently in charge of the shipment of the processed heroin and ATS from the laboratories, working either as contractors or transporting heroin of their own group, as part of their "normal" duties. Part of the deal agreed to by the government and the UWSA, for instance, gave (and, as a matter of fact, still largely gives) the latter's marked trucks unsupervised transit throughout military and police checkpoints (Altsean-Burma, 2004:54–56). In turn, Burmese law enforcement forces cannot enter the areas controlled by the UWSA and the other ceasefire groups without their explicit permission (UNODC, 2002).

Given these advantages and their frequent exploitation for drug-trafficking purposes, it is no surprise that the UWSA is considered by the U.S. government "the largest heroin producing and trafficking organization in the world" and was designated as a "drug kingpin" in 2003 under the Foreign Narcotics Designation Kingpin Act of 1999. Eight high-ranking leaders of the UWSA, including Pao Yuchang, the commander-in-chief of the UWSA, his three brothers, and the three Wei brothers, were indicted on drug-trafficking charges by a federal grand jury in Brooklyn, New York, in January 2005 (U.S. Department of Justice, 2005).

Despite their extensive involvement in drug trafficking, the Burmese government has fully legitimated the leaders of the UWSA and the other CPB splinter groups as "leaders of the national races," inviting them to participate in the National Convention, the Burmese junta's main vehicle for political reform (Ball, 1999:4). The junta also considers the leaders of the ceasefire groups suitable partners in development projects and has allowed them to invest illicit proceeds in the legitimate economy. The UWSA commanders, for example, are accused by the January 2005 U.S. indictment of laundering drug proceeds through the Hong Pang conglomerate, one of the most prominent companies in the Shan State with interests in jewelry, communications, electrical goods, agriculture, mining, and large construction projects (U.S. Department of Justice, 2005).[27]

More generally, the regime has taken no measures to stop the inflow of drug money into the legitimate economy. As a result, Burma was the last country, together with Nigeria, to be removed in 2007 from the blacklist of "non-cooperative countries and territories" of the Financial Action Task Force on Money Laundering (FATF, 2007), the international body that sets guidelines on money-laundering controls. Indeed, the military junta has long promoted the reinvestment of drug proceeds in the legitimate economy. From 1989 onward, for example, the Burmese government has allowed its citizens to lodge money in legal bank accounts with no accounting for its origins. In exchange, it received a "whitening tax" on questionable repatriated funds, levied first at 40% and later reduced to 25% (Davis and Hawke, 1998; Lintner, 2002:267).

Since 2006, the Burmese government has been credited by its U.S. counterpart for intensifying counternarcotic activities and international cooperation even within the regions largely controlled by the ceasefire groups (U.S. Department of State, Bureau of International Narcotics and Law Enforcement Affairs, 2007). Several recent editions of the INCSR (U.S. Department of State,

Bureau of International Narcotics and Law Enforcement Affairs, 2007:244) also maintain that there is "no reliable evidence that senior officials in the Burmese Government are directly involved in the drug trade." The 2002 edition was more cautious:

> No Burma Army officer over the rank of full Colonel has ever been prosecuted for drug offences in Burma. This fact, the prominent role in Burma of the family of notorious narcotics traffickers (e.g., Lo Hsing-han clan) and the continuance of large-scale narcotics trafficking over years of intrusive military rule have given rise to speculation that some senior military leaders protect or are otherwise involved with narcotics traffickers. (U.S. Department of State, Bureau of International Narcotics and Law Enforcement Affairs, 2003: VIII-10)

In fact, NGOs (e.g., Altsean-Burma, 2004:103–107), academic observers (e.g., Ball, 1999), and journalists (Lintner, 2002:266–270) provide abundant detail supporting these speculations, showing that several generals of the Burmese junta maintain personal business links with drug producers (Altsean-Burma, 2004:103–107).[28] Military-controlled companies, particularly the Union of Myanmar Economic Holdings, which is one of the largest companies in the country, are also rumored to be involved in money laundering and in joint ventures with companies set by prominent drug traffickers. Moreover, there are no doubts that lower level officials, especially army and police personnel posted in border areas, are involved in facilitating and taxing the drug trade to maintain order and to attract funds for personal and corporate portfolios (Altsean-Burma, 2004:104–117; U.S. Department of State, Bureau of International Narcotics and Law Enforcement Affairs, 2007:244).

An Unexpected and Neglected About-Face: The Opium Bans in Burma

Given their extensive involvement in the drug trade, the CPB splinter groups would appear as the least likely candidates for engendering a large and sustained reduction in opium production. Yet, this is exactly what they have been doing, despite receiving little attention and even less support from the international community. The three main ceasefire groups have already fully implemented their bans on opium. Lin Ming-xian's Special Region No. 4 around Möng La has been declared opium free since 1997 (UNODC, 2003b). The Kokang Special Region No. 1 under the control of the MNDAA banned poppy cultivation in 2003, after missing a 2000 deadline and is now also considered poppy free by the UNODC (2006:226). Finally, in June 2005, the UWSA implemented a ban on opium in the areas under its control, which traditionally accounted for the bulk of opium production in the Shan State and hence in the whole of Burma.[29] Stiff penalties, including 6 months of imprisonment and heavy fines, have been introduced for whoever is breaking the new disposition (Jelsma,

2005a). The Wa Special Region No. 2 was declared opium free by the UNODC in 2006 (2007a:213).[30]

According to development workers with extensive field experience (e.g., Milsom, 2005; Kramer, 2007), the Wa leaders are convinced that getting rid of drugs is the only way to stimulate regional development, maintain peace, and become part of the international community for the first time. Many international observers tend to place more emphasis on the external pressures received by the UWSA, especially from China, Thailand, the United States, and the Burmese central government itself (TNI, 2005). Other observers explain more cynically the UWSA's willingness to give up its main source of revenue on the rapid increase in ATS production and trade (Altsean-Burma, 2004).

Whatever the reasons behind the bans, they prompted a sharp decline in Burmese opium cultivation and production. According to UN data, the area under cultivation fell from 163,000 hectares in 1996 to 21,500 hectares in 2006—a reduction of 87% (UNODC, 2006:221; UNODC, Central Committee for Drug Abuse Control, Lao National Commission for Drug Control and Supervision and Office of the Narcotics Control Board, 2007). During the same time span, potential opium production decreased by 82% to 315 metric tons (fig. 6.2). However, the decline came to a halt in 2007. Production has expanded in South Shan, where a considerable fraction of the Wa population was forcefully relocated by the UWSA in anticipation of the ban, and to a lesser extent in the eastern Shan State. Although the three special regions remained poppy free, in 2007 the area under poppy cultivation increased in total by 29% in comparison with 2006. The increase in opium production was even greater (49%), because higher yields were made possible, particularly in South Shan, by double cropping, irrigation and fertilization, as well as by favorable weather conditions (UNODC et al., 2007).

There is also evidence that the farmers in the affected regions have sharply felt the consequences of the bans. In Kokang, which gave up cultivating poppy in 2003, many households left the area in search of income and food. From an estimated total population of 200,000 in the year 2000, only 140,000 remained in 2004. Two out of three private Chinese clinics and pharmacies closed; about 6,000 children left school, effectively halving the enrollment rate compared with the previous year (UNODC and Central Committee for Drug Abuse Control, 2004:9). The same negative impact is now being felt on an even larger scale by the households affected by the UWSA ban. According to UNODC surveys, as of early 2007, most villages previously growing poppies faced severe food shortages. Many households had lost more than 31% of their cash income, because the revenue from opium formerly constituted 72% of the annual total and could only be partially replaced by income from other sources (UNODC et al., 2007:92). As a result, the number of vulnerable households doubled in 2007, representing more than 55% of the total (see also Strittmatter, 2004).

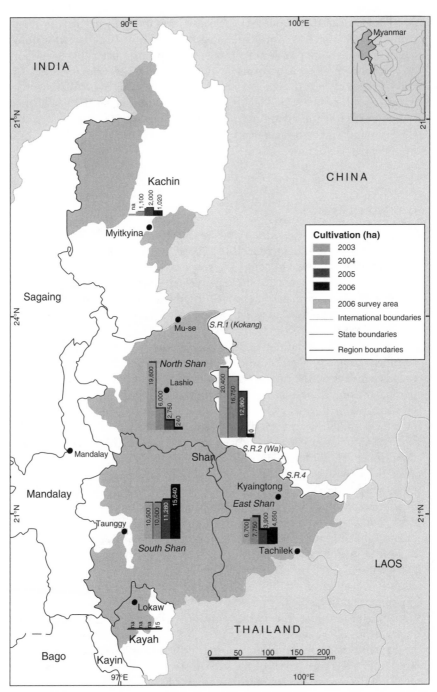

Figure 6.2 Opium poppy cultivation in Burma, 2003–2006.
Source: UNODC et al. (2007).

The needs of these households have all been met only partially by international assistance. The World Food Programme (WFP) estimated the number of food-insecure people at 230,000, of which it had been able to support only 100,000 or 42%. The assistance provided by UN agencies and NGOs is also regarded as "insufficient" by the UNODC itself. This humanitarian crisis throws doubts on the sustainability of the ban in the long term. It has already caused much resentment against the Wa leadership and it is unclear what the UWSA will do if the humanitarian aid and political capital it hoped to gain from the ban is not forthcoming (TNI, 2005).

Concluding Remarks

To what extent are Afghanistan and Burma "narco-states," a label that has often been applied to them (e.g., IMF, 2003:45; Weiner, 2004)? To answer this question, it is necessary to define the very concept of narco-state. This usually includes two main conditions (e.g., Weiner, 2004). First, a narco-state is a country that is economically dependent on the illicit drug economy; second, a narco-state is a country in which the government elites are complicit in the illicit drug trade.

If only the first condition is taken into account, Afghanistan can clearly be considered a narco-state, because it may well be the country most economically dependent on the production and trafficking of illicit drugs (opiates in particular); only Tajikistan might rival it in that respect. The answer is more problematic for Burma, which is much less economically dependent, at least on opiates and likely on illicit drugs taken in their entirety.

The difficulties become inverted when we consider the second condition. Under this condition, Burma would more easily qualify as a narco-state given the extensive corrupt practices linking senior government officials and quasi-state authorities profiting from opiate trafficking and the long-time official accommodating policies, which have only recently begun to take drug and money-laundering control more seriously. With the exceptions of the Taliban regime in Afghanistan and the García-Meza administration in Bolivia, which lasted merely a year (July 1980–August 1981) (Thoumi, 2003:120–121), the official tolerance and protection long endowed on the country's drug industry by the Burmese military juntas find no parallel in the contemporary world.

Afghanistan's case is less straightforward. As shown earlier, there is growing evidence of the capture of key pieces of the nascent state apparatus, such as the Ministry of the Interior, by drug trafficking interests. Unlike Burma, however, the very weakness of the Afghan state undermines the explanatory power of the second condition in the context of Afghanistan, because the central government, as of this writing, has only symbolic sovereignty over large portions of the country.

Given the irrelevance of the state in much of Afghanistan's recent history, it is even more problematic to apply the second condition to the country before 2001. As shown earlier, the state has, for more than 20 years, been a very weak or nonexistent actor in Afghan society in general and in the opiate industry in particular. The evolution of the illegal drug industry in Burma also shows the limits of the concept of narco-state. There, too, notwithstanding its complicity, the state has largely played a marginal role in the opiate industry, because it has never been fully able to exert its sovereignty over the Shan State. In both countries, moreover, a variety of quasi-state authorities have played a pivotal role in developing opiate production and trafficking. Although some of them may have occasionally received support from, or however come to terms with, the central government, quasi-state authorities usually represent a formidable challenge to state power, and these two combined factors—lack of government control and the presence of quasi-state authorities—represent key promoting factors of the opiate industry in both countries.

The opium bans of the former CPB splinter groups may be read—much as the Taliban ban of 2000–2001—as a confirmation of the decisive role played by quasi-state authorities in the upstream phases of the world illicit opiate industry. They also show what can be achieved in drug control by a state or quasi-state authority having no qualms in utilizing authoritarian methods and imposing huge suffering upon its population. As the recent Afghanistan experience shows, it is hard to emulate such successes with democratic methods, especially when the government is weak and corrupt and does not enjoy widespread legitimacy.

7

India

Diversion from Licit Cultivation

(with Molly Charles)

Introduction

The international literature on illegal drug markets makes scant reference to India, but India's role in the world opiate market clearly merits attention. India may be the world's largest consumer of illicit opiates as shown in chapter 5, but it may also be an important supplier. For several decades, India has been the main licit producer and sole supplier of opium (as a final product) to the world pharmaceutical market (INCB, 2005:72); however, as a consequence of significant diversion from licit cultivation, it may, de facto, also be a leading illicit producer. Some foreign and Indian officials conjecture that a substantial share, at least 30%, of India's officially sanctioned production seeps into the illicit market. With the possible exceptions of 2005 and 2006, we find plausible that, in India, 200 to 300 metric tons of opium is illegally diverted yearly, enough to make it the third largest illicit opium producer after Afghanistan and Burma.[1] The prospect that this diverted production never leaves India—the country's internal demand is large enough to absorb it and considerably more—may explain why the country does not figure much in studies, at least supply-side studies, of the world heroin market.[2]

India's opiate market holds additional interest from an international drug control policy perspective, because it has been suggested that Afghanistan should be allowed to supply opiates to the legal market (e.g., Senlis Council, 2005). As discussed in chapter 11, the Indian experience suggests how difficult it is to prevent substantial leakage even in a nation that is relatively well governed let alone one that is not.[3]

Opiate Consumption

Although rough, recent estimates suggest that India's opiate consumption is unrivaled, both in terms of the number of users and the quantity of opiates consumed. Recent survey data and other United Nations-reported prevalence estimates suggest that India has between 2.1 and 2.8 million opiate users, depending on the method of estimation and the year of reference (UNODC and Ministry of Social Justice and Empowerment, Government of India, 2004; UNODC, 2006). At the low end of the range, the UNODC and the Indian Ministry of Social Justice and Empowerment (2004:19–26) extrapolate from the first National Household Survey, which referred to 2001 and covered only the male population, age 12 to 60. In doing so, they estimate that about 1.5 million people regularly consume opium and about 600,000 people regularly consume heroin—the latter figure probably being too low, as household surveys are known to miss many problem drug users (Reuter, 1999). In chapter 5, which uses UN-reported prevalence estimates, we find that opiate consumption in India could have totaled as much as 78 metric tons (pure heroin equivalent) annually from 2001 to 2003—more than twice the amounts consumed by the second and third largest consumer countries, Iran and Russia, respectively.

India has a long tradition of opium consumption, which goes back to the 10th century. From the 16th century onward, poppy was also grown extensively in India, particularly in the northwest, and was an important article of trade with China (see chapter 2). Although opium consumption in India never reached the mass proportions of late 19th-century China, it has never lost—especially in India's rural areas—its embeddedness in popular culture, which both legitimizes and regulates it (e.g., Ganguly et al., 1995; Dhawan, 1998). However, today only a tiny share of India's current opium users are officially registered opium addicts and therefore entitled to purchase opium from state-sanctioned distribution outlets, of which there are also few. In 1997, the last year for which data are available, only about 10,000 people were registered and hence eligible to use 131 outlets (see UNDCP ROSA, 1998:268). Moreover, the opium released to Indian states (ranging from 146–1,240 kilograms yearly in the 1990s [UNDCP ROSA, 1998:270]) is not sufficient to meet the demand of the registered addicts. Thus, the vast majority of India's current opium users—and all its heroin users—must purchase their opiates illegally or instead substitute synthetic products, such as buprenorphine. The literature documents a progressive shift towards synthetic opiates, favored by easy availability and low prices (Dorabjee and Samson, 2000; U.S. Department of State, Bureau of International Narcotics and Law Enforcement Affairs, 2005: 278). However, synthetic opiate users are as a rule distinguished from opium and heroin users in the UN-sponsored surveys and estimates. In the NHS, for example, they accounted for an extra 0.2 percent, corresponding to another 600,000 people (UNODC and the Indian Ministry of Social Justice and Empowerment (2004: 21). The remainder of our discussion focuses on non-synthetic or agriculturally-derived illicit opiates.

Illicit Sources of Opiates

There are four potential sources of agriculturally-derived illicit opiates in India: blatantly illicit domestic cultivation, imports from Afghanistan, imports from Burma, and diversion from licit production. We assess the relevance of each of these sources, first for opium and then for heroin.

Opium

In the case of opium, one source, diversion, appears to dominate. Although ethnographic research indicates that Afghan opium is available in a few exclusive circles of users, law enforcement agencies have no evidence of its regular importation from either Afghanistan or Burma. As stated in the Narcotics Control Bureau (NCB)'s annual reports, in the past few years "there were no cases of opium smuggling into India" (NCB, 2002:15). It is thus fair to assume that the overwhelming majority of the opium needed to satisfy the demand of Indian users is produced domestically. It is not accidental that most opium seizures take place around the licit poppy-growing areas of Uttar Pradesh, Madhya Pradesh, and Rajasthan (e.g., NCB, 2004:7).

Blatantly illicit domestic production also plays a minor part in the market. Since the mid 1990s, the bulk of India's illicit cultivation has been confined to Arunachal Pradesh, the most remote and least developed of the northeastern states (NCB, 2003:15; U.S. Department of State, Bureau of International Narcotics and Law Enforcement Affairs, 2005:277). As of 2005, very rough estimates by local drug control officials put opium cultivation in Arunachal Pradesh at 1,500 to 2,000 hectares. There are no accurate estimates of opium gum yields, but they are thought to be very low, between 2 to 6 kilograms of opium per hectare. As Arunachal Pradesh has no airfields and few roads, and illicit cultivation is confined to isolated jungle, it is likely that much of the opium produced is consumed locally. There is no evidence of local opium being trafficked to other parts of the country (NCB, 2003:15; see also U.S. Department of State, Bureau of International Narcotics and Law Enforcement Affairs, 2000[4], 2004:251).

Thus, we conjecture that a large majority of the opium needed to satisfy the demand of Indian users is produced domestically under licit auspices.

Heroin

The analysis is more complicated in the case of heroin. In the NCB annual reports, Southwest Asia—hence, Afghanistan and Pakistan—is presented as the main source of heroin sold in India. The NCB's claims of the predominance of Southwest Asian heroin are, however, partially undermined by its own statistics. Although Southwest Asian heroin constituted almost half (48%) of the heroin seized in 1997, that share fell to just 5% in 2002. The drop in the share of seizures might be related to the reduction in opium production in Afghanistan in 2001, but data on seizures from Afghanistan's neighbors do not indicate similarly large drops. The absence of data in the NCB's more recent annual report (2004) leaves us with little or no basis for determining whether the percentage of Southwest Asian heroin has rebounded since 2002.

Heroin from Southeast Asia, namely from Burma, accounts for a very small share of India's seizures. According to NCB statistics, heroin that, with certainty, could be traced to Burmese sources represented a minimum of 0.6% and a maximum of 2.1% of yearly total seizures for 1997 to 2002. Although some experts in both India and Burma judge the Indo-Burmese drug trade to be expanding rapidly (e.g., Nepram, 2002), our own data collection in Manipur confirms the NCB assessment of a limited, relatively disorganized inflow of heroin from Burma.

Even if Southwest Asia's share of total heroin seizures in the late 1990s is assumed to represent its share of the Indian heroin market at the beginning of the new century, one may still ask where the rest of the heroin consumed in India comes from. The NCB reports do not explicitly answer this question, and only in one of the more recent issues is a reference made in passing to the diversion of opium from licit production (NCB, 2003:2, 14). The relevance of this source is admitted openly only in the report for the year 2000, which contains the following statements "domestic heroin accounted for approximately 30% of total seizures during the year" (NCB, 2001:9).

Notwithstanding the NCB's ambiguities, evidence on heroin prices and seizures strongly suggests that domestically produced heroin meets a significant portion of the country's heroin demand. If Southwest Asian heroin accounted for a large share of India's consumption and no other sources of heroin were available, then a decline in flows from Southwest Asia (as indicated by the 1997–2002 decrease in the share and amount of Southwest Asian heroin seizures) would result in substantially higher heroin prices. However, the NCB data on heroin prices (NCB, 2002:92, 2003:76–77), show that the apparent decrease in flows from Southwest Asia was not accompanied by an increase in heroin prices either at the retail or at the wholesale levels. Moreover, from 1997 to 2002 a growing percentage—and throughout that period, more than half—of the heroin seizures recorded by the NCB were classified as "of unknown sources." Despite the NCB's official denials, it is plausible that a considerable and preponderant share of such seizures concerns domestically produced heroin (Charles, 2004:6–7).

Interviews with drug users and law enforcement officers in various parts of the country indicate the growing spread of Indian "brown sugar," which usually consists of crude morphine or heroin base. Significantly in Mumbai, drug users report that the *Afghani mal* (the "Afghan stuff," as heroin from Afghanistan is popularly called) has, since the beginning of the 21st century, become increasingly difficult to find and that the local retail market is largely supplied with *desi mal* (the "local stuff")—heroin base produced with opium diverted from licit production (Charles, 2004:79, 86).

The drug users' assessments are also largely shared by law enforcement officials heading or working in narcotics squads in the field (but not by the NCB headquarters, which tends to minimize the extent of diversion [see, for example, NCB, 2002:7]). Given the lack of a standardized heroin signature program in India, the locally based officers interviewed for the study assessed the share of the different sources of heroin on the basis of the investigations they conducted throughout the years and local intelligence. In their opinion, as much as 80% of the heroin consumed in major cities such as Delhi and Mumbai comes from diversion from licit production, whereas Afghan heroin was, by 2004, sold exclusively to a selected clientele. The 2007 edition of the INCSR supports these rough assessments in stating that "morphine base ('brown sugar' heroin) is India's most popularly abused heroin [sic] derivative" (U.S. Department of State, Bureau of International Narcotics and Law Enforcement Affairs, 2007:240). We explore the possibility that domestically produced heroin meets a significant portion of the country's heroin demand below, in relation to our estimates of diversion.

Diversion from Licit Production and Its Share of the Illicit Market

Licit opium poppy cultivation in India is a labor-intensive and geographically dispersed industry, which is inherently difficult to control. In their reports, the Central Bureau of Narcotics (CBN), an agency of the Ministry of Finance responsible for all facets of the opium industry, and the NCB stress the strictness of the Indian licensing and control system (NCB, 2003:13–14; CBN, 2007). However, an analysis of the system of control and qualitative fieldwork in production areas shows that diversion is a routine activity that is openly tolerated and, to a certain extent, even promoted by local cultural norms and social structures. Diversion can occur in four ways. First, cultivators in licit growing regions may plant additional hectares without proper licenses. Second, cultivators may falsely claim that licensed fields in licit growing regions are not harvestable, then sell their harvests illicitly. Third, a properly licensed and harvested field may yield more than the minimum qualifying yield (MQY) and the unreported excess may be sold into the illicit market. Fourth, diversion could occur after the government has purchased or processed the opium, with corrupt agents selling out of the government's inventory. We have found little evidence of additional unlicensed fields or government sales; false claims of unharvestable hectares and excess yields may be important.

The Licit Opium Industry: The Regulatory Process and Its Difficulties

India is the largest producer of opium for the world's pharmaceutical industry. Between 2000 and 2006, India's licit opium production ranged from a low of 332 metric tons in 2006,[5] when 7,252 hectares were licensed, to a high of 1,326 in 2000, when 35,270 hectares were licensed (CBN, 2007) (tables 7.1 and 7.2). India is the only country that permits the legal extraction and export of

Table 7.1

Number of cultivators and area licensed and harvested for licit cultivation, 1996–2006.

Crop Year	No. of Cultivators	Area Licensed (hectares)	Area Harvested (hectares)	Area Not Harvested (hectares)
1996	78,670	26,437	22,593	3,844
1997	76,130	29,799	24,591	5,208
1998	92,292	30,714	10,098	20,616
1999	156,071	33,459	29,163	4,296
2000	159,884	35,270	32,085	3,185
2001	133,408	26,683	18,086	8,597
2002	114,486	22,847	18,447	4,400
2003	102,042	20,410	12,320	8,090
2004	105,697	21,141	18,591	2,550
2005	87,670	8,770	7,833	937
2006	72,478	7,252	6,976	276

Source: U.S. Department of State, Bureau of International Narcotics and Law Enforcement Affairs, 2005:274; CBN, 2007.

Table 7.2

Licit opium production and proportional estimates of diversion in metric tons, 1996–2006.

Crop Year	Licit Production at 70% Solid	Licit Production at 90% Solid	Diversion of 10% of Production at 90% Solid	Diversion of 30% of Production at 90% Solid
1996	1,077	838	83.8	251.4
1997	1,271	989	98.9	296.7
1998	335	261	26.1	78.3
1999	1,382	1,075	107.5	322.5
2000	1,705	1,326	132.6	397.8
2001	995	774	77.4	232.2
2002	1,055	821	82.1	246.3
2003	684	532	53.2	159.6
2004	1,087	845	84.5	253.5
2005	439	347	34.7	104.1
2006	427	332	33.2	99.6

Source: Authors' calculations based on CBN, 2007.

opium gum rather than concentrate of poppy straw ("CPS"), which is much less prone to diversion (see appendix A).

The CBN organizes and supervises the licit cultivation of opium poppy. Before sowing begins, the CBN decides on the quantity of opium it intends to purchase the following year and it determines the expected yield per hectare in each province, referred to as the minimum qualifying yield (MQY).[6] On this basis, the CBN then establishes the area to be planted and the number of licenses to be issued. After the harvest, the CBN collects opium gum from the farmers and operates two processing centers, one in Madhya Pradesh and the other in Uttar Pradesh, where the opium is purified, dried, weighed, and packaged for export or partially refined to supply Indian pharmaceutical companies (CBN, 2007).

With the partial support of the NCB and the state police forces, the CBN also faces the daunting task of monitoring effectively a very labor-intensive and fragmented activity, such as opium cultivation in India (fig. 7.1). As shown by table 7.1, the CBN licensed 72,000 to 160,000 farmers each year from 1996 to 2006. Each licensed farmer is allowed to cultivate a maximum of one fifth of a hectare. If one adds farm workers, about a million people may come into contact with poppy plants and opium gum yearly.

The area licensed for cultivation expanded and then contracted at the turn of the 21st century (table 7.1), as India first tried to increase production during the late 1990s and then to reduce it to keep opium stocks at the levels set by the International Narcotics Control Board (INCB). The level of participation in the licit program, measured in terms of the number of licensed cultivators, also declined, but less so than the area licensed for cultivation, implying that each cultivator can produce less opium for the licit market now than previously. In 2000, the average licensed area per cultivator was just over a fifth of a hectare, the legal maximum; in 2006, it was only a tenth of a hectare. The control of the area under cultivation is made even more difficult by the fact that poppy fields are usually far away from the main roads and that roads are still scarce in parts of Madhya Pradesh, Rajasthan, and Uttar Pradesh.

In late autumn of each year, 800 narcotics officials attempt to measure the licensed but as-yet-unplanted fields, amounting to thousands of hectares of cultivatable land spread over a far greater number of cultivators. Central Bureau of Narcotics officials are also expected to patrol the area under cultivation regularly. Since 2003, the CBN has also begun to estimate the actual acreage under licit opium cultivation by using satellite imagery, and then comparing it with exact field measurements. However, for a month or two prior to the opium collection, which occurs in April, the enforcement activity rests on village headmen (the *lambardhar*). It is up to the *lambardhar* to record the daily yield of opium from the cultivators under their charge. In exchange for their services, the *lambardhar* previously received a commission of 1.5% of the total price of the opium produced. To increase their loyalty, their commission has recently increased to 10% (Mansfield, 2001a:23–24; U.S.

Figure 7.1 Licit opium cultivation areas in India.
Source: Downloaded from www.uwmc.uwc.edu/political_science/opiumprod.html. Accessed October 2007. Modified to erase irrelevant features.

Department of State, Bureau of International Narcotics and Law Enforcement Affairs, 2007:239–242).

The difficulties of enforcement are also evidenced by the persistent discrepancy between the area licensed for cultivation and the area that is finally harvested. As shown by the final column in table 7.1, from 1996 to 2003 this gap oscillated between a low of 3,185 hectares in 2000, amounting to 9 percent of all licensed hectares, and a high of 20,616 hectares or 67 percent of licensed hectares in 1998. The gap declined substantially in 2004, 2005, and 2006, reaching a low of 276 hectares or 4 percent of licensed hectares in 2006 and suggesting that either the Indian government has sharply tightened its controls, possibly reacting to international pressures (U.S. Department of State, Bureau of International Narcotics and Law Enforcement Affairs, 2007:238–244), or that other market conditions have changed, making diversion less attractive. Whereas the 1998 exorbitant discrepancy was largely the result of a cultivators' strike, in other years the gap between the area licensed for cultivation and the area harvested is officially attributed to a variety of causes: drought or, more generally, bad weather conditions, plant diseases, insects, or the Nilghai—a type of cow that is said to eat the poppy crop. Our primary data collection, in contrast, shows that underreporting of hectares harvested and false declarations of opium destruction are relatively frequent—to divert opium to the illicit market or to save it for personal use.

It is usually up to the *lambardhar* to issue a declaration of opium destruction, after they themselves or one of their agents have visited the area under cultivation that has been claimed "unharvestable" and ensured that the crop is burnt. However, according to several interviewees, these officers are often willing to make false statements on the extent of the crop destroyed in return for a "fee." Mansfield (2001a: 23) also singles out the *lambardhar* "as playing a key role in the diversion process."

Sociopolitical Constraints to Law Enforcement

The traditional non-state institutions of caste, kinship, and credit networks, which are still predominant in the rural opium-producing areas, further weaken the control apparatus set by the CBN. Bound by caste and clan ties and embedded in patron–client relationships with local power holders, the *lambardhar* as well as the CBN and state police officers are often unable or unwilling to exercise properly the enforcement tasks that are entrusted to them. In an ethnographic study of the social control of opium production in Rajasthan, De Wilde (2003:3) reports that "the strictness of harvest monitoring and collection, for which the *lambardhar* is responsible, is subject to a variety of extra-legal constraints, and apparently depends more on networks of patronage and credit subject to caste and kinship formations, and less on the letter of the law" (see also Mansfield, 2001a). De Wilde's research in rural Rajasthan in particular shows that, in addition to caste and kinship networks, the members of formal and informal credit institutions are also able to influence the farmers' and regulators' decisions, because many farmers are obliged to borrow money to start the capital-intensive cultivation of opium poppy.

The "extralegal constraints" are most binding when the *lambardhar* have to deal with large and powerful landowners, who usually belong to the upper castes. Working around the official limit of one fifth of a hectare per licensed farmer, large landowners often appropriate a considerable number of licenses, either because many members of their extended families obtain licenses or because poor farmers or sharecroppers officially stand for them to get a license, the latter practice (*benami*) is widespread despite criminalization in 1988. The *lambardhar* as well as the CBN and state police officers often do not investigate or prosecute cases involving powerful persons and are ready to settle amicably the few enforcement actions that are initiated against them. According to our primary data collection, a complacent attitude is also held by members of the judiciary in the few cases in which they are called to adjudicate criminal proceedings involving powerful people (Charles, 2004:26–27; see also Mansfield, 2001a).

Our interviewees' claims are partially supported by official statistics. These show that the chance of being prosecuted for a violation of India's drug law, the Narcotic Drugs and Psychotropic Substances (NDPS) Act of 1985, is very low. According to NCB statistics, between 1994 and 2004 a maximum of 20,138 people have been prosecuted in a year for drug trafficking or selling (NCB, 2003:71). Given India's population of about one billion people and the size of the opiate market (with more than two million users), this is a trivial number. On average, throughout 1992 to 2004, less than a third of them were convicted (NCB, 2003:71).

Minimum Qualifying Yields and the Opium Lobby

One of the CBN's most sensitive tasks is to establish yearly an MQY—the number of kilograms of opium to be produced per hectare in each state. The MQYs are based on historical yield levels from licensed farmers during previous years and are set by the CBN prior to licensing. Simultaneously, the CBN also publishes the price per kilogram the farmer will receive for opium produced that meets the MQY, as well as significantly higher prices for all over-MQY opium turned into the CBN. The purpose of this higher price is to induce the farmer to sell this potentially concealable excess to the government rather than to illicit buyers.

The CBN has almost doubled the MQY since the early 1980s. From a low of 25 kilograms per hectare in 1981 it has risen to 54 kilograms per hectare in Madhya Pradesh and Rajasthan, and to 48 kilograms per hectare in Uttar Pradesh in 2006. Average yields have increased along with the MQY from a low of 30.8 kilograms per hectare in 1984 to a high of 61.2 kilograms in 2006 (all yield figures, here and in the following discussion, are at 70% solid).

The long-term increases in MQY and average yields reflect advances in technology and irrigation. Moreover, they are also evidence of the CBN's increasingly stringent policy. Raising the MQY may be the CBN's most effective means of deterring diversion. If the MQY is too low, farmers can clandestinely divert the excess opium they produce into illicit channels. In its 2005 report, the U.S. State Department, Bureau of International Narcotics and Law Enforcement Affairs (2005:274) thus concludes, "an accurate estimate of the MQY is crucial to the success of the Indian licit production regime." To achieve this goal, in 2001 and 2003, the Indian and U.S. governments conducted a Joint Licit Opium Poppy Survey to develop a methodology to estimate opium gum yield (Acock and Acock, 2003). However, according to the liaison officers interviewed, the survey failed to achieve its main goal because of mistakes in the data collection process and possible data manipulation.

In reality, the setting of the MQY is much politicized. Each year opium farmers and their political patrons try to negotiate the lowest possible MQY. According to many of our Indian and foreign interviewees, the opium farmers' political patrons constitute an effective, although informal, opium lobby, whose members include high-ranking politicians and CBN officers and, in the past, even federal ministers (Sharma, 1999; Tiwari, 2000). During the early 1990s, for example, the MQY was fixed at 34 kilograms per hectare. As the government moved to raise it to 38 kilograms, the opium growers applied considerable pressure and the MQY was then set at 37 kilograms for the crop year of 1993. The case of farmers was openly pleaded by 14 members of parliament belonging to all parties (Sharma, 1999).

If unsatisfied with their patrons' representations, opium farmers can mobilize. During late 1997, 30,000 cultivators went "on strike," voluntarily relinquishing their licenses to demand reductions in the MQYs and increases in the area of cultivation. Although the CBN replaced the striking farmers by issuing 26,000 new licenses in 3 days, the 1998 harvest was one of the smallest on record—about 260 metric tons. Of the 30,714 hectares licensed for production, an extraordinary two thirds was not harvested, strongly suggesting an increase in diversion. To prevent another strike, the following year the MQY was reduced for all three states to 30 kilograms per hectare (U.S. Department of State, Bureau of International Narcotics and Law Enforcement Affairs, 1999).

The amount paid per kilogram of opium at 70% solid rose steadily in nominal terms from 1996 to 2005, from a low of about $14 at the start of the period to a high of $33, falling back only slightly in 2006 to $32 (Bhattacharaij, 2007:15). According to our informants, the price paid on the illicit market is substantially higher, ranging from $107 to $320 per kilogram during 2000 to 2004 (Charles, 2004:28–29). Farmers who submit opium above the MQY are paid a premium, but not nearly enough to bridge the gap between the licit and illicit market.

Calculations of farm revenue and net income for 2000 to 2004—the period for which we have licit and illicit price estimates—further illustrate the relative attractiveness of illicit sales. A farmer cultivating the maximum area (i.e., a fifth of a hectare) may have harvested just more than 11 kilograms of opium at 70% solid, suggesting CBN payments—or a gross income—of about $230 to $350. After subtracting production costs, the net income per farmer—according to our informants—might have been as low as 10% of the gross, amounting to $23 to $35 in our example, although the sale of licit opium by-products (poppy seeds and straw) may have generated more farm income than the opium sold to the CBN, thus suggesting a higher overall net (Mansfield, 2001a:15). If sold on the illicit market, the same opium yield could have generated revenue of about $1,200 to $3,580 and a net income of $990 to $3,260, assuming no differences in production costs and before accounting for the sale of any poppy seeds or straw. If illicit diverters can also sell poppy seeds and straw, the licit and illicit figures are directly comparable. Some Indian government officials have described diversion as "an economic necessity" (Mansfield, 2001a:24; see also Chouvy, 2006a). At the very least, our analysis shows it is economically advantageous.

Attempts to Estimate Diversion

The INCB, U.S. State Department, and others routinely assert that "certain quantities of licitly produced opium continued to be diverted into illicit channels" (INCB, 2005:62). Whereas the INCB does not attempt an estimate, the U.S. State Department (Bureau of International Narcotics and Law Enforcement Affairs, 2007:239) has stated in its 2007 report that "between 20–30% of the opium crop is diverted," although it offers no basis for that claim. Most of the foreign diplomats interviewed in Delhi for the project as well as several Indian law enforcement officers interviewed in different cities by Charles (2004) considered this rate very conservative.

Using the 30% rate, diversion during 1996 to 2006 may have ranged between 78 metric tons in 1998 and almost 400 metric tons in 2000 at 90% solid (see table 7.2). This would imply that during most recent years more illicit opium was produced in India than in all other illicit opium-producing countries, except Afghanistan and Burma. From 1996 to 2005, the three other major illicit producers—Laos, Colombia, and Mexico—produced, on average, 113, 75, and 57 metric tons, respectively (UNODC, 2006:57).

These analyses assume that the amount diverted is a fixed portion of what is actually sold to the government and, by implication, government requirements; if this were the case, then less licensing would lead to less diversion. However, there are plausible scenarios in which the assumption of fixed proportionality might fail. Indeed, under certain circumstances, a reduction in government requirements could lead to an increase in diversion. If farmers are less able to sell legally, they may have more reason to sell illegally—for example, they may not earn enough income through licit sales alone to meet basic household requirements.

A crude test of fixed proportionality takes advantage of the data in table 7.1. As already noted, the "area not harvested" is itself a possible indicator of the extent of diversion, because fields supposedly destroyed before harvest may be harvested unofficially and sold illicitly. If fixed proportionality were the norm, the relationship between the area not harvested, as a proxy for potential diversion, and licensing would be reasonably constant. It is not. Figure 7.2 shows the variability in the relationship between the area not harvested and licensed hectares from 1996 to 2006.

Moreover, in some years, we find evidence of an inverse relationship between the licensed production area and potential diversion (fig. 7.3). For example, from harvest-years 2000 to 2001, government licensing declined by almost 25% and the area not harvested or "destroyed" more than doubled.

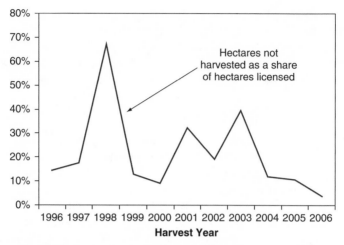

Figure 7.2 Variability in the share of unharvested hectares, 1996–2006.
Source: Authors' calculations based on CBN (2007).

Similarly, from harvest-years 2002 to 2003, licensing fell by 11% and the area not harvested nearly doubled.

Any estimate of illicit flows must be considered speculative. Here we assume that the "truth" involves a mix of diversion from official production and from officially unharvested hectares (table 7.3). From the mid 1990s up until 2004, diversion, based on a 30% rule, could have ranged from 78 metric tons to almost 400 metric tons whereas potential diversion, based only on the number of unharvested hectares (i.e., without any "diversion" from official

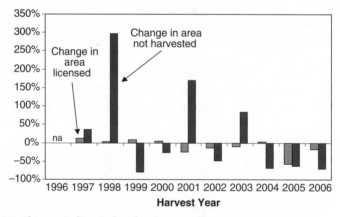

Figure 7.3 Changes in licensed and unharvested areas, 1996–2006. na, not applicable.
Source: Authors' calculation based on CBN (2007).

Table 7.3
Authors' estimates of diversion in metric tons, 1996–2006.

Crop Year	Diversion of 30% of Production	Potential Diversion from Unharvested Hectares	Mix of Diversion from Production and Unharvested Hectares (simple average)
1996	251.4	142.6	197.0
1997	296.7	209.4	253.0
1998	78.3	530.7	304.4
1999	322.5	158.4	240.5
2000	397.8	131.5	264.7
2001	232.2	367.8	299.9
2002	246.3	195.8	221.0
2003	159.6	349.8	254.8
2004	253.5	116.0	184.8
2005	104.1	40.8	72.5
2006	99.6	13.1	56.4

harvests), could have ranged from 116 metric tons to 531 metric tons. Averaging the tonnage figures from the 30 percent rule (column 2) and from the unharvested hectares (column 3) year by year, we conclude that actual diversion may have ranged from about 200 to 300 metric tons yearly through 2004, but has likely declined since then.

If India's illicit opiate demand amounts to 78 metric tons of pure heroin equivalent or 780 metric tons of opium each year, our calculations imply that diversion from licit production accounts for a quarter to over a third of that demand, at least through 2004. Given the NCB's seizure data, the source of the remaining two thirds to three quarters remains a puzzle. There are three possible explanations: the NCB seizure data understate imports from Southwest Asia; many more heroin users routinely use synthetic opiates than officially acknowledged; or we have underestimated diversion.

Heroin Production, Trafficking, and Export

Additional evidence of opium diversion and processing into heroin is given by the dismantling of processing labs and the growing presence of heroin users in or close to production areas in Madhya Pradesh, Rajasthan, and Uttar Pradesh.

Since the late 1990s, 5 to 10 morphine and heroin labs have been dismantled each year; most were located in or close to the opium production areas of the three states (e.g., NCB, 2003:71, 78; U.S. Department of State,

Bureau of International Narcotics and Law Enforcement Affairs, 2005:275). According to the law enforcement officers interviewed and a plurality of other informants, a veritable cottage industry has developed. In primitive labs, villagers process crude heroin from the specified quantity of opium and acetic anhydride provided to them. People are instructed in the method and after a few days the traffickers who delivered the substances come and collect the processed heroin base (Sharma, 1999; Charles, 2004:26). Moreover, since the late 1990s, a limited number of Indian refiners have been able to process better quality heroin (having a beige color and approximating the standards of the Afghan product). Some of this heroin is meant for export, but most of it probably still flows into the domestic market.[7] Seizures of Indian "white" heroin have grown exponentially since the beginning of the 21st century (U.S. Department of State, Bureau of International Narcotics and Law Enforcement Affairs, 2005:275).

Since the late 1990s, opium production areas have also attracted a growing number of heroin users. For example, the city of Kanpur in Uttar Pradesh has evolved into an important transit point and a large, cheap retail market for locally processed heroin (Sharma, 2000).[8] Alternatively, the domestic heroin is brought to final consumer markets in large cities in makeshift ways primarily by independent traders, mostly originating from the production areas, who have contacts with farmers or refiners. According to all Indian and foreign law enforcement officers interviewed, there are no big organizations involved in the business. Although they may occasionally hire "mules" for the risky phases of the heroin transportation into a large city, the traders usually consist of small, mostly family-run, trafficking enterprises.

Only a minor part of the heroin produced with diverted opium as well as a larger, but unknown, portion of the heroin imported from Afghanistan are exported. Since the late 1990s, Sri Lanka has emerged has the main target of heroin exports from India. In 2002, for example more than a third of the heroin seized in India was bound for Sri Lanka; since the late 1990s, the Indian state of Tamil Nadu claims some of the largest heroin seizures each year. Geographic proximity and ethnic links favor smuggling between the eastern coast of southern India and the northwestern coast of Sri Lanka, by sea, mainly by small vessels (e.g., Charles, 2004:38–39; NCB, 2004:18; U.S. Department of State, Bureau of International Narcotics and Law Enforcement Affairs, 2005:276;). As a result of the limited number of seizures carried out in Sri Lanka, it is unclear to what extent the heroin imported from India is consumed locally or exported further.

Indian "brown sugar" heroin is also increasingly available in Nepal, Bangladesh, and the Maldives. Paler, better quality heroin produced either domestically or imported from Afghanistan is exported farther to West Africa and Europe. Every year, a number of West African traffickers are arrested at Mumbai and New Delhi international airports with small quantities of heroin, which are either swallowed or hidden in suitcases (e.g., NCB, 2003:45–57; U.S. Department of State, Bureau of International Narcotics and Law Enforcement

Affairs, 2007:241–242). European nationals are also occasionally arrested while trying to exit the country with small quantities of heroin. Several schemes to send heroin by mail to either Europe or North America have also been uncovered by Indian law enforcement authorities during the past few years. However, the number of foreigners arrested on drug-trafficking charges has remained, throughout the years, surprisingly small, reaching a maximum of 205 persons in 2002 and consistently representing less than 2% of all persons arrested on drug-trafficking charges since the early 1990s (NCB, 2003:70).

There are rumors that some of India's powerful organized crime groups, such as the one headed by Ibrahim Dawood, might be involved in large-scale smuggling of heroin via the sea route (DEA, 2002b; U.S. Department of Treasury, 2003; see also Charles, 2001b). Rumors aside, no seizure of such a type has taken place since the mid 1990s.

Concluding Remarks

Despite the limited involvement of organized crime, our analysis suggests that India is not only the world's largest consumer of illicit opiates but, de facto, also one of the largest illicit opium producers. In contrast to all other illicit producers, India owes the latter distinction not to blatantly illicit cultivation but to diversion from licit cultivation.

The Indian government has, since the late 1990s, been under increasing pressure by the INCB and the U.S. government to monitor licit production and to fight diversion more effectively. Since 2003, the United States has provided the Indian government drug assistance funding worth more than $2.2 million (U.S. Department of State, Bureau of International Narcotics and Law Enforcement Affairs, 2007:244). As shown in the preceding pages, controls may have tightened since 2004. However, the Indian government's recent decision to privatize opium processing and to allow domestic pharmaceutical firms to produce codeine and morphine may represent an unintended setback. Citing India's poor record in monitoring domestic pharmaceutical firms, Dasgupta (2007) reports concern that diversion might increase.

This unprecedented decision may be a reaction to market forces that increasingly challenge the Indian opium industry. U.S. pharmaceutical companies have a keen interest in the revision of the *80/20 rule,* under which they must buy 80% of their morphine from either India or Turkey (DEA, 2006). Like their foreign counterparts, U.S. companies prefer using CPS for ease of extracting narcotic opiate alkaloids, primarily morphine, codeine, and thebaine, the last of which is an important starting material for the production of a number of opioids (U.S. Department of State, 2005: 275). Reflecting that preference, the annual export of raw opium from India has declined by about 50% since the late 1990s, when Australia and France began producing CPS with high thebaine content (INCB, 2008a: 77,79; Dasgupta, 2007). The Indian licit opium industry is dependent on just two countries, the United States and

Japan, which together account for over 96 percent of the international market for licit opium (INCB, 2008a: 79).

In response to these changes, the Indian government is exploring the possibility of a partial shift to CPS, but it may face daunting financial, social, and technological challenges (U.S. Department of State, Bureau of International Narcotics and Law Enforcement Affairs, 2005:275). For example, the countries that currently produce CPS may be reluctant to share the technology with a direct competitor. Moreover, India may have little or no advantage in CPS production, which—unlike opium production—is capital intensive rather than labor intensive.

No matter how the international demand for India's opium evolves, there are voices even within India that question the economic and political sense of the Indian licit opium industry as it is currently organized. The official justification for the industry is that it provides a livelihood for a significant number of farmers and their families (INCB, 2005:72). However, the low earnings of licit opium farmers suggest that one reason why the opium lobby so forcefully promotes licit cultivation is that it provides a cover for participation in the illicit market. Given the low earnings, some Indian observers question the reasonableness of running expensive monitoring and enforcement regimes and protecting an industry that not only helps spread corruption but also enhances local opium and heroin consumption (Samanta, 2002). Transitional financing schemes could provide compensation to currently licensed opium farmers over a period of years as the industry is phased out. Their costs might be reasonable in comparison with the potential gains in reduced corruption and consumption of illicit opiates, but vested interests may hinder change.

8

Colombia

The Emergence of a New Producer

(with Sergio Uribe-Ramirez and Carolina Navarrete-Frías)

Introduction

Although Colombia is a minor producer in the world opiate market, responsible for no more than 2% of total production in most recent years and considerably less in some (see table 3.1, chapter 3), its case is of great interest because it is the only nation to enter the market de novo in the past 50 years. Colombia's entry was unanticipated and it achieved the status of a second-order producer in just a few years. Moreover, although small in the world market, Colombia has been one of the two principal producers for the U.S. market and has provided a substantial share of U.S. consumption (see chapter 5). There is also some evidence that its production has declined abruptly since 2001, for reasons that have not been clearly identified. This chapter provides the first systematic description of the emergence of the Colombian heroin industry.

Why has Colombia been the only country to start illegally producing in the past half century, even as total world consumption was growing? Although no research study can provide an authoritative answer to this question, we suggest that the most important factors were the existence of consolidated drug-smuggling networks servicing the U.S. market; the presence of guerrilla and paramilitary groups in some regions of the country; and, last but not least, the general weakness and corruption of the Colombian government. Colombia was among the many countries capable of producing opiates in the 1990s, but these factors may have led it to exploit the capability.

Supporting this emphasis on existing drug-trafficking capacity, we show that the initiative for starting this industry came not from the farmers, but from the processors and traffickers, who provided the initial seed, training, and finance for peasants to enter the new business. Although the available data are limited, it appears that Colombia's producers frequently rely on the protection of local guerilla groups and, more generally, that the industry has thrived in areas in which central government authority is weak and contested, and effective enforcement therefore limited. The industry differs substantially both from the opiate industry in Asia and from the cocaine industry in the Andes, because it is characterized by small producers working on assignment for small processing and trafficking organizations. It also differs from the Asian opiate industry in that the Colombian government, with substantial assistance from the United States, has made a considerable effort to suppress poppy growing and now destroys a large fraction of what is planted.

Background: Cocaine, Insurgents, and Government Weakness

The sudden development of the opiate industry in Colombia cannot be understood without taking account of three factors: the preexisting drug (predominantly cocaine) industry, the rooted presence of guerrilla and paramilitary groups that fight each other at the same time that they challenge the Colombian state's sovereignty, and the weakness and corruption of the Colombian government.

The Cocaine Industry

The opiate industry in Colombia is part of a larger complex of illegal drug activities in that nation. During the 1970s, Colombia entered the international illicit drug market via its cannabis production, mainly exporting to the United States. The niche for the Colombian entry was created by the spraying of Mexican marijuana with paraquat in the late 1960s. This not only destroyed part of the Mexican harvest, but also made Mexican marijuana uncompetitive, because many U.S. users were concerned that they might be smoking a poisoned product. In the mid to latter part of the 1970s, Colombia also entered the cocaine market, with such success that since the mid 1980s, the country has been the foremost cocaine exporter in the world (U.S. Department of State, Bureau for International Narcotics and Law Enforcement Affairs, 2007b:111–119).

During the 1980s, some of the cocaine-exporting groups became so powerful that they posed a formidable threat to the nation's body politic. In 1989, after the assassination of the leading presidential candidate (Luis Carlos Galan) by the Medellin cocaine traffickers, the national government fought, in effect, a civil war against the major trafficking organizations, which themselves had large gangs of heavily armed men. The result was the dismantling of the Medellin syndicate by 1991 and of the Cali syndicate, another prominent group involving large-scale smugglers, by about 1995.[1] Since then, the cocaine trafficking industry in Colombia has been populated by a set of smaller smuggling organizations (Clawson and Lee, 1996; Thoumi, 2003).

Despite the disruption of the large trafficking organizations, the cocaine industry continues to thrive in Colombia. Since about 2000, the country has become the principal producer of coca leaves, probably reflecting both increased pressure on coca growers in Bolivia and Peru in the mid 1990s, and the displacement (resulting from increasing political violence) of rural Colombian populations from established communities into guerrilla-controlled areas where there are few alternative sources of income (McGuire, 2002).

Guerrilla and Paramilitary Groups

The expansion of coca growing in Colombia has largely taken place in areas characterized by limited or no government authority that are under the more or less contested control of guerilla and paramilitary groups (Vargas, 2005).

Guerrilla organizations have existed in Colombia since the 1960s. The two largest ones are the Revolutionary Armed Forces of Colombia–People's Army (known as FARC, the acronym from the Spanish initials) and the National Liberation Army, (known as ELN). The FARC is present in 35% to 40% of Colombia's territory, most strongly in southeastern jungles and in the plains at the base of the Andes mountains, and has about 15,000 combatants and several thousand more supporters. The ELN is much smaller, with a dwindling membership estimated at 3,000 combatants, and has its strongholds in the northern, northeastern, and southwestern parts of the country (U.S. Department of State, Bureau for International Narcotics and Law Enforcement Affairs, 2007b). Both groups, and particularly the FARC, entered the drug business during the 1980s, enabling dramatic expansion of their resources and geographic reach. Today, the FARC not only extracts protection money from the peasants growing coca and poppies, and from the traffickers trading with the semimanufactured or finished products, but it also has become a key player in the refinement and sale of coca paste. Commenting on these developments, Francisco Thoumi (2003) observes that

> no evidence exists that [guerrilla organizations] have developed
> their own distribution networks abroad or exported directly, but it
> was clear that they profited substantially from the illegal industry. In
> coca growing areas, the guerrilla substituted for the State imposing
> a very authoritarian regime, defining and applying its own laws and
> regulations, and providing education, police, and civil justice to solve
> conflicts among the population. In exchange, the guerrillas charge coca
> production and cocaine export taxes. (p. 88)

According to journalistic estimates, roughly half of the FARC's $300 to $500 million annual income is believed to come from drug profits, mostly from cocaine, not heroin (Miller, 2002).

To counter the growing power of left-wing guerrillas, many paramilitary groups were formed during the 1980s and 1990s, often receiving generous support from drug kingpins. In 1997, most paramilitary groups coalesced into the United Self-Defense Forces of Colombia (known as the AUC, the acronym from the Spanish initials), which has also extensively profited from the drug industry through both extortion of producers and traffickers, and direct participation in the trade (Vargas, 2005:212–214). The AUC almost completely demobilized in 2005 and 2006, but a considerable fraction of its members continues to engage in drug trafficking (U.S. Department of State, Bureau for International Narcotics and Law Enforcement Affairs, 2007:112).

Weakness and Corruption of the Colombian Government

The Colombian state's capacity to enforce prohibitions against drug production and trafficking in large portions of the country is not only directly challenged by a variety of armed groups, but is also further limited by widespread drug-related corruption. Although Colombia's corruption problems precede the development of the drug trade and have broader scope in a tradition of patrimonial rule, the drug trade has greatly intensified the problem (Maingot, 2002; Thoumi, 2003). The most famous scandal, called *Process 8,000*, illustrates how deeply ingrained corruption is in Colombia. The 1994 electoral campaigns of President Ernesto Samper and of many members of the Colombian Congress were said to be financed by the Cali drug syndicate. Allegedly, the Attorney General's Office was able to collect incriminating documentation (including checks from companies of the Cali drug-trafficking syndicate) against approximately 120 current and former members of the Colombian Congress. However, less than two dozen of these were formally charged, only 14 were convicted, and—even among the latter group—several defendants were freed or merely placed under house arrest (Revista Semana, 1997) Drug traffickers seeking to avoid extradition have also been longstanding sources of a good deal of corruption. A few prominent figures, most notably Carlos Lehder, were extradited during the early days of the cocaine trade. During the 1990s, drug traffickers allegedly offered several members of Congress bribes to weaken the extradition law substantially. The administration of President Alvaro Uribe (2002 to the present) has finally begun extraditing large numbers of Colombian citizens charged with crimes in the United States. Between 2002 and late 2007, the Uribe administration extradited 581 individuals, whereas only 66 had been extradited during the previous 15 years (U.S. Department of State, Bureau for International Narcotics and Law Enforcement Affairs, 2008:124).

Even in 2007, despite the strengthening of the criminal justice system under the Uribe administration, these issues continue to reverberate in a long-running scandal that has again involved allegations of payments to members of Congress and of connections between some of them and the AUC. The current scandal has already led to the resignation of the foreign minister and the indictment of 11 members of Congress, two governors, three mayors, and other local officials (Forero, 2007a).

The corruption scandals have also affected other branches of government, particularly the police and the judiciary. Police and military officers and units have also—time and again—been found to be on the payroll of drug-trafficking organizations and paramilitary groups.[2] Prisons are also plagued by corruption problems. Up until the late 1990s, not only were the sentences for major drug traffickers very short (with the average time spent in prisons for drug offenses being 3 years), but the few convicted high-ranking drug traffickers and politicians could easily buy themselves privileged treatment through bribes. According to media sources, these offenders had "unrestricted access to cellular telephones, computers, fax, television and VHS...this allows them to manage their business from the jail" (Revista Semana, 1997).

It has been impossible to obtain information specifically on corruption related to the heroin industry. We offer this discussion of general drug-related corruption as indication that deep drug-related corruption may be an important factor contributing to the emergence of heroin production in Colombia.

The Emergence of the Opiate Industry

Colombia has no tradition of opiate consumption or production. However, starting in 1986, there were signs of small-scale planting of opium poppies in the departments of Tolima, Cundinamarca (where Bogotá is located) and, later on, Santander. Around 1990, law enforcement agencies began to see growth and geographic expansion, with an increasing number of poppy fields detected in the country's central highlands. Initially, not much attention was given to this because Colombia is only between 2 and 4 degrees north of the equator, and most poppy cultivation elsewhere in the world occurs 20 or more degrees north of the equator. Moreover, the altitude of the Colombian fields (between 1,700 and 2,700 meters above sea level) was also much greater than fields found in Asia or Mexico. By 1993, the Colombian National Police (CNP) reported some 6,500 hectares in 14 of the 32 departments or regions of the country, mostly concentrated in the central Andean region (Cauca, Huila, and Tolima). The communities included many in which the Colombian government has been historically weak, ceding power to local governments formed by indigenous communities and subsequently contested by the FARC and the AUC (Thoumi, 2003:91).

It took some time before the international community accepted Colombia's new role. Although the U.S. International Narcotics Control Strategy started reporting Colombian opium production in 1993, and the 1997 *World Drug Report* (UNDCP, 1997: 242) briefly mentioned Colombia's role in heroin production, it was not until 2003 that the country profile, prepared by the UNODC Country Office in Colombia (2003:11) reported that "...Colombia is a newcomer to the cultivation of opium poppy and heroin." That report noted that "[official estimates have] remained at 6,000 to 7,000 hectares. However, according to independent researchers, opium poppy cultivation may be considerably higher, in the range of 15,000 to 20,000 hectares." More recently, the UNODC (2007a) reports opiate production in Colombia starting in 1991 and yielding about 16 metric tons of opium in dry weight equivalent (table 3.1, chapter 3).

There is minimal literature on the early history of poppy cultivation and processing in Colombia. Apart from Ramírez (1993), Vargas and Barragán (1995), and Uribe (1997), information is primarily anecdotal. The data presented in the current study has been gathered by Sergio Uribe from multiple sources in an attempt to cover the 1991 to 2003 period as thoroughly as possible, with some updating for the period since. The project involved 35 interviews with a variety of participants in the market (officials, growers, and local traffickers) to supplement the available official statistics.

Opium Production and Processing

Much less is known about the details of opium production and processing in Colombia than about the corresponding activities in the much larger and older cocaine industry. However, the opium processing stage represents a peculiarity of the Colombian heroin industry, which distinguishes it from that of any other country. In Colombia, the intermediate product is opium latex—that is, raw or liquid opium—not opium gum, as in Asia and Mexico. Opium latex is not consumable.

Poppy Cultivation

Agencies of the U.S. and Colombian governments have at times had very different estimates of the area planted with poppies and their resulting production.[3] The estimates differ substantially in both level and year-to-year change. For example, in the year 2000, the U.S. estimate was 7,500 hectares of poppy harvested. In that same year, one Colombian agency estimated the figure at 6,500 hectares and another at 13,400 hectares. Four characteristics of Colombian production explain the difficulties of developing estimates:

1. The growing season is not well defined. Poppy is cultivated year-round and, although the rainy season is important, it does not appear to be a determinant of farmer behavior.
2. As a consequence of government eradication efforts, the size of fields has been reduced over time, which has made aerial detection and/or remote sensing techniques more difficult; fields are smaller than those used to grow coca.
3. Colombia's climate tends to keep a more or less permanent cloud cover over the regions where most of the poppy fields are located. The lush forest makes satellite detection even more difficult.

4. Growing cycles in Colombia vary among regions from 4 to 7 months, according to the altitude above sea level and the climate during the growing season. This means that on some plots of land, a grower can cultivate and harvest two crops during a 12-month period.

The regions where poppy growers are concentrated have not changed much since the early 1990s. Figure 8.1, which dates from 2002, shows the areas where most poppy fields were found at the beginning of the 21st century.[4]

Processing Latex

The fact that there is no commercial value for opium latex, combined with factors such as the weather (frequent rains and high humidity), have shaped the harvest and trade of raw opium. The collection protocols for liquid latex or raw opium are different from those in Southeast Asia. Rather than the liquid being allowed to dry on the capsules, it is collected 5 to 10 minutes after the capsule has been scored. This liquid is transferred to thin plastic bags and is sold by weight. The latex is contracted for in advance by buyers who have access to the growing regions and who, if necessary, pay a small fee to the local guerilla and/or paramilitary groups. This latex is then processed into morphine base by a local "cook" (who is not a professional chemist). During the early to mid 1990s, there were reports of farmers cheating buyers by diluting latex to increase its weight. As a consequence, buyers now process the latex on the farm, allowing determination of the purity of the latex based on the amount of morphine base. This arrangement also reduces risk, because latex is much bulkier and easier to detect than morphine (discussed later).

The Colombian police have never identified labs for the conversion of latex to morphine. All but one of the few labs shut down—no more than 40 between 1998 and 2002—were set up for processing morphine into heroin rather than latex into morphine. Lab seizure data suggest that heroin labs in Colombia are small operations, because most of the traffic is run by small organizations (often family businesses, according to the police). The small numbers seized indicate that these labs are either very mobile, very small, or both. Most of the lab seizures are in zones close to the growing areas: Cesar Cauca, Valle, Risaralda, and, Guajira. None of the labs found in these departments were located in large cities.[5]

Estimating yields of latex per hectare is even more complex than estimating the area under cultivation. The first question is how many harvests are achieved each year. Up until the mid 1990s, the U.S. government (for instance, National Narcotics Intelligence Consumers Committee [NNIC], 1997) and some CNP reports assumed three harvests. Now the literature reports a consensus that the average number of annual crops of a poppy field in Colombia is two.

Several estimates of latex yields per hectare can be found in different reports published since the early 1990s. There has also been considerable

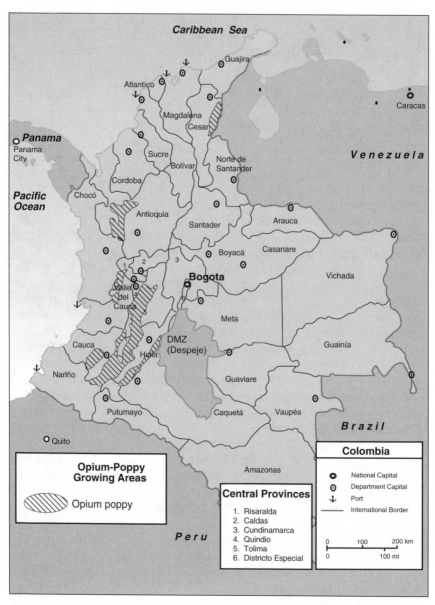

Figure 8.1 Opium cultivation areas in Colombia at the start of the 21st century.
Source: DEA (2002c).
Note: The DMZ was a 50,000 square kilometer demilitarized zone. The Colombian government granted the zone to the FARC from November 1998 to February 2002; it no longer exists.

uncertainty about the yield of heroin from a kilogram of latex. A 1994 study (Uribe, 1997), using data from personal interviews, estimated that the conversion rate was probably between 11.5 and 20 kilos of latex per kilo of market-grade morphine, depending on the region of the country. Prior to 2001 the U.S. government appeared to assume that Colombia produced opium gum just as in Asia, and thus used a conversion rate of 10 (U.S. Department of State, Bureau for International Narcotics and Law Enforcement Affairs, 2000). Operation Breakthrough, conducted by the DEA in 2001 (Guevara, 2002), estimated the conversion rate at 24 kilograms. In 2003, the Departamento Administrativo de Estadístic, Dirección de Cuentas Nacionales (DANE) study reviewed the available data and estimated a new conversion rate of 28 kilograms. The sources interviewed for this study reported that buyers operate on ratios of between 25 and 28 kilos of latex per kilo of morphine.

Combining the estimates of latex per hectare and kilos of latex for a kilo of heroin, the most widely accepted estimate of the heroin yield per hectare comes from the UNODC Country Office in Colombia (2003:14), which in its 2003 Colombia country profile states: "On average, one hectare of opium poppy will produce 1.29 kilogram of heroin per year." However there is no documentation of the basis for these yield estimates. An unpublished 2005 report by Abt Associates (a research organization working for a U.S. government interagency group; 2005) developed an estimate of 2.31 kilograms of heroin per hectare under cultivation. This variation is indicative of the uncertainty surrounding the published estimates.[6] Table 8.1 contrasts Colombia's production estimates as reported to the UNODC[7] with those provided by the U.S. State Department. Again the Colombian estimates, available since 2000, differ in both level and year-to-year change. At the end of this chapter we return to the implications of uncertainty about Colombian heroin production.

Prices from Latex to Heroin

There are no systematic data sources on farm-gate prices for latex over time; data are available for just a few areas and vary from one growing area to the next. This may reflect differences in the charges set by local militia and/or in the market structure at the local level.

Some data for 1998 to 2003 was furnished by the CNP and are presented in the first two columns of table 8.2. They show prices falling in terms of dollar value, during a period in which the Colombian peso fell substantially against the dollar; the price in local currency fluctuated throughout 1998 to 2003.

A series of interviews with local PLANTE (alternative development program) coordinators[8] was undertaken during 2004. These interviews showed that prices have been dropping since poppy production began. For example, in Tolima, the largest growing area in the country, prices fluctuated between 1,200 and 2,000 Colombian pesos per gram during the early 1990s

Table 8.1

Potential heroin production as estimated by the Colombian government/the UNODC and the U.S. State Department (measured in metric tons) from 1994 to 2006.

	1994	1995	1996	1997	1998	1999	2000	2001	2002	2003	2004	2005	2006
Colombian government[*]	6.7	7.1	6.7	9.0	10.0	8.8	8.0	8.0	7.6	7.6	5.6	2.8	1.3
U.S. State Department[†]	NA	NA	NA	NA	NA	NA	8.7	11.4	8.5	7.8	3.8	NA	4.6

[*]Project estimates use data from the UNODC (2005d, 2007a).
[†]Project estimates use data from the U.S. Department of State, Bureau of International Narcotics and Law Enforcement Affairs (2008).

Table 8.2
Price of latex, morphine, and heroin in Colombian pesos and U.S. dollars per kilogram.

Year	Latex (Col$)	Latex (US$)	Morphine (Col$)	Morphine (US$)	Heroin (Col$)	Heroin (US$)
1998	600,000	423	16,000,000	11.285	25,000,000	17.632
1999	750,000	439	18,000,000	10.539	26,000,000	15.223
2000	700,000	341	15,000,000	7.312	25,000,000	12.186
2001	650,000	287	14,000,000	6.194	24,000,000	10.619
2002	900,000	349	16,500,000	6.400	26,000,000	10.085
2003	800,000	283	14,500,000	5.139	22,000,000	7.797

Source: Authors' calculation based on CNP (2004) using Banco de la Republica exchange rates downloaded from www.banrep.gov.co/series. Accessed June 2004.

(1991–1994). From late 1994 through 1998, prices varied between 500 and 800 pesos per gram; after 1998, they dipped to between 400 and 600 pesos per gram. This drop has been even greater in U.S. dollars, because the devaluation of the peso was substantial during this period until about 2000, reflecting high rates of domestic inflation in Colombia.

In its 2003 study, DANE estimated the value of the opium latex harvest at $65.5 million dollars. If costs are subtracted from the total sales estimated in the DANE data (a rough approximation of the costs can be calculated from the same study), this would give a net income, to farmers, of about $30 million—a miniscule figure compared with rural earnings of $15 billion.[9] The value of latex production in 2000 was only about 10% that of cocaine base at the farm level (DANE, 2003). This may reflect the fact that Colombian poppy farmers do not process latex in-farm, whereas more than 95% of coca farmers are estimated to process the leaf onsite, giving more value added to their product. In coca, this could add about 25% to the farmers' income, although estimates vary among authors (Uribe, 2004). There are many reasons why latex is not processed by farmers, but the most important may be lack of skill and buyer concerns about product integrity.

Table 8.2 provides data on domestic prices of the three broad levels of the market in Colombia. It shows some important inconsistencies in the relationship between the price of the raw materials and the price of the finished product. Using the DANE conversion rate of 28 kilos of latex per kilo of morphine along with the police data, the inputs for morphine cost more ($28 \times 800 = 22,400$) than the morphine fetches in the market (14,500). There are no data on the purity of the finished product, however, so it may be that the prices of morphine or heroin do not correspond to very high levels of purity. Most persons interviewed for this study believe the domestic price has remained stable, in pesos, in the years up to 2004.

The Industry Players and Their Relationships

According to the informants interviewed in the Tolima and Huila departments, two arrangements regulate the relationships between farmers and their
financiers and/or traffickers. Known as *consorcio* and *plante* systems, these
arrangements have been instrumental to the spread of opium poppy cultivation in Colombia. As a result of the absence of other empirical studies on the
topic, we do not know to what extent these arrangements are also in place in
other opium poppy-growing areas in Colombia.

The *Consorcio* and *Plante* Systems

In both Tolima and Huila, the initial expansion of opium poppy cultivation
was directed by criminal enterprises, known today as *consorcios* in northern
Tolima, where they are still active. The *consorcios* are formed by small, independent, and sometimes family-based groups that collect morphine base from
the farmers and then sell it to other traffickers or process it into heroin themselves. The *consorcios* first identify rural communities known as *veredas*[10] with
suitable fields and then recruit at least 25 to 30 farmers willing to grow opium
poppy, usually by establishing connections with the local leaders. Because
guerrilla and paramilitary groups were, at least until 2002 (Hutchinson, 2002),
present in the two regions, the *consorcios* have to buy their cooperation by paying a "protection" tax. If the "tax" is not paid, the dominant armed group may
prevent the *consorcio* from operating in the region.

Our research on the *consorcio* still operating in northern Tolima in 2004
suggests that there are two ways in which farmers may associate with a *consorcio*. The first possibility is to allocate or rent a plot of land to the *consorcio*.
Under this system, the farmer gets paid for the land and is at times hired to
work in the poppy field, whereas employees of the *consorcio* provide technical
assistance during the key production phases. A second option for the farmer is
to rent out the entire farm and leave, so as to be able to deny association with
the activity while reaping the benefits.[11]

Consorcios constitute well-articulated mini monopolies. For each *vereda*,
there is a local representative who keeps contact with the traffickers located in
a nearby city and sets the production targets. The *consorcios* in the northern
Tolima region, for example, fix for each farm a minimum amount of land to
be dedicated to growing poppy, usually half a hectare, and set a minimum
latex yield depending on the geography of the field.[12] If these goals are not
met, payment will be restricted to the amount produced, and the farmer will
not be invited to participate in the next harvest.[13]

The local representatives of the *consorcios* regularly visit the fields financed
by the organization to determine the type of fungicides, insecticides, and fertilizers to be used. During the harvest, the local representatives visit the fields
on a daily basis and weigh the latex collected, maintaining strict control and

supervision. In northern Tolima, the *consorcios* go as far as to limit the hours at which latex may be collected (for example, 6 to 9 AM and 4 to 6 PM), to protect the plants and their own investment. If the fields are sprayed by the government, the *consorcios* promptly cover all costs associated with replanting the fields, providing new seeds and eventually additional capital.

The second method of financing poppy fields is the *plante* system. Under this system, a local merchant and/or trafficker finances farmers who wish to grow poppy. The financial backing consists of both money and credit for the grower at a local store, providing access to the basic inputs for the field. In some cases the investors also finance groceries for the farmer's family. In turn, the farmer dedicates a field to growing poppy and takes care of the crop. The harvest is divided between the growers and the financial backer according to proportions to be negotiated on an individual basis. This type of operation is known to exist in southern Tolima and Huila.

A few farmers, at least among the indigenous population in Cauca, have also attempted to operate independently; however, this option is ridden with risks and difficulties. "Independent" growers are more likely to be exploited by both buyers and armed groups, which increasingly appear to be turning more into local warlords with an economic rather than a political agenda. Even if they do not become victims of open exploitation, "independent" farmers face a formidable task when negotiating one-on-one with both the buyers and the armed groups.

Guerrilla and Paramilitary Groups

The areas where poppy is grown are not strongholds of either the guerrilla or paramilitary groups. Nonetheless, at least one of these groups is (or, in the case of the AUC, was) actively present in most growing areas, although their range of activities may be occasionally restricted by the eradication campaigns of the Colombian government and downturns in the fight against another armed group.

A lot is known about the role played by guerrilla and paramilitary groups in the cocaine industry (e.g., Vargas, 2005); much less is known about their functions in the heroin industry. Whenever possible, guerrilla groups require buyers to pay a per-kilo tax on latex purchased from the farmers and they also extract protection money from both poppy growers and local traffickers. In some cases, it has been reported that these groups also charge for the privilege of bringing into a region both precursors and essential inputs (fungicides, fertilizers, and insecticides), suggesting that they have considerable power. Whether armed groups provide some real service for the money they extract is unclear. Several sources consulted for this study suggest that the local armed groups tend to play the role of referees in the agreement between growers, on the one hand, and the *consorcio* and investors of the *plante* system, on the other. They seek to ensure that the farmers meet their minimum production quotas, supervise commitments of both parties, and ensure that the inputs are supplied and that basic needs of the growers are met.[14] Other observers characterize the contemporary action of armed groups as merely parasitic, with no remnants of "social awareness" (Vargas, 2005:212).

Whatever the case, growers are dependent on these "local authorities," because their harvest is worth nothing if they cannot sell it, and buyers cannot access the poppy-growing areas if they do not have the authorization of armed groups. The *consorcios* also seek agreements with armed groups to enforce their local monopolies and thus keep other purchasers out of their growing areas. Both the farmers and the investors linked by a *plante* agreement as well as the few farmers who operate independently, such as the indigenous population in Cauca, are also dependent on armed groups, who must grant potential buyers access to their region.

There are unconfirmed reports that in regions such as southern Nariño, both the *consorcio* and *plante* systems have been replaced by the FARC, who work in much the same way as a *consorcio*.

Links with Cocaine-Trafficking Organizations

When Colombian heroin traffic began in the early 1990s, it seems to have been closely linked to the cocaine trade (Vargas, 1995). Despite the early links between the cocaine and the heroin trade, the government's focus on cocaine may well explain why the heroin traffickers were largely untouched during the 1990s. Indeed, the situation was such that the CNP did not even have the precursor chemicals to test seizures for heroin. In addition, heroin shipments at that time were so small that they could easily slip by at airports. The "invisibility" of heroin trafficking organizations has been further enhanced by the fact that they have largely remained small, low profile, and family oriented as opposed to the large and visible cocaine organizations that emerged in Cali, Medellin, Bogotá, and other cities. The DEA also routinely refers to heroin-trafficking groups as small (e.g., Guevara, 2002).

A close and collaborative relation between Colombian and Mexican Mafias goes back to the late 1980s.[15] Colombian cocaine exports traveled primarily through the Caribbean until that time, when the United States aimed intense interdiction against those routes. This forced Colombians to look for alternatives to reroute their shipments. By the 1990s, Colombian traffickers had become almost completely dependent on Mexico. This made the Mexicans a natural ally at the time when the Colombians entered the heroin trade. Because the Mexican heroin producers manufactured mostly "black tar" heroin, it has been suggested that the Colombians opted for heroin hydrochloride (HCL) to avoid competing. The advantage of HCL was obvious, especially at a moment when the HIV/AIDS epidemic and prevention campaigns were in full swing. Black tar heroin is usually injected, whereas HCL heroin is usually snorted. Colombian heroin dominates the eastern United States, whereas Mexican heroin dominates west of the Mississippi. It is generally inferred that this is the result of a market-sharing agreement, but that—like the claim that the Colombians chose a different product to avoid competition—is no more than a logical inference.

Control Efforts

With the support of the United States, the Colombian government has, during the past few years, greatly intensified efforts to reduce drug production and trafficking.

Eradication

The cultivation estimates discussed earlier (the net number of hectares harvested) are the result of subtracting the hectares eradicated from total cultivation. United States and Colombian authorities differ on the number of hectares eradicated. Additionally, because poppy is a short-term crop, a field sprayed one day may well be replanted within weeks. If eradicators do not monitor the fields every 2 or 3 months, farmers may well get their harvest to market. This situation is unique to Colombia, where most growing areas can

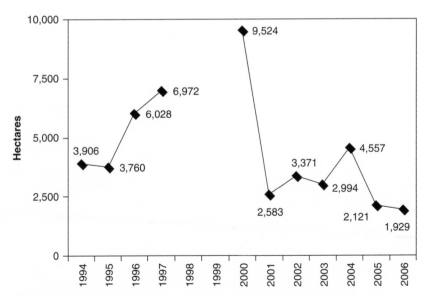

Figure 8.2 Number of hectares of poppy reported as eradicated in Colombia, 1994–2006.
Source: U.S. State Department, Bureau of International Narcotics and Law Enforcement Affairs (2007:120).

generate more than one harvest per year, and makes it very difficult to create an inventory of eradication. Figure 8.2 presents the data reported on these eradication efforts in the country by the U.S. State Department.

Opiate Seizures

Table 8.3 presents seizure data as reported by the Colombian government to the UN drug office from 1993 onward. The three time series for latex,[16] morphine, and heroin show different trends. Although latex and morphine seizures have remained fairly low (except for two peaks in the case of latex in 1993 and 2005), heroin seizures grew steadily through the 1990s to reach a peak of 787 kilograms in 2001. Since then, they have remained fairly stable. In heroin equivalents, total seizures were at their highest at 922 kilograms in 2005, the most recent year for which data are available.

Seizures of latex, usually being transported within each department from growing areas to local processing centers or to local markets, typically net about 10 kilos each. Seizures of latex are few; except for the 2005 spike, since 2000 more than 100 kilos of latex were seized only in 2002, whereas production estimates are between 126,000 and 260,000 kilos. At a national level, the product transported to the final refining installations is morphine, in quantities of 1 or 2 kilos. The small size of the consignments may reflect the types of

Table 8.3
Opium latex, morphine, and heroin seized (in kilograms), 1993–2005.

Year	Latex	Morphine	Heroin	Total (heroin equivalent)
1993	281.3	10.6	44.3	66.6
1994	128.2	85.8	95.4	186.5
1995	144.2	290.2	145.0	441.2
1996	102.8	94.1	80.8	179.2
1997	121.6	87.1	129.7	221.9
1998	100.0	79.1	239.2	322.5
1999	29.2	154.0	514.6	669.8
2000	16.6	107.9	567.2	675.8
2001	3.7	47.4	787.6	835.2
2002	110.3	20.3	776.9	801.8
2003	27.2	78.2	628.8	708.1
2004	57.4	39.3	766.7	808.4
2005	1,623.0	93.0	761.1	921.7

Note: Latex is converted to heroin equivalent at the rate of 28 to 1.
Source: UNODCCP, 2002c; UNODC, 2007b.

installations used to process heroin rather than the effort to avoid internal interdiction.

International shipments are usually in small bundles. Although cocaine is shipped by a wide variety of methods and, in later years, increasingly by conventional cargo (often in loads of hundreds of kilograms), data show that Colombian heroin mostly moves in small shipments. In Colombia, persons who transport heroin are referred to as *mules* or *human couriers,* and they transport (on average) between 750 grams and 1.25 kilograms of the drug at a time. This method has become increasingly popular, especially for small organizations with good connections in the final marketplace, in most cases the United States (U.S. Department of State, Bureau for International Narcotics and Law Enforcement Affairs, 2000).

Reflecting this smuggling technique, most consignments of heroin are seized at Bogotá's El Dorado International Airport and at other air terminals, but they are generally small, ranging from 500 grams to 3 kilograms. The largest airport seizure was 7 kilograms (Ministerio del Interior y de Justicia, DNE, 2002:68). The two largest seizures, each of 80 kilograms, took place at sea in 2002 and 2004 (Uribe, 2004).[17] Of the heroin seizures reported in 2002, 38% involved human couriers, more than any other modality. The U.S. market accounts for almost all the Colombian production, 85% according to the CNP (Uribe, 2004). It is thought that small amounts of Colombian heroin find their way to European markets, yet there is little evidence of a "Colombian connection." It is unlikely that the use of human ingestion is very popular for European traffic, because of the greater time the courier has to travel.[18]

In 2002, seizures of approximately 800 kilograms represented only about 10% of Colombian production. Given that seizures are less than 100% pure, the share of total product seized by Colombian authorities is even less. A simple calculation suggests the challenge of the interdictors' task. Assume that Colombia shipped 8 metric tons to the United States in 2002.[19] On an average day, traffickers would have to deliver only 22 kilos of heroin. This amount can be easily shipped via 22 airline passengers, each of whom has swallowed a kilo of capsules. If approximately 1,800 passengers travel by air to the United States from Colombian cities each day,[20] this would require that only about 1% of passengers be smugglers.

Drug interdiction presents great difficulties generally (Reuter et al., 1988). Traffickers can easily switch from one trafficking method and route to another, involving either air or sea routes and, depending on the size of the country, law enforcement agencies may have to monitor and control millions of square kilometers. Colombia is the only country in South America with a coastline both on the Atlantic and the Pacific oceans. Additionally, the country shares borders with five nations: to the south with Peru and Ecuador, to the north with Panama (as well as sea borders with other central American nations, both in the Caribbean Sea and the Pacific Ocean, and several Caribbean island nations), and to the east with Venezuela and Brazil. These extensive sea and land borders have made Colombia a paradise for contraband runners. Black market activities have been traditional in certain areas of the country since the 1950s.[21]

Finally, substantial quantities of precursor chemicals are seized in Colombia. Although controls of the domestic production and registered imports are thought to be adequate, there appear to be large flows of contraband from Ecuador, Brazil, and Venezuela.

Consumption

There is some domestic heroin consumption in Colombia, but it remains a fairly small problem. One indication is the paucity of data. We offer, here, the few indicators that are available.

National drug use surveys have been conducted three times in Colombia, most recently in 2001. For the first time enough respondents reported heroin use that it was included in the results. Table 8.4 shows the data on heroin, comparing it with marijuana, the most widely used illegal substance, and cocaine.

These data suggest that heroin remained a modest problem in Colombia at the beginning of the century, about 7 years after domestic production became established. However, the data also suggest that the problem is growing. For example, the incidence rate of 3.7 per 1,000 among males age 12 to 60 is higher than in recent United States surveys (Office of Applied Studies, 2006[22]). Moreover, household surveys substantially underestimate rates of chronic heroin use. Studies of HIV in Colombia also reveal the growth of a heroin-injecting population in the major cities (Perez-Gomez, personal communication). The heroin consumption problem may thus worsen substantially in the coming years.

Table 8.4
Prevalence (Prev.) and incidence of major illegal drugs by gender, age 12 to 60, 2001 (percent).

Substances	Life Prev.		Last Year Prev.		Last Month Prev.		Incidence	
	Male	Female	Male	Female	Male	Female	Male	Female
Marijuana	11.52	6.50	8.00	4.5	3.40	1.49	3.94	2.80
Cocaine	6.28	2.88	4.18	1.90	1.53	0.52	2.37	1.30
Heroin	1.43	0.69	0.82	0.35	0.23	0.06	0.37	0.20

Source: Perez-Gomez, 2005:table 4.

Concluding Remarks

Colombia's opiate industry emerged rapidly in the early 1990s but did not expand much after the mid 1990s. As elsewhere, some of the factors that contributed to the development of the industry in Colombia are natural and socioeconomic, such as acceptable geographic and climatic conditions, and the limited options available for small farmers in the countryside. As seen also in the cases of Afghanistan and Burma, however (chapter 6), these factors are not sufficient to explain why Colombia is the only new country to enter the illicit heroin industry as a producer since the 1970s. Three other factors are important: (1) the preexisting cocaine industry, and particularly the existence of established drug-smuggling networks for the United States; (2) the guerrilla and paramilitary groups' effective control over large parts of the country; and (3) the resulting weakness of the Colombian government, which is further intensified by widespread corruption. In this respect it is worth noting that Colombia is a very high-cost producer. The domestic wholesale price of heroin, around $10,000 in 2002, was much higher than the export price from Afghanistan or Burma. This heroin was competitive on the U.S. market because smuggling costs were presumably much lower.

The U.S. government has estimated a sharp decline in the levels of Colombian heroin production since 2001, when it reached a high of 11.4 metric tons (see table 8.1). In 2004, the estimate was exactly one third of that: 3.8 metric tons (U.S. Department of State, Bureau for International Narcotics and Law Enforcement Affairs, 2008:128). No estimate was provided for 2005, because cloud cover prevented effective surveillance. For 2006, the U.S. estimate was 4.6 metric tons—still well below the levels near the turn of the century. The Colombian government's estimates, as reported in the UNODC *World Drug Report* (UNODC, 2007a: 40) are quite different (see table 8.1). They are much higher from 2002 to 2004, but then they decline to a lower level than the U.S. estimates—only 1.4 metric tons in 2006 compared with the U.S. estimate of 4.6 metric tons.

There are two reasons for skepticism about a very large drop in production. First, reported opiate seizures actually increased between 2001 (835 kilograms) and 2005 (922 kilograms). Second, in 2008, the State Department reported that Colombia "remains the primary source of heroin used east of the Mississippi River" (U.S. Department of State, Bureau for International Narcotics and Law Enforcement Affairs, 2008:120). The latter statement cannot be translated into a quantity figure, because there are no estimates of the quantity consumed in specific regions of the country. Moreover, "east of the Mississippi" should be treated as indicative rather than precise. However, as also addressed in chapter 5, it seems unlikely that Colombia, which by U.S. estimates could have exported no more than about 3.6 metric tons of heroin in 2006, net of seizures, could be the primary source for half the U.S. market. The most recent official estimate of U.S. consumption was 13.3 metric tons (ONDCP, 2001:4, table 2).

Yet another reason for some skepticism about this claim of a decline is that estimates of drug cultivation and production have, from time to time, been the subject of large revisions. For example, the United States increased its estimates of the efficiency of Colombian cocaine processing from 45% to 69% in 2001; this led to large increases in estimated Colombian cocaine production. The annual INCSR of the Department of State (e.g., U.S. Department of State, Bureau for International Narcotics and Law Enforcement Affairs, 2007) acknowledges the many sources of uncertainty each year, without attempting to quantify them.

However, our interviews with government officials in the United States suggest that they do believe the decline is real. Both the Colombian and U.S. governments suggest that the decline is the result of effective spraying and interdiction efforts. The fact that export-level heroin prices in Colombia have not risen suggests that the decline is unlikely to be solely the result of eradication and interdiction. It may be that shifts in other sources of supply to the United States have also played a role, if in fact production has declined.

Finally, we note that the emergence of Colombian heroin production is informative about what risk factors might lead to new countries entering the opiate trade. The fact that Colombia had no prior opiate production or consumption shows that the industry can truly develop de novo in a nation. Even more striking, the production developed in areas quite different, by altitude and latitude, from those in Asia and Mexico, and the intermediate product is latex rather than opium gum. Although we note again the lack of any specific information about the relationship between cocaine smugglers on the one hand and either the current heroin smugglers or the original progenitors of the poppy-growing and -processing industry on the other, the principal risk factor for Colombia seems to have been the existence of low-cost smuggling capacity to the United States. The existence of substantial areas in which government power was contested by effective quasi-governments was also a risk factor.

9

Tajikistan

The Rise of a Narco-State

(with Irina Rabkov)

Introduction

Since the collapse of the Soviet Union in 1991, Tajikistan has experienced an extraordinary and devastating expansion of opiate trafficking and consumption, and a near-simultaneous collapse of its legitimate economy.[1] Until the mid 1990s, heroin was virtually unknown in the country and other opiates were not major sources of concern; however, in less than a decade, Tajikistan has become a key transit country for Afghan opiates bound north- and westward, and a major heroin consumer.

Tajikistan now rivals Afghanistan for the unenviable title of the country most dependent on the illicit drug industry. Opiate entrepreneurs, their employees, and the government officials who support and protect them have become dependent on the revenues of the illicit drug trade. Dependency likely extends well into their respective communities. As shown in appendix C, it is unlikely that opiate trafficking adds less than 30% to the recorded GDP.[2] The opiate trade is so important economically that it is central to the political system, which even a decade later is still recovering from 5 years of bloody civil war.

Indeed, the worrying hypothesis this chapter supports is that, since the mid 1990s, Tajikistan has effectively become a "narco-state," in which leaders of the most powerful trafficking groups occupy high-ranking government positions and misuse state structures for their own illicit businesses. Coupled with the ineffectiveness of law enforcement agencies, this superimposition has led to the emergence and consolidation of relatively large and integrated drug-trafficking enterprises controlling an increasing share of the drug-trafficking market—a rare event in the illicit drug industry, signaling lax or non-enforcement of prohibitions against production and trafficking, which we discuss in detail in chapter 10.[3]

Although being exceptional for its pace and intensity, Tajikistan's experience also allows us to investigate the factors determining which countries actually become traffickers. It clearly illustrates that changes for the worse can occur with tremendous rapidity and magnitude, rarely matched by changes for the better. Tajikistan's case is also exemplary of the policy dilemmas faced by impoverished countries in which opium production or, more rarely, as in Tajikistan, opiate trafficking, becomes an entrenched activity.

The Expansion of the Illicit Opiate Industry: Explanatory Factors

Several interrelated geopolitical factors help explain the exceptional expansion of the illicit opiate industry in Tajikistan since the early 1990s. Most prominent among them are geographic proximity and ethnic ties with Afghanistan as well as the Tajik diasporas in both Afghanistan and Russia, a country that has, since the mid 1990s, become the world's third-largest opiate market. Other, more specific socioeconomic, political, and cultural factors—and in particular the implosion of the state during the 1992–1997 civil war and the persistent weakness and corruption of the resurgent state institutions—have converged to give Tajikistan a competitive advantage vis-à-vis other former Soviet republics neighboring Afghanistan. The consequences for the nation have been devastating.

Geographic Proximity and Ethnic Ties with Afghanistan

The most obvious factor of note is Tajikistan's geographic proximity to Afghanistan, the world's largest supplier of illicit opiates. Tajikistan's southern edge and Afghanistan's northern edge abut, creating a porous border of more than 1,200 kilometers. The development of illicit opiate exchanges between the two countries was also facilitated by the common ethnic identities and clan ties of the people, broadly known as "Tajik," living on the two sides of the Tajik–Afghan border on the river Panj (Centlivres and Centlivres-Demont, 1998).

Migration as a Source of Trafficking Links

Migration flows represent another crucial factor in Tajikistan's emergence as the dominant channel for Afghan heroin bound to other Commonwealth of Independent States (CIS) countries and especially to Russia. Between 1992 and 1999, more than 600,000 people left Tajikistan (UNDP, 2000:18). At least 60,000 of those immigrants fled into Afghanistan, a flow that not only revived common ethnic identities and clan ties but also created the basis for future transactions in opiates and other illicit commodities, particularly when most of them returned to Tajikistan in the mid 1990s (DCA, 2004:16).

At the other end of the supply chain, the consolidation of Tajikistan's role as a key transit country for Afghan heroin has been favored by the growth of a large immigrant population in Russia, the principal destination of its heroin exports. It is estimated that more than 800,000 Tajiks go back and forth between Tajikistan and Russia—about one third of Tajikistan's labor force. As former Soviet citizens, most of the Tajik citizens living in or regularly visiting Russia speak fluent Russian, and many have either a Russian passport or residence permit. Despite this, their integration often fails and many immigrants live in terrible conditions; some turn to drug courier services and prostitution for income (International Organisation for Migration [IOM], 2001; Radio Free Europe/ Radio Liberty Transcaucasia and Central Asia Newsline [RFE/RL] 2003).

Tajikistan's opportunity was created by the dramatic growth of heroin demand in many countries of the former Soviet Union since its collapse in 1991. Russia, a minor consumption market in 1995, became one of the largest in the world by 2000 and today has one of the world's highest prevalence rates of opiate use (Paoli, 2005; UNODC, 2005d:55; chapter 3, this volume). Above-average rates of heroin consumption can also be found in most Central Asian republics and eastern European countries, which are also to a large extent serviced by Afghan opiates smuggled through Tajikistan (UNODC, 2004:389–391).

The Civil War and Its Economic Aftermath

The devastation of the Tajik legitimate economy, which followed the implosion of the Soviet Union in 1991 and the subsequent civil war in Tajikistan, provided strong incentives to get involved in the illicit opiate industry. Although it reached its height in 1992, the conflict lasted 5 years, claiming 50,000 lives and displacing almost one fifth of the country's total population of six million. As a result of the war, natural calamities, and the collapse of economic relations with former Soviet republics, Tajikistan's GDP was 57% lower in 1998 than in 1990. With a per capita GDP of only $180, it had then—as it has now—the lowest per capita GDP of all the countries belonging to the CIS.[4] Despite considerable growth since 1997, more than 80% of the country's population still lives below the poverty line and Tajikistan remains one of the poorest countries in the world (World Bank, 2004a). In 2006, Tajikistan's per capita GDP was still only about $290 valued at the official exchange rate and $1,300 valued in terms of purchasing power parity (CIA, 2007). Given the enduring economic difficulties that Tajikistan's residents face, the temptation to become involved in narcotics-related transactions likely remains strong for many.

State Failure and the Rise of Warlords

The civil war also prompted a complete state failure, thus further enhancing Tajikistan's advantage in becoming a key transit country for Afghan opiates.

According to Kirill Nourzhanov (2005:117), the Tajikistan of 1992 resembled the Lebanon of 1975, where "the government does not exist, and whatever part of it exists has no authority, and whoever has authority it is not the government" (see also Zviagelskaya, 1997). Since then, the government of Emomali Rakhmonov, who was elected chairman of the Supreme Soviet in late 1992 and president of Tajikistan 2 years later, has made considerable progress in restoring statehood and reestablishing central authority. However, government personnel and operational procedures are still patrimonial and dominated by interests of a particular regional elite and its changing allies, which leaves them prey to corruption and infiltration by drug traffickers (ICG, 2004b; Nourzhanov, 2005). Indeed, as we show later, circumstantial evidence suggests that several high-level politicians and state officials head (or have headed) some of the country's largest drug-trafficking groups.

Despite being formally included in government structures, some of these civil servants- and politicians-cum-traffickers virtually remain warlords, disposing of their more or less private armies and fiefdoms. The warlords' power is itself a product of the civil war. This not merely entailed an armed struggle between progovernment (former Communist) forces and Islamist and prodemocracy groups, but was also a conflict between subethnic groups of the Tajiks, which represented different regions of the country. The elites and people of Kulob and Gharm, in the south and center of the country, were protagonists of the confrontations, representing the government and the opposition, respectively. Kulobis and Gharmis were respectively aided by ethnic Uzbeks and Hissoris from western Tajikistan, and Pamiris from the eastern region of Gorno Badakhshan (fig. 9.1) (Shirazi, 1997; Nourzhanov, 2005).[5]

As the spiral of internal violence unfolded, a variety of more or less ideologically inspired armed groups emerged, which fought each other. Some were

Figure 9.1 Map of Tajikistan.
Source: CIA (2007) modified to include borders of regions.

based on patronage and consanguineal networks, reviving the traditional custom of blood feud; others resulted from the splitting up of the former Soviet police and military forces; others were veritable criminal gangs, which had engaged in illicit entrepreneurial activities and extortion since the 1980s. By the end of 1992, the real power was in the hands of warlords in most Tajik regions, and they maintained considerable influence over the government restored in late 1992. Rakhmonov's cabinet initially controlled only 40% of the country's territory and had to fight the now-united opposition. Its only available military force was the 20,000 combatants of the People's Front of Tajikistan, which was under the warlords' command.

Other warlords, this time from the Gharm and Badakhshan regions, were included in the government when Rakhmonov signed a peace agreement with the United Tajik Opposition in 1997. Under the terms of the General Agreement on the Establishment of Peace and National Accord, which was brokered by the United Nations, former opposition leaders were integrated into the government, receiving 30% of all government positions, and their militias became part of the Tajik army and law enforcement agencies.

The Problem of Border Control

For much of the 1990s, the Tajik state agencies were unable to protect the country borders and to prevent any type of smuggling, including that of opiates (Pasotti, 1997; Zelitchenko, 1999, 2004). Although they have made considerable progress since the start of the 21st century, substantial problems still remain. As noted in the 2003 INCSR (U.S. Department of State, Bureau of International Narcotics and Law Enforcement Affairs, 2004:462), "the Pyanj river, which forms part of Tajikistan's border with opium-producing Afghanistan, is thinly guarded, and difficult to patrol. It is easily crossed without inspection at a number of points" (see also McDermott, 2002).

A 1993 agreement with Russia entrusted defense of the 1,200-kilometer-long border with Afghanistan to the Russian Border Forces (RBF).[6] They operated for more than a decade in Tajikistan with the support of Russia's 201st Motorized Rifle Division. Tajik troops took over complete control of the border only in July 2005 (Maitra, 2005). The Tajik forces are considered "unequal to the task" by most observers (ICG, 2004b:17–18; U.S. Department of State, Bureau of International Narcotics and Law Enforcement Affairs, 2005:502), and their takeover has had a negative impact on drug interdiction efforts: Heroin seizures decreased by half between 2004 and 2005 (table 9.1). In truth, the RBF also lacked sufficient human and technical means to patrol the long Tajik–Afghan border effectively. During the civil war, many units primarily had to defend themselves from the rioting population, as they supported the Tajik government in their fight against the opposition fighters, and to finance their own living, because their salary was not regularly paid (Atkin, 1997; Machmadiev, 2003).

Given their meager salaries, RBF guards were prey to corruption and, given their inadequate resources and the traffickers' few restraints in using

Table 9.1
Opiates seized in Tajikistan (in kilograms), 1991–2005.

Year	Opium	Heroin
1991	1.9	—
1992	6.7	—
1993	37.9	—
1994	243.6	—
1995	1,571.4	—
1996	3,411.4	6.4
1997	3,515.5	60.0
1998	1,461.9	271.5
1999	1,269.2	708.8
2000	4,778.4	1,882.9
2001	3,664.3	4,239.1
2002	1,624.1	3,958.2
2003	2,371.3	5,600.3
2004	2,315.6	4,794.1
2005	1,104.4	2,344.6

Source: DCA, 2004; UNODC, 2007b.

violence, they could be easily intimidated (DCA, 2000:39; ICG, 2001a:15). Russian soldiers and officials were also repeatedly found involved in heroin-smuggling attempts into Russia (DCA, 2000:17; Knox, 2004). Russian military planes were also used for these purposes (Olcott and Udalova, 2000:18; ICG, 2001a:6, 8).

Tajikistan's borders with former Soviet republics are still less effectively controlled than its border with Afghanistan. Even though Uzbekistan has repeatedly closed and even mined its border with Tajikistan for fear of importing instability, the weakness and limited means of the Tajik border guards and law enforcement agencies and, more generally, the difficulties of establishing effective border controls between the countries that once belonged to the former Soviet Union make the smuggling of even large lots of heroin to CIS countries a relatively low-risk enterprise (Olcott and Udalova, 2000:10–14; Zelitchenko, 2004:301–348).[7]

Corruption

Corruption is not only an almost inevitable by-product of wholesale drug trafficking, but also one of its most powerful breeding grounds. It is a self-reinforcing societal ill. In Tajikistan it existed before the development of the illicit drug industry and, as in other CIS states, flourished during Soviet times and has been further enhanced by the post-Soviet transition (see, for example

Cokgezen, 2004). In Tajikistan, as in other Central Asian republics, corruption has an "eastern" character that shows itself in three forms. First, such corruption is very closely linked to traditional social institutions and relations through family, clan, place of work, and compatriots. Even without the flow of bribes, members of the "in group" are treated preferentially. Second, corruption has a hierarchical structure. The bribe taker, who has often bought his own post, is required to pass a share of his earnings to the boss who helped him. In such a system there is little stigma to a functionary taking a bribe; it is improper only when he takes more than he is supposed to. According to the DCA (2000:72), for example, as of 2000, the position of head of the Interior Ministry Department in one of the districts bordering Afghanistan cost about $50,000. With the bribes extorted from drug traffickers, however, the position holder can quickly earn the money paid in advance and give a share of his revenues to his superiors as well (ICG, 2001a:16). Third, moral views of corruption depend on whether it is "our" or "their" group. It is bad to take bribes from "ours" and it is permissible to take them from "theirs" (Reuter, Pain, and Greenfield, 2003:65).

Such "eastern" corruption powerfully enhances Tajikistan's advantage in the world opiate industry. Coupled with the growing means invested in corruption by drug traffickers, it also undermines the consolidation of democratic and accountable state structures. Despite the limited number of Tajik officials charged on corruption or drug offenses,[8] Tajikistan is regarded as one of the world's most corrupt countries (e.g., Transparency International [TI], 2005). This perception is confirmed by several high-ranking Tajik law enforcement officials interviewed ad hoc for this project. As one official stated:

> Nearly all law enforcement and border-patrolling officers in the border districts are involved in drug trafficking. Some of them smuggle drugs into Tajikistan; others deliver drugs from border districts to other parts of the country; others still "open" the border to traffickers or provide them with crucial information. In other parts of Tajikistan the percentage of corrupted officers is lower. In my opinion, 8 officers out of 10 are corrupted in Dushanbe [Tajikistan's capital]. (Khamonov, 2005:55; for similar assessments, see ICG, 2001a:8, 15, 2001c:14–15).

Even if there might be some exaggeration in this assessment, the few criminal cases that are brought to court are enough to show the extent of drug-related corruption and the involvement of high-ranking civil servants in drug deals. In May 2000, 86 kilograms of heroin and large amounts of foreign currency were discovered in Almaty, the then-capital of Kazakhstan, in cars belonging to the Tajik ambassador and trade representative. The latter was then convicted on drug charges, whereas the ambassador fled Kazakhstan (AFP, 2001). In April 1998, a former Tajik deputy defense minister was imprisoned for using a military helicopter to smuggle 89 kilograms of opium from Dushanbe to Pendjikent in the Soghd region (*Times of Central Asia,* 2002).

Moreover, several officers of Tajik law enforcement agencies as well as diplomats have been arrested and charged in Russia and Kyrgyzstan for wholesale opiate smuggling (Sukhravardy, 2002; Bajun, 2003; DCA, 2004:37). The lavish houses and expensive cars many customs and police officials possess, which they could not have bought on their salaries, provide circumstantial evidence of law enforcement corruption (U.S. Department of State, Bureau of International Narcotics and Law Enforcement Affairs, 2005:502). General Nustam Nazarov (2005), the respected director of the DCA, stated that "corruption in law enforcement bodies became critical and hampered drug control activity."

The Phases of Trafficking

The interplay of the previously mentioned factors can be seen clearly in the evolution of the illicit opiate industry in Tajikistan since the early 1990s. The industry has grown rapidly in quantitative terms, but it has also undergone substantial shifts in the origin and type of opiates trafficked, and in smuggling routes.

Drug Sources: From Local to Afghan Opium

The first years after Tajikistan's independence recorded the rapid expansion of domestic illicit opium poppy cultivation, particularly in the Panjakent and Ayni districts of the Soghd (previously Leninobad) region close to the Uzbek border. By 1995 about 2,000 hectares were cultivated with opium poppy, and from 1991 to 1995 more than half of all reported drug offenses involved the illegal cultivation of drugs (Khamonov, 2005:21–22).

Since 1995, however, local opium and its derivatives have been largely supplanted by cheaper and better quality opiates imported from Afghanistan. The smuggling of Afghan opiates began on a small scale as early as 1992, the first full year of independence and the first year after the expansion of opium growing into the northern regions of Afghanistan. Initially, the traffic was almost exclusively of opium, which was imported mainly into the eastern, autonomous region of Gorno Badakhshan and from there was smuggled to Kyrgyzstan and Uzbekistan. In this mountainous and wild area of the country, opium—as well as other (licit and illicit) commodities—were mainly moved through the Pamir highway linking Khorog, the capital of Gorno Badakhshan to Osh in Kyrgyzstan and Andijan in the Fergana Valley of Uzbekistan. Despite being primarily involved in defending themselves and their families from the rioting population, in 1992, Russian border guards stationed in Khorog managed to seize the first 17 kilos of opium smuggled from Afghanistan. Five kilos of Afghan opium were seized the same year in Kyrgyzstan (Zelitchenko, 1999).

Around 1994, according to our research collaborator, at least 20 metric tons of opium were trafficked yearly from Afghanistan into Tajikistan, primarily in the Gorno Badakhshan region. This generated few criminal cases: a maximum of 53 drug offenses were recorded yearly in the region from 1992 to 1995 (Khamonov, 2005:4).

Entry Points: From East to West

After the shift from local to Afghan opium, a second shift took place in the mid 1990s. Trafficking spread from Gorno Badakhshan to the rest of the country, as Afghan opiates began to be smuggled from Afghanistan into the southwestern Khatlon region, where the cities of Kulob and Qurghonteppa are located (see fig. 9.1). As a result of this shift, Dushanbe and the more populated regions in the western part of the country also became more directly involved in the opiate trade. The lower altitude and better road infrastructure of this region, both in Tajikistan and in Afghanistan, were probably the main factors prompting the shift of routes (UNODCCP Sub-Office in Tajikistan, 2000:16; DCA, 2004:23–24). The shift of routes was accompanied by a further expansion of the volume of opiates trafficked, which have probably exceeded 100 metric tons per year since the late 1990s (Khamonov, 2005:12; see also Townsend, 2006).

Drug Types: From Opium to Heroin

The change of routes and the expansion of the illegal trade were accompanied by a third shift, this time involving the type of opiates smuggled—namely, from opium to heroin. Heroin was seized for the first time in Tajikistan in late 1995. Two lots of 1.9 and 9.9 kilos were recovered in late 1995 by the Russian border guards close to the town of Panj in the Qurghonteppa district of the Khatlon region. In 2000, the UN drug office estimated that about 100 metric tons of heroin may be smuggled yearly from Afghanistan into Tajikistan (UNODCCP Sub-Office in Tajikistan, 2000:9).

The rapid increase in seizures provides further evidence of the rapid expansion of heroin trafficking. Table 9.1 (presented earlier) is based on the data of the Tajik DCA reporting opiate seizures in Tajikistan (which for the early 1990s do not include the seizures carried out by the Russian border guards). In 1996, Tajik law enforcement agencies confiscated the first 6 kilograms of heroin and in 2003 they confiscated 5,600 kilograms. Confiscations have since declined, but have not returned to earlier low levels. In 2003, Tajikistan, a small country of six million people, recorded the world's third largest heroin seizures after China and Pakistan, surpassing even Iran (UNODC, 2005d:260–266).[9] Opium seizures rose from just a few kilograms in the early 1990s to almost 4,800 kilograms in 2000, then declined substantially during the following years, when trafficking shifted primarily to heroin.

By 1998, heroin had flooded the landlocked country of Tajikistan, and its wholesale and retail price had sunk to less than a fifth of its prices in 1996. Whereas a kilogram of heroin bound for export cost $ 17,000 in Dushanbe in 1996, its price plummeted to $ 3,000 in 1998 and became as low as $ 1,000 in 2000 (DCA, 2002).[10]

Tajikistan's Integration into the World Heroin Market

With the growing inflow of Afghan heroin in the late 1990s, Tajikistan became fully integrated into the world heroin market. The process took only a few years. While most of the opium was consumed locally, or at most in the neighboring Central Asian republics, heroin soon became one of Tajikistan's main export goods. In fact, Tajik heroin exports service the entire CIS market, including the booming Russian market and, to a lesser extent, the eastern and western European markets as well.

Estimates of Opiate Flows

In 1999, the International Narcotics Control Board (INCB, 1999:par. 354) estimated that "up to 65 per cent of all Afghan opium, morphine and heroin is trafficked through Central Asia." A year later, the UN drug office (UNOD-CCP Sub-Office in Tajikistan, 2000:6) put the same figure at around 50% of the Afghan opiates intended for export. The truth is that no one knows even approximately the percentage of Afghan heroin that goes through Tajikistan and the other Central Asian republics; there are no strong methodologies for creating such estimates. However, as explained in detail in appendix C, it is plausible that about 50 to 95 metric tons of pure heroin are consumed annually in Russia, the Ukraine, and Central Asia—markets that are served primarily by heroin smuggled through Tajikistan, Turkmenistan, and, to a much lesser extent, Uzbekistan. Adding a share of what is consumed in the rest of Europe and adjusting for seizures, in appendix C we estimate that 75 to 121 metric tons of pure heroin equivalents may flow yearly into or through Central Asia.

An unknown, but probably not very large, fraction of this opiate throughput is smuggled from Afghanistan through Turkmenistan and Uzbekistan. We assume that one third of the throughput is potentially smuggled from Afghanistan into one of the two countries. As a result of this calculation, 50 to 81 metric tons in pure heroin equivalents are left to be potentially smuggled each year into or through Tajikistan, representing about 15% to 25% of Afghanistan's opium production at the time of our calculation and somewhat less more recently. Without corresponding information on purity for the previously mentioned 100-metric-ton supply-side estimate of the UN (UNODCCP Sub-Office in Tajikistan, 2000), a direct comparison is difficult; nevertheless, our range for pure heroin equivalents may be roughly consistent.

Tajik Exporters, Couriers, and Distributors in CIS Countries

During the initial phases of development of the Tajik illegal drug industry, opportunistic smugglers were happy to bring their lots to southern Kyrgyzstan and sell them there to Kyrgyz and other former USSR citizens. Since Afghan opiates began to flow through western Tajikistan, Tajik citizens have increasingly become involved in the export and, to a more limited extent, in the distribution of heroin and other opiates in all CIS countries.

Imitating Nigerian smugglers, many Tajik smugglers initially mastered the skills of the "swallower," transporting drugs in their stomachs or alternatively on their body, their personal belongings, and allegedly even on children. Dozens of such cases were discovered yearly by CIS law enforcement agencies and reported by Russian and Central Asian media (e.g., DCA, 2000:14; *Moskovskii komsomolets,* 2000; MVD, 2000:12; *Times of Central Asia,* 2000). Despite the risks, such trips were quite attractive, because a transporter could earn $200 per trip, a figure within range of a full year's income for many Tajiks (DCA, 2000:12; Khamonov, 2005:43).

At the turn of the century, however, Tajiks became somewhat higher risk drug smugglers. Both in Russia and in Central Asia they received growing attention from customs agents, who had also become more skilled and better equipped. The increased law enforcement pressure led to a two-thirds reduction in the number of "swallowers" detected in 2000 to 2001 at the airport in Domodedovo, Moscow, the principal landing site for airplanes from Tajikistan (Reuter et al., 2003:52).

Since then, smugglers have developed other methods of drug delivery and possibly used transporters from other ethnic groups, as reflected in the decline of Tajik citizens arrested on drug charges in other CIS countries since 2000.[11] Reflecting changes in trafficking groups (discussed later), a growing share of drugs also travels in big consignments in cargo trains and heavy trucks, particularly those transporting cotton and aluminum, Tajikistan's main legitimate export goods.[12] Opiates are also frequently transported on buses, especially those leaving from the northern Soghd region.[13] The smuggling methods are increasingly ingenious. Heroin is no longer simply covered with fruits and vegetables but is transported inside them—for example, inside apricot clingstones, apples, and pomegranates (*Rossijskaja Gaseta,* 2001; Reuter et al., 2003:5).

The Rapid Growth of Local Opiate Consumption

During the second half of the 1990s, the growing availability of heroin prompted the rapid spread of heroin use throughout Tajikistan, displacing opium and, to a more limited extent, even cannabis. An indicator of this trend is given by the dramatic growth of drug users registered in "narcology" centers, which provide treatment for drug addicts. Within a decade, from 1994 to 2003, their number grew more than 10-fold, from 653 to 6,799, with heroin users representing more than 75% of the total in 2003 (DCA, 2004). On the basis of a survey in 2003, the Tajik DCA estimated that there were 55,000 to 75,000 problem drug users (representing more than 1% of the population), 80% of whom regularly used heroin (Khamonov, 2005). As a result of this rapid growth, by 2003, Tajikistan had the eighth highest prevalence of opiate abuse, following Iran, Laos, and several other countries of the former Soviet Union (UNODC, 2004:389–391). There are signs that, since then, the heroin epidemic in Tajikistan has stabilized. This is the result of several factors, among which the most important may be the growing awareness of the negative consequences of heroin use.

To an unknown degree, however, the stabilization of heroin use has also been prompted by changes in the organization of retail distribution, which may have raised retail heroin prices almost fivefold in comparison with 2000 and considerably decreased availability. As a drug user interviewed for this study stated, "You could get any drug quite easily 'til 2000. Everybody sold drugs. Since 2001, only those who have some power behind them have remained in business." Paralleling the evolution of drug-smuggling organizations (discussed later), there has been a downselection of retail drug dealers, too. Only well-connected drug dealers enjoying the protection of high-level law enforcement officials or politicians remain in the market, and their power is allegedly such that they can afford to select customers and raise heroin prices at the same time that they decrease its purity (Khamonov, 2005:24–25).

The price increase and the reduced availability have prompted many users to shift from smoking or sniffing heroin to injecting it, sharply fostering the spread of HIV/AIDS. According to UNAIDS, Joint United Nations Programme on HIV/AIDS (2006:464), the number of people living with HIV in the country in 2005 was probably around 5,000. Although the prevalence (0.1%) is still lower than in other Central Asian and eastern European (not to speak of African) countries, it is increasing rapidly. As it happened earlier in other former Soviet republics, Tajikistan also seems to be on the verge of a major HIV epidemic. In just 1 year, from 2005 to 2006, HIV prevalence among injecting drug users increased from 16% to 24% in the cities of Dushanbe and Khujand (UNAIDS, 2007:26, 28).

Drug-Trafficking Enterprises

Three major types of drug enterprises can be identified in the brief, but dramatic, development of the Tajik drug industry. The relative importance of each type has tended to shift with the development of the Tajik drug trade.[14]

Independent Peddlers

During the initial stages of development (1993–1995), opiates were very frequently traded by individuals or small, unorganized groups of people who had no previous criminal expertise and for whom opiate trafficking represented a means of survival. Tajik researchers estimate that almost half the local young adults (age 18–24 years) were involved in the drug business in 1997 (Iskandarov, 1998). Contrary to established patterns in the western world, many drug dealers were women. They were not only disproportionately unemployed, but were also often left as the single heads of their households, because their partners were dead, fighting, or had migrated abroad. From 1996 to 1999, women made up 27% to 45% of all those convicted annually for drug offenses in Tajikistan (DCA, 2000:12; see also Zelitchenko, 1999).

With virtually no law enforcement, this highly decentralized drug trading hardly needed to involve regular payments of bribes to government officials (although many of them engaged themselves in drug trafficking). The only restraints were moral. Apparently, there was considerable resistance among older family members, who considered drug trading discreditable (Reuter et al., 2003:42).

The independent peddlers were primarily active in the western region of Gorno Badakhshan, often bringing batches of no more than a few kilograms of drugs directly from the Afghan border to Osh or Andijan. With time, some of them also began to sell drugs on retail markets in Dushanbe or other cities and even to export small quantities of opiates directly into Russia, usually relying on the help of relatives, acquaintances, or members of the same village or neighborhood. Although some independent traders still exist, most have been incorporated into larger, more professionally organized trafficking groups (DCA, 2002:14).

Small- to Medium-Size Trafficking Groups

Small- to medium-size trafficking groups appeared simultaneously with the independent peddlers, but largely superseded them as heroin smuggling from Afghanistan expanded. There is no precise information on the number of small- to medium-size trafficking groups operating in Tajikistan. Khamonov (2005:28) estimates that at least 100 of them are active on the border with Afghanistan.

Despite their higher degree of professionalization, the illegal enterprises belonging to the second category rarely consist of more than 10 to 15 persons. Within each group there is some division of labor, but this is quite rudimentary (DCA, 2000:14). Affiliation is based on extended family ties, locality, or membership in a professional association, sporting group, or other traditional male groups. Trafficking and distributing groups with a mixed regional base can be found primarily in Dushanbe, where people from different Tajik regions are used to living together (Khamonov, 2005:40–41, 46). Although Tajiks living abroad are part of some groups, these do not usually have a truly international membership. Many of them are active only intermittently. They come together when opportunity arises, to disband again and possibly reform with a partially changed membership on another occasion.[15]

On average, the monthly heroin turnover managed by small- to medium-size trafficking groups is about 20 to 30 kilograms; it rarely exceeds 50 kilograms. These illegal enterprises are usually specialized in a single phase of the illegal drug industry. Southern groups are frequently responsible for opiate smuggling from Afghanistan; groups based in Dushanbe and other cities take care of the domestic wholesale and retail opiate distribution. Relying on legitimate trade networks, northern groups are frequently in charge of opiate export or wholesale distribution in CIS countries (Khamonov, 2005:40). Unlike independent peddlers, organized trafficking groups usually enjoy some form of government protection, although this may be limited to connections with a few Russian border guards, local policemen, or customs officers.

Criminal Communities: Characteristics…

Since the late 1990s, a third group of drug-trafficking organizations has gained control of a significant—and probably a majority—fraction of the opiate trade. These are large, organized criminal groups, which are usually known as *criminal communities,* a term inherited by most CIS countries from the Soviet penal code (see, for example, Butler, 1997). The most successful ones are able to deal with more than 1 metric ton of heroin a month.

Stable and usually high-level government protection has been critical to the success of these large-scale trafficking groups. Ironically, the progress in border control and law enforcement that Tajikistan has achieved since the late 1990s—thanks to the support of international agencies and foreign donors—has helped the large groups to achieve their success.[16] By 2001, for example, there were 12 to 13 police and custom posts on the route from Khorog to Osh, a distance of only 700 to 800 kilometers. The roads from the Afghanistan border to Dushanbe are checked even more strictly. Rather than create insuperable barriers to drug transportation, this has generated large payments to border and police officials. Small-time individual smugglers are disadvantaged; apparently, there are economies of scale in corruption (Reuter et al., 2003:42–43). This has led to some coalition of corrupted bureaucracy and drug-trafficking organizations. Whereas small- to medium-size trafficking groups rarely enjoy high-level protections, systematic collusion is the characteristic of the organizations belonging to the third category. This variation was candidly described by the DCA (2000) in a report on the illegal drug market in Dushanbe:

> The leaders of all groups have their own relations or other connections with some governmental structures or law enforcement agencies. In many cases these are paid regularly definite sum[s] of money. In some large groups a leader is either a commander of military troops or law enforcement agency. In the largest groups…leader[s] have high position[s] in some governmental structure[s]. (pp. 17–18)

Like the smaller groups, some criminal communities are specialized in one or two phases of the heroin business and, as in the case of smaller groups, their specialization is a function of their location. However, there are also a handful of large and well-connected organizations that involve up to few hundred individuals, including core members and service providers, and operate across a broad spectrum of trafficking activities—from the importation of opiates from Afghanistan up to the wholesale and, occasionally, even retail distribution of opiates in Russia and other former Soviet states.

Most of the latter coincide with the private armies of former civil war commanders turned career or elected public officials. As the DCA (2000) states:

> [T]here are several large organizations in Tajikistan dealing with deliver[y] of drugs. As a matter of fact they all are subject to commanders of military formations, which were formed during Tajik Civil War... some of these formations became parts of armed forces of the country; some are still under the subordination to their commanders and are illegal in their essence." (p. 70, see also 18, 21–22; U.S. Department of State, Bureau of International Narcotics and Law Enforcement Affairs, 2002:128–129)

Little is known on the recruitment criteria and internal division of labor of Tajikistan's most successful drug-trafficking groups. Their core is usually composed of people united by clan or locality ties; however, people from different backgrounds are involved in the less delicate and more risky tasks. Occasionally these large drug enterprises also develop stable partnerships with trafficking groups of other ethnic origin, to which they sell drugs or from which they buy "protection" services in Russia or other CIS countries (Khamonov, 2005:40). As a result of their civil war origins, many of them have a quasi-military organization—a peculiarity that differentiates them from the criminal communities operating in other post-Soviet countries and from the drug-trafficking groups of developed countries with strict prohibition enforcement (see chapter 10). As private armies, they are also well equipped with modern communication means and weapons, including armored vehicles, anti-aircraft rockets, and military planes, and they operate professionally (DCA, 2000:70; Osmonaliev, 2005:21). The largest usually include so-called *protection groups* (i.e., "hit men"), which take care of the most dangerous operations, and particularly the drug import from Afghanistan, and charge "protection fees" from other trafficking groups, when the latter want to operate in their territory (Khamonov, 2005:14–15).[17]

...and Examples

The leaders of Tajikistan's largest trafficking groups belong to both the former People's Front of Tajikistan (PFT), which brought President Emomali

Rakhmonov to power, and the former United Tajik Opposition (UTO), the PFT's main opponent, which was included in the government in late 1997.

The founder of the first large-scale Tajik drug-trafficking group was probably Yaqubjon Salimov, who started his career as a racketeer in Dushanbe in the 1980s and went on to become the lieutenant to *bobo* ("the grandfather") Sangak Safarov, a powerful warlord and the founder of the PFT, and then Tajikistan's Minister of Interior in December 1992 (Nourzhanov, 2005:115–119). From then on, Salimov began organizing opiate smuggling from Afghanistan via the southern Vanch district of Gorno Badakhshan, which he controlled through a relative. Opium and then heroin were allegedly transported by military airplanes to Dushanbe and then by planes or trains to the Russian Federation (DCA, 2000:40; Khamonov, 2005:28–29).

Salimov's drug business long ran undisturbed, because he had control of the police. The Sixth Department of the Ministry of the Interior in charge of combating organized crime was entrusted to an individual who had spent 17 years behind bars. The rank-and-file members of the police were little better; one third of them were purged from the force after Salimov's dismissal in August 1995 (Nourzhanov, 2005:119). Salimov was then made head of the Customs Committee, before siding with an opponent of President Rakhmonov's in 1997, fleeing into Uzbekistan, and being arrested and sentenced to 15 years in prison for state treason, banditry, and abuse of office in early 2005 (Wetherall, 2005).

Having had to finance their fight with illegal means up until the late 1990s, many opposition commanders are believed to have been even more systematically involved in drug smuggling than the warlords of the PFT. In the absence of hard proof, rumors tend to persist, largely without question— so great is the presumption of wrongdoing, irrespective of party affiliations. As a case in point, consider the popular claims that Mirzo "Jaga" Ziyoev, the undisputed military chief of the UTO, is (or at least was) heavily involved in heroin smuggling. As part of the policy of national reconciliation, Ziyoev became Minister for Emergency Situations, a position that was created specifically for him in July 1998. The ministry has a full-size army brigade on its payroll (consisting exclusively of Ziyoev's men). Although his brigade has been permanently deployed in the northern part of the country, Ziyoev allegedly controls, as if it were his personal fief, considerable parts of the Panj district in southern Tajikistan, which is one of the most frequent and easiest entry points for Afghan opiates (Sukhravardy, 2002; Khamonov, 2005:11, 21; Nourzhanov, 2005:124, 127, 130).

Other former UTO commanders-turned-statesmen are also suspected of being involved in wholesale drug smuggling.[18] As much as Ziyoev, all these former warlords retain substantial private armies and largely control pockets of lands in southern Tajikistan, which they consider their patrimony and from which they can organize undisturbed large trafficking deals (DCA, 2000:22; Khamonov, 2005:11; Nourzhanov, 2005:124, 130). Support for these allegations was provided by the drug-related murder of Habib Sanginov, another

UTO commander who had acquired the post of deputy Minister of the Interior. According to the prosecution in his murder case, Sanginov was shot dead in April 2001 because he refused to pay for a delivery of 50 kilograms of heroin worth $100,000 (Gleason, 2001).

Even if the days of Salimov are gone, drug-related corruption is far from being an exclusive characteristic of former opposition members. Several politicians and officials belonging to the former PFT are (or were) also involved in the heroin trade. Two former PFT commanders, for example, were forced to retire from their posts on the Border Protection Committee in January 2002. Although it was not publicly stated, the reason for their dismissal was their systematic involvement in drug trafficking (ICG, 2004b:2; Khamonov, 2005:10). General Gaffor Mirzoev, the former PFT commander and head of the Presidential Guard,[19] was also said to run a powerful drug-trafficking organization up until his arrest on numerous but non-drug-related charges in August 2004 (Institute of War and Peace Reporting [IWPR], 2004; British Broadcasting Corporation [BBC], 2004; Shvaryov, 2004; Khamonov; 2005:13). Russian media sources allege that Mirzoev's long-time business partner was Makhmadsaid Ubaidulloyev, who (as of 2005) was the mayor of Dushanbe and head of the upper house of the Tajik Parliament (for a review, see Reuter et al., 2003:66–67).

In the previously mentioned cases, government officials were often the traffickers themselves. However, there are also a few large independent trafficking groups that merely buy "protection" services from corrupt government officials. Among them there is, for example, an organization led by six brothers from the southern Khatlon region, which is said to export large quantities of heroin in several Russian cities, particularly in the Ural region (Khamonov, 2005:45).

Concluding Remarks

On the basis of the evidence presented so far, one can safely say that Tajikistan has become, in less than 10 years, a veritable narco-state. Drug trafficking heavily pollutes the country's economic and political systems, and seriously threatens its recovery from the ruinous civil war of the 1990s. What is even worse, a preponderant part of its drug trade is conducted not by common criminals or terrorist groups, but by gangs headed or protected by high-ranking government officials. In no other country of the world, except perhaps contemporary Afghanistan, can such a superimposition between drug traffickers and government officials be found (see chapters 6 and 10).

Corrupt high-ranking government officials do not merely represent a few "bad apples," but carry out on a larger scale what significant portions of the population, including many low-ranking law enforcement agents, also do. The key question for Tajikistan is which fraction of the Tajik population profits from the opiate trade. Despite the consolidation process undergone by the drug industry in recent years, it is fair to assume that the share of the population supplementing their legitimate income with opiate revenues is not insignificant. In addition to those directly involved in the trade, one also has to consider those who profit from it indirectly, by working in legitimate companies funded with drug money or by supplying goods and services to wholesale drug traffickers and their families. This means that Tajik leaders face a serious dilemma, because cracking down on heroin trafficking would result in a substantial deterioration of living conditions for a considerable segment of their impoverished people.

Given this and the country's limited means, it is clear that the Tajik government will not be able to control drug trafficking effectively on its own. It will need the continued guidance, supervision, and financial support of the international community.

Part III

Policy Analysis and Implications

10

The Theoretical and Practical Consequences of Variations in Effective Illegality

Introduction

The configuration of the world opiate market is distinctive. As noted in chapter 3, opium is cultivated and refined in a handful of nations, most extremely poor and none rich; transshipped through a few others, most of which are also poor; and consumed in many countries both rich and poor, scattered around the world.

This chapter seeks to explain this configuration and its implications through the development of a theoretical model of variations in effective illegality across countries. The model identifies three stylized cases of enforcement—strict, lax, and non-enforcement—and categorizes countries according to their implementation of international prohibitions on opiate production and trafficking. The model integrates economic, political, and sociological concerns; it explicitly accounts for the actions and inaction of governments in implementing international prohibitions on opiate production and trafficking, and considers their effects on the broader society.

We do not incorporate or evaluate the implications of variations in the implementation of prohibitions on consumption. Our reasons are both methodological and conceptual. A pronounced lack of uniformity of implementation among countries, even countries that we would deem "strict enforcers" of supply-side prohibitions, makes it virtually impossible to apply a case-based approach. Moreover, variations in consumption prohibitions have little practical consequence for what we are focused on—namely, the organization and characteristics of the supply of opiates.

In general, we find that the political, legal, and institutional environment in which producers and traffickers operate plays a key role in determining

- The configuration of the world opiate market, especially the dominance of a handful of opium-producing nations
- The size (understood throughout this chapter as the number of individuals directly involved), organization, and operating methods of the enterprises that produce, process, and distribute opiates in the market
- Broader social impacts of opiate production and distribution, ranging from the legitimacy of opiates, and economic and political relevance of related commercial activities to levels of corruption and violence

Prior assessments of global illicit drug markets produced by international organizations (e.g., UNODC, 2005d) focus on the "law on the books," which is fairly uniform across countries because almost all are signatories to the international conventions.[1] The assessments pay little attention to the "law in action"—in other words, the concrete implementation of international conventions and domestic legislation prohibiting the production and sale of psychoactive substances, including opium and its derivatives, by national and local governments. However, not all governments apply the law to the same degree. Some choose to allocate substantial resources to law enforcement and others do not; some have ample resources to allocate and others do not. Differences also persist in the extent to which the laws prohibiting opiate production and trafficking enjoy popular legitimacy. Thus, most prior assessments neglect the fact that, despite the common prohibition regime, the actions of opiate producers and traffickers are subject to varying degrees of effective illegality across countries.

Our assessment explicitly accounts for differences in implementation of prohibitions on production and trafficking. Governments, through decisions about the enforcement of opiate prohibitions, determine the degree of effective illegality that market suppliers have to cope with, thus enabling or discouraging different activities and organizational forms.

Three Ideal Typical Cases of Prohibition Enforcement

To account for the effects of variations in effective illegality on the world opiate market, we have adopted a Weberian approach and identified three "ideal types"—that is, archetypes, general categories, or stylized cases—of state implementation or non-implementation of opiate prohibition. The three cases are constructed around the notions of strict, lax, and non-enforcement, respectively, with the last category coinciding with state or quasi-state authorities' tolerance or support for opiate production and trade.

We define strict enforcement of prohibition as regularly imposing significant risks of incarceration and asset seizure, so that illegal drug entrepreneurs must take precautions against such risks. In countries approximating this first case, opiate production and trafficking are not only formally but also effectively criminalized. This does not mean that there are not instances of uneven enforcement within these countries—there are—but, in general, the risks of incarceration and asset seizure are real and present for entrepreneurs seeking to engage in production or trafficking. Likewise, there are instances of opportunistic drug-related corruption involving single and low-level officers, but systemic corruption is very rare. The category of strict enforcement is largely built on empirical evidence drawn from drug markets in western Europe, the United States, Canada, and Australia—four settings in which drug prohibition enforcement tends to be strict and considerable drug market research has been carried out. Iran and many Arab countries may fall into this category, but we have not included them in our analysis because of inadequate information.

Lax enforcement involves countries with governments that are weak or unwilling to enforce prohibition strictly. We have developed this category by drawing evidence from two second-tier opium-producing countries (India and Mexico) and from five key transit countries (Albania, Kosovo, Pakistan, Tajikistan, and Turkey). Some of the countries selected as representative of this case—for example, Mexico, Tajikistan, and Turkey—are often praised for aggressively eradicating opium poppy or seizing drugs. However, we describe them as "lax" enforcers because inconsistencies are more the norm than the exception; enforcement is geographically biased, as in Pakistan; or enforcement has undergone major upheavals since the early 1990s—upheaval being an issue for Albania, Kosovo, and Tajikistan. In merely lax environments, entrepreneurs are usually unable to obtain complete immunity from enforcement in the long run and face varying risks of incarceration and asset seizure from either honest law enforcement agencies or potentially corrupt agencies they have not bribed or threatened effectively. In countries close to the second case, opiates are formally illegal, but concrete enforcement depends on law enforcement agencies' strength and integrity, and on enterprises' corrupt connections.

The third case is the rarest and concerns countries (or jurisdictions within them) in which non-enforcement is either the stated or unstated official policy and the government itself (or rivaling quasi-state authorities) tolerates or promotes the production and trade in opiates. Opiates become de facto legal commodities, regardless of whether the countries are parties to the international conventions on opiates and other psychoactive drugs. In considering this case, we draw evidence from Afghanistan and Burma, the two largest illicit opium producers. Non-enforcement may also characterize those parts of Colombia where opium poppies have grown during the past decade, but we have omitted Colombia from our analysis, because we could not find detailed information on the role of the FARC in poppy-growing areas.

We have selected and assigned countries to each case on the basis of data availability and analytical judgment. First, we have included only the countries for which we were able to assemble solid and multifaceted sets of evidence, including both quantitative and qualitative data, drawn from academic, official, and gray sources; we excluded other potentially interesting countries, such as Iran and Laos, for which we could not gather sufficient information for conclusive assessments. Second, we have assigned countries to each of the three cases on the basis of our own and our research collaborators' analyses of the data.[2] We make no claims that the countries chosen meet in every regard the characteristics of their respective type of prohibition enforcement; we do not even expect them to do so, because each category constitutes an ideal type, an abstraction that is not designed to correspond exactly to any single empirical observation.

The Consequences of Strict Enforcement

In this first case, the state has ratified and strictly enforces the international bans on opiate production and trafficking. If these drugs continue to be produced, traded, and consumed for non-medical purposes, an illegal market develops in which the participants are subject to *constraints of illegality* (Reuter, 1983, 1985). These constraints not only prevent the formation of large, illegal enterprises, but also generally shape the operating methods of criminal entrepreneurs. The strict enforcement of prohibitions also reduces the legitimacy of opiates and related market activities, and marginalizes them.

The Size and Organization of Illegal Enterprises

In countries with strict enforcement, illegal opiate suppliers are obliged to operate not only without the benefits of state institutions but, typically, against them. Unlike legitimate entrepreneurs, they cannot resort to state institutions to enforce contracts (Reuter, 1983, 1985). Although private protection services may be provided occasionally by mafia-type organizations (see Reuter, 1983, 1995; Kaplan and Dubro, 2003; Paoli, 2003b), there is usually no sovereign power to which a party may appeal for redress of injury. As a result, property rights are poorly protected, employment contracts cannot be formalized, and the development of large, formally organized, and enduring enterprises is difficult. Moreover, in operating against the state, illegal suppliers also operate under the presumption of overt government hostility—that is, under the constant threat of incarceration and asset seizure. Each participant in an illegal trade may thus try to organize his or her activities in such a way as to reduce the risk of police detection, up to the point that the additional cost of risk reduction just offsets the additional benefit. Incorporating illegal transactions into preexisting social relationships (such as networks based on kinship, friendship, locality, or ethnicity), and reducing the number of customers and employees are two of the most frequent strategies that illegal entrepreneurs use to reduce their vulnerability to law enforcement efforts (Moore, 1974: 15–31; Reuter, 1983, 1985).

In developed countries with effective governments, opiate enterprises are, for all these reasons, likely to be small (in the sense that they involve few individuals directly, such as employees) and not vertically integrated (e.g., wholesale dealers do not also sell retail[3]). Strict enforcement also drastically reduces the geographic scope of illegal enterprises. Because of the difficulty of monitoring distant agents and the higher risks associated with transportation and communication to distant locations, opiate traffickers tend to operate locally; that is, they usually do not include branches in more than one metropolitan area (Reuter, 1985; Mudambi and Paul, 2003).

The threat of incarceration and asset seizure may also result in shorter planning horizons in illegal markets than in legal markets. Illegal entrepreneurs may discount the future more heavily than other entrepreneurs. And, because illegal enterprises cannot be transferred easily, aging illegal entrepreneurs may choose to divert an increasing share of their profits to legal assets that can be passed on to their heirs.

Finally, because they are operating against the state, illegal enterprises are limited in how they can market their products. For example, they cannot build customer loyalty through conventional branding, at least not without attracting the attention of law enforcement (Reuter, 1985). Strong economies of scale, however, are associated with advertising, and the advantages linked to the nationwide marketing of one's own products have long been recognized as a very important factor in the rise of modern large-scale corporations. According to some economists, advertising represents the single most important basis of large-firm advantage (Scherer and Ross, 1990:130–138).

For these reasons, it is unlikely that large, hierarchically organized businesses will emerge in the market for illegal opiates. The factors promoting the development of large bureaucracies in the legal portion of the economy— namely, to take advantage of economies of scale and scope—are outweighed in the illegal markets of most developed countries by the very consequences of product illegality.

The academic literature, the "gray" literature, and other sources all show that in North America, western Europe, and Australia, the great majority of drug deals, even those involving large quantities of drugs, are carried out by relatively small and often ephemeral enterprises.[4] Some of the enterprises are family businesses—that is, they are run by the members of a blood family, who may opportunistically resort to a network of non-kin to carry out the most dangerous tasks. Some are non-kin groups, formed around a more or less charismatic leader, that then acquire a certain degree of stability and develop a rudimentary division of labor. Others are short-term partnerships or collaborations—loose associations of people that form, split, and come together again as opportunity arises.

In line with our analysis, several studies also point out that the success of criminal enterprises frequently rests on family ties and bonds of friendship or locality or, more rarely, common ethnicity (Reuter and Haaga, 1989; Kleemans, van den Berg, and van de Bunt, 1998; Pearson and Hobbs, 2001;

Kleemans, Brienen, and van de Bunt, 2002). Such ties are also the usual foundation of the few larger and more tightly bounded trafficking groups active on either the European or U.S. market. These often have roots in drug-producing or transit countries with less strict enforcement of prohibitions.[5]

The fragmented and decentralized character of drug trafficking and, more generally, organized crime is increasingly accepted even by law enforcement agencies, at least in Europe. In its 2003 annual report, for example, Europol made the following statement:

> [T]he traditional perception of hierarchically structured organized crime groups is being challenged. There is now a development suggesting that a greater percentage of powerful organized crime groups are far more cellular in structure, with loose affiliations made and broken on a regular basis and less obvious chains of command. (p. 8)

There was never much evidence that European organized crime groups ever complied with "traditional perception of hierarchically structured organized crime groups," but Europol has made a clear-cut departure from the Italian mafia model that long dominated the American and European debate on organized crime (for a review, see Paoli and Fijnaut, 2004b).

Criminal investigations and scientific analyses have further undermined the Italian mafia model when applied to illegal markets transactions. According to Paoli (2003b), for example, even Italian mafia groups do not operate as monolithic productive and commercial units when they deal in drugs or other illegal commodities, because they are themselves subjected to the constraints of illegality. On the basis of an extensive review of Italian criminal cases, Paoli (2000:101–104, 132; 2003b:144–148) has shown that mafia members frequently set up partnerships with other mafia affiliates or even with individuals outside the mafia to make drug and, specifically, heroin deals. These partnerships are far from being stable working units and cannot be compared with the branch office of a legal firm. Their composition frequently changes depending on the moment when deals take place or on the availability of single members. After one or a few drug transactions, some teams are disbanded whereas others continue to operate for a longer time, eventually changing their composition.[6]. In sum, in the illegal markets of most industrialized countries, which are governed by relatively strong and efficient state apparatuses, the dominant theme is not organized crime, but poorly organized crime (Reuter, 1983).

Illegal Enterprises' Operating Methods and Market Structure

Strict enforcement presents constraints that powerfully impact the modus operandi of opiate entrepreneurs. For example, to reduce the risks of incarceration and asset seizure, inventories are likely to be modest, because they constitute both a primary asset and potential proof of criminal activity. The analysis of German and Italian criminal proceedings and a number of expert interviews in Germany, Italy, the United Kingdom, and Turkey, for example, show that Turkish importers try to split up large heroin batches as soon as they reach their final destinations (e.g., Tribunale di Milano, 1996).

Ethnic Albanians, who have taken over a substantial share of the heroin import and wholesale distribution activities in Italy, Switzerland, several Baltic countries, and, to a lesser extent, also in Germany (Direzione Centrale per i Servizi Antidroga [DCSA], 2005:32; Europol, 2005:8–12; Nett, 2006:146–157) have developed a more efficient method of managing inventory. According to Italian law enforcement officials, this innovation has been a key factor in the Albanians' success in trafficking opiates (Paoli, 2000:117). Unlike their Turkish predecessors, Albanian traffickers no longer import large batches of heroin into western Europe, but tend to deposit them in eastern Europe, where the detection risk is lower. Albania and Kosovo are still used as warehouses. At least between the late 1990s and early 2004, the Czech Republic and Slovakia were also popular locations for such deposits, mainly because of their convenient geographic position close to large consumer markets in western Europe. Albanian traffickers only allow smuggling into western Europe after they have found a customer; then, western European couriers, traveling in western European cars, bring in the amount required for the transaction, usually less than 10 kilograms of heroin each (Paoli, 2000:117; see also Czech News Agency [CTK], 2003, 2005; BBC, 2006b).

Strict enforcement may also result in less open violence, regardless of whether that violence is used to discourage competitors or to compel employees, suppliers, clients, or any corrupt government officials to respect their contracts. When confronted with the risks of incarceration and asset seizure, illicit entrepreneurs may choose to use less open violence to reduce their visibility, hence their probability of detection. In the words of Pearson and Hobbs (2001:42), "violence and killings attract police attention and leave traces, as well as attracting retaliation. Violence is therefore strictly 'bad for business'" (see also Reuter and Haaga, 1989). Of course, offenders are not always so disciplined as to refrain from using violence for expressive rather than instrumental purposes (Pearson and Hobbs, 2001:41–47). These outbursts of expressive violence can also be read as further proof of the fluid and chaotic nature of drug networks.[7]

Given the high cost of using violence and the small and ephemeral nature of most enterprises operating illegally, it is rare that any of them can exercise quasi-governmental functions. Although they try to make credible threats of punishment in case of non-compliance, opiate entrepreneurs in particular are all vulnerable to the risks of being cheated by employees, suppliers, clients, and corrupt government officials, and have to rely largely on monetary rewards to control the risks of being betrayed or tipped off to the police. Monetary rewards are the entrepreneurs' principal method for securing the compliance of state representatives. However, under strict enforcement, illegal enterprises are unable to influence the decisions and actions of government and, specifically, of law enforcement agencies systematically. At most, they may be able to corrupt a few individual law enforcement officials or, even less likely, politicians.

Again, empirical evidence from the scientific literature and from law enforcement agencies supports U.S. and western Europe's placement in the first category. Although local U.S. police departments were prone to systemic corruption up until the late 1950s (Landesco [1929] 1968; Reuter, 1995), in the United States, Canada, Australia, and most European countries there is no evidence more recently of a systematic pattern of corruption and infiltration of political and government institutions by drug-trafficking (or other organized crime) groups (Paoli and Fijnaut, 2004a:614–616). To quote (again) Europol (2003:10):"politically, few OC [organized crime] groups pose a direct threat to Member States."[8]

For all these reasons—the absence of economies of scale and scope in illegal operations, the disincentives to use violence to discourage competition or compel respect, and the inherent inability of illegal enterprises to influence government enforcement systematically—the development of monopolies or oligopolies in opiate markets is highly unlikely. In other words, in countries with strict enforcement, the relationships among these illegal enterprises generally involve a reasonable degree of competition. Empirical evidence again supports these hypotheses. Despite finding that some traffickers deal with very large drug quantities and have enormous incomes, no researcher has found evidence—except on the most local basis (e.g., a few blocks) or in the strongholds of mafia groups in southern Italy—that a drug enterprise has the ability to exclude others or to set prices, the hallmarks of market power (Katz and Rosen, 1994:chap. 13). The best evidence against control is simply the ease with which new sellers enter and the speed with which dealers depart. Throughout Europe and North America, moreover, drug-dealing enterprises are price takers—that is, none of them is able to influence opiate prices appreciably by varying the quantity of the output they sell. The continuing decline of prices for more than a 20-year period at all levels of the market in heroin in many of the major consumer countries (UNODC, 2006:363–367) suggests that, if market power ever existed, it has now been dissipated (see chapter 3).

Legitimacy and Sociopolitical Impact

Regardless of whether it is reinforced by prohibitions against the use and possession of opiates, the strict enforcement of prohibitions against production and trafficking reduces the legitimacy of opiates. Coupled with an inhibiting effect on availability, delegitimization and the fear of legal sanctions reduce opiate attractiveness. Most experts agree that the removal of prohibitions would almost certainly increase both their availability and legitimacy, thus fostering an increase in their consumption, although there is no consensus on the amount of the expected increase (for an overview of the different estimates, see MacCoun and Reuter [2001:72–100]).[9]

The bad reputation associated with dealing in opiates and the high risks of incarceration and asset seizure also tend to marginalize the supply of these commodities socially. Only a few educated persons with the prospect of a career in legitimate business or government are willing to risk their reputation, freedom, and physical safety by becoming involved in the production or trade of opiates. The apparently high earnings of drug dealers in western countries—recent studies of the U.K. drug markets found that some mid-level dealers earned hundreds of thousands of pounds sterling annually (Pearson and Hobbs, 2001; Matrix, 2007)—represent compensation for both the low repute of drug-related business activities and the risks of incarceration, loss of property, and physical injury deriving from the action of law enforcement agencies and other participants in the business (Reuter and Kleiman, 1986). The same high risks and costs are also faced by government officials who are offered bribes by opiate entrepreneurs.

Even if democratic regimes cannot completely eliminate opiate markets in the context of free and open societies, in countries with effective government structures and strictly enforced prohibitions, the related economic activities—production, trafficking, and consumption—are very unlikely to expand so much that they supersede legitimate ones or endanger the stability and legitimacy of the state. Substantial illegal opiate markets can coexist with an effective state committed to strict prohibition enforcement, but these markets are very unlikely to become a major component of the economy as a whole. For example, in the United States, a retail heroin market of approximately $12 billion in 1999 (ONDCP, 2001) would have amounted to barely one 10th of a percent of the nation's GDP of $9,268 billion (Council of Economic Advisers, 2007:table B-1).[10]

The Consequences of Lax Enforcement

In the second case, the state formally prohibits opiate production and trafficking, but it is too weak or corrupt or simply unwilling to enforce the ban consistently. Although the market is formally illegal, its agents are partially freed from the constraints of illegality. Lax enforcement also fosters the legitimacy of opiates. It may enable their production and trade to expand to the detriment of legitimate economic activities and, if the illegal industry reaches a certain critical dimension, may even slow down the consolidation of effective and democratic state structures.

Tajikistan, a transit country, best exemplifies this second case; other opiate-transit countries, such as Pakistan, Turkey, Albania, and Kosovo (a highly autonomous province of Serbia from 1999–2007, which became independent in early 2008) are also strong candidates. Mexico is the only important illicit opium producing country—a second-tier producer—that falls into this class.[11] With its extensive diversion from licit opium production, India also illustrates what happens in a producer with low levels of enforcement.[12]

Lax enforcement can be the result of either state weakness or of extensive corruption in a state that is not necessarily weak but, for example, authoritarian. Although weakness and corruption very often accompany each other, it is worthwhile to keep them distinguished analytically, because they have different consequences for the size, organization, and operating methods of illegal enterprises.

The Size and Organization of Illegal Enterprises

Lax enforcement partially frees opiate entrepreneurs from the constraints of illegality. At least in the short run, many (if not most) can operate without the constant threat of incarceration or asset seizure—that is, they do not need to operate against the state. In principle, they may still face the "constraints of anarchy:" that is, like their counterparts who operate under strict enforcement, but for entirely different reasons, these drug entrepreneurs may have to do business without the benefit of state institutions to enforce contracts or to prosecute contract violations. Whether they find themselves operating without such protective services will depend in part on whether lax enforcement arises from state corruption or weakness.

If corruption is the prime cause, the constraints of anarchy may be overcome by enterprises able to secure either a blind eye or, even more, active support, especially in the form of outright protection, from corrupt high-level government officials, law enforcement authorities, or, possibly, from insurgent groups. As we demonstrate later, the protection reaches its peak when an opiate enterprise is closely linked or virtually coincides with a government agency or an insurgent group. Under these conditions, large enterprises can readily develop. When corruption underlies laxity, well-connected opiate suppliers may be better able to act like legal enterprises than under strict enforcement, but with the added expense of bribes and payoffs.

However, even with strong ties to corrupt officials, agencies, or insurgents, the drug entrepreneur's position is not as completely secure as it is in the third case of non-enforcement. It is always possible that the corrupt officials or agencies that currently turn a blind eye toward illegal activities or provide protection to illegal entrepreneurs will be overruled by other officials or agencies, perhaps at the insistence of the international community or more powerful nations, as has happened time and again in Mexico and Tajikistan, for example. Alternatively, insurgent groups, especially if they have not yet attained firm territorial control, may not be able to offer continuous or reliable protection. Thus, under lax enforcement, a well-connected opiate enterprise will still face the threat of disruption and will never operate entirely like a legal enterprise.

Alternatively, if lax enforcement is largely the result of the weakness of the state, all entrepreneurs, both legal and illegal, lack regular access to state provision of protection and contract enforcement. As a consequence, legal and illegal business enterprises may operate quite similarly. In both sectors of the economy, the lack of institutional support will discourage the development of formally organized modern "corporations," and economic exchanges will tend to be embedded in preexisting social relationships. Tajikistan, Albania, and Kosovo, all of which have experienced recent civil unrest if not outright civil war, illustrate this point. In each, the rampant informal economy has long marginalized the formal one, with many informal and thoroughly criminal enterprises operating in a similar way and relying on preexisting social relationships to achieve stability (Corpora, 2004; Pugh, 2004). Enterprises might be large or small, but their success and stability would depend on the strength of those relationships, whether among family members or within ethnic groups. In a cross between the two scenarios, the stability of some illicit enterprises founded on preexisting social relationships may be reinforced by the direct involvement or at least the open and systematic support of corrupt government officials or agencies.

In practice, the intermingling of both conditions—laxity because of corruption and state weakness—is most common. In the seven countries selected as exemplary of lax enforcement, we find many small operations based on family, friendship, or local ties. In Turkey, for example, drug smuggling is largely a family business. In an extensive and well-documented study of the Turkish mafia, Frank Bovenkerk and Yücel Yesilgöz (1998) report that police investigations in various countries have produced evidence that entire Turkish families in western Europe supplement their incomes by investing in the heroin-smuggling business. "Mom and pop" operations are also active in Mexico in the cultivation of opium poppy, heroin processing, and smuggling, working independently or contracted by individual traffickers or trafficking groups (DEA, 2000:3).

In these seven countries, however, we also find enterprises that are much larger and more stable than those operating under conditions of strict enforcement. Some of these large enterprises have their core in family-based, local relationships; others have, instead, bureaucratic traits and, specifically, quasi-military structures.

Clans and Tribes

Opiate enterprises derive from—and sometimes are one and the same as—extended families, clans, and tribes in Pakistan, Turkey, Albania, Kosovo, and Mexico. Some of the Pashtun tribes spanning the Afghan–Pakistan border, such as the Afridi and the Shinwari, have been engaged in large-scale heroin production and trafficking since the 1980s (UNDCP, 1998b; see also Abbas, 2006).[13]

In Turkey, too, some of the most lasting and successful opiate enterprises also have an extended family or clan at their core. The most prominent example is the Kurdish Baybasin clan, which is reputed to be one of the largest suppliers of heroin for the western European market. According to Interpol, the Baybasin family has been involved in large-scale heroin smuggling in Britain, Germany, the Netherlands, Italy, and Spain (Thompson, 2002). From the late 1970s onward, the Baybasin clan has also manufactured heroin in secret factories around its home town of Lice in southeastern Turkey.

The clan, with at least 40 people constituting the core members of its various drug-smuggling enterprises, has long been led by Huseyin Baybasin with the support of his three brothers.[14] According to his own statements, Baybasin made his first trip to Europe to smuggle heroin in 1982 and was active in this business up to his 1998 arrest and subsequent sentence of life imprisonment in the Netherlands. Throughout this period, the Baybasin clan appears to have enjoyed high-level political and government protections. These ties were probably established in the 1970s, when Huseyin Baybasin was a member of the Grey Wolves, Turkey's main ultranationalistic movement. Despite his later siding with (and generous funding of) the Kurdistan Workers' Party (usually referred to by its Kurdish acronym of PKK), he was allegedly able to maintain many of these high-level political connections.[15]

Large, longstanding trafficking enterprises, based predominantly on extended family ties, can also be found in Mexico. One of the most resilient is the Herrera organization from the northwestern state of Durango, which has been in operation since the mid 1950s. The organization is reported to be comprised of multiple families, all of which are related to the core Herrera family through either blood or marriage. In the 1960s and '70s, the Herrera family enjoyed such wide-ranging political connections that it was not subject to the standard extortionate police practices of the "plaza system," and its members were long considered untouchable (Lupsha, 1992:179; see Appendix D). Unlike smaller players, the Herrera organization manages the whole cycle from opium poppy cultivation to heroin distribution in the United States. According to the DEA (2000:3–4), it is a polydrug enterprise. In addition to heroin, the Herrera organization is involved in trafficking large quantities of cocaine and, on a smaller scale, marijuana and methamphetamine (*Washington Post*, 1978).

Although today's most notorious contemporary Mexican "drug cartels" draw most of their revenues from smuggling Colombian and Peruvian cocaine into the United States, many have their roots in the opium poppy-cultivating areas of the western Sierra Madre and started their businesses with heroin production and smuggling. Despite their high degree of professionalism and sophistication, these "cartels" are also largely based on family ties. Six brothers, for example formed the core of the Arellano Felix group, which has claimed control over Tijuana, the main drug gateway into the western United States, since the 1980s (DEA, 2003b:20). The Arellanos also exemplify the shift from the heroin to cocaine business, as they moved to Tijuana from the opium-producing state of Sinaloa.

Despite the common reliance on family ties, the size and the stability of illegal businesses operating under lax enforcement sometimes far exceed those of enterprises operating under strict enforcement, as the case of the Arellanos clearly demonstrates. At its peak, the Arellano trafficking group had 200 or more members in the Mexico base, with hundreds of additional members throughout the organization's network (Finckenauer, Fuentes, and Ward,

2001). Thanks to lax enforcement, virtual criminal dynasties can emerge. The six Arellano brothers were not only the offspring of a well-known heroin-trafficking family but also cousins of Miguel Angel Felix Gallardo, regarded as Mexico's most powerful drug trafficker before his 1989 arrest for the murder of an American drug agent (Golden, 2000; DEA, 2003b:8).

Although relatively new, only emerging after the collapse of the Soviet Union, ethnic Albanian drug-trafficking enterprises frequently also rest on—and disguise themselves in—the typical ethnic Albanian extended families, which at their core may well include up to 60 members with 150 surrounding relatives. According to ethnographers (e.g. Giordano, 2002; see also Barth, Bickerich, Grossekathoefer, Onneken, and Schlamp, 1999), in fact, many Albanian men can still recount relatives of their 7th to 10th degree and expect to rely on them, if they need support in either licit or illicit businesses. As Italian mafia groups did (and partially still do) in Sicily and Calabria, ethnic Albanian groups reflect—and profit from—the widespread phenomenon of "amoral familism" (Banfield, 1958) or, more correctly, "double morality" (Hess, 1973:23–52), whereby family interests and values are put first and pursued even at the expense of the interests of the larger communities and in defiance of state rules. Ethnic Albanian organized crime groups have been described recently as "hierarchical, disciplined and based on exclusive group membership" by Europol (2004:8).

Quasi-Military Organizations
In countries with lax enforcement, large opiate enterprises may also involve quasi-military structures, typically challenging the state and its authority, but sometimes built into the state. As seen in chapter 9, Tajikistan's largest and most sophisticated drug-trafficking organizations—that is, those that are capable of importing heroin from Afghanistan and exporting it to other former Soviet states—usually coincide with the private armies of former civil war commanders turned career or elected public officials.

According to some sources (International Strategic Studies Association, 2004), the Kosovo Liberation Army (KLA) has been involved directly in heroin trafficking. Although these allegations are unproved, intelligence, journalistic, and scholarly sources agree that the KLA has relied on money derived from drug trafficking and other illegal businesses to purchase its weapons, and that many of its members, both before and after the NATO liberation of Kosovo in spring 1999, were involved in illicit activities, including the heroin trade. Anecdotal evidence shows that these criminal entrepreneurs-turned-KLA combatants exploit their KLA contacts and membership for widening their spheres of action and establishing a reputation of violence and criminal competence, effectively opposing the restoration of law and order (Arsovska, 2006b; Zaremba, 2007).[16]

In some countries, intelligence agencies have also entered the drug trade directly or, at least, have let their members participate extensively in it. An example of participation is provided by the Direccion Federal de Seguridad

(DFS), a Mexican government antiguerrilla force that is accused of having tortured and killed hundreds of Mexicans considered threats to the regime before being disbanded in 1985. According to evidence presented during the trial for the murder of a DEA agent, DFS commanders not only accepted lavish bribes and gifts from narco-traffickers, but also made direct investments in the plantations and trafficking ventures of a major drug-trafficking organization, the so-called Guadalajara cartel (Lupsha, 1992:180–181, quoting extensively the proceedings of the previously mentioned trial; Reuter and Ronfeldt, 1992:102–103).

Pakistan's military intelligence agency, the ISI, also has been repeatedly suspected of involvement in illegal heroin trafficking from Afghanistan. There is consensus among Afghan scholars and journalists that, during the 1980s, the ISI routinely condoned heroin manufacture and sales by some Afghan guerrilla groups, with some of its officials getting involved in heroin smuggling themselves (e.g., Coll, 1991; Rubin, 2003:196–199). Some sources, including a 1993 CIA report that was leaked to the press, also allege that the ISI itself went into the heroin business after the Soviet retreat from Afghanistan in 1989. After that event, foreign governments—chiefly the United States—stopped funneling money and arms through the ISI to Afghan mujahedin guerrillas fighting the Soviet-backed Kabul government. The heroin trade allegedly became one of the ISI's alternative sources of funds to continue the same level of operations in other areas, including aiding militants fighting Indian troops across the border in Kashmir (Royce, 1993; Khan, 2004:38–41). The ISI's plans to enter the drug business were revealed by Pakistan's former prime minister Nawaz Sharif in a 1994 interview with *The Washington Post* (Anderson and Khan, 1994).

Whatever the ISI's exact involvement in the heroin trade, it is clear that as governments, such as those in Tajikistan and Kosovo, increasingly tolerate the participation of quasi-military organizations and even state agencies in the illicit opiate industry, they get closer to the case of non-enforcement, with state (or quasi-state) tolerance and support of opiate trafficking. With the exception of the ISI and DFS, the enterprises that we have reviewed in this section are not fully modern bureaucracies; nonetheless, many of them clearly have a size, stability, and protections that illegal enterprises operating under strict enforcement can only imagine.

Illegal Enterprises' Operating Methods and Market Structure

Lax enforcement also affects the operating methods of criminal entrepreneurs. If a state is unable or unwilling to enforce prohibitions strictly, certain risks for opiate producers and traffickers are much lower. The risks of incarceration and asset seizure may even (at least in the short run) become negligible for well-connected dealers. For them, the risks of being cheated by their counterparts or by corrupt authorities may also decline significantly. However, no enterprise operating under lax enforcement can completely eliminate the risks of operating against and without the state in the long run. In such a context, market participants may rationally choose behaviors, such as cultivating opium poppy, processing its derivatives, and holding large inventories that would be too costly in the first case, but cannot ignore the possibility of enforcement or of being cheated.

Each of our seven "lax" countries provides supportive evidence. Although large-scale opium cultivation is concentrated in countries with almost no enforcement, Mexico's experience demonstrates that small-scale cultivation of opium poppy is possible in countries with only lax enforcement. However, Mexico's experience also shows the difficulties faced by growers under such circumstances: Law enforcement agencies' eradication efforts impinge on cultivation, which is extremely fragmented and mainly concentrated in remote regions along the spine of the Sierra Madre Mountains in western Mexico.[17] At least partly reflecting the related risk, opium farm-gate prices are also much higher in Mexico than in Asian opium-producing countries without enforcement. Lower risk-adjusted smuggling costs to the U.S. market enable Mexico to be a major supplier in competition with low-cost Asian production countries.[18]

Opium poppies have also been traditionally cultivated in the Afghan border regions of Pakistan and were cultivated in Tajikistan during the first chaotic phase of the civil war at the beginning of the 1990s. Given the virtual absence of law enforcement, these two contexts must be seen as intermediate between the second and third cases.

Large quantities of opiates are processed into heroin and possibly held as inventories (although the evidence for this latter claim is weaker) in most of the seven countries with lax enforcement. Pakistani labs long refined a substantial share of the opium produced in Afghanistan, and their recent demise, as well as the lack of opiate processing in Tajikistan, should not be read as proof of unfavorable local sociopolitical conditions, but must be related to the comparatively ideal conditions found in Afghanistan. Massive diversion from licit opium production and large-scale heroin processing routinely take place in India. Since the late 1970s, refineries in southeastern Turkey have transformed morphine base into heroin, and local traffickers sometimes hold large inventories of opiates in one single place, as indicated by the seizure of 7.5 metric tons of morphine base close to Istanbul in April 2002 and other multiton seizures carried out in Turkey (Frantz, 2002; Atasoy, 2004:19). Despite the absence of large seizures, a number of western European law enforcement officers we interviewed report that large inventories of heroin are also kept in Kosovo and Albania. Heroin is also cut and repackaged there, before being smuggled farther into eastern or western European-consuming countries.

In countries with lax enforcement, well-connected criminal entrepreneurs can lead very comfortable lives, publicly enjoying their wealth and circulating in high society in the company of high-level politicians. In Turkey, for example, pictures in the press show Urfi Cetinkaya, suspected of exporting tons of heroin into Germany, Portugal, Belgium, Spain, and the Netherlands, and eventually arrested in his villa in Istanbul, meeting a deputy parliament speaker at a gala dinner (*Turkish Daily News,* 2000).

Some criminal entrepreneurs do not just circulate among politicians, they also hold public office. During the 1980s in Pakistan, one of the most notorious drug barons, Ayub Afridi, built a large fortress estate and a private army in the legendary Khyber Pass area bordering Afghanistan with the revenues of smuggling heroin and other commodities from Afghanistan (Anderson, 1993; Burns, 1995). In the mid 1980s, Afridi was indicted twice for drug trafficking, but he never appeared in court and was declared an absconder. Arrest warrants were issued, but the Pakistani police said they could not serve them because Afridi lived in a tribal area where they had no powers. Not withstanding this track record, Afridi sat as an elected member of parliament from 1988 to 1990, enjoying parliamentary immunity and dropping out only when a new ordinance barred known drug traffickers from running in an election (Anderson, 1993; Burns, 1995; Kessler, 1995).

At least circumstantially, it seems that many successful drug traffickers in Tajikistan, some in public office, also have few qualms about showing their wealth—they drive expensive cars, fly helicopters, and live in luxurious villas (Khamonov, 2005).

Likewise, in Mexico, the leaders of the most powerful drug organizations live well and, before 2000, were only seldom targets of the very selective Mexican drug law enforcement (DEA, 2000:3–4; Golden, 2000). Up to his arrest in 1986, for example, Miguel Angel Felix Gallardo was a friend and associate of two Sinaloa state governors. While the DEA sought to arrest him, he not only served on the board of one of Mexico's leading banks, but he and his family had an active social life among the political elites of Sinaloa, Sonora, and Jalisco (Lupsha, 1992:187–188). In addition to state protection, some Mexican drug enterprises still have deep roots and enjoy considerable popular support in their home regions. Joachin "El Chapo" (Shorty) Guzman, one of Mexico's drug kingpins, who escaped in 2001 from a federal high-security prison, allegedly hides in his home state at his ranch in the Sierra Madre Mountains. Although he often throws catered parties, locals do not usually acknowledge his presence and, if they talk about him at all, they praise him for his benevolence and generosity (Boudreaux, 2005; see also Sullivan and Jordan, 2005).

It seems likely that instrumental violence is more commonplace in the case of lax enforcement than in the case of strict enforcement—for example, to settle conflicts arising from illegal transactions and possibly to intimidate government officials. It has, however, been impossible to find systematic supporting evidence. Some of the countries selected as "lax enforcers" tend to have higher murder rates than those selected as "strict enforcers," but others do not. According to the *European Sourcebook of Crime and Criminal Justice Statistics,* for example, between 1995 and 2000, Albania recorded one of the highest rates of completed homicide in Europe, reaching the staggering rate of 46.5 per 100,000 (compared with Germany's 2.0 and Italy's 1.6) in 1997, a year of heavy rioting. In contrast, during the same period, Turkey's rate of completed and attempted homicide was lower than that recorded in most western European countries (WODC, 2003:35–36).

Leaving aside the difficulties of comparing criminal statistics across countries, it has been impossible to estimate the murders in any given year that are either drug- or organized crime-related, even in data-rich nations such as the United Kingdom and the United States. There are a few research studies of specific cities and periods (see, for example, Goldstein, Brownstein, and Ryan, 1992). Anecdotal evidence does show that in some of the selected countries, drug traffickers do not hesitate to use weapons to defend their interests from law enforcement officers, maverick business partners, or competitors. Armed conflicts are very frequent on the Afghan–Tajik border between traffickers of both sides and the Russian or Tajik border guards. In 2001, moreover, the then-deputy minister of the interior, Habib Sanginov, was murdered because of his failure to pay a drug shipment.

Since the 1980s, Mexico's drug traffickers have killed hundreds of lawyers, judges, police officers, politicians, and journalists who have challenged them. And countless bystanders have simply been in the wrong place at the wrong time. In 1993, the Roman Catholic cardinal of Guadalajara was gunned down in crossfire between rival drug-trafficking groups. Especially in border areas, police officers trying to reduce corruption become victims of deadly attacks, as happened twice, in 1994 and 2001, with the Tijuana police chief and, in 2005, with two police chiefs of New Laredo, another busy border crossing farther west (Thompson, 2005a). Drug-related violence cost more than 1,500 lives in Mexico, including those of police, rival drug traffickers, and civilians in 2005 alone (Roig-Franzia, 2006) and has escalated since then. Mexican drug enterprises are particularly brutal against their competitors or members of their own ranks who betray them. Small-scale massacres in vendettas by one drug-trafficking or criminal group against another are quite frequent. In February 2001, for example, a massacre in a small village in the state of Sinaloa left 12 men and boys dead (Finckenauer et al., 2001).

Although data on drug-related violence in Turkey could not be collected in the country itself, evidence from western European countries indicates that Turkish criminal groups resort to violence more frequently than groups of other nationalities. Several reports of the Dutch police, for example, point to "the extremely violent nature of Turkish criminal organizations in comparison with other criminal organizations" (KT-NON, 2002:62). Ethnic Albanian criminals also have a reputation for their ruthlessness and violence both in their home regions and in western Europe (Hysi, 2004; Arsovska, 2006a, b). In contrast, possibly because the illicit opiate industry derives from the legal one, the level of opiate-related violence seems to be quite low in India.

It is plausible that in countries with lax enforcement illegal enterprises enjoying the protection of powerful state representatives may be able to secure an oligopolistic position in the local market, particularly if they can direct the attention of law enforcement agencies to less protected competitors. Evidence for such a case can be found for both Mexico and Tajikistan. In Mexico, large drug-trafficking organizations run large shares of the opiate and cocaine export markets, staging violent turf wars to maintain control of the most convenient border crossings (DEA, 2000, 2003b). In Tajikistan, too, several large and well-connected enterprises have, since the late 1990s, gained hold of a significant—and probably a majority—fraction of the opiate trade. Their market power usually rests on two assets: the protection or, more often, the immediate involvement of a high-level politician and the control of segments of the Afghan border. However, in neither context do these large enterprises seem able to fix drug prices or to exclude smaller competitors, as indicated by the contemporaneous existence of a multiplicity of heroin-smuggling enterprises.

Legitimacy and Sociopolitical Impact

Lax enforcement fosters the legitimacy of opiate-related economic activities. If opiates may be produced, traded, and consumed in daylight with very limited fear of police intervention, these activities themselves will eventually lose the stigma of illegality and may come to be considered socially acceptable.

Three of the selected countries provide possible evidence of effectively legitimized consumption; the others do not. Pakistan has experienced a major increase in heroin use since the early 1980s, when heroin became available and began replacing opium. With 500,000 hard-core users, Pakistan now has the 10th highest prevalence of opiate abuse, according to the United Nations Office on Drugs and Crime (UNODC, 2004:389–391). In its worst-affected cities, prevalence of heroin abuse was estimated at the turn of the century to be as high as 4% in the male population age 15 to 45—a figure that, according to the UN drug office, "by most countries' standards would be considered unrealistically high" (UNODCCP, 2002b:xiii).[19] The progression of heroin consumption in Tajikistan has been at least as dramatic, because the country did not have a significant heroin-using population before the mid 1990s. However, by 2004, Tajikistan recorded the eighth highest prevalence of opiate abuse (UNODC, 2004:389–391). Although at a less sensational pace, India also has recorded a rapid increase in heroin consumption since the early 1980s, whereas opium consumption is still, by and large, socially accepted.

In Turkey and Mexico, in contrast, heroin consumption has remained limited, despite the two countries' selective enforcement against trafficking and the resulting heroin availability (Institute of Forensic Sciences, Istanbul University, 2000; Atasoy, 2004; DEA, 2000). There are no empirical data on heroin consumption on either Albania or Kosovo, but consumption in the former is said to be on the rise (U.S. Department of State, Bureau of International Narcotic and Law Enforcement Affairs, 2006:304).

As for opiate supply, all seven countries provide supporting evidence that lax enforcement can increase the legitimacy of opium production and trafficking. In the tribal areas of Pakistan, as in Tajikistan, in southeastern Turkey, Mexico, Albania, and Kosovo, a substantial minority of the local population has apparently no misgivings in dealing with opiates. This is even truer for India, where the legality of opium exclusively depends on the buyer. In traditional cultivation districts, opium is a legitimate commodity and it acquires an illegal status only when it is sold to non-state agents. Particularly in countries that have been disrupted by civil war, some of the people involved in the lower levels of the illegal drug industry have (or had) no viable income-earning alternatives. As a police officer working in the eastern Gorno Badakhshan region of Tajikistan emphatically stated, in the mid 1990s "we wouldn't have survived without opium. I knew a lot of people who brought drugs to Osh [in Kyrgyzstan] and returned with butter, bread or other food. The police could do absolutely nothing" (Khazoev, 2004). The "success stories" of large-scale traffickers mentioned in the previous section further increase the legitimacy of formally criminalized activities.

In countries with lax enforcement, opiate production and trade may expand to the detriment of legal economic activities, although they may also profit from the sheer lack of legitimate alternatives, as in postcivil war Tajikistan and Kosovo. After it has reached a critical level, the illegal drug industry may frustrate or distort the state-building process. When a large number of politicians and government officials profit directly or indirectly from an illegal trade, they acquire a personal interest in its continuation, thus blocking attempts to enforce the prohibition on such commodities or to create a more authoritative and effective state apparatus.

Again, each of the seven countries provides supporting evidence, especially the countries with smaller economies. Opiate trafficking and drug-related corruption have already become so pervasive there, that in chapter 9 we defined Tajikistan as a narco-state. Although no precise estimate exists of opiate trafficking's share of GDP in either Albania or Kosovo, there are no doubts that both of their economic and political systems are also heavily affected. According to the Council of Europe Parliamentary Assembly (2004:8, 2), for example, organized crime and corruption, of which drug trafficking represents a major component, constitute "the single most important problem for Albania" and "the single most important threat to the functioning of democratic institutions and the rule of law in the country." Considerably larger, Mexico, Turkey, and Pakistan are less affected by opiate processing and trafficking, which are rooted in geographically limited sections of the three countries. However, even in these countries, drug-related revenues allow the implementation of government practices that are incompatible with the rule of law and, in Turkey and Pakistan, may also finance insurgency (see appendix D).

The Consequences of Non-enforcement

In the third case, the state, or quasi-state authorities effectively substituting for the central government in some parts of a country, willfully choose to ignore international prohibitions on opiates and openly tolerate or even profit from their production or trade. This case does not require the authorities to be directly involved in opiate production or commercialization; for example, it suffices if they systematically profit from these activities, by "taxing" independent producers and traffickers.

Even allowing for a broad definition of non-enforcement, this is the least commonly occurring case. Nonetheless, the two major illicit opiate producing countries—namely, Afghanistan and Burma—have long met, at least regionally, most of its conditions (as shown in detail in chapter 6). In addition, state tolerance of opium production and trade previously characterized Laos and may also characterize those parts of Colombia where opium poppies (and coca) are grown.

The Size and Organization of Illegal Enterprises

Under conditions of state tolerance and support, opiate entrepreneurs do not have to operate against the state. Unlike their counterparts in the second case, they may be entirely freed from the constraints of anarchy (i.e., the lack of accepted and effective mechanisms for enforcing contracts and prosecuting violations). The degree to which these constraints are effectively removed, however, depends on two variables.

The first variable is the extent of the state or quasi-state authority's direct involvement in the opiate industry. Even between and within the two selected countries, considerable differences can be found. According to most sources, for example, the Taliban as a whole never attempted to organize the opium trade but merely taxed cultivators and traffickers. In contrast, from the early 1960s to the late 1970s, Kuomintang (KMT) forces aimed to control a large share of the Burmese opium trade, although they also sold protection and transportation services to independent traffickers. For much of the 1990s, the same could be said for the Eastern Shan State Army (ESSA) of Lin Ming-Xian, which rules over the crucial triborder area of Möng La on the Burmese, Chinese, and Laotian borders (Lintner, 2002:273–274). The other quasi-state authorities that are active in Burma's production areas profit from the illegal opiate industry through both direct involvement and taxation.

The second important variable is represented by the extent of consolidation and sophistication of the state or quasi-state institutions. As in the case of lax enforcement, the strength of governing institutions, be they state or quasi-state, will affect the size and structure of the enterprises. Afghanistan and Burma illustrate two extremes. The Afghan mujahedin of the 1980s and early 1990s were never able to consolidate their power beyond the warlord stage. They were unable to provide the citizens and enterprises of the areas under their control with most of the services typical of a state, except for the imposition of taxes. In contrast, the United Wa State Party (UWSA) and other splinter groups of the Communist Party of Burma (CPB) are mini states, whose existence and borders are de facto recognized by the Burmese central government, with which they have maintained ceasefire agreements since 1988.

Arguably, the Burmese government itself could represent the most sophisticated state institution supporting the illegal opiate trade, dating back to the abolition of the opium monopolies in Indochina and Thailand in the 1950s, depending on whether one accepts the thesis that its long tolerance of the drug trade in the Shan State has not just been the result of its lack of control in the area but a strategic choice (Altsean-Burma, 2004). Some circumstantial evidence supports this thesis; however, the Burmese government has worked predominantly through the proxy of militias or insurgent rebel groups. It is also unclear the extent to which key segments of the Karzai administration have been effectively captured by powerful drug-trafficking enterprises. Nonetheless, in the rest of this section. we deal largely with quasi-state institutions.

In a market for a legal commodity, the constraints of anarchy can be off-set effectively by the emergence of a strong state providing a fair and effective legislative and judicial framework for competition among private enterprises. This is not a possibility, though, in the current illicit opiate market. The quasi-state authorities openly supporting the drug trade have no ability or interest in filling the governance or oversight roles we almost automatically ascribe to the state in our contemporary democratic and market-oriented societies. Not even the Burmese regime, for example, has ever done so. For this reason, we hypothesize that the constraints of anarchy are at a minimum when a strong and effective quasi-state authority directly plans and controls key phases of the illegal opiate industry. Under these conditions, the factors promoting the development of large, enduring modern bureaucracies—namely, to take advantage of economies of scale and scope of operations—can exercise their influence; the development of large-scale hierarchical enterprises becomes more likely.

Although 40 years have elapsed, the enterprises created the two KMT Generals Ly and Tuan for smuggling opium and heroin from the Shan State into Burma remain the largest and most hierarchical ones ever found in the illegal opiate industry and probably in the whole illegal drug industry. In their heydays, Ly and Tuan arranged caravans of up to 600 mules carrying up to 30 tons of opium from the Shan State's production areas into Thailand. Largely consisting of the KMT Third and Fifth armies (manned with about 1,400 and 1,800 men, respectively), these smuggling enterprises had a strict military organization and approached most closely the model of modern bureaucracies. The two generals' armies maintained a string of radio posts that stretched for hundreds of kilometers from the two army headquarters in northern Thailand to the opium production areas in the northern Shan State. Each post was guarded by 80 to 100 KMT soldiers, who also worked as opium brokers and purchasing agents (Kamm, 1971; McCoy, 1991:353). The KMT convoys also provided transportation and protection services to independent traffickers, who traveled with them (Cowell, 2005:10).

Unlike the KMT armies, the even larger militias set up by Khun Sa during the early 1990s and later on by the UWSA and the other CPB splinter groups do not appear to have been systematically involved in opiate trafficking (Kramer, 2005:46–48). The armed groups and illegal enterprises appear to have been distinct entities, although precise information on the latter's functioning has been hard to find. However, there are no doubts that the trafficking enterprises of the militia leaders profited greatly from the militias' protection and logistical services.

In contrast, large illegal enterprises may not develop if the supporting authority is weak and unstable. As in the case of lax enforcement, illegal enterprises mirroring their legal counterparts are likely to develop, and the former tend to be operated like the latter, reflecting local economic, social, and political conditions and development. It may be possible for opiate producers and traffickers to form large enterprises under these conditions, but nothing in the environment would encourage them, and the constraints of anarchy might discourage them.

In Afghanistan in the 1980s and 1990s, the opium trade was largely the prerogative of a class of traders who usually dealt both in opium and other legitimate commodities, and who enjoyed full visibility and recognition in the local society. Indeed, until 2001 they openly traded opium in the local bazaars.[20] Reflecting local tribal patterns, a small number of large-scale opiate traffickers organized the opium trade and heroin processing in the east, whereas the opium trade was decentralized in the south (UNDCP, 1998b). During the 1980s and first half of the 1990s, several mujahedin groups entered the trade themselves, exploiting their military logistic channels to organize shipments of opium and heroin out of the country. As Akhundzada's experiment in the Helmand Valley exemplifies (Rubin, 2003:245), their attempts to centralize production and trade were usually short-lived (see chapter 6).

The Taliban had only slight, direct involvement in the trade. Nevertheless, by pacifying the country and providing effective security, they had a positive impact on the opium industry, even if their law enforcement and judicial systems were not sophisticated enough to enforce contracts and property rights. The Taliban rule constitutes the closest example in the illegal opiate market to the case of a governing body supportive of the industry, yet even the Taliban experience remains fundamentally different from the performance of most contemporary states.

In more recent developments, the concentration of the opium industry in Afghanistan at the beginning of the 21st century almost paradoxically reflects the process of state reconstruction and the concentration of drug-related enforcement since 2002 in the corrupt Ministry of the Interior. In addition to what was discussed earlier in chapter 6, we provide an explanation for this apparent paradox in the final section of this chapter.

Illegal Enterprisea' Operating Methods and Market Structure

State or quasi-state tolerance or support also affects how opiate enterprises operate. As the risks of incarceration and asset seizure each become negligible, opiate entrepreneurs are free to carry out visible and bulky activities, such as cultivating the formally illegal opium poppy, processing its derivatives, and holding large stocks, without concern for the costs that would accompany those risks in the cases of strict or lax enforcement. Absent a strong state or quasi-state authority, participants may still face the constraints and associated risks of anarchy, but it is no coincidence that the two countries most closely approaching non-enforcement are the two largest illicit opium producers.

Afghanistan and Burma also host a growing and preponderant share of the world's illicit morphine- and heroin-processing. Replacing opium, heroin has accounted for a progressively larger share of illegal exports since the 1970s in the case of Burma and since the mid 1990s in Afghanistan. This change mirrors similar processes in legitimate markets that have shifted manufacturing to countries with low labor costs. In the case of opium, the advantages of processing the agricultural product close to the field are increased by the fact that opium is much bulkier than its derivatives. Ten kilograms of opium are conventionally thought to be necessary to produce a kilo of morphine or heroin, although the actual ratio may vary from 8 to 12 kilograms, depending on the opium quality and humidity (UNODC, 2003c:132–135). As interdiction risks are largely a function of volume, this means that smuggling heroin is much less hazardous than smuggling opium.

Intelligence sources (UNODCCP Sub-Office in Tajikistan, 2000) suggest the possibility of large inventories of opium and heroin in Afghanistan.[21] Our own analyses in chapters 3 through 5 lend weight to the claim of substantial inventories in the supply chain, at least with regard to the pre-Taliban ban, but not necessarily to more specific claims of large holding areas. Indeed, even the current analysis suggests otherwise in cases of state weakness, because large holdings may be difficult to protect and are subject to risk of theft. Nevertheless, according to the UN drug office, aerial satellite photos taken during the year 2000 in northern Afghanistan showed the existence of at least 40 stockpiles allegedly capable of supplying 20 tons of narcotics (UNODCCP Sub-Office in Tajikistan, 2000:9).

With the official tolerance or support of their criminalized activities, illegal entrepreneurs have no need to hide themselves or their criminal revenues and are free to reinvest the latter in their enterprises or in the legitimate economy. This is particularly clear in Burma, where the official government openly tolerates the ceasefire groups' involvement in the drug trade and has shown no interest in prosecuting former drug kingpins. Several UWSA and former CPB leaders with proven involvement in the drug trade are suspected of having become some of the largest entrepreneurs of the Shan State, with interests in jewelry, communication, mining, and large construction projects. Li Hsing-han and Khun Sa (who died in 2007), two of Burma's most infamous drug traffickers, were also granted immunity from prosecution by the Burmese government and were allowed to reinvest drug money in a range of legal and semilegal economic activities.

With the opium industry adding perhaps as much as 50% to Afghanistan's legitimate GDP in recent years (UNODC, 2005b:1), the boundaries between the illegal and legal economies are even less distinct. Almost inevitably, all the participants in the opium supply chain, and specifically the wholesale traffickers who receive most of the income, reinvest their money in legitimate economic activities. Many observers believe that the construction boom that has occurred in Kabul and other Afghan cities since 2002 has been at least partially funded with drug money (Anderson, 2007). Indeed, even though the Karzai administration has condemned all forms of opium trafficking since its formation in January 2002, some of the commanders involved in the drug trade have so much power and money that they have gained high-ranking government positions in the local and central administrations.

How much violence is used depends on the authorities' strength, including their degree of consolidation and sophistication, and the extent of their involvement in the opiate trade. Powerful authorities may have an interest in reducing violence in the opiate industry and the ability to do so, but, as previously noted, they do not tend to fill mainstream oversight or governance roles. None currently provides fair or effective protective services to independent entrepreneurs. The regime of the pre-Taliban ban represents the only approximation to this circumstance, and even that was remote.

Authorities' interest in peace is probably highest when they are directly involved in the opiate trade and thus have not only a political but also a direct economic interest in keeping drug exchanges peaceful and smooth. The UWSA and the other CPB splinter groups seem to illustrate this case, although the evidence is anecdotal (Strittmatter, 2004). However, to subdue competitors, powerful quasi-state authorities may adopt violent and even brutal means, because they are not bound by democratic constraints. The fight that erupted in 1967 between the KMT forces, Khun Sa's militia, and the Laotian troops of the corrupt general Ouane Rattikone has gone into history books as the "Opium War" and, according to Thai police reports, left at least 150 people dead (McCoy, 1991:355–361). As even powerful quasi-state authorities seldom constitute a homogeneous bloc, conflicts may also arise within their leaderships for control of political or economic resources.

If the authority is weak, the participants in the opiate industry, like their counterparts under lax enforcement, have to defend themselves and their properties from attacks of competitors and robbers. According to field studies carried out by the UNDCP in Afghanistan in the late 1990s, most traffickers in southern and eastern Afghanistan behaved in such a way during the mujahedin's rule during the 1980s and early 1990s. As traffickers' experience during the mujahedin's rule suggests, violence may reach its peak when there is no dominant quasi-state authority, and entrepreneurs, be they legitimate or illegitimate, are left vulnerable to robberies and extortion by competing warlords.

The extent of bribery also depends on the same two variables. Bribes are not necessary if the authority is itself coordinating the drug production or trade. They may instead become substantial if opiate entrepreneurs have to deal with weak and competing quasi-state authorities, each with its hand out and the potential to interfere with commerce, as in the mujahedin's phase of Afghanistan's recent history.

The same is true for the emergence of monopolies and oligopolies. If the state or quasi-state authority is weak (regardless of its involvement in the opiate trade), enterprises controlling a preponderant share of the opiate market are unlikely to consolidate. Under conditions of state or quasi-state weakness, illegal enterprises are likely—as in the second case of lax enforcement—to rely upon preexisting social relationships. They may become large businesses, but they are unlikely to grow enough in a situation approximating anarchy to establish real market power.

Quasi-state authorities may themselves form an oligopoly or even a monopoly, when they are powerful and directly engaged in the opiate trade. For example, by providing protection and transportation, the semiprivate armies of the two KMT generals effectively controlled, although they did not own, a large chunk of the Burmese industry up to the mid 1970s. Ten to fifteen years later, Khun Sa's refineries were also said to process a major portion (according to the DEA, 80% [McCoy, 1991:311]) of Burma's opium. Anecdotal evidence additionally shows that until the implementation of the opium bans in the late 1990s, the leaders of CPB splinter groups profited directly or indirectly from much of the opium and heroin trade taking place within their mini states. Particularly the ESSA also made some efforts to monopolize heroin smuggling (Lintner, 2002:271–273).

As the ongoing bans in the Shan State show and the Taliban ban on poppy growing in 2000 to 2001 demonstrates, illegal enterprises operating with approval of an authority are dangerously at the latter's mercy. Because quasi-state authorities do not usually consider themselves bound by the rule of law, in the short run at least they can be much more effective than any democratic regime in repressing the production and commercialization of illicit commodities (see chapters 4 and 6).

Legitimacy and Sociopolitical Impact

The state or quasi-state authority's tolerance or support of opiate production and trade inevitably enhances the legitimacy of these activities, thus further facilitating their expansion. In Afghanistan, for example, the increasingly supportive attitude toward opium of most indigenous leaders during the two last decades of the 20th century, except for the Taliban's final turn in July 2000, did more than create a favorable environment for the illicit opium economy but also helped overrule the reservations of traditional Islam.

The growing legitimacy of formally illicit opiates, coupled with widespread availability, may also promote consumption. Support for this thesis can be found in both Afghanistan and Burma.

Opium and even heroin use has been spreading in Afghanistan since the late 1990s, despite Islamic prohibitions on intoxicants. The first Afghan

nationwide survey carried out in 2003 by the UNODC and the Afghan Ministry of Counternarcotics estimated that there were 150,000 opium and 50,000
heroin users, representing 0.6% and 0.2% of the total population, respectively
(UNODC Afghanistan, 2003; UNODC and Government of Afghanistan,
Counter Narcotics Directorate, 2005). Opium and increasingly heroin, which
was virtually unknown in Afghanistan until the early 1990s, have become the
means for small but growing fractions of the Afghan population to cope with
the pain, both psychological and physical, of losing family members, home,
job, well-being, and even country, in the case of refugees (UNODC Afghanistan, 2003).

In Burma, too, despite strong Buddhist injunctions against taking intoxicating or psychoactive drugs, opiate consumption is rising, especially in cities.
There, too, a shift has occurred from opium smoking to heroin injecting—a
habit that is more addictive and poses a greater public health risk. According to a joint UNODC/UNAIDS/WHO study, there are between 30,000 and
130,000 injecting drug users in Burma, mostly men on heroin (U.S. Department of State, Bureau of International Narcotics and Law Enforcement Affairs,
2006:245). Other sources reach even higher estimates. According to the Burnet Institute, the number of injecting drug users in Burma may lie between
150,000 and 250,000 (Reid and Costigan, 2002). The widespread sharing of
injecting equipment (such as needles) by drug users and the government's
initial lack of response have been major factors driving Burma's HIV/AIDS
epidemic, which is one of the worst in Asia (UNAIDS, United Nations Joint
Programme on HIV/AIDS, 2006:28; see also ICG, 2004a).

An authority's "benevolent" attitude toward a generally criminalized
activity also impacts the authority itself and the society at large. States or
quasi-state authorities openly supporting an illegal industry are bound to
be marginalized from the international community, losing their credibility
and status, and being considered ineligible for international assistance and
funding. Quasi-state actors may even become the target of foreign repressive
attacks. This stigma and attached negative consequences then reverberate
throughout the whole society.

Although not exclusively for their policy toward drugs, most of the current and past leaders profiting from the opium industry in Afghanistan and
Burma have either been denied recognition or considered pariahs by the
international community. The United States and other western countries' long
toleration of the KMT's and Afghan mujahedin's involvement in opium trafficking are exceptions (McCoy, 1991; Rubin, 2003). The overall international
community has shown much less tolerance for their successors, and particularly the United States has invested much energy in hampering the activities
of key foreign drug traffickers and their protectors, even trying to subject
them to U.S. prosecution. In Burma, for example, the UWSA leaders have all
become targets of U.S. federal indictments (U.S. Department of Justice, 2005).
And both the Taliban and the UWSA have had problems convincing the international community of their sudden commitment to enforce their bans on

opium and collecting the funds necessary to alleviate the consequent sufferings of the local population.

Two Theses on the Role of Governments in Opiate Markets

Two theses summarize the main findings of our analysis.

Thesis One:The Distribution of Illegal Opiate Production across Countries

The degree of effective illegality to which opium and its derivatives are subject typically rises from producing areas in Asia and Latin America to consumer markets in neighboring countries and the developed world.

This thesis appeals to common sense, yet it has not been articulated clearly in past research or analysis. The bulkiest and most visible market activities, particularly growing opium poppy, generally take place in countries or jurisdictions with scant enforcement of prohibitions and supportive local leaders. Many countries can produce opium as a purely technical matter. Australia and France do so now for the legal market, whereas the list of past producers includes China, Iran, Macedonia, Taiwan, and Turkey. Yet, despite the vast distances to the wealthiest consumer markets, Afghanistan and Burma emerged as the dominant illicit producers of opium during the last two decades of the 20th century, largely because they provided supportive contexts for illicit opium production.

Countries with no national enforcement of prohibitions or maverick local leaders that flout enforcement have an advantage in attracting opium cultivation vis-à-vis countries with a strict enforcement of prohibitions (Thoumi, 2003). The lower risks of incarceration and asset seizure sharply reduce the costs of production and distribution. Conversely, the relatively efficient government apparatuses of most developed countries and their stricter enforcement of prohibitions make growing opium poppy so risky that the compensation for such prohibited activity becomes—to make a bad pun—"prohibitive." Economically, it then makes sense to import opiates, especially heroin, produced thousands of kilometers away to supply consumers in western markets; heroin bundles can always be hidden much more easily than poppy fields.

Risk-related cost differentials also help explain why the prices of opiates in producing countries are only a negligible fraction of the final retail prices in consuming countries. Ten kilos of opium, approximately what is needed to produce 1 kilo of pure heroin, cost about $500 to $1,000 at the farm gate in Afghanistan in the late 1990s and, more recently, closer to about $1,500. Once cut and sold in small doses in a European retail market, the same kilo of pure heroin could sell for as much as $500,000 (UNODC, 2004). As in the case of other agricultural products, part of the farm-to-retail price spread represents more ordinary processing and transportation costs. In the case of heroin, however, the size of the spread primarily reflects the higher costs of illegality further down the supply chain (Reuter and Greenfield, 2001).

The degree of effective illegality may also affect the distribution of trans-shipment routes through its effect on relative costs, but to a lesser extent than in the case of production. The emergence of the Central Asian route, for example, has been enhanced by the weakness, ineffectiveness, and low legitimacy of governments in the region, but the Central Asian republics' geographic proximity to, and cultural and commercial ties with, Russia almost predestined them to service the booming Russian heroin market.

Thesis Two: Illegal Business Operations and Social Outcomes

The strictness of governments' enforcement of prohibitions—in other words, the degree of effective illegality to which opiate production and trafficking are subject—is the most important single factor to shape how the illicit opiate market is organized in a particular country and the behavior of its suppliers. The degree of effective illegality also has significant consequences for the perceived legitimacy of the prohibited activities, their impact on the surrounding society, and the state itself.

The degree of effective illegality affects not only the distribution of opium production across countries, but also the size, organization, and operating methods of emerging enterprises. For example, when enforcement is lax or absent, larger enterprises are more likely to emerge and consolidate; moreover, they may assume modern bureaucratic (for example, military) organizational forms and exercise government-like functions. In addition, the strictness of enforcement may influence the levels of inventories that entrepreneurs choose to hold, the ways in which they interact with other illicit entrepreneurs, and the nature of their relationships with government officials. Lastly, it may also affect illicit entrepreneurs' use of violence, although such violence occasionally has expressive and thus non-strategic roots.

The core point of this thesis is that whenever prohibitions are effectively enforced, agents dealing with opiates are subject to the powerful constraints of illegality (Reuter, 1983, 1985), which, in turn, impinge on their business practices. These constraints progressively slacken as the enforcement of prohibitions becomes less effective. They may disappear almost completely, if enforcement becomes negligible and the local state or quasi-state authorities themselves become involved in opiate production and trade.

As for broader social outcomes, the issue of "causality" merits discussion. On the one hand, our analysis suggests that strict enforcement affects broader societal conditions, including the authority of the state; on the other hand, broader societal conditions may, at least in part, determine the extent of enforcement.

In general, strict enforcement is heavily dependent on the degree of stability, effectiveness, and legitimacy of the national states called to enforce international prohibitions. Whatever their intentions, leaders of weak and resource-poor governments receiving little or no support from local populations will not be able to enforce prohibitions on opiate production and trade effectively. We acknowledge these differences across countries but we do not investigate them here; for the purposes of this analysis we have considered prohibition enforcement as an independent variable. In the country studies in chapter 6 through 9 and in appendix D, however, we provide a historical reconstruction of the reasons why the national governments of several countries playing a key role in the world opiate market today are weak and ineffective, and thus unable to enforce strictly prohibition on opiate production and trafficking.

Strict enforcement is also linked by a reciprocal relationship to the perceived legitimacy of opiates. Where the production and distribution of opiates have become well established in society—in particular, where they are hardly even concealed—it is difficult to enforce prohibition stringently. Moreover, changes in the perception of opiates preceded and indeed facilitated the passage of restrictive legislation both nationally and internationally (see chapter 2). Although the relationship between enforcement and perceived legitimacy is clearly reciprocal, we consider here the strictness of enforcement as the independent variable for several reasons. First, enforcement is the variable that most direcly affects the organization and operation of illegal enterprises. A second, more substantive reason is historical and concerns both developed countries with strict enforcement and the countries with lax enforcement or none. In the former group, opiates and their related market activities have long had low popular legitimacy. This negative perception is reinforced by strict enforcement, which has confined opiate use to marginal social groups, by raising opiate prices and restraining their availability. With the partial exceptions of India and Turkey,[22] none of the countries selected as exemplars of lax and non-enforcement were traditionally large-scale producers, traders, or consumers of opiates. The current, partial acceptance of opiate production and trafficking (and in some countries consumption as well) thus appears to be the product, among other factors, of deficiencies in enforcement and not vice versa.

The impact of opiate production and trafficking on the surrounding society and the state itself is at least in part mediated through its effect on the allocation of resources, including land, labor, capital, and entrepreneurial skill. If the production of opiates expands (e.g., because of the laxity of enforcement), then the production of other goods that require one or more of these resources may contract, until the point at which the producers can do just about as well in any activity.[23] The important effect is not the influence on the use of land and labor, which are in chronic excess supply in poor countries such as Afghanistan and Burma. Rather, the issue is that, over time, in countries that do not strictly enforce international bans, illegal entrepreneurial activities may replace legitimate ones, become an increasingly important source of funding for the government and its corrupt officials, and may even

Table 10.1

Summary table. The degree of effective illegality and its impact on the opiate enterprises, the larger society, and the state.

Case	Status of Opiate Markets and Related Risks	Sociopolitical Environment	Relationship between State and Enterprises	Key Characteristics of Enterprises		Legitimacy and Sociopolitical Impact	Illustrative Countries
				Size and Organization	Operating Methods		
Strict enforcement	Formally illegal, with medium to high risks of incarceration and asset seizure	Strong states with little or no systemic corruption and occasional local corruption; mostly democratic, but not necessarily so	State directly opposes illegal operations, enterprises face constraints of illegality	Small, fragmented, and unstable operations; rooted in preexisting social relationships, (e.g., family)	No cultivation or processing and limited short-term inventories; occasional use of violence and bribes; competition; criminal activities and entrepreneurs are concealed	Delegitimization of opiate production and trafficking; negative effect on consumption; little or no effect on strength of state or economy	Western European countries, United States, Canada, and Australia
Lax enforcement	Formally illegal with low short-term risks of incarceration and asset	States with widespread systemic and local corruption; mostly weak	State inconsistently opposes illegal operations and may even provide some enterprises	Small to large operations, often founded on preexisting social relationships	Limited, small-scale cultivation, processing and inventories possible; moderate to pervasive use	Partial legitimization of opiate production and trafficking; consumption may be more attractive than under strict	Pakistan, Turkey, Albania, Kosovo, Mexico, Tajikistan, and India

230

	seizure; potentially higher long-term enforcement risks	but not necessarily so	with limited institutional services (e.g., protective) through corrupt channels. The latter enterprises may thus be freed from the constraints of anarchy at least in the short run. However, constraints of illegality cannot be excluded in the long run.	(e.g., family). Large enterprises may develop, if they enjoy stable, high-level protections; some of them may also have bureaucratic (most often quasi-militaristic) traits.	of violence and bribes; potential for oligopoly; criminal activities and entrepreneurs may be visible	enforcement; weakens state, largely through support of corrupt individuals or agencies; may encroach on other economic activity	
Non-enforcement	Formally illegal with no enforcement and no short-term or long-term risks of incarceration or asset	States unable to control portions of the country or uninterested in enforcing prohibition or both; thus often failed states or	State or quasi-state is unable or unwilling to oppose illegal operations and may tolerate or actively support enterprises. Enterprises do not have to	Small to large operations rooted in relationships (e.g., family), and/or quasi-militaristic; large, consolidated enterprises	Large-scale cultivation, processing and large-scale inventories possible; use of violence and bribes depend on role of state/quasi-state; potential	Full legitimization of opiate production and trafficking; consumption may be more attractive than under lax enforcement; financially supports but politically delegitimizes state or quasi-state authorities; may	Afghanistan and Burma

(*continued*)

Table 10.1
(*Continued*)

Case	Status of Opiate Markets and Related Risks	Sociopolitical Environment	Relationship between State and Enterprises	Key Characteristics of Enterprises		Legitimacy and Sociopolitical Impact	Illustrative Countries
				Size and Organization	Operating Methods		
	seizure (de facto legality)	effectively "criminalized" states or quasi-states	operate against the state and are at least partially freed from constraints of anarchy; extent depends on state or quasi-state's involvement in industry and sophistication.	more likely to emerge if they are closely linked or coincide with state or quasi-state	for monopoly; criminal activities and entrepreneurs enjoy full visibility	encroach on other economic activity	

prevent the consolidation of effective state structures. Table 10.1 synthesizes the second thesis, by comparing and contrasting the conditions under which strict, lax, and non-enforcement arise and their implications.

Concluding Remarks

We discuss the policy implications of our model of varying effective illegality in chapter 11. We conclude here with some observations on the "optimal" institutional conditions for illegal opiate enterprises and two caveats.

Our model shows that, aside from opium poppy cultivation, not all forms of non-enforcement offer the best conditions for illegal drug businesses. As Thomas Hobbes (1968) pointed out more than 300 years ago, anarchy hinders businesses, whether licit or illicit, because it makes their environment unpredictable and risky. As shown by the mujahedin phase of Afghanistan's recent history, illegal entrepreneurs, too, have incentives to avoid countries with no central authority or failed states—as do their legitimate counterparts. If no central authority is able to guarantee a minimum of peace and security, entrepreneurs become prey to a variety of self-styled representatives of the central government and rivaling quasi-state authorities demanding bribes from them.[24]

A state authority not directly involved in illegal trades and providing effective protective services for commodities and contracts probably represents the ideal circumstance for illegal (and other) entrepreneurs. There are no examples of this in the contemporary world opiate market. In it, the largest, most stable, and therefore most potentially challenging illegal enterprises tend to develop

- When the enterprise and a state bureaucracy or quasi-state-authority merge, as can happen under no enforcement. Burma, with a variety of quasi-state authorities involved in the drug business, illustrates this point.
- When the enterprises under conditions of lax enforcement have entered into lasting protection and profit-sharing agreements with high-ranking government officials or "pieces" of the government apparatus. This is exemplified by Mexico in much of the 1980s and 1990s, and the contemporary "capture" of the Ministry of the Interior in Afghanistan.

In both cases, these enterprises enjoy a formidable advantage vis-à-vis their competitors and may exploit economies of scale and scope of operations. There is, however, an important difference between the two cases. In the first one, the quasi-state authority directly running the trade may have the potential to establish a monopoly (or an oligopoly, if, as in the Shan State of Burma, several drug-trafficking quasi-state authorities exert control over neighboring areas). In the second case, the consolidation of monopolies is highly improbable, and even oligopolies can be built only if the protectors of the dominating drug enterprises can each control substantive portions of the whole state machinery.

We conclude with two caveats. First, nations that strictly enforce prohibitions on opium production and trafficking usually operate under the rule of law, but there are important exceptions. China's successful elimination of opiate production, trafficking, and consumption in the early 1950s, the Taliban's cutback of 2000 to 2001, and the more recent experience in the Shan State demonstrate that authoritarian regimes can be very effective in enforcing prohibitions on opiate production and trafficking and, at least in the short run, may be more effective than democratic nations. However, although not necessary from an analytical point of view, the identification of strict enforcement and rule of law remains a fundamental objective in policy terms in all societies that want to call themselves democratic and in which enforcement of state prohibitions should be perceived as legitimate by the majority of the population.

Second, our findings do not represent an endorsement of the drug control policies carried out by the countries that we regard as strict enforcers or of the international drug control regime in which they operate. With our analysis, we have demonstrated only, albeit importantly, that strict enforcement—defined as the regular imposition of significant risks of incarceration and asset seizure—can reduce the harms of opiate production and trafficking, framed in terms of violence, corruption, and instability within the current drug control regime. The construction of ideal types has made it possible to ignore the idiosyncrasies and shortcomings of particular countries. For example, we are well aware that "strict enforcement" does not necessarily equate fully to even-handed or fair enforcement; recent press reports from any of our strictly enforcing countries could validate this claim. Moreover, our analysis does not exclude the possibility that the harms of opiate production and trafficking could be better reduced through other means—potentially means that require substantial changes in the terms of the regime itself. In the next chapter we investigate a range of potential approaches, some involving only a modest shift in emphasis and others involving a reversion from current prohibitions to the regulatory measures of past centuries.

11

Synthesis of Findings and Lessons for Policy Making

One hundred years have passed since the International Opium Commission adopted its final resolutions in Shanghai in February 1909, laying down the cornerstone of the contemporary international drug control regime. Although the regime initially emphasized the regulation of supply, during the past 50 years it has become increasingly prohibitionist, so much so that we now face a predominantly illegal market for opium and its derivative products.[1] The simultaneous approach of the centennial anniversary of the Shanghai conference and a high-level UN meeting to evaluate the past decade's drug control efforts provides ample reason to assess the current state of the world opiate market and possible futures. In the first 10 chapters of this book we have collected and analyzed key facts about the market and its operation. In this chapter, after synthesizing the main findings of our analysis, we discuss their policy implications and consider possible futures for drug policy.[2] In doing so, we focus on supply-side policy measures not only because the Taliban cutback first motivated our research, but more fundamentally because they have featured very prominently in the deliberations and actions of the international drug control regime since its inception.

Findings on the World Opiate Market

In many ways, the contemporary world opiate market looks and functions like a typical agriculturally based market, but drug control policy, especially

Table 11.1
Determinants of production, trafficking, and consumption.

Form of Market Participation	Determining Factors		
	Policy	Socio-economic and Cultural	Geographic
Production (very few countries)	++++	++	++
Trafficking (few countries)	+	+++	++++
Consumption (many countries)	+	++++	++

Note: Ranked by relative importance of factor from least (+) to most (++++). Some socioeconomic and geographic factors are prerequisites for production, but they are not difficult to satisfy.

governments' enforcement of prohibitions on production and trade, and properties of addiction can help explain important differences, largely through their divergent effects on production, trafficking, and consumption. For example, governments' policies toward opiates play a central role in determining whether and how individual countries engage in production; however, in the case of trafficking, they play a secondary role, with geographic proximity to producers and consumers, and commercial and demographic ties mattering more. In the case of consumption, proximity to producers may increase the likelihood of use, but probably not as much as other socioeconomic and cultural factors.

These distinctions shed light on the distribution of production, trafficking, and consumption across countries and bear directly on policy choices. If, for example, policy plays a central role in determining the location of production, then by implication it may be possible to elicit change through policy. Table 11.1 provides a basis for comparing the importance of policy and socioeconomic, cultural, and geographic factors in determining the location of production, trafficking, and consumption activities.

Production

After meeting some basic climatic and socioeconomic needs, the role of governments, particularly effective illegality, constitutes a major determining factor in the location of opium poppy cultivation. All else being equal, cultivation tends to concentrate in countries with no effective enforcement of opium prohibitions and with local government or quasi-government tolerance or support for opiate production and trade. Afghanistan and Burma, the world's two leading opium producers, most clearly illustrate this principle. Even so, data on production in several other second- and third-tier producers (e.g., Mexico, Pakistan, and possibly Laos) demonstrate that opium poppy cultivation can also occur under the less than optimal conditions of merely lax enforcement. Prices may be higher under lax enforcement than under non-enforcement, to compensate producers for the additional risks of detection and punishment, and production may be much more scattered and tenuous. Still, consistent with the general premise, opium poppy fields do tend to concentrate in the areas where the enforcement of prohibitions is least intense.

Few countries in the world offer the same "ideal" conditions for illegal opium poppy cultivation as Afghanistan and Burma, suggesting a possible lack of close successors if Burma's decline in opium production continues and if Afghanistan curbs its production. Among Afghanistan's neighbors, no one country offers an equally hospitable environment of non-enforcement. Turkmenistan may be a candidate, but we have too little information about the country to form a compelling assessment.[3] To find non-enforcing countries with government tolerance of production and trade, one would have to move to sub-Saharan Africa; however, the transplanted industry would likely require a few years' time to become operational, with potentially significant disruptions for Afghanistan's and Burma's current customers.

Does this mean that opiates are not subject to the so-called *balloon effect* (i.e., the notion that squeezing the opiate industry in one location will shift it to another)? Unfortunately it does not, because, as the examples of Mexico, Pakistan, and Laos show, cultivation also occurs under subideal conditions of lax enforcement. And, as the example of Colombia has shown, new producers can still enter the market. Given this, the list of potential successors, even among Afghanistan's neighbors, is much longer. Tajikistan leads, given its previous experience with opium cultivation and the trafficking know-how and contacts available to its largest opiate traders. Kyrgyzstan, which was the main supplier of legal opium for the entire Soviet Union up until 1973 (Zelichenko, n.d.), could also follow suit. The country has not only been heavily involved in Afghan opiate trafficking since the mid 1990s but, after the so-called Tulip Revolution of March 2005, has been heading toward anarchy (Madi, 2004; *Economist,* 2005; Marat, 2006).

If a sustained reduction of Afghan production were possible, poppy fields could, at least technically, expand in Pakistan as well, which has already lost the nearly opium-free status it had acquired from 1999 to 2002. It is doubtful, though, that the Pakistani government would tolerate the resurgence of large-scale opium poppy cultivation in frontier areas. Iran's stringent record of enforcement in recent decades (Raisdana and Nakhjavani, 2002; UNODCCP, 2002d) suggests that it is also an unlikely host for renewed large-scale production. Moving beyond Afghanistan's immediate neighbors, there are many countries with weak governments that could eventually host illicit production, if traffickers or others take the initiative to import the know-how.

The cutback in Afghan opium production in 2001 and the more recent cutbacks in production in Burma and Colombia demonstrate that sharp reductions in illegal opium production at the national level are possible in the short term. However, these sudden and substantial reductions have occurred, at least in the cases of Afghanistan and Burma, with high levels of coercion by an authoritarian regime or quasi-state. Moreover, the 1-year-long Afghan cutback was considered by most experts to be unsustainable over a longer period without international assistance. Likewise, most observers have called the sustainability of the Burmese opium bans into question, agreeing that the Wa and other Shan State parallel authorities can maintain them only at the cost of tremendous suffering for the local poppy-growing population. In the case of Colombia, we know less about the causes of the reduction in opium poppy cultivation, but believe that a change in the country's political dynamic may have enabled the government to reclaim some authority—hence, strengthen enforcement—in producing regions.

Even to the extent that the Taliban, Wa, and others can succeed in dramatic cutbacks in opium production, this analysis strongly suggests that new producers will eventually enter the market to take their place. They may be less efficient and thus produce at a somewhat higher cost, but the difference in cost is likely to have little effect on retail prices and consumption, especially in richer countries.

Trafficking

Proximity to major producing and consuming countries, and strong commercial and demographic connections usually override all other factors in determining which countries become principal transit countries. State weakness, complicity, and the non-enforcement of the global prohibition regime encourage trafficking, much as they do cultivation, but our analysis demonstrates that geographic proximity and strong commercial and demographic ties are even more important.

Some countries seem almost predestined to become major transit countries because of their locations. The most prominent are Thailand for Burmese opiates; Pakistan, Iran and, more recently, Tajikistan in the case of Afghan opiates; and, at the opposite end of the supply chain, Mexico for the U.S. market.

The case of Iran is exceptionally striking in so much as it demonstrates the inability of even the most stringent and severe enforcement efforts to eliminate or redirect trafficking.[4] Since the 1980s, the Iranian government has aggressively enforced opiate prohibitions and imposed very high penalties on drug trafficking. Iran typically accounts for more than a quarter of the world's opiate seizures and, during the second half of the 1990s, Iranian authorities executed more than 400 drug traffickers annually (Ashouri and Rahmdel, 2003:28–9). During the years after the Islamic Revolution of 1979, more than 3,700 police officers have been killed in Iran in fights with drug traffickers (Ashouri and Rahmdel, 2003:22), also suggesting a substantial political and social commitment to drug control. However, despite this tough record on enforcement, Iran has long represented the main route for smuggling heroin into Turkey and Europe, its primacy being only recently challenged by the emergence of the so-called "Silk Road" route across Central Asia as the principal channel to Russia.

Legitimate trade and flows of immigrants and transitory workers can enhance the illicit trade in opiates by providing cover—the illicit trade can merge with and hide in these flows. As a consequence, countries having such commercial or migratory ties with key producing and consuming countries likely enjoy an advantage in opiate trafficking. For example, the benefit of Tajikistan's proximity to the expanding heroin market in Russia has been enhanced further by the large diaspora of its citizens in Russia. Likewise, heroin loads can be easily disguised in the constant flow of exchanges linking the 5 million Turkish citizens and the almost 1.5 million ethnic Albanians living in Europe to the relatives and friends living in their home countries (Stiftung Zentrum für Türkeistudien, 2003; Arlacchi, 2004:6–7).[5]

The current division of the market between Turkish and ethnic Albanian drug traffickers in the European wholesale heroin trade may be best explained by the relative strength of the two diasporas. Turkish groups have remained the dominant supplier of heroin in the countries, such as the Netherlands (KLPD, 2006) and the United Kingdom (SOCA, 2006:27), in which stable Turkish communities exist and the presence of Albanian migrants is limited. In comparison, Albanian trafficking groups have claimed the upper hand in those countries that received large migration flows from Albania during the 1980s and '90s, such as Italy, Switzerland, and the Nordic countries. Unsurprisingly from this perspective, the situation is more fluid in Germany, a nation that hosts large diasporas from both countries. Although Turkish traffickers seem to maintain the lion's share of the heroin wholesale trade in Germany, their predominance is now being challenged effectively by Albanian (and Macedonian) counterparts in several cities, such as Frankfurt (Paoli, in press).

As the pipelines of regular commerce and traffic change, so do the channels of drug trafficking. For example, as a result of changes in immigration policies, Australia now has large Chinese and Vietnamese populations. This, in turn, has created new routes of trafficking to the Australian heroin market. At the same time, Australia's imports of legitimate products from both countries have also grown. The case of Africa also illustrates the relevance of geographic proximity and intense commercial and migratory ties with either producing or consuming countries. Despite the weakness and ineffectiveness of most African governments, no African country has so far attracted substantial illicit opiate trafficking, although some African nationals, particularly the Nigerians, are extensively involved in the trade elsewhere in the world.

Our analysis suggests that, once established and supported by neighboring or affiliated producers and consumers, drug trafficking is robust and unlikely to respond to policies that uniquely target it, except under exceptional circumstances.[6] Successful trafficking organizations usually acquire specific expertise and "relational capital" (referring to the stock of existing connections among traffickers, see chapter 3) that allows them to function more effectively than potential competitors in other countries and along other routes. The established national industry is thus advantaged relative to new-comers, creating a significant but not insurmountable barrier to entry for traf-fickers from elsewhere and reinforcing market segmentation (i.e., the division of the global market into "submarkets" in which producers in one country or region serve consumers in another through set distribution channels).

Consumption

Opiate consumption occurs on every continent, with the majority of con-sumption in tonnage occurring in Asia, in part because of proximity to production and the large population base, and the majority in dollar value occurring in western nations. Westerners have led the world's shift to heroin consumption, but their non-western peers have been following close behind. Opium and compote are still popular in some Asian and eastern European nations, but heroin and other refined products now dominate.

In contemporary opiate markets, especially those for heroin, demand tends to grow rapidly at the onset of an epidemic as a market takes shape. Rates of initiation then fall rapidly as the market saturates and "matures," and a period of relative stability ensues. During this period, demand is unlikely to expand rapidly, but it is also unlikely to contract rapidly—heroin addicts in particular cannot shed their habits easily or quickly. A substantial increase in global demand would require a new epidemic in a new market, as occurred in the 1990s in Russia and parts of Central Asia. A substantial decrease in global demand in the short run is unlikely.

The historical evidence also suggests that restrictive policies aimed at users, some stemming from international agreements, may have played a part in the sharp reductions in opium consumption that occurred during the first half of the 20th century, but changes in societal and, notably, physicians' perceptions of opiates played the greater part. Moreover, some restrictions unintentionally worsened certain aspects of opiate use. For example, at the beginning of the 20th century, the adoption of the first prohibitionist provisions on opium use engendered a shift from opium to heroin in several countries, including China and the United States. Heroin is much more compact than opium, hence it is a more practical illegal drug. Restrictions on opiate use also promoted inject-ing, which is a much more efficient delivery method, and prevented—and, in stringently prohibitionist regimes, may still prevent—some users from seek-ing medical attention.

Policies that address supply may have only modest effects on consump-tion and demand, limited ultimately by the responsiveness of users to changes in market conditions. Even the U.S. and Swedish governments, both of which have devoted considerable energy to supply-side efforts, have had little success in reducing use (Boekhout Van Solinge, 2002; Boyum and Reuter, 2005). That is not to say that supply-oriented policies have no effect. For example, policies that disrupt the market and substantially reduce availability may result in less consumption in the short run, induce some consumers to enter treatment, and even prevent others from entering the market or becoming habituated. The higher elasticity of demand and fragility of markets that are less mature make the potential for consumption and demand reductions greater. Moreover, strict enforcement of prohibitions on production and trafficking may have the added benefit of further delegitimizing opiates and discouraging use.

One recent episode does encourage the belief that supply controls can make a difference even in a mature market; however, the episode may not be easily replicable. In late 2000 Australia experienced a sudden tightening in the supply of heroin, referred to as the heroin "drought." Although the exact cause of this tightening is still not known, it may have been related to seizures and arrests by the Australian Federal Police aimed at major heroin smugglers from Southeast Asia. The consequent decline in Australian heroin consumption has been sustained for more than 5 years. Although indicators show some recovery from the low of early 2001, immediately after the proposed precipitating events, they still suggest substantial reductions in heroin consumption compared with 1999 (Degenhardt, Day, Hall, and Bewley-Taylor, 2007). The Australian heroin market is not small (roughly 70,000 addicts in the late 1990s), but Australia is a remote island nation with limited accessibility, which may allow for more effective control than is the case in most major heroin-consuming nations.

Organization and Operation of Illegal Enterprises

The size, organization, and operating methods of enterprises that produce or traffic illicit opiates are important because they influence the adverse consequences of the trade both within and beyond the market. For example, large and visible enterprises, which have amassed political power and social credibility, can threaten the authority of the government. These characteristics largely depend on the degree of effective illegality (i.e., on the strictness of the national or subnational governments' enforcement of prohibitions against opiate production and trafficking).

In countries with strict enforcement, traffickers and producers are obliged to operate not only without the protections of state institutions, notably the court system, but against those institutions. Illegality then means that the businesses are likely to be small, ephemeral, and not vertically integrated, relying largely on preexisting social relationships, such as family ties or bonds of friendship or locality. The factors promoting the development of large firms in the legal portion of the economy—namely, to take advantage of economies of scale and scope—are outweighed in illegal markets by the threats that a strong government poses and the need to reduce visibility.

Strict enforcement also imposes constraints that powerfully affect the operating methods of illegal entrepreneurs. For example, to reduce the risks of incarceration and asset seizure, illegal entrepreneurs are likely to avoid producing opiates, hold very modest inventories, rarely resort to open violence, and make no claims of quasi-governmental functions. Opiate production and trafficking are also likely to remain concealed criminal activities without popular legitimacy. For these reasons, strict enforcement will likely engender competitive markets with small enterprises and little or no opportunity for the development of monopolies or oligopolies.

Lax enforcement, the intermediate case, allows no firm prediction regarding the organization and operation of illicit enterprises. Constraints of anarchy, the difficulty of operating where there are weak forces of order, may lead to small firms. In contrast, if the state is strong enough and corrupt enough to provide effective protection for those that purchase it, the result may be open and large-scale operations.

Under conditions of non-enforcement, with state tolerance or active support, illegal entrepreneurs do not have to operate against the state. Moreover, unlike their counterparts in settings of lax enforcement, they may also be freed entirely from the "constraints of anarchy." The degree to which these constraints are effectively removed, however, depends on the state or quasi-state authority's sophistication and direct involvement in the opiate industry. Enterprises are likely to remain small and rely on preexisting social relationships if the state or quasi-state authority is weak or unstable. They can become large and secure, and assume bureaucratic characteristics if they are closely linked or coincide with a powerful state or quasi-state authority.

Non-enforcement also has some broad effects on the operating methods of businesses. As the risks of incarceration and asset seizure each tend toward zero, opiate entrepreneurs are free to carry out visible and bulky activities, such as cultivating opium in large fields, processing its derivatives, and holding large stocks. As mentioned earlier, this helps account for the fact that the world's two dominant illicit opium producers have conditions approaching non-enforcement and active support. Opiate production and trafficking may, with time, come to be considered legitimate, and their organizers are likely to acquire social and even political legitimacy. The extent of violence and bribery also depends on the strength and involvement of state or quasi-state authorities. Violence may be high if the supporting state or quasi-state authority is weak; it may be low if the state or quasi-state authority is strongly institutionalized and directly involved in the drug trade. With powerful and engaged state or quasi-state authorities backing them up, opiate enterprises may form oligopolies or even monopolies. The potential for outright monopoly tends to be the greatest when the authority and firm are one and the same.

Segmentation and Change

Two characteristics of the world opiate market, taken as a whole, further suggest both the possibilities and the limitations of supply-oriented drug control policies. First, the market is segmented in the short run, which may temporarily amplify the effects of supply-based policy interventions in specific countries or regions. The segmentation of the world opiate market is largely the result of the illegal status of its commodities and the close geographic, commercial, and demographic ties on which trafficking depends. In an illicit market, information travels much more slowly and inefficiently than in a legitimate market, and exchanges are predominantly carried out by enterprises founded on preexisting relationships—a fact that increases their cohesion but also renders them less capable of major strategic change.

Our analysis of the Afghan cutback suggests that production interruptions, even if not sustained for long, can, with the help of segmentation, make a difference in affected destination markets. Given the high level of coercion necessary to implement the cutback, it is not a policy experiment that we would advocate repeating, but it—and the market's response to it—may provide an upper bound for gauging the potential achievements of short-term production interventions in other settings. Indeed, a smaller cutback in a year when stocks are lower could have as much effect.[7]

Second, notwithstanding its tendency toward short run rigidity, the world illicit opiate market can and does change over time. Very occasionally, under the right conditions, it changes both radically and rapidly, even by the standards of legitimate markets. Our review of the history of the market during the past 200 years in chapter 2 and the more recent experiences of Afghanistan, Burma, Pakistan, Colombia, the Central Asian republics, especially Tajikistan, and Russia all provide concrete examples of change, some of it occurring rather quickly.

In the early-to-mid 1990s, for example, Colombia entered the world opiate market as a substantial grower of opium poppy. Its production placed it almost immediately among the second-tier producers of opium poppy, where it has remained for more than a decade. However, given recent reports of substantial declines in production, its future among the second-tier producers is in question. Russia, a relatively minor heroin consumer in 1995, became one of the world's largest consumers by the turn of the century and has remained so to the present. During the same period, Central Asia saw the emergence of a major heroin problem, both in trafficking and consumption.

Each of these events has an explanation. In addition to fulfilling some basic preconditions (e.g., amenable climate and the availability of land and labor), Colombia likely was at risk because of the existence of integrated drug-smuggling networks servicing the U.S. cocaine market; the presence of guerrilla and paramilitary groups in some regions of the country; and, last but not least, the general weakness and corruption of the Colombian government. Russia was undergoing a painful transition to a market economy, and an epidemic of illegal drug use is not historically rare at such times.[8] Russia was most efficiently supplied through Central Asia, given geography, migration patterns, and the minimal border controls between the Central Asian republics and Russia. Transshipment also encouraged the increase in consumption in Central Asia.

The catalogue of comings and goings also indicates a disturbing bias in the nature of change. Absent draconian measures, conditions most typically worsen more quickly than they improve. The market may be sufficiently rigid to open a small but meaningful window for supply-based policy interventions, but, in general, "bad things," including market entry, still happen faster than "good things." Changes for the better are difficult to achieve, because they are usually linked to long-term changes in the very perception of opiates and the creation of alternative income-earning opportunities for farmers that have become socially and economically entrenched in production, or to economic development more generally. Moreover, whether government leaders impose draconian measures, adopt gradualist approaches, or take positions somewhere between the two, the gains can slip away quickly. Farmers in Afghanistan resumed and expanded opium poppy cultivation during the aftermath of the Taliban regime and, to a much lesser extent, farmers in Pakistan have also returned to cultivation.

Can the World Supply of Opiates Be Cut and with What Consequences?

These observations bring us back to the question that first provoked our interest in the cutback in Afghan opium production—whether the world opiate supply can be cut and with what consequences. In summary, we find that supply-oriented policy can have only a limited influence on the world market. We refer here to reductions in the world supply in total. This is not to say that longer term reductions are not possible in individual countries or regions, including or especially through more democratic means. We address this possibility in the discussion of policy opportunities.

- It is possible to reduce the world supply of opiates in the short run, Xmost visibly through harsh policy measures; however, if production falls in one region, production—as well as illegal diversion from ongoing licit production—will probably expand in other regions eventually, with the magnitude and speed of the expansion depending in part on growing conditions, land and labor availability, effective illegality, and the extent and persistence of market segmentation.
- New production—and increased diversion—will likely be somewhat costlier than old production, because it may occur under less than optimal conditions (relating to geographic, socioeconomic, and most notably policy factors), but not dramatically so.
- New production, depending on its location, may also need to find new and potentially costlier trafficking routes, which in turn may lengthen the duration of the adjustment process.
- The initial reduction, eventual expansion, and modest cost increase would likely lead to a small reduction in consumption and demand (some current users may choose to consume less or enter treatment and some potential users may be discouraged from entering the market), but

market segmentation could temporarily amplify the effects of the initial reduction on consumption and demand in specific countries or regions.
- Expansion of production in other regions may entail substantial costs for those regions (e.g., relating to increases in corruption and violence).

Suggestions for Leveraging Limited Policy Opportunities

Our book appears at the time of a discussion of the resolutions of the 1998 UN General Assembly Special Session which aimed at "eliminating or significantly reducing the illicit cultivation of...the opium poppy by the year 2008." (UNGASS, 1998: clause 19)[9] Our analysis makes clear that the goal was unrealistic in the first place, will not be met in 2008, and has little chance of being achieved in another 10 years. These propositions are hardly controversial.

Ultimately, we see the greatest potential for supply-oriented policy in achieving reductions in local—national or regional—production and offer a number of suggestions for making the most of those opportunities. The gains may be very important to individual countries or regions, if not to the rest of the world.

Lasting national or regional reductions in opiate production will require a long-term perspective, heavily weighing institution building and economic development, and sustained international support, particularly in societies that have become socially and economically entrenched in cultivation. As already noted, among the many countries in the world that could produce opium on the basis of geography, labor availability, and other socioeconomic conditions, cultivation has gravitated to a handful of countries with little or no enforcement; this suggests a possible opening for effective national or regional interventions. If production is attracted to conditions of lax or non-enforcement, then it may be discouraged by conditions of strict enforcement. However, cultivation has become entrenched in the livelihoods of millions of people in producing countries and cannot be eliminated hastily in a democracy that has concern for the well-being of its citizens and its own longevity. The following discussion focuses initially on what can be accomplished nationally or regionally rather than globally.

The Taliban regime and Wa authorities have achieved dramatic reductions in production in relatively short periods of time through draconian measures, but no democratic government can rightfully use the same degrees of coercion. A democratic government must, instead, persuade a population of farmers to shift to other activities through a mixture of positive incentives and threats that fall within the framework of a transparent and honest system of criminal and civil sanctions. These are difficult objectives for the governments of impoverished nations with weak institutions and limited claims to legitimacy. The international community, consisting of international agencies and foreign governments, would need to provide adequate and long-term support to countries involved, simultaneously fostering development and the creation of a fair and effective law enforcement system.

The record of development agencies during the past half century makes clear that this is a major challenge, but there is at least one success story. Over a period of 30 years, through a mix of more or less democratic means, including substantial development assistance, Thailand has all but ceased opiate production. Thailand's success has entailed extensive use of alternative development and local community empowerment in addition to drug elimination measures. Thailand's efforts to eliminate opium poppy cultivation have also profited tremendously from the overall democratization and economic development of the country, which has offered realistic and sustainable alternative livelihoods to the opium-growing peasants (Renard, 2001). We draw less insight from Colombia's more recent and relatively rapid reduction in production because we know less about the circumstances surrounding it and because it is difficult to describe Colombia as having become entrenched in cultivation to the same extent as either Afghanistan, Burma, or Thailand; its foray into the opiate marketplace will have been brief if the reduction persists.[10]

Indeed, effective drug control may be "preconditioned" on critical amounts of effective economic development, institution building and, in conflict-ridden contexts such as Afghanistan and northeast Burma, political stabilization. In their absence, disruptive drug control interventions, such as forced eradication, may deprive farmers of their only source of income, further alienate them from seemingly non-responsive government institutions (and western donors), and eventually push them into the arms of self-proclaimed protectors, ranging from the Taliban to the FARC.

The recent experience in Afghanistan is instructive in this respect, as summarized in Buddenberg and Byrd (2006), a UNODC–World Bank publication. There, increased eradication and in-country enforcement have devastated the lives of thousand of households, as the promises of alternative development did not materialize in time. These efforts have further weakened the shaky legitimacy of the government, and of the tribal elites who had agreed to eradication. They have been distorted by corruption, have targeted disproportionately the poorest and least-protected farmers and traffickers, fostering a dangerous consolidation of the Afghan drug industry, and have provided financial means and political legitimacy to armed groups—ranging from the resurgent Taliban in the south to many smaller militias throughout the country, which are willing to offer protection to peasants and traffickers. Byrd and Buddenberg (2006:6) conclude: "All these considerations point strongly toward 'mainstreaming' the counter-narcotics dimension in national development programs."

Thus, drug control cannot be seen in the major producing nations as solely a law enforcement issue, and attention must be given to the potentially disruptive effects of coercive measures. Policy must support affected regions in strengthening and legitimizing their political institutions—an extraordinary challenge—and creating alternative income-earning opportunities for farmers within the framework of a long-term opium elimination program. Acknowledging the diversity of the opium economy, counternarcotic efforts should first target areas that offer alternative opportunities and be postponed in remote, poor areas that are heavily dependent on the opium economy (Mansfield, 2006). As again recognized in the UNODC–World Bank publication, in such areas "premature efforts to eliminate [the opium economy] will be hard to sustain and could likely prove counterproductive" (Byrd and Buddenberg, 2006:19).

The rationale for policy making in this area can be found in the Feldafing Declaration, which, in a key recommendation states: "Alternative Development should neither be made conditional on prior elimination of drug crop cultivation nor should a reduction be enforced until licit components of livelihoods strategies have been sufficiently strengthened" (Feldafing Declaration, 2002:2).[11] Experience from alternative development projects in Thailand and Burma also shows that affected communities need to be involved and have a say in their own development process. Local empowerment is crucial not only for the success of alternative development projects, but also for achieving genuine rule of law, in which communities view state prohibitions as legitimate and meaningful (Renard, 2001; TNI, 2002).

However, strengthening the institutions and legitimate economy of a producing country such as Afghanistan, Burma, or Colombia could lead ultimately to a shift in production to other countries. Historically, such a shift—the "balloon effect"—may be the best interpretation of Thailand's success; Burma became a lower cost supplier even for Thailand's own opiate market. As production in Burma has declined, production in Afghanistan has risen, possibly displaying a similar form of production relocation; whether Laos or any other neighbors of Burma will increase their production or enter the market over time remains to be seen. Nevertheless, our pessimism about the *global* effects of supply interventions does not mean that individual producing countries cannot benefit from them. Thailand, as noted earlier, is a country that has shifted from substantial opium production to almost no production and has benefitted greatly, even if some or all of that production has shifted elsewhere. Later, we consider some of the costs that could be associated with a shift in production from one location to another.

The most effective means of reducing trafficking in a specific country or region may be an effective intervention against production or consumption in neighboring countries or regions.[12] Trafficking tends to gravitate to those countries in close proximity to producing or consuming nations, particularly those with strong demographic or economic ties. As such, trafficking interventions may gain little traction, absent a reduction in production or consumption in those countries or a severing of those ties.[13]

Moreover, for some trafficking countries, the conditioning realities of an entrenched activity, relative poverty, and weak states are the same as for producing countries. In a small number of trafficking countries, most prominently Tajikistan, trafficking involves large numbers of low-level participants for whom this activity is the best available economic pursuit, although leaving them little better off than their neighbors. In other, somewhat richer countries, such as Turkey, trafficking may be important in poor regions where other economic opportunities are slight. Leaders of trafficking nations, like those of producing nations, may lack the political will to crack down on the activity because of its importance to impoverished communities. Certainly, this seems to be a contributing factor to the increase in trafficking in Tajikistan.

Market segmentation offers a policy opportunity for reducing consumption and possibly longer term demand in specific countries or regions. In a segmented market, a substantial production cutback or trafficking disruption in one area can have large effects in the individual countries or regions it services even if global production and trafficking are not much reduced. Over time, the market will either restore or reconfigure itself, but, at least in the short run, the local effects may be noteworthy.

For the time the market takes to adjust, a major break in supply (i.e., one that severely limits local availability) may open small windows of opportunity for consuming countries or regions, as indicated by the successful poppy eradication in Mexico in the late 1970s and the much more recent Australian heroin "drought." The short term may see reductions in heroin use and related harms, an increase in the number of users willing to enter treatment, and a decrease in the number of new initiates, with potentially longer term consequences.

Similarly, the ban on opium implemented by UWSA in June 2005, following bans imposed by other, smaller, quasi-state authorities of northeastern Burma, may help China, Australia, and other Southeast Asian and Pacific markets, even if Afghan production expands.

Strict enforcement of prohibitions on opiate production and trafficking can, in the long term, reduce drug-related corruption, violence, and instability. Governments can substantially influence the risk assessments and actual behaviors of enterprises that produce or traffic illegal opiates. If governments can enforce prohibitions with sufficient rigor, they can prevent the consolidation of large and stable enterprises, some of which may have political ambitions, and openly challenge state authority. Small and ephemeral illegal enterprises are very unlikely to infiltrate or corrupt government apparatuses systemically; moreover, with typically short-term planning horizons they may be less likely to develop or implement revolutionary or terrorist plans. Strict enforcement can also lessen the appeal of widespread and open violence, although violence is likely to remain an occasional component of the illegal drug market.

However, for countries that have become accustomed to lax or non-enforcement, a shift toward strict enforcement may imply a worsening of drug-related corruption, violence, and instability in the interim. Recent developments in Afghanistan clearly demonstrate the potential for worsening conditions. Powerful drug-producing and -trafficking organizations are using all available means to oppose state efforts to enforce prohibition more rigorously and fight for the "right" to continue their established businesses. This struggle is dangerously undermining the process of state consolidation and legitimization. Afghan drug organizations have strong support from local communities that are economically dependent on opium production; they are corrupting key elements of the nascent government apparatus and many of them have sided with the remerging Taliban.

Strict enforcement of prohibitions on opiate production and trafficking may well reduce the adverse consequences of the illegal opiate industry in the long run. However, the path from lax or non-enforcement may be rough. It is not just a question of political will alone. Much more than that, as in the case of lasting local reductions in opiate production, it is largely the result of long-term economic development and political institution building.

Possible Futures for International Drug Policy

In sum, our analysis does not augur well for the international drug control regime. We find little reason to predict success in reducing the world supply of opiates and only limited opportunities to affect national or regional conditions.

The apparent difficulty of achieving success under the current regime leads almost inevitably to questions about possible futures for drug control policy. Does the regime require reform and, if so, what direction might it take? Can old approaches be reinterpreted for the current era or can new, possibly unorthodox, approaches be implemented within current structures?

Lessons from History

First and foremost, history suggests that change is possible. Two centuries of opiate history clearly demonstrate that the world opiate market and the domestic and international policies that have been adopted either to regulate or control it have undergone radical change. Historical research on opiates "demonstrates that the concepts, the reactions, the structures of controls which are now taken for granted are not fixed and immutable" (Berridge, 1999:230).

Our historical analysis further shows that the current drug control system was developed primarily by western policy makers informed by western values, cultural practices, and interests. Since the Hague Convention of 1912, this system has largely reflected western elites' and, later, the western population's will to reduce non-medical consumption of psychoactive drugs, such as opiates, that were not well entrenched in western habits. Despite the initial focus on opium consumption in China, the main aim of the western nations soon became preventing or containing the consumption of heroin and morphine, which had been extracted by western chemists, produced and distributed by western pharmaceutical companies, and are more powerful and addictive than opium itself. These drug control efforts often overlooked that opium had been ingrained in the culture of Asian populations for centuries and that much occasional or even regular opium consumption (as is true of alcohol in western countries) was compatible with a normal lifestyle and did not produce severe health consequences. The western colonial powers were themselves happy to supply and tax opium consumers in most of their Asian colonies even after 1912 and, in the case of France, as late as the 1950s—a fact that should lead to more understanding for the dilemmas currently faced by poor opium-producing and -trafficking nations.

The development of the international drug control regime and parallel domestic legislation has been an episodic and opportunistic process. For example, the studies of several historians[14] show that influential personalities (e.g., Bishop Charles H. Brent, Hamilton Wright, Malcolm Delevingne, Harry J. Anslinger), epochal events (such as World War I), and slim majorities (the 1919 U.S. Supreme Court sentence banning drug maintenance policies was a five to four decision [Musto, 1987:131–132]) have all, sometimes unexpectedly, contributed to major policy turns.

Even more important, the international drug control regime has not been fully prohibitionist throughout its history. From its inception in 1909 and up until World War II, the regime, by and large, favored regulation over prohibition, with considerable leeway left to national governments to address both supply and demand. Only in the 1950s did the tone and provisions of the treaties become increasingly prohibitionist, mainly at the insistence of the United States. The 1961 Single Convention on Narcotics Drugs and the 1988 Trafficking Convention epitomize the prohibitionist approach. However, the international drug control regime has, throughout its history, maintained a clear and consistent supply-side focus, a point recently made by the executive director of the UNODC (Costa, 2008:13). Notwithstanding a slight increase in attention to demand in the 1970s, paralleling the sudden resurgence in illicit drug use—and a UN pledge for a balanced approach—demand control, treatment, and prevention have remained largely domestic issues. At the level of international policy, traditional supply-oriented goals still account for the majority of energy and funding.

History does not just provide a much-needed grounding for the contemporary debate on the future of the international drug control regime. It also offers a largely unexploited inventory of policy experiments and potential alternatives to the current regime. During the course of the past two centuries, one can find an extraordinary variety of policies concerning both opiate supply and demand, ranging from an almost complete absence of regulation to almost complete prohibition. Historical evidence also allows for examination of the advantages, drawbacks, and risks of the different policy options. Because this book primarily concerns the supply side of the market, we largely limit our observations here to past policy initiatives aimed at supply.

Among them, the most interesting may be the regulatory regimes of the colonial era. These regimes clearly presented advantages for users and may have lessened drug use-related harms; however, governing bodies faced substantial conflicts of interest in reconciling demand reduction with revenue maximization. Despite these conflicts, some such regimes, most notably that in Formosa under the Japanese occupation, were able to reform themselves and help reduce the consumption of opiates.

Would a regulatory regime be possible today? Although they are not called so, the heroin maintenance programs introduced since the 1990s by several European nations (including Switzerland, The Netherlands, Germany, and the United Kingdom) for heroin addicts not responsive to other treatment methods can be considered embryonic state monopolies for quasi-medical opiate distribution.[15] Given their very modest enrollment, though, these maintenance programs have limited capability of reducing parallel illegal markets. The issues surrounding a broader based regulatory approach, one that might encompass production, are more complex and require deeper consideration. For example, it may be much more difficult to control production and distribution in the global market of the current era than in the mostly regional markets of the colonial era. India's experience with "leakage" from regulated pharmaceutical production also suggests substantial practical barriers, particularly in countries with weak governing institutions, and the likely persistence of a parallel illegal market. Nevertheless, the League of Nations was, despite its limited powers, quite successful in curbing the legal production of opiates in the 1920s and early 1930s exactly because the main producers were legal pharmaceutical companies vulnerable to adverse publicity. Needless to say, finding answers to this question goes beyond the scope of this book.

Non-traditional Drug Policy Options

Here we present and briefly comment on three non-traditional or "unorthodox" approaches to supply control that originate, not from our own research, but from discussions we have had with others in recent years.

Buying up the Crop

One non-traditional policy option would involve the preemptive purchases of opiates in dominant producing countries, primarily in Afghanistan. The total cost of the purchase of all Afghan opium production prior to 2001 might have been no more than $250 million,[16] a small fraction of what is spent by wealthy nations to deal with the problems of their heroin addicts. A preemptive purchase, if it substantially limits the availability of heroin or other opiates, might drive many users into treatment or lead them to desist from or reduce their use for a period of time.

There are two standard objections to preemptive purchases. The first objection is that it would be impossible to make this preemptive purchase discreetly. Traffickers would soon become aware of the new entrants in the market and would bid against them. The price of opium in Afghanistan would soar and the program would end up costing taxpayers a great deal more and still not prevent some opium from continuing to flow into the illegal market, albeit at higher prices. No doubt it would be difficult to do this discreetly, but the program does not have to prevent all opiates flowing into the illegal market. If stocks were not large and the program took, say, 75% of production off the market, it might do substantial good for a year, even more so in a segmented market.

The second objection is that the intervention would exacerbate longer term problems both for Afghanistan, if it were the target of the buy-up, and for the world opiate market more generally. In the face of the increase in demand at the farm gate, growers would now plant more, absent effective restrictions on new planting, thus further increasing the Afghan economy's dependence on opium. The additional production and resulting dependency would leave the Afghan economy markedly vulnerable, particularly if the program were to end abruptly, and could encourage global consumption. If unprepared for the termination of the program, farmers who previously participated in the buy-up program might find themselves with no other outlet for their harvests but the illicit market. In such a way, the world would face a temporary increase in illicit supply when the program ended. And, even with effective restrictions on new planting in Afghanistan, other countries or regions might begin to enter the illicit market, attracted by increases in farm-gate prices.

Nevertheless, the program might still have merit for consumer countries, especially those with mature markets.[17] For them, the temporary increase in illicit supply that might occur when the buy-up ended would lead only to modest increases in use, the costs of which might be outweighed by the benefits of the initial decrease in flows to the illicit market.

Moreover, some of the negative effects for Afghanistan could be lessened if the time horizon of the program was made clear from the start and if the phase-out was accompanied by well-planned and executed alternative development initiatives, including the provision of basic security in contested areas and the creation of effective alternative income-earning opportunities for the affected farmers. However, selling one's own production exclusively to the program and accepting the progressive phasing out would have to be made conditions for participation in the program; this would require both enforceability and a credible commitment to the phase-out.

Strategic Location

Given the destructive tendencies of drug production and trafficking, one might ask whether it is more desirable to have production dispersed across many countries or concentrated in a few, much as it is today; whether it is more desirable to have production stably located in specific countries, much as it has been in recent years, or to move it around; and whether it is even possible to determine which countries would suffer least (e.g., in terms of violence and corruption) from remaining or becoming major producers and traffickers.

In the 1990s, some economists, including the then-chief economist of the World Bank and future U.S. Treasury Secretary, Lawrence Summers, raised similar questions with regard to the location of the world's polluting activities and prompted a heated debate over a possible movement toward *pollution havens* in developing countries.[18] Much of that debate was understandably couched in moral terms, with concern for damage to the developing countries strongly outweighing other considerations. A difference for opiates may be that production and, to a slightly lesser extent, trafficking are already highly concentrated in a small number of countries.

Upon analysis, the concept of strategic location in the world opiate market may be every bit as unacceptable as the idea of the pollution haven, but it may be worth considering the differences in circumstances and whether the answer might be any different because of them.

Here we focus principally on issues of dispersion and relocation. What would be the balance of costs and benefits, if, for example, half or all of Afghanistan's opium growing were to shift to Turkmenistan?[19] Although there is no way to provide a definitive answer to this question for any pair of nations, it is possible to identify at least three factors that could affect the costs.

First, the adverse consequences of drug production are not likely to be proportional to size. The corruption and undermining of government authority will not fall by half if production falls by half; some of the bad effects are simply the consequence of a substantial engagement in illegal production. Turkmenistan will incur those "fixed" adverse consequences by hosting an industry half the size of that in Afghanistan currently; Afghanistan will not shed half those burdens. The effect of the transfer of the drug-related corruption and loss of authority on the recipient country, in this case Turkmenistan, will depend in part on the initial strength of the state.

Second, some of the adverse consequences can be reversed only over time. Indeed, even if all of the industry shifted to Turkmenistan, the bad effects on Afghanistan's development (both economic and political) would take time to correct. There might even be violent conflict among the warlords fighting over the declining market, although that is less certain. If, instead, the shift away from production in Afghanistan were the result of institution building and economic development that lessened the appeal of opiate production (as occurred, for example, in Thailand), then the adverse consequences might diminish before or with the shift.

Third, a crackdown, if necessary to reduce production, could itself have adverse effects. With effective institution building and economic development, a crackdown would not be necessary and the problem would not arise. However, alternative development programs may, as they did in Thailand, require decades to take hold. Any decline in Afghanistan during the next few years would more likely be the result of tough enforcement aimed at producers.

These crackdowns have historically generated their own violence and corruption; they are likely to do so in the near future.

These three factors also bear on consideration of the balloon effect. Although many analysts, including the current executive director of the UNODC (Costa, 2008), have noted the effect, there has been no systematic analysis of its consequences. In fact, it may have profound consequences for policy choices.

Giving Afghanistan Poppy Growers Access to the Legitimate Market

During the past few years, the Senlis Council (2005), a European NGO, has intensively lobbied the UN system to license cultivation of opium poppy in Afghanistan for medical purposes—a proposal that has attracted considerable media attention (e.g., Szalavitz, 2005; Kamminga and van Ham, 2006) and some political backing.[20] As much as buying up the crop, such an experiment, if implemented on a sufficiently large scale, could benefit Afghanistan by providing a legal income to thousands of Afghan farmers, freeing them from the grip of warlords imposing protection taxes on them, weakening the legitimacy of the resurgent Taliban and maverick politicians who more or less explicitly sponsor illicit opium production and trade, and, conversely, strengthening the legitimacy of the Afghan government and the rule of law (Felbab-Brown, 2007a).

However, at least as much as buying up the crop, giving Afghanistan's farmers access to the legal opiate market seems to have little promise of reducing supplies to the illicit market. Because the current area of cultivation represents only 3% of Afghanistan's arable land, even licensing the entire area would not exclude the possibility of an equally large area of illicit cultivation (Felbab-Brown, 2007a). As routinely occurs in India, drug traffickers would easily outbid the government and stimulate opium diversion. As shown in chapter 7, India may be the world's third largest illicit opium producer. If a country like India cannot effectively prevent diversion, it seems quite unlikely that Afghanistan, with a nascent state administration unable to control large portions of the nation's territory, could do so. Moreover, the economic, political, and social costs that one might reasonably associate with extensive diversion, such as those arising from drug-related corruption and lobbying, may be less than those associated with widespread illicit production, but nevertheless substantial.

The Indian experience also draws attention to the economic shortcomings of the proposal. Unless subsidized or accompanied by the reliable sale of licit by-products (poppy seed and straw), Afghan farmers may not earn enough from licit opium production to meet basic needs. The licit market price may be too low. To offer farmers a more reasonable income—in absolute and relative terms—and thus encourage the success of the licensing scheme, the Afghan government would also have to address the full range of economic factors that drive illicit opium cultivation, including, for example, farmers' access to credit (Mansfield, 2006; Felbab-Brown, 2007a).

Lastly, the Senlis Council's (2005) proposal is based on the false assumption that there is a large, unsatisfied opiate demand waiting for Afghan opium.

This confuses potential needs and actual demand. Although there may be too little opiate available in Third World countries, this is primarily a result of decisions by regulatory and law enforcement authorities, not the limited amount of production. Were developing countries to modernize their health-care delivery systems, it is possible that their demand for morphine and, eventually, imports could grow, but even that would not guarantee demand for Afghanistan's proposed licit production. Pharmaceutical companies increasingly prefer to buy the principal opium alkaloids and above all thebaine not from India, the only country producing and exporting opium gum, but from countries that have adopted the poppy straw concentrate (CPS) processing method. This preference favors Australia and France, countries that, since the late 1990s, have been able to produce CPS with high thebaine content (Chouvy, 2006a; appendix A, this volume).

Opportunities for Future Research

The research base for drug policy, especially international supply control, is slight. We hope we have added to it, but much remains to be done. We suggest two lines of research, the first would consider the applicability of our findings to other drugs; the second would consider costs and benefits of the current regime.

Applicability of Policy Lessons to Other Drugs

Where does our analysis leave us with regard to markets for other drugs? Determining whether the lessons we draw for opiate policy are transferable to other drugs would require a similarly thorough investigation of the nature of the markets, particularly international markets, for these drugs. Such a study would also have to examine the role of governments and the international control regime in shaping the markets. This investigation is well beyond the scope of our study; however, we offer a few remarks on the potential for cross-market learning.

Intuitively, the transferability of our findings seems more likely for other agriculturally based illegal drugs (i.e., cocaine and cannabis), than for synthetic drugs such as ATS, including Ecstasy and methamphetamines. Additionally, there are more parallels for cocaine than for cannabis.

Like opium, coca (the plant that gives rise to cocaine) grows in only a few relatively poor countries, although technically speaking it could grow in many other countries and has historically been grown in Java, Taiwan, and Bengal. None of the three major coca-growing countries (i.e., Colombia, Peru, and Bolivia) strictly enforces prohibitions on cultivation in growing regions. Moreover, the export price of cocaine from producing countries is a tiny fraction of the retail price in consuming countries for the same reasons (including the substantial risks of incarceration and asset seizure) that the export price of heroin is a tiny fraction of the retail price.

In contrast, cannabis cultivation occurs in many countries, including some rich countries such as the Netherlands, Switzerland, the United States, and Australia, which are able to satisfy substantial shares of their demand with

domestic production. In the United States, one of the world's largest cannabis producers, the share may be about two thirds (UNODC, 2005d:82). The
markup from farmer to user is also very much smaller, in part, because traffickers face less risk en route. They have less need to cross national borders
and many countries enforce prohibitions on production, trafficking, and consumption relatively laxly or do not maintain prohibitions. A few jurisdictions,
mostly in Australia, have removed criminal penalties for cultivation of a small
number of plants for own, personal use; the Netherlands has moved to de
facto legalization of the retailing, although not the production, of the drug.
However, the worldwide spread of cannabis cultivation also provides confirmation for our model of effective illegality. Large-scale cannabis cultivation is
concentrated in northeastern Morocco, where it has long enjoyed the benevolent tolerance of the local authorities (UNODC, 2005d).

Illegality and enforcement seem to have similar effects on the size and operating methods of cocaine- and cannabis-trafficking enterprises as they have on
opiate-related firms. Adding weight to this claim, in chapter 10 we built our
case of strict enforcement on the basis of literature not focusing exclusively on
opiate trafficking, but also dealing with drug trafficking in general and occasionally including other illegal markets. We have done so not just because the
literature focusing on opiate trafficking is scant, but also because most scholars
repeatedly highlight the strong parallels between opiate and other illegal markets. The effects of lax and non-enforcement also seem intuitively to apply to
other illegal markets. For example, large and stable cocaine-trafficking organizations having no qualms about openly challenging state sovereignty have
consolidated in countries lacking consistent enforcement of prohibitions, such
as Colombia and Mexico. With some additional adaptations, the analysis concerning the impact of varying effective illegality could eventually be extended
to the enterprises producing and dealing with synthetic drugs.

Even within the family of agriculturally based illicit drugs, though, there
are differences among the three main substances in several important dimensions. For example, the poppy is an annual and, when it flowers, it is highly
conspicuous in most growing environments. Coca is a perennial plant, which
implies a substantial initial investment decision and a future stream of annual
harvest decisions, and is slightly less conspicuous. Cannabis is more easily concealed than either poppy or coca and has a much higher yield per acre in terms
of the active ingredient of the drug. In addition, coca in its raw form is much
more perishable than opium and cannot be stored for long periods; cannabis
also has a short shelf life. Moreover, cannabis, unlike either coca or opium,
requires almost no processing and relatively little labor to do so. Although the
direct transferability of our results to other drugs would have made for a more
satisfying conclusion to our research effort, we see a need for additional study,
at least to investigate the implications of these differences.

Assessing the Current International Control System

An even more ambitious goal for future research is to initiate an assessment of
the balance and distribution of the costs and benefits of various components

of the global prohibition regime. This analysis should consider the costs and benefits of important elements of the current system, including tough enforcement of penalties against producers and traffickers, such as incarceration and asset seizures. This assessment must consider not only specific drug control objectives, such as the containment of illegal drug consumption and the resulting health and social costs, but also the impact of illegal drug production and trafficking and their prohibition on state-building and socio-economic development in the most affected producing and transit countries. Although it may be impossible to assess prohibition in toto, as MacCoun and Reuter (2001) show, it should be possible to examine whether the benefits outweigh the costs of specific elements of the existing regime and to identify the winners and losers in each case.

The data collection and weighing problems would be daunting, but attention to this issue is crucial for the long-term legitimacy of the international drug control system. We believe that such an assessment will not remain an academic exercise, but should provide a much needed empirical ground to the determination of future drug policy. To date, even the longstanding acrimonious debate between "legalizers" and "warriors on drugs" has focused largely on the rationale and the costs and benefits of the current policy regime in developed consuming nations. At least for opiates, no systematic attempt has ever been made to weigh costs and benefits more globally.

The Path Forward

In our view, the main rationale for long-term policy should be to minimize the adverse consequences associated with opiate production, trafficking, and consumption in terms of human health, welfare, violence, corruption, and conflict. Whether the current regime requires reform, either through the reinterpretation of old approaches or the adoption of new ones, possible solutions should emerge from the broad assessment of the costs and benefits of the current regime and through a similarly broad assessment of the alternatives. Law enforcement indicators, such as hectares eradicated, quantities seized, laboratories destroyed, and arrests made, cannot provide a sufficient basis for assessing the effectiveness of the options.

To achieve a broader perspective it would be prudent to involve other UN agencies, such as the WHO, the UNDP, the World Bank, and UNAIDS[21] in the policy review process and, beyond that, in drug policy formulation and implementation. Arguably, these agencies play only a marginal role in shaping drug control policy, although they have had to deal with the negative consequences of drug markets and, in some instances, drug policy itself—again a point recently made by the UNODC executive director (Costa, 2008). Too often, instead, restrictive interpretations of the conventions and sharp criticisms of single states' initiatives are taken alone by the INCB and accepted uncritically by the Commission of Narcotics Drugs, the main UN forum for discussion and decision making on drug policy. The Commission might be better able to react critically were its membership drawn from a more diverse community.

Currently, the member state delegates composing it are drawn overwhelmingly from the foreign affairs and law enforcement disciplines. With a view to minimizing the harm of drug markets and drug policies, it would also be prudent to include NGOs and, in particular, NGOs that represent or have experience working with opium growers and drug users, in the review process and in drug policy formulation and implementation.

Without abandoning international coordination and cooperation, it might also be useful to consider reintroducing some of the flexibility of earlier eras in allowing countries to adapt policy to their own circumstances. This could also lower the impatience that an increasing number of European nations have for some of the very restrictive interpretations of the conventions imposed by the INCB. As mentioned earlier, some European countries have gone as far as to neglect the latter's sharp criticisms and to introduce heroin maintenance programs for heroin addicts not responsive to other treatment methods. Such experimentation has, so far, largely concerned the demand side of the market, but some alternatives, as discussed earlier, may be possible on the supply side. A political will for reform may be slowly coalescing. A growing number of policy makers in Europe and elsewhere informally agree that the time may have come for an assessment of the drug control regime, including the possibility of a new, more flexible Single Convention (see, for example, Jelsma, 2005b). It is not yet clear, however, if their efforts will gain momentum or even persist, because the procedures for treaty change are complex, time-consuming, and riddled by political barriers.

In keeping with our suggestion for an assessment of costs and benefits of the current regime, it will be important to determine the balance of the costs and benefits of any proposed reforms and to identify potential "winners" and "losers." It may also be worth weighing the effects of the reforms against those of other non-drug-related policy options. Given the inherent scarcity of national and international resources, would these reforms deliver a reasonable or acceptable return?

Finally, we note that both the United Nations and the United States have recently made the case for the current control system by comparing the level of opium production in the contemporary market with levels 100 years ago. For example, a 2007 publication by the U.S. ONDCP (2007:16) noted: "Global opium production once stood at more than 30,000 metric tons, annually, with many nations involved (such as Iran, China, India, Pakistan, Thailand, Burma and Turkey). Today the global figure for total production is an estimated 7,000 metric tons, a 77 percent reduction since [1907]…according to the United Nations' Global Drug Report" (see also UNODC, 2006:7). The frivolity of the comparison, because so much has changed apart from the formal controls, is indicative of the difficulty of providing a positive gloss to the performance of the current international system in reducing opiate supply. Perhaps matters would be worse without the system in place, but the past 10 years have seen no global supply-side improvements; production has increased. The challenge remains to develop controls that balance the laudable goal of reducing world illicit opiate production and consumption—or more realistically, the harms deriving from them—with the costs and limits of most of the current interventions.

Appendix A

Legal Production of Opium

The focus of this book is the illegal market for opium and its refined products. A legal market, which services the pharmaceutical industry, exists alongside the illegal market. Except for India, which we examine in chapter 7, there is little evidence of leakage from legal to illegal markets in producing countries.[1] Nonetheless, because there are occasional proposals that current illegal producers be allowed into the legal market as a method for reducing the supply to illegal markets (e.g., Senlis Council, 2005), it is useful to provide a brief account of that market.

The International Narcotics Control Board (INCB), a UN organization established in 1968 in accordance with the 1961 Single Convention, strictly regulates legal production. The INCB allocates to individual countries the right to produce specific quantities of opium and many other psychoactive substances. The set of countries allowed to produce opium has changed over time. The 1953 Opium Protocol allowed seven countries to produce for the export market: Bulgaria, Greece, India, Iran, Turkey, the USSR, and Yugoslavia (McAllister, 2000:179–184). The list now is very different. Of the original seven, only India and Turkey are still licensed producers. The other nations with quotas are Australia, France, Spain, and Hungary (INCB, 2008a:78–81). A few other nations, including China and Japan, produce small amounts for their own medical use. India is the only country that permits the legal extraction and export of opium gum; all other large-scale producers, including Turkey, have adopted the concentrate of poppy straw (CPS) processing method, which is.much less prone to diversion.[2] For this reason, the opiates now licitly produced are formally called *opiate* (INCB, 2008a) or *narcotics raw materials*

(NRM) (DEA, 2006). In 2006 total production of opiates for the international licit market consisted of a total of 490 tons of morphine equivalent (39 tons in morphine equivalent of opium production plus 451 tons in morphine equivalent of morphine-rich poppy straw) and of 72 tons in thebaine equivalent of thebaine-rich poppy straw (INCB, 2008a: 79–81). Thebaine is, like morphine, an alkaloid of opium; unlike morphine, it is not used therapeutically but is converted industrially into a variety of compounds, including the painkiller oxycodone.

The INCB attempts to balance supply and demand by obtaining regular estimates from each country on their consumption of various kinds of opiates. The allocation among producer nations is a purely political process. There is no claim, for example, that these are the lowest cost producers or that this configuration helps minimize illicit production. India is a high-cost producer but bases its claim for a higher allocation on the risk of diversion. Australia is a low-cost producer with minimal diversion risk. Efforts to gain substantial quotas for illicit producers (e.g., Burma in 1964 and Afghanistan in 2005) as a way of reducing black market supplies have been unsuccessful.

Since 1979, the UN Economic and Social Council has repeatedly called on importing countries to support traditional suppliers of NRM and to limit imports from non-traditional suppliers. In response to such a resolution, in 1981 the U.S. DEA (2006) published a final rule specifying certain source countries of opiates; the rule is frequently referred to as the *80/20 rule*. Under that rule, opiates can be imported from one of only seven countries. Traditional suppliers, India and Turkey, must be the source of at least 80% of the U.S. requirement for opiates. Five countries—France, Poland, Hungary, Australia, and, in the past, Yugoslavia as well[3]—may be the source of not more than 20% (DEA, 2006). The 80/20 rule has had a profound impact on the licit opiate market, because the United States is by far the largest importer.

Up until the late 1990s, India's market-leading position was further reinforced by the fact that thebaine could be extracted only from opium gum, which India alone produced. Because thebaine is not naturally present in CPS, the CPS producing countries were effectively excluded from the thebaine market. However, since the late 1990s, technological progress has threatened India's dominance. Since that time, in fact, Australia and France have begun producing CPS with high thebaine content and, as a consequence, many countries, including the United States, have been importing an increasing fraction of their legal opiates from Australia and France instead of India, as opium rich in thebaine is not included in the 80/20 rule (see chapter 7). According to interviews with foreign liaison officers in Delhi, U.S. pharmaceutical companies have also been lobbying the U.S. government to revise the 80/20 rule. So far, their lobbying efforts have not been successful, given that the 80/20 rule was confirmed anew in 2006 (DEA, 2006). Despite this, India's opium exports have followed a downward trend since the 1990s and its overall market share has considerably declined (INCB, 2008a:78–79; see chapter 7).

Appendix B

Average Consumption and Purity

The analysis of opiate markets is complicated by the lack of good estimates of the quantities consumed by an opiate user each year. The issue comes up at a number of points in our analysis. For example, we need the quantity estimate to compare total production and consumption, and to establish whether opiate inventories have been growing or shrinking. Similarly, to estimate the share of Afghanistan's production that flows through Tajikistan, we must estimate total heroin consumption in Russia and other markets supplied through Central Asia. For each nation, we need figures on the number of users and on how much each consumes on average in a year. Official statistics provide only estimates of the number of users.

Too few data exist to permit nation-specific estimates of average consumption for most countries of interest, other than the United States. To fill in the gaps and to provide a basis for benchmarking the nation-specific estimates that we have constructed, we have developed a "default" rate for average annual consumption in countries outside the United States (i.e., 30 grams). For the United States, we use a 15-gram estimate that is both consistent with U.S. government estimates of U.S. heroin consumption and with the uniquely high price of heroin in that country. This appendix describes the basis for the default rate and the U.S. estimate, and compares our figure with other aggregate studies. It also summarizes the small number of articles that include data permitting estimation of consumption by heroin users in specific samples. The focus on heroin is a result of the fact that no contemporary studies except for Iran (Cultural Research Bureau, 2001) have attempted to estimate average opium consumption.[1]

Methodological Issues

The difficulty in developing consumption estimates arises largely from that fact that a user cannot report how much of an illegal drug he or she purchases. Sales are often made hurriedly in clandestine settings with little or bad information. No sale comes with a meaningful guarantee regarding the quantity or purity of the drug; in some nations, retail purity varies a great deal. Buyers can report only how much they spent or, in the case of heroin, how frequently they injected, smoked, or inhaled.

To use data on spending, one needs purity-adjusted price data to calculate the quantity of heroin each user consumes; such price data are available on a regular basis only in the United States. Within Europe, the EMCDDA reports "typical" retail purity as lying between 20% and 45% (EMCDDA, 2002a:26) but does not report a purity-adjusted average price. The great variation in observed street-level purity and unadjusted prices, and the lack of data on the correlation between them, creates a great deal of uncertainty in an estimate that simply divides average price by average purity.

To convert reports of use frequency to estimates of quantities, it is necessary to have an estimate of the standard quantity in a dose. The size of a dose is also not available on a systematic basis. Consider, for example, what was available for Russia. A doctor specializing in drug treatment in Moscow, who was interviewed for a related project, believed that addicts in her clinic injected two to four times daily. Paoli (2001) reports that the usual selling unit is 100 milligrams; the two to four times injection per day would then suggest a figure of 200 to 400 milligrams per day. Unfortunately, no purity data are available.

Purity is a major problem for the analysis of opiate markets. We believe that purity declines as heroin moves along the distribution chain, reflecting cutting with diluents by successive dealers. For example, for Turkey, as shown in chapter 4, the average purity in multikilo shipments in 2002 was about 40% whereas in Germany, in 2002, 45% of retail seizures were less than 10% pure and only 9% were more than 30% pure (REITOX [Germany], 2003:54) However there is substantial variation at all levels of the market. Reuter and Caulkins (2004) reported that from 1987 to 1991, approximately one eighth of the U.S. DEA's U.S. retail purchases had purity less than 5% whereas more than 10% had purity greater than 75%. In U.S. low-level wholesale markets (more than 10 grams, raw quantity), the reported interquartile range in 2002 was 34% to 62% (ONDCP, 2004).

Our Procedure

Absent national consumption estimates, we have developed a "default" rate for consumption outside the United States—an average, expressed per user in pure heroin equivalent grams—using U.S. and other evidence. We started with the United States, because it provides the most systematic evidence on consumption quantities. The U.S. ONDCP (2001) reports that U.S. heroin addicts consume roughly 15 grams of pure heroin per year, or about 50 milligrams per day when actively using, which we assume to be about 300 days per year, allowing for sickness, a few days in a local jail or treatment program, and other short-lived breaks in use.

For our non-U.S. default rate we assume that opiate users in other countries consume twice as much per capita as those in the United States (i.e., 30 grams of pure heroin equivalent per user per year), reflecting the lower prices outside the United States. The increase gives nod to price responsiveness, absent a full cross-country analysis of prices and demand elasticities. We believe that an estimate of 100 pure milligrams per user per day—consistent with an annual estimate of about 30 pure grams—for countries with opiate prices that are, relative to average earnings, much lower than the United States, is reasonable and not inconsistent with judgments of experts.

Other Aggregate Studies

A few other studies have attempted to develop population-level estimates. The UNODC (2005d) reports a global average of 28 grams per annum and a European average of 58 grams. For validation of the higher figure, the UNODC cites the results of a U.K. study on people entering treatment in 1997, which it states implies 68 grams[2] (Gossop, Marsden, and Stewart, 1997). However, treatment research (e.g., Anglin and Hser, 1990) has consistently found that users enter treatment at times of peak use; thus, reports of use in the period immediately before treatment entry will overstate average use rates. Moreover, treatment entry is itself not randomly distributed across dependent users; those with more severe problems have a higher probability of being referred to treatment as a consequence of arrest. Thus we believe that the figure is too high. The UNODC figures for other regions are based on estimated total consumption from an input/output model, divided by estimated prevalence. The regional figures vary from 10 grams in South America to 56.5 grams in Oceania; for most regions, the figure falls between 15 grams and 33 grams.

Bramley-Harker (2001) estimated total pure heroin consumption in 1999 in the United Kingdom at about 11 metric tons,[3] which for a population of 275,000 heroin addicts amounts to about 40 grams per addict per annum, nearly three times the U.S. figure of about 15 grams and a third higher than our 30-gram non-U.S. default rate. Although heroin is unusually cheap in the United Kingdom, a number of assumptions used in the estimating procedure may have biased the numbers upward. For example, the study assumed that the number of days of active consumption was 52 times the number reported the previous week by users not in treatment or prison. In fact, heroin users spend a good deal of their careers in treatment or prison; thus, the number of days of use will be substantially lower.

A later estimate for the United Kingdom (Singleton, Murray, and Tinsley, 2006) showed a lower total figure of about 8 pure metric tons for 2003, representing differences in methodology and data sources. On the basis of a relatively sophisticated analysis of a survey of arrestees, the study estimated that intensive users consumed the equivalent of 160 to 240 adulterated milligrams per use day (48–72 grams per annum) and non-intensive users consumed 100 to 185 milligrams per use day (30–55 grams per annum) (Singleton et al., 2006:67). The figures were lower if the user was in treatment. With an estimated heroin-using population of 280,000 opiate users (Singleton et al., 2006:28), the implied annual consumption per user was approximately 29 grams per annum, a figure remarkably close to our default rate.

Microstudies

We have found only four studies outside the United States that report enough data to permit even a rough estimate of annual consumption. Atha and Davis (2003) report purity-adjusted data from a list of customers in northern England showing a median of 280 milligrams of heroin per day but a skewed distribution with a substantially higher average (e.g., the 75th percentile was 515 milligrams). These data came from records in a prosecution and required the strong assumption that each customer had no other dealer.

The other three studies draw on samples of users in treatment. Jimenez-Lerma, Manuel, Landabaso, Iraurgi, Calle, Sanz, Gutiérrez-Fraile (2002) report in a study of 80 addicts in a treatment clinic in the Basque region of Spain that their patients consumed an average 512 milligrams of heroin per day. The study does not report purity but, according to the Observatorio Español sobre Drogas (2005:172), the purity of a dose of heroin has consistently remained above 20% since 1998. Similarly, Smolka and Schmidt (1999) report average daily consumption of 740 milligrams per day for a sample of 22 addicts in treatment in Berlin. They do not present purity data. For Germany, heroin retail purity has generally oscillated, from 1996 to 2004, between less than 10% and 20%, with substantial variation across cities (BKA, 2005b:40). Gossop et al. (1997) report data on 1,075 treatment admissions in 1995 in the United Kingdom. Average monthly heroin consumption at admission varied by treatment modality, ranging from 9.4 grams (inpatient) to 16.4 grams (methadone reduction). The weighted average was approximately 12 grams per month, using data from the 809 respondents who reported at the 6-month follow-up.

Table B.1 attempts to array the results in a consistent fashion. However, because each study reported the results in a different fashion, we have had to use different procedures to develop the annual pure gram estimates. For example, Gossop et al. (1997) included figures on total monthly consumption at street purity and the number of days used per month, whereas Jimenez-Lerma et al. (2002) reported directly the average quantity per day. We have

Table B.1
Individual study estimates of heroin consumption.

Study	Location	Sample Description (size)	Quantity per Day (grams)	Estimated Purity (%)	Implied Annual Consumption Pure Heroin (grams)
Atha and Davis, 2003	Northern England	Customers of a single dealer (92)	280	40	40
Jimenez-Lerma et al., 2002	Basque country	Treatment sample (80)	512	25	38
Smolka and Schmidt, 1999	Berlin	Treatment sample (22)	740	15	33
Gossop et al., 1997	Britain	Multisite treatment sample (809)	550	38	55

also had to make assumptions for some studies about the number of days used per annum and we corrected for inconsistencies in data presentation. The results are thus quite approximate.

Given the bias that we believe arises from use of treatment samples to estimate average use, we draw comfort from these studies. They suggest that the 30 grams of pure heroin per annum, at least for western Europe around the end of the 20th century, may be a reasonable approximation.

Caveats

Note that national prevalence estimates are often not well defined in terms of the frequency of use of the included population; they might include not only those dependent on opiates, but also occasional users. The official U.S. estimate for 2000 was roughly 900,000 chronic users (using at least eight times per month) and approximately 250,000 occasional users (ONDCP, 2001:9, table 3).[4] Other nations do not have consistent series on the numbers of occasional, dependent, or chronic users. Moreover, the national estimates also include users of opium and morphine, who may consume large quantities by weight because their consumption methods, such as smoking in the case of opium, are less efficient. Absent reliable data, we rarely make any adjustment for users of opiates other than heroin, but, except for a few countries, it is thought that they constitute a small share of the total outside Asia.

Annual consumption per user might be expected to vary over time and across countries. For example, the inflation-adjusted price of heroin has fallen in many western nations during the past 20 years. This should lead heroin users, on average, to consume somewhat more of the drug in recent years, unless the price of other, substitute drugs has fallen even more. In some western nations, heroin addicts are eligible for income support as a result of their poverty; in others, they are not. It is plausible that addicts in the former, with higher incomes, would consume more heroin. We offer these observations not as predictive statements, but as indicative of the factors that might lead to variation in quantities consumed—a topic that has not yet been examined.

Moreover, it may well be that in some nations, where opiates are particularly cheap in absolute and relative terms, the correct figure is higher than 30 grams per annum. Occasionally, reports provide some measure of the relative cost of a dose of heroin. For example, in Dushanbe, the capital of Tajikistan, in 1999 a 150-milligram dose sold for $0.60, a kilogram of rice cost $0.33, and a kilogram of cooking oil cost $0.66 (DCA, 2004), which suggests that heroin is relatively cheap for addicts in that country. It is unclear what would serve as counterpart commodity measures for a U.S. heroin addict, but with heroin costing the average user about $30 per day (ONDCP, 1999:13), the cost of a heroin habit may be higher as a ratio of the goods needed for survival, making it relatively more expensive in the United States in real terms.

As a possible upper bound on the amount that a user might consume, there are data from heroin maintenance programs launched since the late 20th century in several western European countries. In Switzerland, for example, addicts could consume as much heroin as they desired for a fixed payment (i.e., the cost was not related to the size of the dose) and daily consumption averaged about 500 milligrams per day or 150 grams per year (Rehm, Gshwend, Steffen, Gutzwiller, Dobler-Mikola, and Uchtenhagen, 2001). No illegal market will generate figures close to that.

Appendix C

Central Asia

Trafficking Revenues and Economic Dependency

Introduction

Much of the concern about drug trafficking in Central Asia[1] rests on the assertion that it has become a major economic force in the region, particularly in Tajikistan. Drug trafficking may draw hard currency into the region and offer income-earning opportunities to residents facing very limited alternatives, but it also fuels corruption, as we addressed in chapters 9 and 10, and may help finance other illicit activities.

This appendix reproduces an earlier analysis[2] that systematically assesses the economic dimensions of opiate trafficking in Central Asia, focusing especially on Tajikistan, to ground discussions of both the significance of trafficking and possible policy responses. It estimates Central Asia's income from opiate trafficking in GDP-like terms for a representative year—specifically, the year 2000. It follows the conventions of national income and product accounting to facilitate comparisons with existing estimates of the region's legitimate market GDP.[3]

To the extent possible, this analysis uses quantity and price data for the year 2000. We chose 2000 over 2001 largely because of its relative stability.[4] Extraordinary political and military events in Afghanistan led to a dramatic decline in production in 2001 and contributed to substantial intra-annual variation in regional wholesale prices. For these reasons, a calculation of opiate income for Central Asia for 2001 would have been more speculative than for 2000 and less likely to provide insight into the economic implications of drug trafficking in other years. Admittedly, the year 2000 might not be fully representative either, because it immediately followed a "boom" year for Afghan opium production, but it might yield more robust estimates than 2001.[5]

This analysis yields estimates of the region's opiate income ranging from less than $500 million to more than $1.5 billion annually in GDP-comparable terms. The breadth of the range reflects substantial weaknesses in the underlying data. Moreover, because the range is GDP comparable, it does not include the potentially large backflows of drug-related wages and earnings from operations outside the region. For example, Central Asians distributing drugs in Russia might repatriate hundreds of millions of dollars annually. Nevertheless, the estimates are substantial, equating to roughly 1.5% to 5% of the region's reported GDP. If, as the evidence suggests, Tajikistan is Central Asia's primary drug trafficker, then its opiate income may be equivalent to 30% to 100% of its reported GDP. Even the low end would be much higher than has been estimated for any other nation other than post-2001 Afghanistan. For Peru and Bolivia, at the height of their involvement in the cocaine trade and in the midst of the Latin American debt crisis, no credible estimates have exceeded 10% to 15% (Alvarez, 1995).

Reviewing Previous Income Estimates

We begin by noting how difficult it is to estimate illicit drug income. Estimation requires a combination of quantity and price data or, for domestic consumption, extrapolation from surveys of expenditures among frequent opiate users. The United Nations offered the first systematic, documented, and published estimate of Central Asia's opiate earnings in 2003 (UNODC, 2003c), reckoning that the region's gross drug profits amount to about $2.3 billion annually. Given considerable uncertainty and substantial methodological differences, it may be reassuring that the United Nations' figure is only 50% larger than our high-end figure; we discuss some of the methodological differences underlying the figures after presenting our own estimates.[6]

Prior to the UNODC report, widely quoted revenue estimates, generally with little or no documentation, fed the policy debate. For example, Olcott and Udalova (2000:13) cite an obscure Russian report and state that "Central Asia seems to be 'catching up,' and it has already been reported that several million are involved in the production, refining, sale, and trafficking of drugs with an annual turnover of $14 billion."[7]

Our estimates may not be correct either (indeed, they probably are not), but they are among the first with explicit documentation of their origins and the only ones that derive from standard economic accounting practices. To that extent we are confident that they represent an improvement over existing figures.

Estimating Opiate Availability, Consumption, and Seizures

In addition to serving their own market, Central Asian traffickers provide a bridge between producers in Afghanistan and consumers in Central Asia and elsewhere. Thus, Central Asia's drug-related income depends not only on how much opium Afghanistan produces and sells each year (hence, availability), but also on where it gets consumed and seized. In addition to its own consumption, Central Asia is an attractive export route for some, but not all, markets. For example, it is likely that Central Asia services significant shares of the Russian, Ukrainian, and other European markets. However, it is highly unlikely that opiates consumed in India and Pakistan would pass through Central Asia. Although doglegged routes are not unknown in the drug trade, the commercial and transportation links between Central Asia and India and Pakistan are not good. Data on seizures are also important—for example, enough opiates must transit Central Asia to account for both consumption and seizures in destination markets.

The Availability of Afghan-Originating Opiates

Central Asia does not currently produce opium; rather, it handles opium and opium derivatives that originate in Afghanistan.[8] As such, the Afghan production estimate provides an anchor for the Central Asian income estimate.

As noted previously, Afghanistan has, in recent years, become the world's leading opium producer. In the boom year of 1999, Afghanistan alone accounted for almost 80% of global opium production, with harvests amounting to about 457 metric tons in pure heroin equivalent units, applying a standard conversion ratio of 10 units of opium for every 1 unit of heroin or morphine (see chapter 3). In 2000, when Afghanistan's opium production fell back to 328 metric tons, a level nearer to other prior years, the country still accounted for nearly 70% of global production. To the extent that farmers and traders held inventory from the 1999 harvest, the 328 metric ton figure may understate total opium availability, so that the year 2000 may be less typical than a simple production estimate would otherwise suggest.[9]

The Taliban ban, which was announced in 2000, did not affect the year 2000 harvest, but the year 2001 harvest plummeted—to return to prior peak levels since then (see chapters 3–6). Perhaps ironically, the only lasting effect of the Taliban ban may have been an increase in cultivation in the north—the region nearest to Central Asia—which may have facilitated the growth of the drug trade in and through Central Asia.

The Consumption of Opiates in Central Asia's Markets

Unfortunately, the data on consumption are not as transparent as those on production. National consumption estimates are not available or well documented for most countries (Reuter, 1998; chapters 3 and 5, and appendix B, this volume).

In view of the data deficiencies, we proceed by developing annualized, year 2000 estimates of opiate consumption for each of the markets that Central Asia services: Russia, the Ukraine, the rest of Europe, and Central Asia itself. Market by market, we report on existing estimates of national consumption or, when none exist, derive estimates of our own, using data from United Nations and other available reports to derive national totals—the product of (1) prevalence (the number of persons who use opiates during the year) and (2) the amount they typically consume gives the total pure heroin equivalent consumption for each market. Derivation is challenging because it requires information on both prevalence and quantity; information on prevalence is weak and information on quantity is even weaker (see appendix B).

As in previous chapters and working with the same evidence and assumptions, we also use a default rate for the annual consumption of the typical non-U.S. user of 30 grams of pure heroin per annum (see chapters 3 and 5, and appendix B). We use the default rate as a proxy in our calculations of national consumption when country-specific data are missing. We also use it as a basis for comparison, a "benchmark" to evaluate our estimates, when the data are especially weak.

Russian and Ukrainian Consumption

In this section we develop a consumption estimate for Russia, which has become the single largest market served primarily through Central Asia, and we use the estimate to extrapolate a consumption estimate for the Ukraine.[10] The Ukraine is a smaller market than Russia, but it is still significant in its own right.

Estimating Russia's opiate consumption—increasingly as heroin—is critical to understanding Central Asia's role in the opiate trade. Heroin consumption in Russia was slight until the later years of the Soviet occupation of Afghanistan (Paoli, 2001). Numbers for all drug-related problems (overdoses, arrests, treatment episodes, and AIDS cases) have risen dramatically since then, particularly in the late 1990s. For example, the number of persons entering treatment rose from 244,000 in 1996 to 452,000 in 2000 and 507,000 in 2001 (UNODCCP, 2002a:20).

The Prevalence of Use and Addiction   Estimates of the total number of heroin users in Russia have a weaker evidentiary base than those developed in the United States and western Europe. For purposes of estimating total consumption, the number of persons frequently using heroin is most important; frequent users may average an annual consumption 5 to 10 times that of occasional users (ONDCP, 2001). Of the 452,000 registered drug users entering treatment in 2000 in Russia, 298,000 were classified as addicts (UNODCCP, 2002a:20); the others may have been occasional users attempting to reduce the severity of criminal justice punishments.

Although expert opinion is often cited as supporting an estimate of about 2.5 million heroin addicts in 2000, the number appears to include both regular and occasional users (see, for example, Paoli [2001:85], citing Russian Ministry of Interior estimates of 2.5 million to 3 million users) and also may include compote users.[11, 12] Here, in this analysis, we use an estimate of about one million addicted heroin users in 2000,[13] which is more than three times the number of those registered in Russia as drug addicts. One million generates a high heroin addiction prevalence rate when compared with any western nation—roughly twice that of Switzerland (Rehm, Gshwend, Steffen, Gutzwiller, Dobler-Mikola, and Uchtenhagen, 2001), which is a country with a significant heroin problem, or of the United States.

The fragility of current estimates of the number of Russian heroin users is also indicated by the very high prevalence of heroin use among young persons. A survey of 15- to 21-year-olds in Moscow, the Russian city believed to have the highest prevalence in Russia, found 6% reporting having used heroin at least once; for no other country was the figure higher than 2% (Paoli, 2001, citing Vishinsky, 1998). The one million figure for 2000 might increase rapidly in the near future, although it is important to remember that epidemics can also end quite rapidly (Caulkins, 2007).

The Quantity of Consumption   There are no official estimates of individuals' annual consumption, but studies provide a basis for crude estimation. According to a doctor specializing in drug treatment in Moscow, who was interviewed for a related project, addicts reported about 500 to 1,000 milligrams daily, but that was at street purity, which is low and variable. The doctor believed that they injected two to four times daily. Because addicts are more likely to be able to report injection frequency rather than quantity consumed, we rely on that for our rough calculations.

Paoli (2001) reports that the usual selling unit is 100 milligrams. Injections of two to four times per day would then suggest a figure of 200 to 400 milligrams per day. Unfortunately, no purity data are available and, as noted in appendix B, in other nations observed purity ranges from 5% to 75%. If purity is 50%, the previous figures generate an estimate of 100 to 200 milligrams for the average daily consumption of pure heroin per addict. This, in turn, yields an estimate of 30 to 60 grams per addict per year, compared with the 30-gram benchmark, assuming that addicts actively consume, on average, 300 days per annum. With one million addicts, total Russian consumption would amount to about 30 to 60 metric tons of heroin, accounting for as much as 10% to 20% of Afghanistan's opium production in 2000, measured in pure heroin equivalent units.[14]

These figures are very rough, but they are still informative. They suggest that Russian consumption accounts for a significant share of total Afghan production, implying that Central Asian traffickers may handle a significant share.

Although less of the Ukraine's heroin may flow through Central Asia than Russia's, we use the consumption estimate for Russia to develop a consumption estimate for the Ukraine. We believe that the analogy is reasonable, given the two countries' proximity and historical socioeconomic linkages. To derive the Ukrainian estimate, we simply adjust the Russian total for the smaller Ukrainian population. The Ukraine's population is about one third as large as Russia's (World Bank, 2002), implying a total consumption of about 10 to 20 metric tons.

Other European Consumption

Few systematic estimates of quantities exist at the national level in Europe.[15] Bramley-Harker (2001) estimated total pure heroin consumption in 1999 in the United Kingdom at about 11 tons,[16] which for a population of 275,000 heroin addicts amounts to about 40 grams per addict per annum—nearly three times the U.S. figure of about 15 grams and a third higher than our 30-gram benchmark.[17] Heroin is unusually cheap in the United Kingdom, but a number of assumptions may have biased the estimate upward.

For the moment, however, we take the U.K. figure at face value and extrapolate to the western European market as a whole. A study from the EMCDDA (2002b) reports fewer than 1.5 million problem drug users in Norway and European Union member states, excluding Greece.[18] Adding estimates for Greece and Switzerland, derived from United Nations' reported prevalence rates, the total remains under 1.5 million.[19] Taking 1.5 million as a high-end but plausible estimate and using the U.K. 40-gram figure, this would suggest about 60 metric tons of pure heroin consumption annually. Alternatively, applying the 30-gram benchmark, the total for western Europe would result in a figure of about 45 metric tons.

Central and East Europe report moderately serious drug problems, but with a population base of about 125 million, excluding Russia and the Ukraine, much of which exists outside the global economy, the region is unlikely to generate even another half million addicts.[20] (A countervailing factor is the large flow of heroin through the Balkan route.) Another EMCDDA study, this one on the drug situation in European Union candidate Central and eastern European countries, reports a prevalence rate of problem drug use of 0.25% of the population age 15 to 64 years for Poland, the largest country and one of the few for which systematic, albeit old, data are available.[21] Four other nations had rates of around 0.5%. High rates were reported for two of the smaller nations, Estonia and Latvia (EMCDDA, 2002c:17–18).[22] Taking 500,000 as another high-end but plausible estimate of opiate users and applying the U.K. figure of 40 grams per addict per year, the total amount consumed would be about 20 metric tons of pure heroin. The total for the 30-gram benchmark adds up to about 15 metric tons.

Central Asian Consumption

As already noted, opiate consumption has increased sharply in the nations of Central Asia itself. Table C.1 gives United Nations' prevalence figures for drug addiction at the time of this analysis.[23] They may exaggerate the growth, but lacking a basis for refinement we use them for our calculations. The Kazakhstan and Kyrgyzstan prevalence rates, if taken to refer primarily to opiate use as regional circumstances might merit, are among the highest found anywhere

Table C.1
Estimated number of drug addicts in Central Asia, ca. 2000.

Market	Actual Number	Population	Rate per 100,000 Inhabitants
Kazakhstan	165,000–186,000	14,860,000	1,110–1,251
Kyrgyzstan	80,000–100,000	4,867,000	1,644–2,054
Tajikistan	55,000	6,131,000	897
Uzbekistan	65,000–91,000	24,813,000	262–367
Total	365,000–432,000	50,671,000	720–853

Note: The data are reported as "preliminary findings" on the extent of the drug problem in Central Asia; they are not attributed to a particular year.
Source: UNODCCP, 2002d:25.

in the world. They are also much higher than the rates previously reported for these two countries in the United Nations' *Global Illicit Drug Trends 2002* report (UNODCCP, 2002c).[24]

Data for Turkmenistan are less recent; however, it has such a small population that its addition would seem to make little difference. In our estimate we use the prevalence rate found in the United Nations' *Global Illicit Drug Trends 2002* report (UNODCCP, 2002c), which was 0.3% for the adult population in the late 1990s. This yields a total of about 10,000 opiate users. For comparison, we also apply Tajikistan's prevalence rate to Turkmenistan, yielding what might be regarded as a high-end estimate of the possible in that highly authoritarian regime. That raises the country's total to more than 45,000 opiate users. Adding in the estimates for Turkmenistan to those for the rest of Central Asia, the total number of opiate addicts in the region is then about 375,000 to 480,000. Because regional data on quantity are absent, we apply the 30-gram-per-annum benchmark, bringing the total consumption for the region to about 11 to 14 metric tons, after rounding.

Seizures of Opiates That Enter or Transit Central Asia

Estimating seizures is simpler than estimating consumption. The United Nations provides estimates of opiate seizures by country and product type (i.e., opium, morphine, or heroin) for each country along the Central Asian supply chain. Apart from concerns about seizures reentering the market, the most significant complication arises in converting them to pure heroin equivalent units. First we convert them to heroin equivalent units using a ratio of 10 units of opium to 1 unit of heroin or morphine. Then, to adjust for purity, we treat seizures occurring early in the supply chain (i.e., in Central Asia) as "pure" units; we treat seizures occurring later in the pipeline as progressively less pure. Specifically, we assume that seizures occurring in Russia are

75% pure and seizures occurring in the Ukraine and the rest of Europe are 50% pure.

Table C.2 presents seizure figures for Central Asia, Russia, the Ukraine, the rest of Europe, and various other countries (for context) in heroin equivalent metric tons and, for Central Asia, Russia, the Ukraine, and the rest of Europe, with purity adjustments, in pure heroin equivalent metric tons.

The combination of consumption and seizures amounts to the total shipments that must enter each of the markets that Central Asia services, and only a portion of which will travel through Central Asia. In the next section, we posit market shares and use the consumption and seizure estimates to track the flows of opiates into and through Central Asia, preliminary to estimating Central Asia's opiate income.

Table C.2
Opiate seizures in Central Asian and other countries (in metric tons).

	1995	1996	1997	1998	1999	2000
Central Asia						
Kazakhstan	0.02	0.05	0.14	0.06	0.07	0.28
Kyrgyzstan	0.08	0.18	0.17	0.04	0.04	0.36
Tajikistan	0.16	0.35	0.41	0.39	0.84	2.36
Turkmenistan	0.00	0.00	2.09	0.64	0.70	0.43
Uzbekistan	0.09	0.20	0.31	0.39	0.66	0.88
Central Asia total	0.36	0.78	3.11	1.51	2.31	4.30
Russia	0.13	0.20	0.05	0.64	0.85	1.20
The Ukraine	0.01	0.02	0.00	0.01	0.02	0.04
Europe	6.68	6.78	7.04	7.31	8.32	11.81
Other countries						
Pakistan	21.70	6.61	6.89	3.87	6.61	10.38
Iran	25.78	26.19	37.18	40.63	49.24	44.86
Turkey	4.41	5.60	4.18	5.42	4.65	8.57
Purity-adjusted figures						
Central Asia	0.36	0.78	3.11	1.51	2.31	4.30
Russia	0.09	0.15	0.04	0.48	0.64	0.90
The Ukraine	0.01	0.01	0.00	0.00	0.01	0.02
Europe	3.34	3.39	3.52	3.65	4.16	5.90

Note: Opiates are measured first in heroin equivalent units, assuming a 10:1 ratio of opium to heroin or morphine, and then adjusted for purity. Europe includes western and Central and eastern Europe, except Russia, the Ukraine, and Turkey. The purity adjustment for Europe, so defined, is 50%; the purity adjustments for Russia and the Ukraine are 75% and 50%, respectively.
Source: Authors' calculations based on opium, morphine, and heroin seizures reported in UNODCCP (2002c).

Tracking Opiate Flows into and through Central Asia

Central Asia serves four major markets in part or in whole: itself, Russia, the Ukraine, and the rest of Europe. Here, we posit plausible share allocations for each of these markets, drawing largely from expert opinion. We apply the shares to our estimates from the previous section to calculate flows into and through Central Asia.

The vast majority of heroin consumed in western Europe has been produced in Afghanistan. The route from Iran, through Turkey and the Balkans, the so-called *Balkan route*, has been the most prominent. However, the Balkan route, with its innumerable variations, is not the only route leading from Afghanistan to western Europe. Some Afghan-originating heroin travels directly from Pakistan, facilitated by the large Pakistani immigrant population in Britain. Nevertheless, some also travels indirectly through Russia. Entry into Russia through Central Asia appears to involve little risk to smugglers, and entry into other parts of Europe from Russia appears to involve only moderate risk.

In the following calculations, we assume that one third of consumption in Europe, excluding Turkey, Russia, and the Ukraine, is supplied via Central Asia and Russia. This may be a high-end figure, given European statements about the share coming through Turkey and the Balkans.[25] Note that total shipments include opiates—primarily heroin—that are seized in Europe; this adds another 6 metric tons of potential throughput in pure heroin equivalent units.[26] Furthermore, we assume that all opiates destined for Russia travel through Central Asia and that two thirds of all opiates destined for the Ukraine also travel through Central Asia. Finally, we assume that Central Asia fully serves its own market. Table C.3 summarizes our calculations, based on

Table C.3
Estimated opiate flows into or through Central Asia in 2000 (in metric tons unless otherwise stated).

Market	Consumption	Seizures	Share into or through Central Asia	Flow into or through Central Asia
Europe	60–80	6	0.33	22–29
The Ukraine	10–20	0	0.66	7–13
Russia	30–60	1	1.00	31–61
Central Asia	11–14	4	1.00	15–18
Total	111–174	17	—	75–121

Note: Opiates are measured in pure heroin equivalent units, assuming a 10:1 ratio of opium to heroin or morphine. Europe includes western and Central and eastern Europe, except Russia, the Ukraine, and Turkey. The Ukrainian seizure estimate rounds to zero.
Source: Authors' calculations and UNODCCP (2002c) for data on opiate seizures.

these assumptions, for total flows of opiates into and through Central Asia, by destination.[27]

The calculations indicate that Central Asia may handle a substantial share of Afghan-originating opiates and a significant, albeit somewhat less noteworthy, share of global production. The estimated flow into or through Central Asia—75 to 121 metric tons—would amount to about 23% to 37% of Afghanistan's opium production, and about 16% to 26% of total world production in 2000.

Estimating Opiate Trafficking Income

Ultimately, the economic scale of opiate trafficking matters at least as much as the quantity for policy purposes, because much of the damage caused to society by trafficking is a function—a complicated function—of how much money it generates. By valuing transactions at successive stages of the supply chain, it is possible to produce an estimate of Central Asia's opiate income in roughly GDP-comparable terms.[28]

A comprehensive GDP-comparable measure of opiate income would consist of three components: final consumption expenditures; merchandise exports valued at the export frontier; and any associated service exports, possibly including cross-border transportation and guard services. However, the attribution of the smuggling margin—the difference between the trader's sale price at the export frontier and the first purchase price in the importing country, part or all of which might which might constitute a service export—adds considerable uncertainty to the estimation process, because it depends on the residency of the smuggler or "service provider" (OECD et al., 2002:156).[29]

If, for example, an Afghanistan-based smuggler were to carry opiates across the border into Tajikistan, the value of his or her services would be credited to Afghanistan's national income as a service export—up to the point of the first in-country transaction.[30] Note, though, some smugglers are based outside the country. For example, Mansfield and Martin (2000) note that opium prices were sometimes quoted in Turkmen or Pakistani currencies, suggesting that some of the buyers were from those countries. Absent an empirical basis for attributing the service value, we assume at this and all other points in the supply chain that half of the smuggling margin accrues to the exporting country.

Smuggling assumptions aside, we draw on basic principals of economic accounting, as set out in the *System of National Accounts 1993*, or *SNA* (United Nations et al., 1993), and the IMF's *Balance of Payments Manual* (IMF, 1993). The Organization for Economic Cooperation and Development (OECD) discusses the application of these principles, especially the SNA, to illegal activities, including drug trafficking, in a handbook for measuring the non-observed economy (OECD et al., 2002). Shcherbakov (2000) specifically addresses the challenges associated with evaluating foreign trade transactions in a study of

Russian drug trafficking. As suggested earlier, our calculation requires information on three basic income-accounting elements:[31]

1. Final consumption expenditures in Central Asia, consisting of the value of all opiates consumed in Central Asia
2. Central Asia's exports to Russia (including opiates flowing through, en route to Europe), consisting of the "free on board" (f.o.b.) value of all opiates shipped from Central Asia's export frontiers to Russia and the value of the services provided by Central Asian-based smugglers in moving the opiates across the border[32]
3. Central Asia's imports from Afghanistan, consisting of the f.o.b. value of all opiates shipped from Afghanistan's export frontiers to Central Asia and the value of the services provided by Afghan-based smugglers in moving the opiates across the border

Our income calculation is intended to be GDP comparable, but we offer a cautionary note on its use and interpretation. Here, as elsewhere in this analysis, adding a GDP-like estimate of drug-related income to a county's or region's reported GDP, without any adjustments, could overstate its overall income, resulting from the possibility of the implicit inclusion of illegal activities in the reported figure and other double counting (for a more thorough treatment of this issue, including several examples of double counting, see OECD et al. [2002:157–158]).

Although not part of a GDP-like measure, we are also interested in another type of income: Central Asia's share of the income from opiate distribution within Russia. To the extent that Central Asians work for Russian-based distribution networks or establish their own satellite operations or "foreign affiliates" in Russia, some of their wages and earnings may eventually flow back to Central Asia. Such earnings, which are counted in gross national product, may also affect the regional economy.

For each of these calculations we need prices at different points in the supply chain. Although we do not have export and import prices per se, we do have border and wholesale prices that we can use as proxies. Unfortunately, we have little basis for allocating the value of trade in services (i.e., the smuggling margin). As noted earlier, we attribute 50% of the margin to the exporting country. For example, we attribute 50% of the difference between the Afghan export price and the Tajik import price to Afghanistan's service exports, which are equivalent to Tajikistan's service imports, and we attribute 50% of the difference between the Tajik export price and the Russian import price to Tajikistan's service exports.

Price data are extremely sketchy, but table C.4 presents rough estimates of prices as a kilogram of heroin flows from Afghanistan to Russia. The table provides ranges for prices at each market level, because anything else would suggest false precision. To the extent possible, the figures refer to observed or reported price estimates for the year 2000. We have culled data from a variety of sources, including official government reports, United Nations studies,

Table C.4
Price of a kilogram of heroin along the supply chain.

Location and Point of Sale	Price
Afghanistan	
Export	$700–$1,000
Tajikistan	
Import	$1,000–$1,500
Export	$1,500–$2,000[*]
Retail	$2,000–$5,000[†]
Russia	
Import	$15,000–$30,000
Retail	$75,000–$300,000

Note: Prices are reported as per kilogram for pure heroin equivalent units; retail sales typically occur in volumes of less than 1 gram. [*]Most sources indicate a range of $1,500 to $2,000; however, the DCA (2002) also reports a low of $1,000 at unknown purity. [†]The DCA (2002:66) reports the retail price as about $4,000 per pure kilogram, when sold in 0.15-gram units; it also reports prices of $3,000 to $5,000 in a separate table. The UNODCCP (2002c:195) reports prices of $1,700 to $2,000 at 90% purity.
Source: Various government reports, United Nations studies, press reports, informal interviews, and expert opinion were used as sources. See "Note" for information on some specific price ranges.

press reports, and informal interviews, and combined it with expert opinion. Although any price within a range seems about as likely as any other, we use the endpoints for calculations.

For a combination of substantive and practical reasons, we use Tajikistan as the reference country for calculating the value of Central Asia's trade and consumption. For the trade calculation, we use Tajikistan because there are many indications that it is the initial entry point for a majority of the Afghan heroin passing through the region. However, for the consumption calculation, we use Tajikistan, only because we have very little price data for other countries. This second reason is especially dissatisfying, because, as indicated in table C.1, Tajikistan probably accounts for a relatively modest share of Central Asia's total consumption.

Even for Tajikistan, there are few observations and their documentation is often incomplete. A research unit in the Tajikistan DCA (2002), working in collaboration with the United Nations provides one of the most complete descriptions. The UNODC, formerly the UNODCCP, also provides data separately, including national reports on wholesale and retail prices in the region; These data are, at best, impressions from police agencies and are not based on analyses of individual observations. In addition, the United Nations presents price data in various special reports, including a publication on the drug situation in the regions neighboring Afghanistan (UNODCCP, 2002d). These data indicate considerable variability over time in reported prices at all levels of the market. For example, the wholesale price of a kilogram of heroin in Tajikistan fell from $5,150 in 1998 to $1,575 in 2000, but rose to $3,900 by December 2001 and fell to $3,400 by February 2002.

For transactions that occur in Central Asia, the income has two principal components (1) payments to the couriers, dealers, and smugglers, mostly for taking legal and physical risks; and (2) payments to corrupt officials.[33] Although not included in a GDP-comparable estimate of income, some earnings are generated outside of Central Asia and repatriated by Tajiks or other Central Asian nationals involved in trafficking further along the distribution chain. Tajiks appear to play a prominent role in Russia, both at the smuggling and low wholesale levels. The GDP-like estimate reflects their role in smuggling heroin into Russia, but not their role in distribution within Russia. Still, the latter role may generate significant earnings for Tajiks because the markups, in absolute terms, are so high. It may also have very different political and social consequences, depending in part on whether the earnings are repatriated to Tajikistan, remain in Russia, or go elsewhere.

For illustrative purposes, we also attempt to calculate the additional "income" from drug-related activities undertaken by Central Asians in Russia and include it as a separate line item in table C.5, labeled "Russian distribution." As a rough approximation, we attribute a fixed share of the earnings from distribution within Russia (i.e., the difference between the Russian import prices and the retail price) to Central Asian labor. However, we may have even less basis for making this allocation than in the case of the smuggling margin (arrest records that report central Asian or Russian citizenship provide limited guidance). We attribute 15% of the value added in Russia to Tajiks and other Central Asians, reflecting our view that the large majority of in-country earnings accrue to Russian residents. Table C.5 gives our estimates of total earnings for Central Asian residents active in the drug trade, by sector, with a separate line for Russian earnings. The plausible range is large, driven more by uncertainty about prices than quantities.

As should be obvious from the figures in table C.5, the lion's share of drug-related income accrues in the export sector, of which the overwhelming majority is derived from the provision of smuggling services. We find that our results are not especially sensitive to the weaknesses of Central Asia's domestic retail price data, but are highly sensitive to the weaknesses of international price data. Moreover, the results suggest the utmost importance of improving our understanding of the organization of smuggling operations, including the residency of participants, to allocate income properly to one country or region. If, for example, the smuggling margins attributed to exporting countries were 75%, not 50%, Central Asia's income would have been about 45% higher, with an additional $200 to $700 million.

Having performed the basic income calculations, it is useful to compare the results with various economic indicators for the region and, to the extent possible, individual republics. Although we have no basis for

Table C.5

Gross domestic product-comparable estimates of Central Asia's opiate-related income (by component of income for 2000).

Income Component	Unit Price (dollars per kilogram)	Quantity (metric tons)	Value ($millions)
Central Asian (CA) consumption			
Kazakhstan	2,000–5,000	5.0–5.6	10–28
Kyrgyzstan	2,000–5,000	2.4–3.0	5–15
Tajikistan	2,000–5,000	1.7–1.7	3–8
Turkmenistan	2,000–5,000	0.3–1.4	1–7
Uzbekistan	2,000–5,000	2.0–2.7	4–14
Total consumption	2,000–5,000	11–14	23–72
CA exports			
Goods	1,500–2,000	60–103*	90–206
Services	6,750–14,000	60–103	405–1,442
Total exports	8,250–16,000	60–103	495–1,648
CA imports			
Goods	700–1000	75–121	53–121
Services	150–250	75–121	11–30
Total imports	850–1,250†	75–121	64–151
CA net exports	NA	NA	431–1,497
CA total income	NA	NA	454–1,568
Addendum			
Russian distribution	9,000–40,500	30–60‡	270–2,430

Note: Opiates are measured in pure heroin equivalent units, assuming a 10:1 ratio of opium to heroin or morphine. *Export quantity calculated as Central Asian imports (75–121 metric tons), less Central Asian consumption (11–14 metric tons) and Central Asian seizures (4 metric tons). †Multiplying by Afghanistan's entire 328-metric-ton pure heroin equivalent production estimate, this range would generate an export value of about $280 to $410 million, but exports to other destinations (e.g., Iran and Pakistan) may yield higher unit returns. ‡The quantity, 30 to 60 metric tons, is the amount consumed in Russia.
Source: Authors' calculations.

systematically allocating Central Asia's export earnings to the individual republics, there are many indicia to suggest that Tajikistan is the principal transshipment country out of Afghanistan. Tajiks are also much more prominent than other Central Asian groups in Russia's domestic distribution system. On this basis, we chose to allocate two thirds of the region's export earnings to Tajikistan and the remaining third to Kazakhstan, Kyrgyzstan, Turkmenistan, and Uzbekistan, taken as a whole. We allocate Central Asia's earnings from distribution activities within Russia along the same lines (table C.6).

Table C.6

Gross domestic product and opiate-related income estimates for Central Asian republics (in millions of U.S. dollars for 2000).

	Reported GDP	Final Consumption Expenditures	Opiate-Related Income		Earnings from Russian Distribution
			Net Exports	Total	
Kazakhstan	18,200	10–28	NA	NA	NA
Kyrgyzstan	1,300	5–15	NA	NA	NA
Turkmenistan	4,400	1–7	NA	NA	NA
Uzbekistan	7,700	4–14	NA	NA	NA
Subtotal	31,600	19–63	144–499	151–523	90–810
Tajikistan	1,000	3–8	288–998	303–1,046	180–1,620
Total	32,600	23–72	431–1,497	454–1,568	270–2,430

Source: Authors' calculations and World Bank (2002:208–210, table 4.2) for GDP reported at annual average official exchange rates.

The results for Tajikistan are especially striking. Its estimated "opiate income" could be equivalent to 30% to 100% of its reported GDP. Data on government expenditures and trade in legitimate products provide additional bases for comparison. Tajikistan's total government expenditure was only $196 million at the turn of the century (CIA, 2002). If bribes to officials constituted only 10% of the $303 to $1,046 million, they would amount to 15% to 55% of the total government expenditure, suggesting a potentially substantial increment to officials' salaries. If as much as one quarter went to bribes, the increment to officials' salaries would be huge. Export earnings from legitimate products totaled $640 million in 1999; $330 to $1,100 million[34] from heroin exports would have provided a considerable boost.

These estimates are for the year 2000 specifically, resting largely on ad hoc price observations for transactions in and through Tajikistan. For earlier years, prices were higher, but quantities flowing through Central Asia were substantially smaller. Without going through the same detailed set of calculations, it is not possible to determine whether revenues in 2000 were higher or lower than for 1997 to 1999. We have no firm basis for extrapolating to later years, but have no reason to believe that Central Asia, Tajikistan in particular, has become much less dependent on income from drug trafficking. In the years postdating the Taliban ban, Tajikistan's economy has grown, but so have Afghanistan's opium production and, possibly, Tajikistan's engagement in trafficking. Moreover, the use of Tajik price data as the reference point may have biased the regional estimates downward. The smattering of evidence for the other Central Asian republics suggests that prices may have been somewhat higher elsewhere in the region.

Comparing the 2003 United Nations' Income Estimate

The UNODC's estimate of regional gross drug profits, about $2.3 billion annually (UNODC, 2003c), is roughly 50% higher than our $1.5 billion estimate of regional GDP-like income. Given a high degree of uncertainty in any estimate and substantial differences in methodologies, the two estimates seem not inconsistent; however, some of the methodological differences make the figures difficult to compare.[35] These differences arise in both the estimation of quantity and value.

The United Nations extrapolates from production and seizure data to develop quantity estimates, whereas we start with probable demand. First, we estimate opiate consumption in each of the major markets served at least in part by Central Asia, including Russia, the Ukraine, the rest of Europe, and Central Asia itself; then, we add the seizures in each market to arrive at their total in-flows. Next, we posit Central Asia's share of each market (see table C.2). We use the shares to estimate the quantity of opiates that flow into or through Central Asia. The seizure data are important only in so much as they arithmetically affect trade and sales volumes. Moreover, we do not distinguish between opium and heroin or morphine in our calculations; rather, we define a single product in heroin equivalent units, which trades in all markets.

Finally, with regard to income estimation, we attempt to allocate the earnings from international transactions in GDP-like terms by distinguishing between trade in goods and services, and by accounting for the residency of the service provider. Using standard accounting practices, we separately identify the export value of the goods, measured f.o.b., and the additional value of the services that move them across each border. Ordinarily, we might describe the landed value of a product in terms of cost, insurance, and freight. In this case, the smuggling margin can be thought of as a payment or premium for protection, or "insurance." Although the United Nations allocates the entire markup from the Afghan–Tajik border to Moscow to Central Asia's gross profits, we allocate only the share of the markup that accrues to Central Asian residents for services rendered. Attributing the full markup is tantamount to assuming that Central Asian residents provide all the trafficking services from Central Asia into Russia and through to Moscow, without any transactions occurring en route.

Concluding Remarks

The findings of this analysis are generally consistent with widely held views on the volume and value of drug trafficking in Central Asia. We may differ on some or even many of the specifics, but our conclusions are similar in nature: A substantial fraction of Afghanistan-originating heroin may well flow through Central Asia and it contributes significantly to the region's economies, especially Tajikistan's. At any point in our range, the drug trade would be a major economic force in the region and a dominant activity for Tajikistan. Were the estimates at the high end of our range "correct," the economic significance of the drug trade would be extraordinary.

However, it is our view that the high-end estimates of Central Asian's earnings in Russia are much too high. They depend on retail price estimates that are very high relative to those reported in richer countries in western Europe. (The same could—or should—be said of the high-end estimates of Central Asia's exports to Russia, because they depend on what, we believe, are overstated wholesale price estimates.) Moreover, simply adding the Russian earnings to a GDP-comparable measure would be inappropriate and potentially misleading. At the very least, internal consistency would require netting out the analogous earnings of Russian nationals operating in Central Asia. If the Russian nationals' earning were omitted from the Central Asian income estimate, the difference might be substantial (for possible reasons, see chapter 9).

We conclude with a few general observations on methodology: In this appendix we have reproduced an earlier analysis that uses national income and product accounting conventions to assess the economic significance of Central Asia's participation in the drug trade. The approach is noteworthy in its own right. It allows a systematic evaluation of illegal market activity and draws attention to key aspects of the drug trade, including the predominance of smuggling services in income accrual. The approach also underscores the need for more credible information in at least three areas: (1) drug consumption in major markets to estimate throughput better; (2) border, wholesale, and retail prices to estimate the value of shipments better at each stage of the supply chain, and (3) the organization of drug-smuggling operations to understand better the distribution of income along the supply chain.

Appendix D

Examples of Countries with Lax Enforcement

In chapter 10 we presented seven countries as exemplars of lax enforcement of prohibitions against opiate production and trafficking. We discuss the cases of India and Tajikistan at length in chapters 7 and 9, respectively; here we provide some brief background information on Pakistan, Turkey, Albania, Kosovo, and Mexico to demonstrate that they, too, satisfy the conditions of lax enforcement.

Pakistan

As a result of Pakistan's federal structure, the diversity of its administrative systems, and the weakness and low legitimacy of its central government, Pakistan is far from implementing international prohibitions against opiate production and trafficking uniformly or strictly. Virtually no prohibition enforcement is found in the Federally Administered Tribal Areas (FATA), a north-to-south mountainous strip forming a 1,200-kilometer wedge between Afghanistan and the settled areas of the Northwest Frontier Province (NWFP) and other Pakistan provinces.[1] Limited and often symbolic enforcement is also carried out in the southwestern province of Balochistan, which borders Afghanistan to the north and is the largest in the country by geographic area (fig. D.1).

In the FATA, the federal government is represented by political agents whose mode of administration is regulated by treaties, agreements, and understandings with the local Pashtun tribes. Laws of Pakistan or the NWFP do not apply in the FATA unless extended to them through a special notification by

Figure D.1 Map of Pakistan with provincial details for the Federally Administered Tribal Areas (FATA), Northwest Frontier Province (NWFP), and Balochistan. *Source*: Downloaded from www.hopeforlife99.com/. Accessed October 2007. Modified to erase excessive detail.

the president of Pakistan. Although national drug law has, under international pressure, been extended to the FATA, its enforcement is not even symbolic. Unlike the fully administered districts, there are no police forces, regular or irregular, and no courts—civil or criminal—in the tribal areas (UNDCP, 1994:74–77; Khan et al., 2000; Abbas, 2006).

In 2002, the Pakistani government sent thousands of troops into the FATA to hunt for Osama bin Laden and other Al Qaeda fugitives from Afghanistan. This unprecedented action in Pakistani history, however, did not foster general law enforcement or compliance. Coupled with some coordinated operations carried out jointly by Pakistani troops and U.S. forces, which led to civilian casualties, it instead antagonized most local tribes, fueling a veritable insurgency in Waziristan

(Abbas, 2004; Coghlan, 2004; BBC, 2006a). In 2005 and 2006, the Pakistani government and the pro-Taliban tribes of South and North Waziristan signed peace agreements in which the tribes and the Taliban based there agreed to cease cross-border attacks into Afghanistan and assaults on Pakistani security forces, public servants, and state property in exchange for a reduced presence of Pakistani troops (Niazi, 2006a). Despite the agreements, attacks and clashes have continued.

Large portions of the vast province of Balochistan are also subject only to limited control of the central government. In the so-called *B zones,* covering most rural areas, notified federal and provincial laws apply but are enforced by a political agent or deputy commissioner supported by tribal levies (UNDCP, 1994:73). As the FATA, this western province is also inhabited by fiercely autonomous tribes—in this case, Baloch and Pashtun. Moreover, Balochistan has repeatedly fought for independence (Titus, 1996). After bloody fighting with the Pakistani army in the mid 1970s, low-level armed struggles began again in 2003 and escalated in 2006. When General Pervez Musharraf, then Pakistan's president, reacted to them by crushing the progressive nationalist movement in Balochistan and assassinating its leader, the Baloch National Jirga (the assembly of tribal elders) was convened for the first time in 130 years and called for revisiting the accession of Balochistan to Pakistan (BBC, 2006c; Niazi, 2006b).

The FATA and Balochistan's geographic proximity to Afghanistan and their lack of meaningful enforcement explain why illegal opium poppy cultivation and heroin processing have concentrated there since the 1970s (UNDCP, 1994). Pakistani control efforts and, more important, the more favorable conditions for illegal opiate production in neighboring Afghanistan largely drove out poppy cultivation and heroin processing from Pakistan during the 1990s. After being declared a "poppy-free nation" by the United Nations in 2001, however, opium poppy cultivation has resurged modestly, again concentrating in the FATA and Balochistan (Khattak, 2003; U.S. Department of State, Bureau of International Narcotics and Law Enforcement Affairs, 2004, 2006:226).

Since the 1970s, Pakistan has also become a major conduit for Afghan opiate exports, with Pakistani traffickers playing a major role in the business. Local traffickers also supply a large domestic market, as opiate users are estimated in at least 700,000 (UNODC, 2007a). As the U.S. State Department contends, "to a very significant extent, when it comes to opiates, Pakistan is part of the massive Afghan opium production/refining 'system.' Relatively modest drug cultivation/production in Pakistan frequently means that financiers in Pakistan have judged circumstances in Afghanistan more favorable to investments there, as opposed to Pakistan" (U.S. Department of State, Bureau of International Narcotics and Law Enforcement Affairs, 2006:226).

Turkey

Turkey is usually referenced in the drug control literature for its successful shift from licit opium to poppy straw production and resulting control of opiate leaks into the illicit market during the early 1970s. Moreover, Turkey's seizures—on the basis of total tonnage—are among the world's largest (see table 3.2). Nonetheless, Turkey's enforcement of the international drug prohibition regime has been weak, corrupt, and inconsistent. These deficiencies have allowed the country to acquire and maintain a pivotal role in the trade of Afghan heroin to Europe. In addition to weak enforcement, two other factors must be mentioned: (1) Turkey's geographic position, bridging Asia and Europe, and (2) the wide diaspora of its citizens in western Europe—five million Turkish citizens[2] live in Europe (Stiftung Zentrum für Türkeistudien, 2003).

Our assessment of Turkish enforcement of the international drug prohibition regime is based on a growing (but still slight) scientific literature (Bovenkerk and Yesilgöz, 1998, 2004; Robins, 2008), the report of our Turkish collaborator (Atasoy, 2004), European and Turkish judicial investigations, reports of Turkish parliamentary commissions of inquiry, Turkish and foreign media and NGOs, our own limited data collection in Turkey and other European countries, as well as specific events in Turkish political and public life.

These sources show that in their strenuous fight against left-wing protesters in the 1970s and, later, against Kurdish separatist groups, several Turkish cabinets and the military developed shady alliances with ultranationalist paramilitary groups and with Kurdish clans, allowing them to engage in criminal activities, including heroin processing and smuggling into other European countries. In particular, since the early 1980s, several Kurdish clans have become prominent in the international opiate trade largely as a result of their roots in southeastern Turkey, the natural entry point for Afghan opiates from Iran. The entrepreneurial transformation of some of these clans was inadvertently fostered by the Turkish government itself and particularly by the Özal cabinet, which in 1985 created the village guard system to support the fight against the Kurdistan Workers' Party (usually known under its Kurdish acronym of PKK).[3] In the village guard system, certain clans were hired by the state to secure their villages against attacks and infiltration of the PKK and to support the Turkish armed forces in their operations against the PKK. For this purpose, the state not only paid considerable sums of money to the clan leaders, but it also provided the necessary weapons. Parts of these armed groups, sometimes working jointly with government officials, then became engaged in drug trafficking, arms sales, and other illegal activities (Atasoy, 2004:167; Kramer, 2000).

Two scandals brought these and other such alliances to light. The first scandal erupted when a truck crashed into a limousine near the town of Susurluk in western Turkey in early November 1996. In the accident, three people were killed: a high-ranking police official; a former leader of the Grey Wolves (an ultranationalist paramilitary group of the 1970s), who also was a convicted heroin smuggler and a wanted Interpol murder suspect; and the former leader's girlfriend. A member of parliament, who controlled a progovernment Kurdish militia and allegedly received monthly funds from the government to fight Kurdish separatists, was also in the car (Hermann, 2001). According to a report prepared by the Turkish prime minister's office, the state used ultranationalist gangsters and allied Kurdish clan leaders as death squads in its fight against the PKK. Under state protection, these same gangsters' drug smuggling, casino gambling, and money-laundering rings had been allowed to flourish, the report claimed. Officials from the police and intelligence agencies, which were also given extraordinary powers to fight the Kurdish insurgency, had allegedly joined forces with the gangsters and enriched themselves during the process. Although the report was not made public, it was partially leaked to the press and the then-prime minister confirmed most of the published accounts in a television interview (Couturier, 1998; Kinzer, 1998; see also Bovenkerk and Yesilgöz, 1998).

The second scandal, also in 1996, was provoked by a botched kidnapping case, which revealed the so-called Yuksekova gang in the town of the same name on Turkey's southeastern Iranian border. The gang included several members of security force special counterinsurgency teams and village guard contingents, and had been responsible for drug trafficking, kidnapping, and numerous murders in the Kurdish region (Couturier, 1996). According to the unconfirmed allegations of a PKK defector and former gang member, several tons of heroin were transported from Yuksekova to Diyarbakir, the largest city of Turkey's southeastern region, and then to Istanbul under the instruction of several gendarmerie officers in official cars, tanks, and helicopters (Godze, 2001).[4]

In the case of heroin trafficking, the benign neglect or support shown by some parts of the Turkish law enforcement and intelligence communities for drug traffickers allied in the fight against Kurdish separatism might have been eased by the fact that the heroin trade long had minimal negative repercussions on Turkey itself. Despite the large flow of opiates through the country, the domestic heroin addiction problem has remained surprisingly low (Atasoy, 2004:57–66; *Turkish Daily News,* 2005), while the country has profited from the heroin exports of its criminal entrepreneurs. Only since the end of the 20th century, according to Robins (2008) and several foreign liaison officers interviewed in Turkey in 2004, has the fight against heroin trafficking become more thorough and effective, and Turkey's international police cooperation has improved significantly. Both endogenous and exogenous factors have fostered such a change, including Turkish military and political elites' determination to safeguard state stability by severing ties with ultranationalist gangs, the growing criticism and pressure of the international community, and Turkey's effort to obtain membership in the European Union.

Albania and Kosovo

Serious gaps in the enforcement of drug prohibition can be found not only in transit countries close to opium production, but also at the doorsteps of final consumers, as Albania and Kosovo demonstrate. In both instances, local government authorities have largely been unable to enforce law and order, much less the international drug prohibition regime, at least since the fall of

Albania's totalitarian communist regime in 1990 and the NATO bombing campaign in Kosovo in spring 1999, respectively. Until its declaration of independence during early 2008, Kosovo, although formally remaining a part of Serbia, was administered as a UN protectorate outside the control of Serbian authorities.

Despite recent improvements, these two territories predominantly inhabited by ethnic Albanians have long been a veritable "gangster's paradise," as *Newsweek* defined Albania in an article of March 2001 (Hammer, 2001). Although neither Albania nor Kosovo played a major role in opiate transshipment before 1990, both have since become hubs for trafficking in opiates and other illegal commodities. As mentioned in chapter 10, ethnic Albanians from both Albania and Kosovo have become key players in the heroin import and wholesale distribution in many western and eastern European countries (Europol, 2004:8, 12).

The rapid expansion of all illegal activities experienced by Albania since the early 1990s and particularly the phenomenal growth of previously unknown crimes, such as trafficking in drugs, weapons, and human beings, were made possible by the weakness, corruption, and incompetence of the local law enforcement agencies and judiciary. As Albanian scholar Vasilika Hysi (2004:540) notes, "the police, prosecutors' offices and courts were long unable to repress or even control these new phenomena. Quite on the contrary, state organs were often exploited by politicians to pursue their own personal goals; there was a general lack of professionalism and law enforcement officers often favoured a political party or accepted bribes from criminals and common citizens to secure their positions or to make some extra money." The political class was no better and, despite the scarcity of judicial proof, high-level corruption is acknowledged by all observers (HDPC, 2002:21; U.S. Department of State, Bureau of International Narcotics and Law Enforcement Affairs, 2006:303–304). According to the unconfirmed accusations reciprocally launched by leading politicians, some of the politicians are also directly involved in drug trafficking. On the matter of political involvement, the current prime minister of Albania, Sali Berisha, who was also president of Albania from 1992 to 1997, stated the following: "Let's be honest: Albania . . . could only become an Eldorado for heroin and cocaine, because the state was behind it" (*Der Spiegel*, 2005:87; see also Simpson, 2002).

Kosovo's rise in the international heroin markets during the second half of the 1990s was also favored by its growing lawlessness. Guerrilla fighting by the Kosovo Liberation Army (KLA) increasingly eroded Serbian control of the province, even before the NATO bombing campaign of spring 1999. First NATO, then the United Nations Interim Administration Mission in Kosovo (UNMIK) were long unable to restore law and order, with the KLA turning from an ally into a serious obstacle to Kosovo's peace process. In 2001, when the KLA tried to foment an uprising of ethnic Albanians in neighboring Macedonia, a top Macedonian government official described the situation in Kosovo bitterly: "There's no rule of law, no ethnic tolerance, no human rights.

Not even an economy, except foreign aid and organized crime" (Nordland, Terzieff, Gutman, Barry, Mironski, Cirjakovic, 2001). Despite their emphasis, these assessments are by and large confirmed by academic research (see, for example, Arsovska, 2006a).

Since then, Kosovo has achieved some progress. However, despite the optimistic assessments regularly published by the UNMIK (see, for example, UN Security Council, 2005), law enforcement, particularly as it relates to drug-trafficking activities, is still far from strict. In 2004 Pino Arlacchi (2004:11), former executive director of the United Nations Office for Drug Control and Crime Prevention, and a consultant for the European Agency for Reconstruction in Kosovo, maintained: "The principal weaknesses and limitations of the Kosovo criminal justice systems are concentrated in the area of the fight against major crime...the fight against it in Kosovo is just in its initial stage. Resource allocation is in this area largely insufficient, technical assistance and capacity building have to be substantially increased, and a stronger commitment by UNMIK and the PISG [Provisional Institutions of Self Government] is indispensable" (see also Arsovska, 2006a; Zaremba, 2007).

In addition to lax enforcement, the rise of Albania and Kosovo in the international heroin markets has been favored by other factors, including their location on the main smuggling route linking Afghanistan's opium poppy fields to western Europe's heroin consumers (the so-called *Balkan route*); the existence of a large ethnic Albanian diaspora;[5] and some particularly relevant sociocultural characteristics of the ethnic Albanian population, particularly the strong sense of collective identity, the importance of extended family ties, and the continued persistence of an honor code in place of written law (Arsovska, 2006b). As shown in chapter 10, all these factors directly affect the operation of Albanian and Kosovo criminal enterprises.

Mexico

Unlike the weakened or failed states of Tajikistan, Albania, and Kosovo, Mexico is a conventional modern state with unquestioned authority almost throughout its territory. Its government invests considerable human and financial resources in the fight against drug trafficking, seizing large amounts of drugs and eradicating a substantial proportion of marijuana and opium poppy crops each year (UNODC, 2005d:251–292). In 2005, for example, a record 20,803 hectares of opium poppy were eradicated—a 30% increase over 2004 (U.S. Department of State, Bureau of International Narcotics and Law Enforcement Affairs, 2006:49). However, Mexico's commitment to enforce the international drug control regime has been undermined by the extensive corruption of its public administration—specifically, its police and prison authorities. As the 2005 Investment Climate Statement of the U.S. State Department (U.S. Department of State, Bureau of International Narcotics and Law Enforcement Affairs, 2005) states more generally: "[C] orruption has been pervasive in almost all levels of Mexican government and society."[6]

The pervasiveness of corruption is a by-product of the authoritarian, "patron–client" political system that dominated Mexico for seven decades, being centered—up until the epochal election of July 2000—on the political monopoly of a single party, the Partito Revolucionario Institucional (PRI). In such a system, as Alejandra Gómez-Céspedes (1999:356) explains, "Mexican police forces were created not to protect but to control the population, and they were granted permission to repress, steal, and extort bribes in exchange for loyalty to whoever was in authority."

Dating back at least as far as the 1960s, according to most sources (Lupsha, 1992; Reuter and Ronfeldt, 1992; Astorga, 1996; Gómez-Céspedes, 1999; Pimentel, 2003), drug producers and traffickers have been the most rewarding, if not the primary, targets of police and politicians' extortions.[7] Before the late 1970s, opium poppy and marijuana growers and traffickers merely had to pay off the officials of the local *plaza* (town) to buy their license to operate. As the illegal drug industry expanded, a percentage of the profits was sent, usually on a monthly basis, to superiors and political party representatives in Mexico City, and direct contacts were established between the most successful drug traffickers and national civil servants and politicians.

The involvement of the political center in the web of corrupt relationships linking state representatives and drug traffickers was not the only change that occurred during the 1980s. The power ratio between the two also changed. Although state representatives long had, with few exceptions, the upper hand, from the late 1980s onward they were no longer able to dictate the terms of corrupt agreements and to exert tight control on illegal entrepreneurs. Two sets of processes contributed to this change: (1) the start of the democratization process in Mexico and the consequent weakening of the PRI and its authoritarian ruling system, and (2) the tremendous expansion of the illegal drug industry and the consequent accumulation of wealth, military, and political resources by the most successful drug-trafficking organizations. The democratization process culminated in the election of Vicente Fox, the leader of an independent party, in the presidential election of July 2000. During the preceding 15 years, drug traffickers profited from the progressive breakdown of the PRI's authoritarian regime, gaining autonomy from their corrupt "protectors" and becoming more aggressive and violent. From the late 1980s onward, they have had no qualms assassinating both their competitors and the few police officers and prosecutors who go after them.

At the same time, however, the transition from authoritarianism to democracy has also exposed, through investigations and scandals, the corrupt ties linking drug traffickers and government representatives. During the Zedillo administration (1994–2000), for example, state governors were dismissed in connection with criminal activities. Hundreds of police officers from local and federal police forces, including the Mexico City police, were suspended, fired, or charged with crimes because of corruption or direct involvement in drug trafficking. Even General Jesús Gutierrez Rebollo, Mexico's drug czar in the mid 1990s, was arrested and convicted for accepting bribes from a leading drug trafficker (Gómez-Céspedes, 1999). The fight against corruption and drug trafficking intensified since Fox came to power in late 2000 and has been furthered by Fox's successor, Felipe Calderón, who also belongs to the National Action Party. In addition to the arrest and dismissal of thousands of local and federal law enforcement agents, in 2003 the elite federal antidrug unit was shut once again because of the corruption of its very leaders (Sullivan, 2003; see also Weiner, 2002). Since 2001, Mexico has also made unprecedented advances in its fight against drug cartels by capturing many of the most powerful kingpins. However, many analysts say that the new leaders' vows to wage "the mother of all battles" against drug traffickers are being undermined by outdated laws, lenient penal policies, and corruption inside the jails.[8]

Although systematic corruption has provided a fertile breeding ground for the illegal drug industry in Mexico, it does not fully explain the industry's expansion during the last quarter of the 20th century. The reasons for the expansion lie largely in Mexico's proximity to the United States, one of the world's largest markets for illicit drugs. Mexico is, today, the principal transit country for cocaine entering the United States, with 70% to 90% of the cocaine destined for the United States passing through the Mexican mainland or the country's periphery. Mexico also serves as the main foreign source of the marijuana and methamphetamine consumed in its big, northern neighbor (DEA, 2000, 2003b).

The strong incentives to service the large drug-abusing population of the United States also explain the rise and resilience of the Mexican heroin industry.[9] With estimated potential opium production averaging almost 80 metric tons a year from 2001 to 2005, the five most recent years for which data are available (UNODC, 2007a:40), Mexico belongs to the group of the second-tier illicit opium producers (see discussion and table 3.1 in chapter 3). According to the U.S. government and the UNODC, net heroin production in Mexico averaged 4 to 6 metric tons of heroin during the 1990s and has increased slightly since then, despite the growing eradication efforts (DEA, 2003b:9; UNODC, 2007a:40). The peculiarity of the Mexican opiate industry is that it is exclusively oriented toward the United States: the vast majority of Mexican opium is converted into heroin and is smuggled into the United States, accounting for a substantial but uncertain share of the market (see chapter 5).

Notes

Chapter One

1. Indeed, after the completion of our data collection in spring 2008, the United Nations reported that world production had risen to a new record of 8,870 metric tons, implying an increase of more than 100% since 1998 (UNODC, 2008:38).

2. In 1989, the military government changed the name of Burma to Myanmar. For the sake of consistency in this book, we have chosen to use *Burma*, because we refer to many events that predate 1989.

3. For the most part, we do not address issues of distribution within consuming counties.

4. Papers published in Hough and Natarajan (2000) provide a sense of the limits of research on the domestic distribution of drugs.

5. "Golden Triangle" and "Golden Crescent" are expressions frequently used to point to the two traditional areas of illicit opium production and early-end trafficking, which are centered in Burma and Afghanistan, respectively. The Golden Triangle traditionally included the triborder regions of Burma, Laos, and Thailand, although China is also occasionally considered part of it in recent years. The Golden Crescent originally stretched from Turkey to Pakistan. Because neither the Golden Triangle nor the Golden Crescent ever constituted homogenous areas, and some of the cited countries no longer produce opium for the illicit market, we rarely use the two expressions.

6. In the late 1990s, the UNDCP launched a study on local illegal drug markets in 17 non-western European and non-North American cities. Although the fieldwork was carried out on the basis of the same research protocol and the findings were thus potentially comparable, practical and organizational problems hindered the overall study and no final comparative analysis was published.

7. Arguably, the data on trafficking, largely derived from data on seizures, are the least strong, but the data on consumption pose the greatest analytical challenges.

8. We chose these countries for their importance in understanding the market and because we were able to identify local researchers with whom collaboration might be possible. A complete list of our research collaborators is presented in "Acknowledgments."

Chapter Two

1. Clearly, there are important differences in market conditions. For example, the international controls arising in the early 20th century were designed to deal with a fundamentally different problem from that faced today, and they focused on opium rather than on heroin. Moreover, they largely set out to address the behavior of governments themselves, as regulators and promoters.

2. French Indochina consisted of a federation of protectorates (Tonkin and Annam, which now form the northern part of contemporary Vietnam, as well as Cambodia and Laos) and one directly ruled colony (Cochin China, the southern part of today's Vietnam). French Indochina was formed in October 1887 from Annam, Tonkin, Cochin China, and the Kingdom of Cambodia; Laos was added after the Franco-Siamese War of 1893. The federation lasted until 1954.

3. Codeine, another active ingredient in opium, was first isolated from opium in 1832. Its antitussive properties were discovered in 1875. However, its availability remained very limited up until 1886, when codeine was synthesized for the first time from morphine by a German chemist, Albert Knoll. From then on, the Knoll AG began to produce codeine in large quantities (de Ridder, 2000:24–25).

4. Ironically, at Bayer, the invention of heroin is ascribed to Felix Hofmann, the same chemist who also synthesized acetylsalicylic acid, the active ingredient in Aspirin. And in an even more ironic twist of history, the invention of aspirin was initially neglected, whereas heroin was immediately marketed as a "heroic" medicine (de Ridder, 2000:73–74).

5. Newman (1995) is the most authoritative source of total consumption estimates, but even careful estimates must be treated as rough approximations. Technical problems are rife. For example, the opium smoker generated an ash that had morphine in it. The ash was recycled by the owner of the opium den (Newman, 1995). Thus, it is difficult to know what total morphine content was actually consumed from a given total quantity of opium. Similarly, some opium was reexported to other nations through China, confusing calculations based on production and import figures.

6. Albeit the Chinese opium was only 30% to 70% as potent, in terms of morphine content, as 21st-century opium (Dikötter, Laamann, and Zhou, 2004:8–9).

7. Newman (1995) estimates that the number of heavy users (consuming 20–30 grams daily) was comparatively modest: 4.8 million. Regular or moderate users (consuming between 2.2 grams every 3 days and 7.5 grams daily) constituted another 16.2 million.

8. Ethnographic research (e.g., Dhawan, 1998; Ganguly, Sharma, and Krishnamachari, 1995) shows that to a certain extent this is possible even today. Similarly, the coca leaf, chewed or consumed as tea, has beneficial nutritional and medicinal properties that have been recognized by traditional Andean societies for centuries (Greenfield, 1991).

9. It must be stressed, however, that the 2000 ONDCP estimates are only for heroin and do not include other opioids, such as OxyContin. Data from a household

survey (Office of Applied Studies, 2005) show that the estimated number of chronic users would more than double if the consumption of other opioids were taken into account.

10. Chinese migrants predominantly stuck to opium. Initially they were satisfied with Asian products. From 1909, when opium smoking was prohibited, their demand was increasingly supplied with opium produced in Mexico (Astorga, 1996).

11. China ratified the Hague Convention of 1912 as early as 1915, but did not underwrite later drug control treaties until the Single Convention of 1961.

12. See U.S. Census Bureau (2006a, b) for 1930 and 2004 population estimates. The authors calculated tonnage estimates for 2004 from UNODC global consumption figures (UNODC, 2005d:133) and potential illicit opium production figures (UNODC, 2006:57), assuming that heroin and morphine account for about 70% of all opiate use (the UNODC [2006: 57] provides an estimate for the share of heroin use). Note, applying recent prevalence rates (UNODC, 2006:75) to the 0.04- to 0.05-gram estimate implies average annual consumption of about 15 grams annually per chronic user, which is conservative (see appendix B).

13. For example, Greenfield (1997) discusses the use of information and "sunlight" in the context of the development and application of international labor standards.

14. For acknowledgement of the decrease in supplies from legal manufacturers see, among others, de Ridder (2000:138–147) and Meyer and Parsinnen (1998:29–32).

15. The 1906 edict on opium can be read in Baumler (2001:66–71).

16. The term *addict* is used in historical documents by westerners reporting on regular users in Asia. It may well have been inaccurate, as Newman (1995) carefully documents.

17. The addict register is described in Johnson (1975).

18. Given their trade relationship and the Anglo-Chinese opium treaty of 1907, the decline in Chinese consumption had large effects on the Indian opiate industry; prices fell and stocks accumulated, requiring the British government to step in and provide temporary price supports in 1913 (Newman, 1989).

19. The leader of the cartel and of Shanghai's most powerful criminal group, the Green Gang, was Tu Yueh-sheng, who came to be known as the "Opium King of the Nation" in the early 1930s. Thanks to a close alliance with Chiang Kai-shek, Tu controlled the entire opium and heroin commerce and production process in Shanghai, with thousands of tons of opium being sent along the Yangtze River from the southwestern cultivation areas to tens of heroin laboratories (Wang, 1967).

20. Wright (1958) claims that the number of users was 1.5 to 2 million in a population of 19 million; he offers no documentation.

21. We explain the concept of *epidemic* in detail in the next chapter; here, we note that it refers to the disease-like spread or growth of demand—use begets use—in a particular market.

22. The expansion of heroin use, coupled with some abuses in the prescription of heroin and cocaine, led to the tightening of the British System in 1968. Although maintenance policies were upheld, physicians lost the right to prescribe heroin or cocaine to their addicted patients, unless specially licensed (Spear, 2005).

23. Despite the associations the term may evoke, Nixon proved to be pragmatic and pursued a multitrack drug policy. The most innovative part of Nixon's drug war involved demand reduction through treatment, which expanded significantly during the early 1970s. Almost unimaginable by today's standards, in 1974 more than 60% of

federal funds went toward demand reduction, and particularly toward the expansion of methadone maintenance (Courtwright, 2001a:170–174).

24. The seven producer states were Bulgaria, Greece, India, Iran, Turkey, the USSR, and Yugoslavia.

25. The Single Convention required parties to submit estimates-of-need and statistics concerning drugs, imported, exported, manufactured, retained in stock, and consumed. From this point onward these data had to be sent to the INCB. The import certification system remained in force. Governments were required to license manufacturers, traders, and distributors, and all who handled drugs had to maintain records of their transactions.

26. Schedules II and III were less strict and contained primarily codeine-based synthetic drugs.

27. National governments and antiprohibitionist activists and organizations still debate whether the prohibition of drug possession included in Article 36 requires criminalization of drug possession for personal use (United Nations, 1972:18). A summary of the debate can be found online at http://en.wikipedia.org/wiki/Single_convention_on_narcotic_drugs#Possession_for_personal_use. Accessed April 2007.

28. Setting transitional reservations, Article 49 of the Single Convention required parties to eliminate completely all quasi-medical use of opium, opium smoking, coca leaf chewing, and non-medical cannabis use within 25 years of the coming force of the Convention. All production or manufacture of these drugs was also to be eradicated within the same period. Only parties for which such uses were "traditional" could take advantage of delayed implementation; for others, prohibition was immediate. Since the transitional period ended in 1989, these practices are fully prohibited today, and the drugs may be used only for regulated medical and scientific purposes (Senate of Canada Special Committee on Illegal Drugs, 2002:451–455).

29. The Convention on Psychotropic Substances placed hallucinogens under fairly stringent controls, but applied considerably weaker limitations to the trade in the drugs manufactured by western pharmaceutical companies, such as stimulants and depressants (McAllister, 2000:225–234).

30. For example, the UN (1949) survey of world opium production in the 1930s and '40s suggested that Afghanistan's opium production may have been about 75 tons in 1932.

31. India's illicit production (i.e., what it diverts from licit production) most typically flows into the domestic market; India's licit production primarily flows into the export market (see chapter 7).

Chapter Three

1. For the purposes of this analysis, we define the supply side in terms of *producers* (i.e., opium poppy growers) and *traffickers,* and we define the demand side in terms of retail *consumers.* We generally use the term *traffickers* as an all-encompassing term for the middlemen who sell drugs at various market levels, but we sometimes distinguish between cross-border traffickers, also known as *transshippers* or *smugglers,* and domestic traffickers. We occasionally refer specifically to retail sellers as *dealers.* The term *trader* has different connotations in different settings. For example, in Afghanistan, it often but not always refers to those who purchase opium directly from farmers.

2. *Relational capital* refers to the stock of existing connections among traffickers. For similar uses of the term see Kale, Singh, and Perlmutter (2000).

3. Just as the United States tends to do a large share of its business with its neighbors in licit markets, it may be more likely to do business with its "neighbors"—Mexico and Colombia—in the illicit opiate market.

4. The United States operates satellite and aerial surveillance programs that provide data on cultivation in some of the growing areas in some of the major growing countries. The United Nations undertakes well-documented "ground-truthing" studies, such as surveys of grower intentions for the forthcoming season in Afghanistan and Burma.

5. For example, Operation Breakthrough in Colombia led the U.S. Drug Enforcement Agency (DEA) to revise production estimates because new evidence suggested that most poppy fields are harvested only twice annually, not three times (Drug Availability Steering Group, 2002:59).

6. We cite cultivation and production estimates from the UNODC, unless noted otherwise.

7. Laos is an outlier among these producers in that much of the opiates that it produces remain in the country. The UNODC (2003a) estimates that about one third of total production in Laos is consumed domestically, primarily in the form of opium.

8. Some of the individual producer countries are discussed in detail in part II of this book.

9. The 2003 and 2006 Afghan opium prices are not directly comparable. For 2003, the UNODC reports the price of fresh opium, which has substantial water content; for 2006, it reports the price of dry opium. The change in measurement suggests an even greater decline in price since 2003.

10. The UNODC did not publish this information for 2003. As a caveat to these comparisons, the reporting of prices for the second- and third-tier producers, such as Columbia and Mexico, show great inconsistency. The DEA (2000) reports a much higher farm-gate price per kilogram of opium in Mexico, compared with the UNODC. Similarly, Sergio Uribe (2004), our Colombian research collaborator, shows varying estimates of the heroin content of opium latex (Uribe, 2004; chapter 7, this volume).

11. Differences in costs of production might reflect underlying differences in factor productivity; the productivity of land and labor may differ across locations.

12. Without the offsetting differences, the comparatively low-cost producers would eventually drive out the comparatively high-cost producers.

13. We address the issue of risk in more detail in chapter 10 in the context of effective illegality. However, in conventional economic terms, a difference in risk (e.g., more risk, as might arise from more stringent enforcement) creates an additional cost, requiring additional compensation and making some routes costlier than others. In effect, the risk-related cost differences serve as de facto tariffs.

14. See Townsend (2006) for a discussion of the risk that Afghanistan will become a major source of opiates for the Chinese market. Indeed, our own analysis (see chapter 5) suggests that at least some Afghanistan-originating opiates may flow eastward with the reduction in Burma's production.

15. The number of international trafficking arrests might also provide some information, but the data are at least as poor as those on the amount of seizures.

16. Russia reported heroin and morphine seizures of 3.3 metric tons in 2003, almost 4 metric tons in 2004, and 4.7 metric tons in 2005. The seizure figures for all opiates, including opium, are somewhat higher.

17. The flow model presented in chapter 5 provides additional supporting evidence. Iran accounted for about 25% of world seizures in 2002 and 10% of world consumption for 2001 to 2003, Pakistan accounted for about 16% of world seizures and 6% of world consumption, and neither Tajikistan nor Turkey even ranked among the world's major consumers. China's seizures and consumption were more evenly matched in percentage terms.

18. Abt researchers (1999) analyzed both the Heroin Signature Program, which provides data on large seizures, and the Domestic Monitor Program, which contains data on retail-level seizures, to estimate the origins of U.S. heroin from 1993 to 1999. Although in 1993 they estimated that Mexican and South American (Colombian) heroin accounted for less than 60% of those samples for which an origin could be assigned, by 1999 it accounted for more than 80% (Abt Associates, 1999:6). Our own analysis, presented in chapter 5, suggests that a smaller but still very substantial share of U.S. heroin originates in Latin America.

19. Until 2003, this publication was known as *Global Illicit Drug Trends*.

20. The prevalence rate refers to the percentage of the population, age 15 to 64, that uses the drug in some time period, most typically a 12-month period prior to data collection (UNODC, 2006:404). The UNODC refers to these figures as estimates of the annual prevalence of "abuse" and uses them to calculate numbers of "abusers"; however, we believe that the terms *use* and *users* are more accurate. Although many people who use opiates, especially heroin, suffer and cause serious harm, not all do.

21. Among those that now regularly conduct general population surveys and attempt to estimate the number of *problematic drug users,* a term coined by the European Monitoring Center on Drugs and Drug Abuse, are Australia, the Netherlands, Switzerland, and the United Kingdom. There are good-quality annual data from school surveys of 15- to 16-year-olds in almost all European nations under the European School Project on Alcohol and Other Drugs. Information about the project can be found at www.espad.org.

22. The UNODC describes the variety of problems and its approaches to addressing them in a chapter on methodology in the *World Drug Report* (see, for example, UNODC, 2006:403–416).

23. For example, the official U.S. estimate for 2000 was roughly 900,000 chronic users (using at least eight times per month) and approximately 250,000 occasional users (ONDCP, 2001:9, table 3). Although the series for the number of chronic users was stable for 1992 through 1998, that for occasional users was not. Other nations do not have consistent series on the numbers of occasional, dependent, or chronic users.

24. Successive estimates sponsored by the U.S. ONDCP have been inconsistent with respect to trends. The most recent study, published in 2001 and reporting estimates for 1988 to 2000, showed a decline of about one third in the number of frequent users of cocaine and of heroin during that period. Earlier estimates had shown a decline in the early 1990s and then a recovery to the level of 1988 by the late 1990s. Estimates for Europe show a mixed pattern, with some countries showing increases between 1995 and 2005, and others showing stability (EMCDDA, 2006: 67–72; see also the EMCDDA Reitox National Focal Points' annual reports from individual nations, which can be found at www.emcdda.europa.eu/?nnodeid=435).

25. In chapter 5, we adjust the Russian prevalence figure to account for compote use.

26. On this basis, the United States accounts for a smaller share of global consumption than estimates of users would otherwise imply. The official estimate of U.S.

heroin consumption, less than 15 metric tons in 2000, is likely less than 5% of world illegal opiate consumption, even though with an estimated 1.2 million past-year users, the United States accounts for almost 8% of all users. (The ONDCP [2001:4, table 2] shows 13.3 metric tons of U.S. consumption for 2000, down from more than 14 metric tons in the preceding 2 years. The ONDCP has not published a more recent estimate.) World output of illegal opium in 2000 was approximately 4,700 metric tons. This does not include diversion from India's licit production. If about 20% is seized, as occurred in that year, and nothing is stored, that generates about 3,760 metric tons in consumption, equivalent to about 376 metric tons of heroin. Even for a calculation based on the higher rate of seizures in 2004, the United States would still have accounted for less than 5% of consumption; however, storage would imply a smaller figure for total consumption and an equivalently larger share for U.S. consumption. A rough calculation indicates that at least half of world output would need to be taken out of circulation, through a combination of seizures and storage, for the U.S. share of consumption to rise to 8%.

27. Were consumption distributed evenly across all countries, including the United States, Asia would still account for more than half of total consumption (table 3.3).

28. Although a small share of the Afghan-originating $58 billion retail figure, the $1 billion farm-gate value still represents a higher share than might have been found just prior to the Taliban ban in 2000.

29. Note that the ratio of export-to-farm-gate value has been substantially higher in recent years. In 2004, the export value was 4.7 times higher than the farm-gate value (UNODC, 2005d:181); in 2005, it was 4.8 times higher (UNODC 2006:212); and, in 2006, it was 4.1 times higher (UNODC, 2007a:195).

30. Our analysis of drug-related incomes in Central Asia (see appendix C) lends further weight to this statement. In that analysis, we estimate trafficking income in Central Asia for the year 2000 at $500 million to $1.5 billion at a time when the UNODC estimated, using a broader definition of income, Afghan earnings of about $1 billion. Yet in the year 2000, Central Asia accounted for a minority of Afghanistan's opiate exports, most of which went through Iran or Pakistan.

31. Production in Latin America, especially Colombia, presents exceptions to many of the descriptive statements in this section about growing conditions, harvest technologies, and so forth. For a detailed discussion of production in Colombia, see chapter 8.

32. As noted previously, we are not addressing synthetic opiates, although we recognize that they provide close substitutes for heroin and morphine and thus may affect the market.

33. In Southwest and Southeast Asia, the surface of the caplet is scored by hand with a small-bladed knife and the opium gum oozes out through these cuts. Scoring may occur several times during the harvest, because the caplets ooze over a period of days. For details, see http://www.shaps.hawaii.edu/drugs/dea20026/dea20026.html, which reprints a DEA booklet that is no longer readily available from that agency (DEA, 2001). Mansfield (2004a:8–9) indicates that opium poppy cultivation requires about 8.5 times as much labor as wheat cultivation per hectare. He also notes that poorer farmers may stagger planting within a season to avoid hiring outside labor for harvest.

34. Refining opium into heroin is a multistep process that involves basic chemicals and tools, but requires little specialized knowledge or facilities. For a more detailed explanation, see McCoy (1991:21–23) and the previously mentioned DEA (2001)

booklet reprinted at http://www.shaps.hawaii.edu/drugs/dea20026/dea20026.html. The CIA offers details and photos on these matters at www.cia.gov/cia/publications/ heroin/flowers_to_heroin.htm#Link08.

35. The opium poppy has been described as a hardy plant, requiring little by way of fertilizers and pesticides (Booth, 1998:2–3). As has been reported in some districts of Afghanistan (Mansfield, 2004a:18), farmers may also choose to multicrop, wherein a single plot of land simultaneously or sequentially accommodates opium poppy and other, oftentimes edible and soil-rejuvenating crops, such as beans and peas, both to garner additional outputs from the land and to offset the soil-depleting effects of long-term opium growing (for additional information, see Booth, 1998:3).

36. Indoor production, which is obviously invariant to seasonality, has been reported in cannabis markets in the United States and other developed countries, but not in illicit opium markets.

37. The opium poppy grows under a variety of conditions, but it prefers a climate that is "temperate, warm with low humidity and not too much rainfall during early growth" and sandy loam soils (Booth, 1998:2). It also requires ample sunlight.

38. The United Nation's *Myanmar Opium Survey 2004* describes the growing season as, "field preparation," ranging from mid August to mid September; "sowing," ranging from early September to early October; and "harvest," ranging from late December to late February (UNODC and Central Committee for Drug Abuse Control, 2004:15, table 9).

39. The UNODC (2006:212, 221) estimates that 309,000 households were involved in opium cultivation in Afghanistan in 2005 and that 193,000 households were involved in Burma.

40. Burma's production has declined substantially in past years, but the Wa's decision to exit the opiate market does not appear to have been intentionally manipulative (see chapter 6).

41. Here, economists' use of vocabulary departs from other use. Economists may define the *short run* as a period during which supply and demand are not moving, in that no one enters or exits the market, which, in the case of poppy cultivation, might amount to a single growing season or less; however, society-at-large might view a new growing season or two (i.e., the amount of time required for farmers in other regions to begin planting opium poppy) as a short period of time.

42. Labor scarcity does not seem to be a constraint, as evidenced by the very rapid development of an opium-growing and heroin-producing industry in Colombia, with much more costly labor and no prior experience in opium production, in the early to mid 1990s (see chapter 8).

43. Most countries have had just one "typical" heroin epidemic during the past 40 years, but the United Kingdom appears to be an exception. Although the typical epidemic involves a sharp upturn in new use followed by a downturn, a number of studies estimate that U.K. heroin initiation rates grew steadily from about 1975 to 2000 (see, for example, De Angelis, Hickman, and Yang, 2004).

44. Smoking is less efficient than injecting heroin, so that samples of heroin smokers report higher daily dosages than samples of heroin injectors (e.g., Smolka and Schmidt, 1999).

45. Nothing is known about the daily consumption levels of compote users.

46. *Shiray* is a residue of smoked opium that can be eaten or smoked again, after being boiled several times and reduced to a black or dark-brown, thick substance. Smoked with a special pipe, shiray constitutes a peculiarity of Iran and is fairly popular

there. *Shiray* users may have numbered 100,000 addicts and 50,000 recreational users during the late 1990s (Cultural Research Bureau, 2001:11, 79–80).

47. Opium consumption is less efficient than either heroin injection or smoking.

48. This is not a mere statistical artifact from the inclusion of some of those in treatment; many patients remain active heroin users (National Drug Monitor, 2003). Similar statements may hold for Australia and Switzerland, two other countries committed to a generous supply of treatment services. France, which for a long time provided only counseling and psychiatric services for addicts, may constitute a partial exception to this general pattern. In 1994, concerned about HIV among intravenous drug users, mostly heroin addicts, the French government changed policy and made substitute drugs for heroin users readily available. Emanuelli and Desenclos (2005) show that this led to very sharp reductions in many indicators of heroin problems, but do not offer any direct measures of the prevalence of heroin addiction.

49. For European estimates, see the website of the European Monitoring Center on Drugs and Drug Abuse (www.emcdda.europa.eu) and, for U.S. estimates, see the ONDCP (2001).

50. From 1980 to 2000, it is estimated that the price of heroin in the United States fell by approximately 80%, from $2,000 per pure gram to $400 per pure gram, in constant dollars (ONDCP, 2004). There is no evidence that this led to an increase in initiation.

51. For example, the ONDCP (2001) shows a substantial increase in total heroin consumption between 1994 (10.8 metric tons) and 1998 (14.5 metric tons), even as the estimated number of addicts was falling.

52. In this way, an opiate market eventually behaves like a typical market for an ordinary product. In the short run, economists tend to think of consumers as responding to changes in prices by moving along—up or down—a particular demand curve, not by relocating the curve.

53. Nordt and Stoller (2006) provide a particularly compelling example. They analyze the pattern of initiation into heroin use in Zurich from 1990 to 2002.

54. Many studies in western nations report mortality rates of about 1% to 2% (e.g., Hser et al., 2001).

55. Policy may have some impact, depending on its form. For example, treatment with methadone or other opiate agonists and antagonists can reduce the total quantity of heroin consumed or, at least as in the case of heroin maintenance, commercialized through illicit channels.

56. These are all examples of "negative" changes; alternatively, production cost, enforcement penalties, or trafficking costs could decrease and the analysis would reverse itself.

57. Users have not been subject to very high rates of arrest or penalty in the United States; however, heroin addicts frequently are arrested for the crimes they commit to fund their heroin purchases.

58. Although the origins of the event are unclear, addicts reported that it was much more difficult to find heroin during the event than it had been before (Day, Degenhardt, and Hall, 2006).

59. Although popularly referred to as a *drought*, the event had nothing to do with a lack of rainfall.

60. In recent years, the United Nations and others have adopted a vocabulary distinction, referring to agriculturally oriented programs as *alternative development programs* and broader economic programs as *alternative livelihood programs*. We do not draw this distinction here.

61. See Jelsma (2001), for example. The claim is controversial, with the U.S. government insisting that the herbicides pose no risk to human health. For a review supporting that claim, see Inter-American Drug Abuse Control Commission (2005).

62. Mexico reported in 2001 that it had eradicated 15,350 hectares out of the estimated 19,750 hectares of opium poppy that were in production (DEA, 2003b), but there has not been a consistent decline in Mexico's estimated potential opium production.

63. Infrastructure development may also have unintended and counterproductive effects. It is believed that the creation of better roads in the Chapare Region in Bolivia in the 1980s, intended to help the distribution of legitimate agricultural products, had the effect of providing easier access for small planes to pick up coca paste (Greenfield, 1991; Riley, 1996).

64. For example, in some parts of Bolivia's Chapare Region, rubber turned out to be more profitable than coca leaf (Mansfield, 1999). However, earlier attempts to induce shifts to citrus and other perishable or semiperishable agricultural commodities were not as successful (Greenfield, 1991).

65. We are unaware of any studies that have examined the effects of interdiction in trafficking countries on heroin availability. A very limited number have attempted to do that in the case of cocaine. Reuter, Crawford, and Cave (1988) built a simulation model in which cocaine smugglers used past interception data to make decisions about which routes to pursue. Given the low export price of cocaine and low inputs of both equipment and personnel per gram, it turned out to be difficult to increase retail prices substantially with more aggressive interdiction. Crane, Rivolo, and Comfort (1997) examined the effects of temporary spikes in seizure rates in source zones and found that they did increase retail prices substantially, but the effect faded with time. There has been considerable controversy about the researchers' development of a price series and of their approach to modeling the short-run effects of interdiction events to reach this conclusion (Manski, Pepper, and Thomas, 1999).

Chapter Four

1. An analysis carried out by the UN drug office in 2002 with the data that were then available further supports this conclusion (UNODCCP, 2002c:11–42).

2. The 1999 decree was preceded by two earlier, fruitless attempts at a ban. When they first conquered Qandahar in late 1994, the Taliban declared that they would eliminate all illicit drugs. However, they soon realized that they needed the income from poppies and could not afford to ban opium cultivation and trade. Instead, from the beginning, they banned cannabis, imposing harsh penalties on transgressors (Griffin, 2001:152–153; Rashid, 2001:118–119). The justification for this differentiation was that hashish was an Afghan vice, whereas opium and heroin, although being recognized as *haram* (forbidden) as hashish, were (erroneously) not perceived as drugs misused in Afghanistan and thus exclusively intended for export (Lintner, 2001; Macdonald, 2005).

In late 1997, after entering negotiations with the UNDCP, the Taliban agreed to ban heroin trade and consumption and, at a later stage even opium cultivation and trafficking in exchange for a potential payment of $250 million over a decade for alternative development. Up until September 1999, however, no concrete steps were taken by the Taliban to implement such declarations, and the UNDCP could secure only a fraction of the sums promised from the international community (Transnational Institute [TNI], 2001; Rashid, 2001:123–124).

3. Risen (2006:155) states that DEA officials believe that the Taliban had large stores of opium in 2001.

4. One participant in meetings with the regime in 2001 reported that the Taliban had been informed that there were three issues that the West cared about: expulsion of Osama Bin-Laden, the status of women, and opium production. He thought the leadership had chosen the last as the least painful to their dignity (personal communication with a member of the international delegation).

5. This is notable because Burma had produced substantially larger quantities in years prior to 1999 and 2000, and therefore may have had both the productive and distributional capacity to yield a globally significant addition, with sufficient warning.

6. We offer here no comments on India as a producer of opiates for the illicit market. Diversion is substantial, and our estimates in both chapters 5 and 7 suggest that India is comparable with other second-tier producers. Chapter 7 also describes a modest increase in potential diversion from the licit to the illicit market in 2001, but the increase is less than 60 metric tons of opium or 6 metric tons of heroin equivalent.

7. The growing regions in northern Afghanistan, which were previously of minor significance, have continued to yield substantial quantities of opium ever since.

8. The UNODC reports prices of $700 per kilogram in Nangarhar and $650 per kilogram in Qandahar on September 10, 2001; it reports prices of $657 and $446 in each province a month earlier.

9. The turmoil would simply mean that there was great uncertainty and that prices conveyed little or no reliable information.

10. From *The Economist* website, "The common tendency of prices in financial markets initially to move further than would seem strictly necessary in response to changes in the fundamentals that should, in theory, determine value. One reason may be that in the absence of perfect information, investors move in herds, rushing in and out of markets on [rumor]. Eventually, as investors become better informed, the price usually returns to a more appropriate level. Overshooting is especially common during significant realignments of exchange rates." Accessed December 27, 2006, from www.economist.com/research/Economics/alphabetic.cfm.

11. Arguably, imperfect information should be especially relevant in an illicit market, but to the extent that Afghanistan was not enforcing provisions against opium production, it may have been no more relevant to price formation in this market than in any other Afghanistan market.

12. Adjustment for agricultural inflation in the United States does not change the result.

13. To the extent that the Afghan economy depends on opium earnings, it may be difficult to separate these particular events. That is, changes in exchange rates and wages may be driven in part by changes in opium prices and vice versa. However, the price and exchange rate data show a substantial difference in Afghan- and U.S. dollar-denominated farm-gate opium prices, which seems to indicate that the temporary appreciation of the Afghani was at least partially independent on opium price trends.

14. See the UNODC (2003c) for additional evidence of modest trader margins.

15. Pakistan may have also seen an increase, but our efforts to document this were unsuccessful.

16. Dr. Raisdana provided annual data for 1992 to 2003 and first-quarter data for 2004.

17. The heroin prices are not purity adjusted. The decline in the ratio of heroin to opium prices may reflect declining purity of heroin, but that itself is an indicator of decreasing availability.

18. It is difficult to compare these quarterly observations with the estimates presented in table 4.1, because they are annual averages and may obscure quarterly fluctuations.

19. The purity data come primarily from seizures of 1 kilogram or more. Given that Turkey has a small domestic heroin market, these are likely to be seizures related to the international trade.

20. No. 3 heroin is the less pure smoking form. No. 4 is the purer form that is usually injected.

21. Average purity was 37% in the second quarter of 2000. (H.M. Customs and Excise, United Kingdom, provided unpublished data.) Earlier data from the U.K. Forensic Science Service are discussed by the UNODCCP (2002c:33).

22. Customs and Excise seizures are more likely to be of larger quantities, so the police data provide more information specific to the retail market.

23. Neither the German nor U.K. data include the distribution by size of seizure prior to 2002. Thus, an actual purity decline might be masked by a shift to seizures of smaller quantities. However, there is no reason to believe that such a shift occurred.

24. Ingeborg Rossow provided the data in this paragraph by personal communication.

25. The flow model results, which cover production, consumption, and seizures for 1996 to 2003 and are presented in the chapter 5, indicate a substantial excess supply of opiates globally during 1996 to 2000. That is, production far exceeded the total of estimated consumption and reported seizures. In 2001, the production deficit equaled about half the excess of the previous 5 years. Global production levels from 2001 to 2005 have been comparable with those in the 1990s; only in 1994 and 1999 did the total noticeably surpass the levels of 2002 and 2003. We estimate that the total of consumption and seizures in 2002 and 2003 was moderately smaller than production, not allowing much inventory buildup. Rough calculations using data for 2006 suggest a much greater potential for accumulation.

26. Indeed, according to the UN drug office, aerial satellite photos taken during the year 2000 in northern Afghanistan showed the existence of at least 40 stockpiles allegedly capable of supplying 20 metric tons of narcotics (UNODCCP Sub-Office in Tajikistan, 2000:9).

27. As addressed in chapter 11, the benefits of opening a window of opportunity with a supply-side intervention must be weighed carefully against the costs, both in terms of the impacts on opium growers and others who may depend on the opium economy, and the actual, direct costs of the interventions.

Chapter Five

1. In the rest of this book the use of the word *region* is context specific—sometimes referring generically to an area or place that is not a particular country. In this chapter we identify and analyze market activities for a set of 15 specific geographic subregions (North

America, South America, Central America, Caribbean, Transcaucasia, Central Asia, East and Southeast Asia, Middle East and Southwest Asia, South Asia, North and East Africa, Southern Africa, West and Central Africa, Central and eastern Europe, western Europe, and Oceania), and for a smaller set of aggregate regions. In the data tables and figures that accompany the text in this chapter, totals may not jibe as a result of rounding.

2. The Taliban announced the ban in 2000; it affected plantings in 2000 and actual harvests in 2001.

3. The UNODC published the 2003 seizure data in 2005 (UNODC, 2005d).

4. The U.S. State Department also cited this range (10%–30%) in several earlier editions of the INCSR; however, in a much more recent report, postdating our analysis, it raised the lower bound without explanation: "Although there is no reliable estimate of diversion from India's licit opium industry, clearly, some diversion does take place. It is estimated that between 20–30 percent of the opium crop is diverted" (U.S. Department of State, Bureau of International Narcotics and Law Enforcement Affairs, 2007:239). In chapter 7, on the Indian market, we consider a range of options for calculating diversion, including one that accounts for some diversion from hectares that have, at least officially, been declared "destroyed." Each of these options results in a larger tonnage figure than the 10% diversion rate. At the close of this chapter we offer some initial observations on the implications of adopting different assumptions.

5. In the years after the completion of this modeling effort, Afghanistan's opium production increased dramatically and has surpassed earlier levels (see chapters 3, 4, and 6).

6. In more recent years, production in Laos has declined and India would generally rank third, even with the more conservative 10% diversion rate. Notwithstanding a substantial decline in Burma's production, it remains the world's second largest opium producer after Afghanistan.

7. Allegations have been made that the DCA has either overstated its seizures in recent years or that the heroin it has destroyed has been of much lower potency, with the original seizure sold by some of its officers back to the traffickers (Khamonov, 2005).

8. The United Nations refers to these figures as estimates of opiate "abuse" rather than "use." As noted in chapter 3, we believe that the latter term is more accurate.

9. Appendix B provides a more detailed discussion of the development of the 15- and 30-gram estimates, and the role of price and income elasticities in determining consumption.

10. See chapter 3 and appendix C for more information about the development of the Russian heroin epidemic. Roughly consistent with UN reports, we assume that 75% of Russian opiate users were poppy straw (compote) users between 1996 and 2000, and that 50% were poppy straw users (compote) between 2001 and 2003. We make corresponding downward adjustments in Russia's reported prevalence rates to eliminate poppy straw from the estimate.

11. Indeed, postdating the completion of the research for this chapter, China's reported prevalence rate rose from 0.1% to 0.2% (see UNODC [2005d:365] for the new figure and chapter 3 in this volume for a very brief discussion of the change). The increase would serve to reinforce our finding of the importance of China as a major consumer, and the dominance of Asia in the world market.

12. Our estimate of 880,000 opiate users is roughly consistent with our collaborator's estimate of 740,000 heroin users (Institute of Public Security, Chinese Ministry of Public Security, 2004); however, prevalence rates in neighboring Asian countries are considerably higher. The more recent, higher estimate of China's prevalence rate would reduce the gap.

13. Asia is the world's leading consumer in terms of aggregate tonnage, but not total revenue.

14. Note that the actual seizure rate for 2003, 110 metric tons or about 23% (UNODC, 2005d: 48), was higher than the 1996 to 2000 average. On that basis, the surplus for 2003 would have been smaller and the surplus share of production would have been the same in 2002 and 2003.

15. Indeed, the reported increase in China's prevalence rate would support this conclusion, although a downward adjustment in India's prevalence rate (as suggested earlier) or an increase in its diversion rate within the reported range would result in even larger annual surpluses.

16. Many other routes exist, but, as a rough approximation and for tractability, we focus on these routes, which we believe to be dominant and potentially representative. In this analysis, we assume that the India-originating opiates that India diverts to the illicit market remain in India to satisfy its domestic needs, but address the possibility of exports in chapter 7.

17. We are unaware of any evidence that opiate markets outside the Americas are regularly supplied by either Colombia or Mexico, nor are we aware of any evidence that Latin America receives opiates from Asia.

18. We did not attempt to apply the 16% 1996 to 2000 global average seizure rate to this analysis because of the substantial differences in seizure rates across countries and regions.

19. The combined figure for Colombia and Mexico is still higher in 2003 than in 2001 or 2002 even after accounting for the recent revisions in the UNODC's production estimates for Latin America. (See chapter 3 in this volume and the UNODC [2007a:40] for the new production data.) The new, higher combined totals for 2001, 2002, and 2003 are 17.1, 13.4, and 17.7 metric tons, respectively. However, the combined production figures for Colombia and Mexico in 2004, 2005, and 2006 are somewhat lower than for the earlier years, dropping to 12.9, 9.9, and 8.5 metric tons for each year, respectively. The 2004 to 2006 figures suggest that potentially smaller shares of U.S. consumption originated in Latin America during those years than in the prior years.

20. On the basis of the revised Latin American production estimates, imports from other sources would have amounted to 46% and 68% of U.S. consumption in 2001 and 2002, respectively, with seizures; and 27% and 49% of that consumption without seizures, all else being equal. Even with the increased estimates of production, a large share of U.S. consumption would have originated elsewhere.

21. We assume a somewhat higher share in appendix C for a year 2000 calculation.

22. As noted previously, we assume that India's diverted production remains in India.

Chapter Six

1. In chapter 10 we provide a more theoretical and general explanation of the distribution of opiate production, by pointing out that the bulky phases of opium poppy cultivation and processing tend to take place in areas with very lax or no government enforcement of prohibition on production and trafficking. Here, in this chapter, we follow a more historical and country-specific approach.

2. In the 1920s and '30s, Afghanistan did report the production of small amounts of opium to the League of Nations, primarily from the provinces of Herat in the west, Badakhshan in the north, and Jalalabad in the east. However, the amounts produced were still very small compared with other reporting countries or the amounts produced by Afghanistan since the 1990s. No production was reported, at that time, from the southern provinces of Helmand and Qandahar, which from the mid-1990s onward accounted for more than half of Afghanistan's total opium production (UNODC, 2003c:87–88).

3. Afghanistan was never part of the British Empire, but was invaded twice by British troops during the 19th century. By the end of the Second Anglo-Afghan War in 1881, it had fallen within the British sphere of influence.

4. It is a telling detail that, by 1957, Burma had the highest murder rate in the world. According to official statistics, which in the words of a senior police officer described only "half the story," Burma recorded more than 120,000 deaths in the first 9 years of independence. These figures did not include insurgent-related deaths, which were recorded separately and were far higher (Smith, 1991:97).

5. The Taliban are a transnational Islamist movement, which consolidated in the *madrasas* (Islamic academies) in the Afghan–Pakistan border areas from the early 1980s onward. At the beginning of the following decade, they developed into a political force with the support of foreign sponsors, above all from Pakistan. For more information on the Taliban, see Maley (1998, 2002), Rashid (2001), and Griffin (2003).

6. In 1959, for example, the then-democratic government of independent Burma recognized that in those areas "administrative control has not been fully established yet" (Renard, 1996:42).

7. It must be stressed that these identities (tribal, ethnic, and local), which are usually referred to with the protean word of *qawm* in Afghanistan, are not fixed since time immemorial, but are often a matter of negotiation (see Glatzer, 1988; Centlivres and Centlivres-Demont, 2000; Rubin, 2003:25).

8. Since the 1980s, a not insignificant fraction of opium traffickers in Afghanistan are mullah (i.e., Muslim religious authorities), owing to their traditional right to exact the 10% tithe levied on all farm produce, including opium, in exchange for their religious duties (Griffin, 2003:124).

9. The systematic involvement of quasi-state authorities in the illegal drug economy is a peculiarity shared by Afghanistan and Burma with only one other country of the world: Colombia. In that South American country, several guerrilla organizations and paramilitary groups directly and indirectly profit from heroin and cocaine production, "taxing" growers, refiners, and traders; and, since the late 1990s, even organizing drug processing and export (Thoumi, 2003:102–107; chapter 8, this volume). It is certainly not accidental that since the intensified involvement of quasi-state authorities in the drug trade Colombia has become the world's largest producer of coca and a significant, albeit recently declining, second-tier producer of opiates (UNODC, 2005d:41, 61).

10. In 2006, the export value of Afghanistan's opium amounted to just 46% of Afghanistan's legitimate GDP; the export value rose from $2.7 billion in 2005 to $3.1 billion in 2006, but Afghanistan's legitimate economy grew more rapidly (UNODC, 2007a:195).

11. The existence of a vast pool of competent workers trained in the delicate task of lancing poppies now gives Afghanistan a substantial advantage relative to other

potential producers (IMF, 2003:41). As most of these laborers employed in opium poppy fields are itinerant, they have also significantly contributed to the rapid propagation of poppy growing. Having acquired the know-how to cultivate poppies and having established the necessary contacts to sell the opium that they usually receive as payment, many itinerant laborers, once back in their home villages, started to experiment with opium production (UNDCP, 1999b).

12. This is the profit margin estimated by Pain in 2006. According to the 1998 UNDCP's findings (1998b:10–12), the markup on the rapid turnover trade, when traders purchased opium from farmers to sell it quickly again in various bazaars, taking advantage of local price differentials, ranged between 9% and 26% in eastern Afghanistan and 3% to 7% in the southern provinces of Helmand and Qandahar.

13. To the extent possible, we have tried to reconcile the findings of the UNDCP's (1998b) and Pain's (2006) ethnographic studies with the more criminological picture of drug trafficking drawn by Shaw (2006) on the basis of interviews primarily with Afghan and foreign government representatives, representatives of NGOs, and civil society, but also with an unspecified number of individuals involved in, or at the margins of, the trafficking networks.

14. The Taliban's largest source of income was represented by the taxation of the so-called *transit trade*. Under the Afghan Transit Trade Agreement, which went back to the 1950s, listed goods could be imported duty free in sealed containers into Pakistan for onward shipment into land-locked Afghanistan. As a matter of fact, already in the 1980s and even more so in the 1990s, most of the goods were sold in smugglers' markets in Pakistan—the transit trade already being a major source of income for the mujahedin. Under the Taliban's aegis, duty-free consumer goods began to be smuggled directly into Afghanistan on their way to Pakistani black markets from Dubai, either by air or by land via Iran. A World Bank study estimated the value of unofficial reexport to Pakistan at $2.2 billion in 1997 (out of a total of $2.5 billion in exports), the first year after the Taliban had captured Kabul. The same study estimated that the Taliban derived at least $75 million in 1997 from taxing the Afghanistan–Pakistan transit trade (Naqvi, 1999; see also Rubin, 2003:xxii–xxiii; UNODC, 2003c:12–13).

15. According to *sharia* (Islamic law), *zakat* is a tax on wealth levied at 2.5% and should be distributed to the poor. It is unclear on what legal basis the Taliban imposed this tax at a much higher rate and on a flow of commerce rather than a stock of wealth. It is also unclear whether the *zakat* was assessed on gross income or on profit (Rashid, 2001:118; Rubin, 2003:xxxiv).

16. The different organization of the trade in eastern and southern Afghanistan was also, at least in part, the result of the different products being traded. In eastern Afghanistan, centralization was fostered by the growing incidence of heroin processing, which favored large-scale traffickers having access to the necessary chemical precursors and skills. In southern Afghanistan, on the contrary, no such incentives were at work, as opium remained the key product to be smuggled into either Pakistan or Iran up until the turn of the century (UNDCP, 1998b).

17. After losing 3 metric tons of opium to three cross-border traders, for example, a respondent in the southern region kidnapped two family members of his maverick business counterparts to try to regain his lost opium or the money he was owed (UNDCP, 1998b).

18. In addition to the studies already quoted, see, for example, Moreau and Yousafzai (2003); Dahlkamp, Köbl, and Muscolo (2003); Muench (2004); Burnett (2004); Watson (2005); TNI (2005:10); and Blanchard (2006:13–15).

19. Two prominent examples of this merging of roles of trafficker and government official are Hazrat Ali and Gul Agha. The former, a well-known wholesale drug trader since the early 1990s (Harris, 2001) and a tactical ally of U.S. troops in the Bora Bora operation of late 2002, was made chief of the police in Nangarhar. Despite his shaky credentials (or possibly because of them and the harsh methods he is famous for [see Human Rights Watch (HRW), 2003]), he was very successful in enforcing opium eradication in the province in 2005 (TNI, 2005:9). Likewise, Gul Agha Sherzai was first appointed governor of Qandahar, a major southern opium-producing region next to Helmand, and then urban development minister in the Karzai administration, despite his known involvement in the opiate trade (Moreau and Yousafzai, 2003; Weiner, 2004:27, 59). As a western diplomat stated, "It's inconceivable that warlords like Hazrat Ali and Gul Agha are not profiting handsomely from the drug production and trafficking taking place right under their noses" (Moreau and Yousafzai, 2003).

20. Daud himself might be an example of a warlord-turned-politician closely associated with the drug trade. According to many journalistic accounts, in fact, Daud himself used to be, and his family still is, directly involved in heroin manufacturing and smuggling. Daud was finance secretary of Ahmed Shah Massoud, the Northern Alliance leader who was assassinated two days before the September 11 attacks. From his family and military strongholds in Kunduz, he has been in a privileged position to exploit, both through his own family enterprises and the provision of protection services to other traffickers, the growing flows of opiates from Afghanistan's northeast into Tajikistan (Moreau and Yousafzai, 2003; Muench, 2004; Watson, 2005).

21. A glimpse of the trafficking and processing income may be drawn from the estimates published by the U.S. Embassy in Rangoon in 1996, according to which in the fiscal year 1995–1996 there were at least $600 million that could not be accounted for in terms of official trade. Revenues from the drug trade were thought to make up for the preponderance of this huge statistical discrepancy (Lintner, 2002:267–268).

22. "Necessity knows no law," General Tuan explained to a British journalist in 1967. "That is why we deal with opium. We have to continue to fight the evil of communism and to fight you must have an army and an army must have guns, and to buy guns you must have money. In the mountains, the only money is opium" (*Weekend Telegraph* [London], March 10, 1967, quoted in McCoy, 1991:352).

23. Among the KMT's powerful supporters, there was General Kriangsak Chamanan, who was installed as Thailand's prime minister in 1977 by a military coup and ruled until 1980. For 10 years up until 1973, General Kriangsak had been the liaison officer between the Thai supreme command and the KMT, and had allegedly been an economic partner and personal friend of both KMT generals (Weintraub and Lawton, 1978; McCoy, 1991:416–420).

24. A paradigmatic example is the Shan National Army (SNA), a loose coalition that was founded in 1961 and eventually included most of the rebel bands operating in Kengtung state. According to McCoy (1991:348), the SNA never hauled more than 1% of the Burmese opium exported into Thailand and Laos. However, the profits and arms drawn from the opium trade were sufficient to produce a dramatic shift in the balance of forces in Kengtung. In 1960 to 1961, most of the rebel units in Kengtung were little more than bands of outlaws hiding in the mountains. Thanks to the opium–arms commerce, the SNA's seven major commanders had, by 1965, an estimated 5,000 soldiers under their command and they controlled most of Kengtung. Despite the impressive short-term gains, in the long run their involvement in the opium trade turned out to be a source of internal corruption for the SNA (as for most other rebel

groups), alienating commanders from their troops and prompting ranking officers to fight each other for the spoils (McCoy, 1991:346–348).

25. For a detailed history and assessment of the UWSA and UWSP, see Kramer (2007).

26. During the following years, similar ceasefire agreements were reached with a total of 17 armed groups. The details of the verbal deals were never made public and vary from group to group, depending on their military (and hence bargaining) power (Hawke, 1998).

27. For a list of other companies funded with drug proceeds, see Altsean-Burma (2004:112–117); Davis and Hawke (1998); Hawke (2004); Maung (2001); Fawthrop (2005); and Chao (2005).

28. The current vice-chairman of the Burmese junta, General Maung Aye, for instance, was close to Khun Sa from when he was the commander of Eastern Command in the southern Shan State. Lieutenant General Khin Nyunt, the former prime minister, is also alleged to have profited from the business relationships he developed with Lo Hsing-han, when the latter acted as a go-between in the negotiations between the Burmese government and the CPB splinter groups. Allegedly, Nyunt also had business links with Lin Ming-Xian, the head of the ESSA, and held shares in ATS laboratories close to Möng La (e.g., Altsean-Burma, 2004:104).

29. In 2004, potential opium production in Wa Special Region No. 2 still represented 39% of the production in the Shan State and 36% of the national total (UNODC and Central Committee for Drug Abuse Control, 2004:13).

30. With its independent satellite surveys, the U.S. government confirms this sharply negative trend, although it cautions, as do several international NGOs (World Food Program [WFP] and Japanese International Cooperation Agency [JICA], 2003) and independent observers (TNI, 2005) that "none of the regions is truly opium-free" (U.S. Department of State, Bureau of International Narcotics and Law Enforcement Affairs, 2007:241). The UNODC (2007a:212–213) also reported considerable increases since 2006 in opium output in the southern Shan State, where a considerable fraction of the Wa population has been forcefully relocated by the UWSA in anticipation of the ban, and where farmers have begun planting outside the typical opium poppy season (thus potentially escaping the UN and U.S. surveys).

Chapter Seven

1. As in other chapters, and consistent with UNODC practice, we work with "90% solid" estimates of the opium content of India's harvests, whereas the Indian authorities usually publish "70% solid" data (CBN, 2007). We note exceptions as they arise.

2. Our analysis relies on an extensive data collection carried out primarily by Molly Charles at eight different sites in India. Data for the study were collected with both qualitative and quantitative methods; however, given the sensitive nature of the topic, qualitative methods dominated. Charles conducted in-depth interviews and participant observation in Mumbai (formerly Bombay), Delhi, Chennai (formerly Madras), Kota, Amritsar, Chandigar, Gawlior, and Manipur. In total, she interviewed 20 national law enforcement officials and lawyers, seven health professionals, 30 users of heroin and other hard drugs, and five petty dealers and other informants

specifically for this project. Paoli also interviewed four Indian top law enforcement officers, five foreign liaison officers, and one diplomat in Delhi and Mumbai. Information was also drawn from all standard secondary sources and the analysis of about 180 drug-related criminal proceedings reviewed by Indian High Courts and the Supreme Court from 1985 to 2001. This chapter additionally builds on extensive fieldwork carried out particularly in Mumbai by Charles and colleagues during the late 1990s (Charles, Nair, and Britto, 1999; Charles, Nair, Das, and Britto, 2002). Detailed insight into Mumbai's illicit drug market, drug users' careers, and patterns of consumption were then gained through in-depth interviews with drug users and the analysis of 737 files of clients of a drug treatment center. The original extensive report (Charles, 2004) is available at http://laniel.free.fr/INDEXES/PapersIndex/ INDIAMOLLY/DRUGSDYNAMICSININDIA.htm.

3. Note that India is not the first country to have difficulty controlling leakage. See chapter 2 for a brief discussion of Turkey's experience with leakage and control in the 1970s.

4. Before 2001, the INCSR of the U.S. State Department are available only in html format and therefore no page reference is possible.

5. "Opium years" straddle 2 calendar years, from October 1 to September 30. When only 1 year is mentioned, it is the harvest year.

6. A farmer who fails to achieve the MQY is ineligible to receive a license for opium growing the following year.

7. In our calculations in chapter 5, we assume that India's diverted opiates remain in India to meet the needs of domestic consumers. This assumption is, by and large, reasonable for the periods of analysis in chapter 5. However, were we to update the model, we might allow for a small fraction of export.

8. The availability of heroin in the rural areas of Uttar Pradesh was also shown by the ad hoc thematic study of the national survey on drug abuse among the rural population. With 43.9% of heroin users of the total of the drug users contacted, Uttar Pradesh scored a rate of heroin abuse three times as high as the average rate recorded in the six states sampled (UNODC and Ministry of Social Justice and Empowerment, Government of India, 2004:53).

Chapter Eight

1. Both groups are routinely referred to as *cartels*. Because there is no evidence that they were able to raise prices and prevent entry of others, we prefer to use a more neutral term, such as *syndicate*.

2. In September 2007, for example, an investigation by the Colombian Defense Ministry revealed that coalitions of drug traffickers and the FARC had infiltrated the U.S.-backed Colombian military, paying high-ranking officers for classified information to help them elude capture, continue smuggling cocaine, and organize guerrilla attacks (Forero, 2007b).

3. Even the 2007 INCSR (U.S. Department of State, Bureau for International Narcotics and Law Enforcement Affairs, 2007a) contained major internal inconsistencies. The INCSR reports estimates of Colombian cultivation in two places: first in a section titled "Policy and Program Developments" and then in a section specifically on Colombia. The figures for cultivation for 1998 to 2000 are as follows:

	1998	1999	2000
Policy and program developments	6,100	7,500	7,500
Country report	4,050	5,000	5,010

It is worth noting that the different figures cannot be the consequence of differences in interpretation of the series (e.g., gross or net of eradication), because they are essentially identical for the years immediately before and after these 3 years.

4. There was some disagreement among the experts consulted on the location of opium poppy fields. The DEA map represents the results of our best efforts.

5. Although labs have been hard to come by in Colombia, storage houses like those found in Asia are completely unheard of. Local authorities deny that they exist (personal interviews). Because poppy is a year-round crop, there is no need for such facilities. This is very different from the situation confronted by other growing regions, such as Afghanistan or Burma, where there is only one crop per year and all farmers in a region produce at the same time, giving them an incentive to hold some product back for sale when prices are higher.

6. Notwithstanding this uncertainty, it is very likely that Colombia is less productive than Afghanistan, where the average yield for 2002 to 2006 was about 4.0 kilograms per hectare per year. Colombia may, however, be as or more productive than Burma, where yields during the same period averaged about 1.1 kilogram.

7. The Colombian estimates are taken from the *World Drug Report 2005,* which reports Colombian production as opium tonnage and uses a factor of 10 to convert from tons of opium to tons of heroin.

8. PLANTE closed in 2003; the interview subjects were former PLANTE employees.

9. Based on figures reported in Earth Trends (http://earthtrends.wri.org/pdf_library/country_profiles/eco_cou_170.pdf; accessed July 4, 2007).

10. A *vereda* is a municipal administrative unit that usually grows around an elementary school and is composed of 25 to 40 families. Article 22 of Law 388 of 1997 regulates the participation of communities in the territorial organization of municipalities and allowed representation by *veredas* or rural boroughs. *Veredas* are based on tradition, and their geographic limits and structure do not have a legal basis (Martínez-Muñoz, 2004:188–189).

11. Most farmers in poppy-growing regions have taken possession of the land, but lack formal ownership. This situation facilitates this type of agreement, because the legal owners of the land could be prosecuted if illicit crops are found in their farms.

12. According to our interviewees, the goal set by the *consorcios* varies between 5 and 8 kilos per half hectare. This implies production of no more than 16 kilograms latex per hectare, yielding barely half a kilogram of heroin per hectare. This is substantially lower than the figures cited in other studies for heroin per hectare.

13. If the *consorcios* receive a large order during the harvest, they attempt to fulfill it by any means possible. Usually they instruct the farmers to score even the immature capsules, thus lowering the yields. Under such circumstances, the *consorcios* do not penalize the growers and pay them the expected production of the field—say, 5 kilos—although the advance harvest may lead to a yield of only 4 kilos.

14. Occasionally, local armed groups also attempt to protect natural resources, by limiting the amount of forest that can be destroyed to plant poppy. There have been cases of farmers who destroyed water sheds to plant poppy and were forced to replant the area by the guerrillas. This happened, for example, in El Plateado, part of the municipality of Argelia, Cauca, in 1994.

15. Some marginal comments about this relation can be found in Torres and Sarmiento (1998) and Escobar Gaviria (2002). No in-depth study of this relationship has been conducted.

16. The UNODC reported seizures of latex under the category "Opium (raw and prepared)," making no distinction between the opium latex seized in Colombia and the opium gum seized elsewhere.

17. In contrast, there have been individual cocaine seizures as large as 10,000 kilograms.

18. Swallowing the packages exposes the courier to the risk of death if the package ruptures; the longer the trip, the greater the risk.

19. We use, here, the estimate of 8 metric tons of production but make two compensating adjustments: We assume that only 85% of Colombian production is destined for the U.S. market, but that it travels at 85% purity.

20. Colombia has direct daily flights to Miami from four cities: Bogotá, Cali, Medellin, and Barranquilla. Other daily international connections go to Atlanta, Houston, and New York. Heroin can also be easily shipped to the United States from the international airports of Quito, Panama, Mexico, and Caracas. In 2004, 658,000 passengers flew from Colombia to the United States, according to the U.S. Bureau of Transportation Statistics (www.bts.gov/publications/national_transportation_statistics/html/table_01_42.html; accessed May 2008).

21. As Pablo Escobar's brother admits (Escobar Gaviria, 2002), his brother's first illicit activity was running contraband from Uraba, on Colombia's Caribbean coast almost at the Panamanian frontier to Medellin.

22. The National Survey on Drug Use and Health reports 147,000 new initiates in 2001 in the population of 12 years of age and older. Even if all were males, this would still produce an incidence rate of less than 3 per 1,000 males. (Office of Applied Studies, 2005:table 4.4A).

Chapter Nine

1. A stand-alone version of this chapter was first published in the *Journal of Drug Issues* 37 (4):951–980. We thank the journal for allowing us to reprint a modified version of the article.

2. Matthew Kahane, the UNDP head in Tajikistan, estimated that the drug trade accounts for 30% to 50% of the economy (International Crisis Group [ICG], 2001c:19). Kahane provided no description of his methodology.

3. The chapter draws on a detailed report on opiate trafficking prepared by the Analytical Center of the Drug Control Agency of Tajikistan (DCA, 2004), a specialized law enforcement agency founded in 1999 that has since been working with the financial support and guidance from the UNDCP/UNODC. The chapter also rests on a candid report of an experienced and high-ranking Tajik law enforcement officer, who carried out detailed field observations and interviews with more than 20 of his colleagues specifically for the study, but who has adopted a pseudonym for fear of retaliation (Khamonov, 2005). As far as possible, the data drawn from Tajik sources have been cross-checked with interviews with officers of international agencies stationed in Tajikistan, secondary sources, and, in particular, through an extensive analysis of English- and Russian-speaking media in Russia and Central Asia.

This case study also builds on a previous research project on the contribution of drug trade to the Central Asian economy, which was carried out by Peter Reuter, Emil Pain, and Victoria Greenfield (2003).

4. The CIS includes all the former Soviet Union republics, less Estonia, Latvia, and Lithuania.

5. The northern elite from Khujand and its province, the Leninobad (now Soghd) *oblast,* which had been predominant under Soviet rule, initially remained neutral and then accepted an ancillary role in the government restored in late 1992 and dominated by Kulobis (Nourzhanov, 2005).

6. Tajik citizens composed 71% of the 11,700 RBF's contract soldiers and 99% of its conscripts, but only 7% of its officers (ICG, 2004b:17).

7. A 2005 assessment of the effectiveness of border protection policy in Russia offered the following, worrying results: "[The total] length of the Russian border is 60,932 kilometers. The land border is 14,509 kilometers; 405 check points including: 175 motor checkpoints, 58 railroad checkpoints, 81 airport checkpoints, 76 seaport checkpoints and 15 river check points. Most of the checkpoints are located 10–40 kilometers from the border. There are only 660 customs officers specially assigned to counter drug trafficking units. Most of the units lack personnel and equipment. None of the border checkpoints are equipped with either mobile or fixed x-ray machines.... Nine separate departments and ministries share responsibility for border control and monitoring border checkpoint procedures, and the infrastructure is funded by different organizations" (UNODC Russian Federation, 2005:9–10). If this is the situation of the RBF, one can only imagine the conditions under which the border control agencies of the other, less developed, CIS countries operate.

8. According to official data, a maximum of 27 civil servants were charged yearly during 1997 to 2003 for drug offences in Tajikistan (Khamonov, 2005:56–58).

9. Tajikistan would have ranked fifth after Pakistan, Iran, China, and Turkey, had morphine been included in the measure (UNODC, 2005d:54, 267–271).

10. The DCA (2002) does not provide information on purity.

11. In 1997, 657 Tajik citizens were arrested in Kyrgyzstan, Uzbekistan, Kazakhstan, or the Russian Federation. Within 3 years, this figure almost tripled, only to fall back to 669 in 2003 (DCA, 2004:14–15).

12. On June 30, 2001, for example, 135 kilograms of heroin was seized in the Russian Astrakhan region on a train transporting raw cotton, which was en route from Qurghonteppa to Ilichevsk (Ukraine) and then to Switzerland (Borisov, 2001). In November 1999, more than 730 kilograms of opium along with smaller quantities of heroin and cannabis were seized from a truck driven by a Tajik citizen in Uzbekistan (DCA, 2004:30). In July 2003, 420 kilograms of heroin were seized near Moscow from the hidden compartments of a truck driven by three Tajik nationals (*Itar-Tass,* 2003).

13. In late 1999, for example, 40 kilograms of heroin were seized close to the Russian city of Chelabinsk on a bus travelling from Khujand to Yekaterinburg (DCA, 2004:27–31).

14. Contrary to what is maintained by other scholars (e.g., Cornell, 2005; Engvall, 2005), we have found no convincing evidence that several radical Islamist groups are also major players in the Tajik drug industry. True, the most prominent of these groups, the Islamic Movement of Uzbekistan (IMU), was involved in the drug trade up until 2001. However, since then, the IMU's strength has dramatically declined and, even at the height of its power, its role in the regional drug trade was overestimated (ICG, 2001b).

15. This is a pattern typical of many drug-dealing enterprises all over the world (Paoli, 2003a; chapter 10, this volume).

16. The same path can be observed in Afghanistan. There, too, the shift from a situation of virtual anarchy (what we define as *non-enforcement* in chapter 10) to that of lax prohibition enforcement has enabled the consolidation of large trafficking enterprises enjoying high-level protections in the government (see chapters 6 and 10).

17. Clashes between smugglers and Russian border guards have been reported frequently since the late 1990s and often ended up with heavy casualties on both sides (Osmonaliev, 2005:21).

18. Among them, there were some who held, as of 2005, the positions of chairman of the State Customs Committee, first deputy Minister of Defense of Tajikistan, deputy chairman of the State Committee of Border Protection, and the chairman of the State Oil and Gas Committee (Khamonov, 2005:11).

19. For much of the 1990s, the Presidential Guard was President Rakhmonov's main militia, although its loyalty lay primarily with Mirzoev, who paid his men out of his own pocket, using income from the largest casino of Dushanbe, which his family owned (Nourzhanov, 2005:119–120).

Chapter Ten

1. One hundred eighty-three states are currently parties to the three main drug conventions (see www.unodc.org/unodc/en/treaties/index.html for more information on the conventions themselves; see chapter 2, this volume).

2. Ideally, we would use a quantitative indicator of state implementation or non-implementation of the global prohibition regime vis-à-vis state or quasi-state authorities' tolerance or promotion of opiate production and trafficking. For example, one might calculate the probability each drug producer or trafficker faces of being arrested and convicted for his or her illegal activities (see Caulkins and Reuter [2006] for U.S. calculations). Unfortunately, although we have collected useful data for most of the countries selected, we cannot claim to have complete—or even minimally adequate—data for this calculation. Our evidence is only piecemeal. For some countries included in the second category, the available data interestingly suggest very low rates of incarceration and conviction rates for drug-trafficking offenses. In Turkey, for example, about 1,200 people were arrested for heroin trafficking in the year 2000, and 4,000 to almost 8,000 people were prosecuted yearly from 1994 to 2002 for drug trafficking and possession (Atasoy, 2004:119–124), corresponding to the very low rates of 1.7 suspects per 100,000 inhabitants in the case of heroin-trafficking offenses and between 5.6 and 11.3 suspects per 100,000 in the case of the broader category of general drug offenses. In contrast in Germany, with a roughly equal population, 16,216 heroin-trafficking offenses and 244,336 total drug offenses (thus including both trafficking and possession) were reported in 2000, (respectively, 19.7 and 296.5 per 100,000 inhabitants [BKA, 2002:191–192]). The extremely low rates of drug-related arrests and prosecutions in India have already been discussed in chapter 7.

3. Some heroin businesses occupy very narrow niches—for example, connecting one dealer who can buy 10-kilo bundles with two or three dealers who buy 5-kilo bundles (Reuter and Haaga, 1989).

4. Although not focused specifically on opiates, empirical research carried out in the United States and a number of western European countries provides indirect

support for our findings. After Patricia Adler's seminal ethnographic study (1985) of an upper level dealing and smuggling community in California during the 1970s, studies involving interviews with convicted drug traffickers were carried out in the United States (Reuter and Haaga, 1989), Australia (Ovenden, Loxley, and Mcdonald, 1995), the United Kingdom (Dorn, Oette, and White, 1998; Pearson and Hobbs, 2001), and Canada (Desroches, 2005). In the mid 1990s, Bovenkerk (1995) wrote the biography of a Dutch female go-between in the cocaine trade, whereas Zaitch published (in 2002) an ethnographic study of Colombian drug entrepreneurs in the Netherlands. In addition to several other studies on high-level drug trafficking with a more limited primary data collection and a bourgeoning journalistic literature, a substantial body of field research has accumulated during the past two decades that describes characteristics of various low-level markets, primarily for cocaine and heroin (see, for example, Dorn, Murji, and South [1992]; Ruggiero and South [1995]; Klerks [2000]; Ruggiero [2000]; Gruppo Abele [2003]; Bovenkerk and Hogewind [2003]; Dorn, Levi, and King [2005]; and Van Duyne and Levi [2005]; Spapens, 2006; Spapens, van de Bunt and Rastovac, 2007). At least for a few U.S. and western European cities, a good deal is known about who retails these drugs, the size and the stability of the organizations in which they work, their careers, the prices they charge, and the incomes they earn. (For the vast U.S. literature, see, for example, Preble and Casey [1969]; Johnson, Goldstein, Preble, Schmeidler, Lipton, Spunt, and Miller [1985]; Reuter, Maccoun, and Murphy [1990]; Bourgois [1995]; and Jacobs [1999]. For Europe, see Arlacchi and Lewis [1990b, c]; Ruggiero [1992]; Korf and Verbaeck [1993]; Paoli [2000]; Colombié, Lalam, and Schiray [2000]; and Braun, Lory, Berger, and Zahner [2001]).

In Europe there is also a rapidly growing literature on organized crime (see Fijnaut and Paoli, 2004). Drug trafficking usually receives attention, both because it is perceived to be the largest activity in terms of revenue and people involved, and because there is a larger amount of information available on it than on other illegal activities. Particularly in Germany (Rebscher and Vahlenkamp, 1988; Weschke and Heine-Heiß, 1990; Sieber and Bögel, 1993; Pütter 1998; and Kinzig, 2004) and the Netherlands (Fijnaut, Bovenkerk, Bruisma, and van d Bunt, 1998; Kleemans et al., 1998; Klerks, 2000; Kleemans et al., 2002) but to a lesser extent also in Italy (Paoli, 2003b), several empirical studies have addressed organized crime, primarily relying on an analysis of criminal cases or interviews with law enforcement officers (see also Colombié, Lalam, and Schiray, 2000 for France). As described in chapter 1, a limited primary data collection was also conducted for this study in several European countries.

5. In the western European heroin market, these are usually Turkish or Albanian groups, which (according to intelligence sources) control the lion's share of imports for most countries (Europol, 2004:12; BKA, 2005:26; National Criminal Intelligence Service [NCIS], 2005; see also Paoli and Reuter, 2007). However, several European nations, particularly the Netherlands and Germany, also report cases of heroin import involving citizens of countries located on the so-called Balkan route, such as Serbs and Macedonians, and, occasionally, Nigerians. The latter usually import heroin (and even more frequently cocaine) by carrying small quantities on or in their own body and traveling by air (BKA, 2005:30; Europol, 2005:10).

6. Emblematic in this respect is the large-scale transcontinental heroin trafficking, which was organized by Sicilian Cosa Nostra members in the late 1970s and early 1980s and was described in the first Palermitan *maxiprocesso* (maxi trial) of 1985. Notwithstanding popular images of a unified Cosa Nostra-led operation, judicial papers reveal that different stages of the operation were run by members of various mafia

families who, far from considering themselves part of a single economic unit, were very jealous of their own networks of clients and suppliers. Investigative judges state the following: "De facto autonomous, but functionally linked, structures have been created inside Cosa Nostra, running the different phases making up the complex drug trade, while the 'men of honor' who do not have operational responsibilities in the trade may financially contribute to it, sharing profits and risks to different degrees" (Tribunale di Palermo, Ufficio Istruzione Processi Penali, 1985:1887). By creating a climate of trust, common membership in Cosa Nostra enhanced the development and consolidation of business exchanges. These exchanges, however, can hardly be likened to the relationships among the departments of a single business company. They were, instead, transactions among enterprises so distinct that, despite the mafia brotherhood ties, the respect of contracts was guaranteed by all the means open to them, including the threat and the use of violence (see Paoli, 2003b:144–147).

7. Whatever the purpose of violence, illicit entrepreneurs learn to minimize its use when they operate under conditions of strict enforcement. Interestingly, Jana Arsovska (2006b) reports that, since the late 1990s, ethnic Albanian organized crime groups operating in western Europe have adopted more fluid organizational structures and have learned to maintain a lower profile by, for example, reducing the use of violence to avoid prosecution by western European law enforcement agencies.

8. Italy presents exceptions. Mafia groups' conditioning of Italian public life finds no parallel in western or even in eastern Europe. From the late 1970s to the early 1990s, the Sicilian Cosa Nostra assassinated dozens of policemen, magistrates, and politicians. However, mafia "pacts" with high-level politicians were not drug related nor were most mafia murders. High-level political connections are generally used by mafia bosses to acquire control of legal markets and public money flows, whereas the assassinations of high-ranking politicians and public officials were dictated by the Cosa Nostra's desire to reduce general law enforcement pressure. The Cosa Nostra has occasionally sought to halt drug-related cases, but has focused more typically on cases involving either its internal organization or murder. Moreover, Cosa Nostra members have been largely marginalized from wholesale drug trafficking since the late 1980s (Paoli, 2003b). Particularly since the early 1990s, the illegal drug industry, including remaining mafia businesses, has been subject to strict enforcement (Arlacchi and Lewis, 1990b, c; Paoli, 2000; Gruppo Abele, 2003; Paoli, 2004; see also DCSA, annual).

9. For example, the steep increase in cannabis prevalence use in the Netherlands during the early 1990s has been convincingly linked with the de facto legalization of cannabis retail sales in the mid 1980s (MacCoun and Reuter, 2001:238–263; see also Hall and Pacula, 2003), even though Dutch cannabis use remains well below the level of some other European countries with more standard prohibition regimes (EMCDDA, 2006:42).

10. Expenditures on cannabis, cocaine, heroin, and methamphetamine would in total have been a little more than one half of 1%.

11. Laos, another second-tier producer, may now also come close to lax enforcement, having come much closer to meeting the conditions of state tolerance and nonenforcement in the past, but because information on Laos is limited, we do not discuss the country at length in either case. According to McCoy (1991) and other sources (Lintner, 1992), Laos virtually enforced no opium prohibition at least up until 1975, when the Communist party took control of the government. Up to that point, corrupt elites—ranging from high-ranking military officers, such as the infamous General Ouane Rattikone, to members of the royal family, such as the Prince Sopsaisana (in

whose suitcase 60 kilograms of heroin were found at a Paris airport in 1971)—were directly involved in the opium trade (McCoy, 1991:374–377, 283–285). Although evidence for the following years is scant, the control of opium production and trade does not seem to have become a priority of the new socialist leaders until the 1990s. A section prohibiting drug trafficking as well as manufacture of heroin and other narcotics was introduced in the Penal Code in 1990; it was only in 1996, however, that production and possession of opium were made illegal. In 2000, the Opium Elimination Program was approved and, in 2001, the National Party Congress made opium elimination a national priority. Opium cultivation area decreased by about 55% between 1998 and 2003, but enforcement is unlikely to be consistent across the country. Opium poppy cultivation remains concentrated in the north of the country, where 55% of all villages are inaccessible to vehicles (UNODC, 2003a).

12. For more information on Tajikistan and India, see chapters 9 and 7, respectively; in appendix D, we discuss the features of Pakistan, Turkey, Albania, Kosovo, and Mexico that qualify them as "lax enforcers."

13. Unfortunately, no information is available on their internal divisions of labor.

14. Much information on the Baybasin clan is drawn from Frank Bovenkerk's and Yücel Yesilgöz' book on the Turkish mafia (1998; see also 2004). The two authors interviewed Huseyin Baybasin at length (see also Carlson, 2005).

15. His criminal record tends to confirm his statements. Baybasin was arrested in 1984 in London with a large consignment of heroin and was sentenced to 12 years of imprisonment. After 3 years behind bars, he was transferred to Turkey and immediately released, prompting allegations of corruption at the highest levels of the Turkish government (Thompson, 2002). According to Baybasin's own statements, during the 1980s the Turkish state was directly involved in the drug trade, helping him find channels to bring heroin revenues back to Turkey and extorting a tax in exchange for protection services from the largest heroin smugglers, including the Baybasin clan itself (Bovenkerk and Yesilgöz,1998, 2004). If Baybasin's allegation are true, as Bovenkerk and Yesilgöz who interviewed him repeatedly tend to believe, they would suggest conditions closer to our third case—namely, non-enforcement, including state (or quasi-state) tolerance and support.

16. According to the Turkish government, the PKK was, at least in the 1980s and 1990s, responsible for much of the illicit drug processing and trafficking in Turkey (Embassy of the Republic of Turkey in Washington DC, n.d.). This claim must be considered an exaggeration. There is no clear evidence that the PKK or its high-ranking militant members have ever run drug businesses. However, numerous sources, including the DEA (2002b), show that the PKK has, since the late 1980s if not earlier, received large donations from Kurdish drug-trafficking families. In some cases, PKK cells both in Turkey and abroad may have gone as far as to extort Kurdish illegal entrepreneurs regularly (Atasoy, 2004:36–37; Robins, 2008).

17. Even in the problem area of the state of Guerriero, the average field size is just more than 2,000 square meters in size. Mexican opium poppy growers also often use non-traditional cultivation patterns or use terrain-masking and nearby vegetation for cover. Some growers reportedly pluck the brightly colored petals off the poppy plant, after it has flowered, to avoid detection from eradication forces (DEA, 2000:5).

18. At the Mexican farm gate in the late 1990s, a kilo of opium cost, on average, $1,000 with occasional spikes up to $5,000, according to the DEA (2000:8). Even if

only the average price is considered, this amounts to about 10 to 25 times the cost in the same years in Afghanistan.

19. This figure is much higher than those presented elsewhere in this book, because it refers exclusively to the male population, at the age most likely to consume drugs, in the worst-affected cities.

20. Consistent with these observations, UN reports indicate that local opium traders earned modest incomes in the 1990s, no greater than those of other traders in local bazaars (UNDCP, 1998b:10–12).

21. Under conditions of strict and even lax enforcement, we would look for examples of large seizures for evidence of large stocks, but in the case of non-enforcement, we do not have this opportunity; almost by definition, "non-enforcers" are also "non-seizers."

22. India is a special case because its illicit opium output overwhelmingly results from diversion from licit production (see chapter 7). Turkey is also only a partial exception because the areas where opium poppies used to be grown differ from the southeastern border areas where opiate processing and trafficking have been largely located since the 1960s (Atasoy, 2004).

23. For empirical evidence, see Greenfield (1991), which finds that Bolivian coca farmers earn incomes close to national averages.

24. This conclusion is also backed by the case of Somalia, which has not become a major producer or transit point for opiates or other illegal commodities, although it has had no central government since the early 1990s. Illegal entrepreneurs' lack of interest in Somalia may be explained in part by its peripheral location from the standard opiate and, more generally, commercial routes. Also important probably is the absence of an effective central government since the early 1990s, which has resulted in general anarchy and in the near-total collapse of the commercial infrastructure, and the banking and judicial systems (Heinzelmann, 2006; Perras, 2006).

Chapter Eleven

1. Only under highly restricted circumstances and with the preventive approval of the INCB may opium be produced, and its derivatives extracted and used for medical purposes (see appendix A).

2. This chapter draws not only on our own analyses but also occasionally and explicitly on other studies of related issues. It also incorporates some insights from studies of other drug markets.

3. Information about this country is scarce and contradictory. On the one hand, Turkmenistan is a country dominated by a very oppressive and corrupt dictatorship. Since the late 1990s, its political and military regime has been very uncooperative with international drug control agencies, and at the beginning of the 21st century was said by many observers to be heavily involved in the opiate business (Safronov, 2002; ICG, 2003a:9–10, 18). On the other hand, neither the UNODC nor other sources suggest that Turkmenistan has become a major conduit for opiates from Afghanistan onward, certainly not to the same extent as Tajikistan—as it might if the institutional conditions were so attractive. Moreover, the sudden death of Turkmenistan's absolutist ruler, Saparmurat Niyazov, in December 2006 makes prognoses about the country's drug control course even more difficult. Turkmenistan's new president, Kurbanguly

Berdymukhamedov, who was sworn in in February 2007, has promised and slowly begun to introduce reforms, including unlimited access to the Internet, better education, and higher pensions (BBC, 2007). At the time of this writing, it is too early to assess whether a professed interest in domestic reforms will carry over into other arenas, such as drug control.

4. China provides another such example.

5. No doubt the longstanding tradition of trade—and general smuggling—across the Afghanistan–Pakistan border has also contributed to the success of those opiate trafficking routes (Asad and Harris, 2003).

6. We note one such circumstance in our discussion of the so-called Australian heroin "drought."

7. The analysis also suggests that the effects of a cutback that is even moderately longer than that achieved by the Taliban might be greater, depending largely on the responses of current and potential producers in other regions. In the wake of the Taliban cutback, the global distribution system was able to run down stocks over a 12-month period and largely meet demand, perhaps reflecting the bumper crops and inventory accumulation specific to the late 1990s. A second year might have produced a sharper increase in prices in both regional and downstream markets, although it also may have afforded opportunity to other producers in other countries or regions to increase their output or enter the market anew.

8. For example, Conroy (1990) describes a cocaine epidemic in Russian cities during the upheaval at the end of World War I and the early years of the Soviet era.

9. The same objectives were set for the coca bush and the cannabis plant and have not been achieved either, as evident in the annual production statistics found in the UN *World Drug Reports*.

10. In addition, supporting the general premise that alternative economic activities are crucial, Colombia's economy certainly presents better options than either Afghanistan's or Burma's. The experience may suggest that a producing country is better able to exit the market the less time it has spent in it; in this way, the experience would also support the demand-side hypothesis that immature markets are more susceptible to change, hence policy action, than mature markets.

11. The Feldafing Declaration is the outcome of a conference convened in 2002 by the UNODCCP, the German Federal Ministry for Economic Cooperation and Development (BMZ), the German Foundation for International Development (DSE), and the German Agency of Technical Cooperation (GTZ).

12. Such an approach is not unknown in other international policy arenas. In the 1980s, for example, the Swedish government invested in pollution control in East Germany because much of its air pollution came from East German electrical power plants.

13. Trafficking interventions, without complementary policy measures in consuming or producing countries, are unlikely to affect whether one country or another engages in transshipment. However, as explained later, this does not mean that supply-oriented interventions in trafficking nations hold no value, because they may well affect the size, organization, and operating methods of trafficking enterprises and, through these variables, the negative impact of trafficking on the larger society.

14. Key sources include Berridge (1984, 1999), Musto (1987), Bewley-Taylor (1999), and McAllister (2000).

15. The heroin given to addicts is provided from INCB-authorized production.

16. The figure would have been higher in the years immediately after the ban; however, since the peak of 2003, prices have fallen and may eventually return to their preban levels (see chapter 4).

17. This is one instance in which a mature market may be more amenable to policy intervention than an immature market, albeit through indirect means.

18. Summers apparently signed an internal (World Bank) memo that addressed the issues on December 12, 1991. Summers later argued that the memo was taken out of context, but in the words of a Harvard *Crimson* reporter "it has tailed him ever since it was leaked to the *Economist* in 1992" (Theodore, 2003: online edition, available at www.thecrimson.com/article.aspx?ref=348802). The memo was "immortalized into song by a Yale music professor," in a piece written for two sopranos and titled, "Mortgaging the Earth" (Theodore, 2003). For a copy of the leaked memo, see www. mindfully.org/WTO/Summers-Memo-World12dec91.htm.

19. A similar analysis might apply to trafficking.

20. In October 2007, for example, the European Parliament (2007:4) issued a recommendation to the European Council to look at "the possibility of pilot projects for small-scale conversion of parts of the current illicit poppy cultivation into fields for the production of legal opium-based analgesics."

21. UNAIDS is the joint UN program on HIV/AIDS.

Appendix A

1. There is a great deal of diversion further down the chain. In the United States, such drugs as oxycodone (sold under the trade name of Oxycontin) and hydrocodone, have entered the black market through diversion from regular distribution channels.

2. In the CPS process, poppy pods are dried on the stalk in the fields and then crushed to remove the seeds. The seeds are used for a food product and the crushed pods are processed in a factory to extract the alkaloids. In India, however, farmers lance poppy pods in the fields to remove opium. Farmers then turn in the collected opium gum to the government (INCB, 2008a:78–80).

3. In late 2006, the DEA (2006) proposed to replace Yugoslavia with Spain.

Appendix B

1. Very detailed estimates of opium consumption in China spanning the nineteenth and twentieth centuries have been provided by Newman (1995; see chapter 2 this volume).

2. There are some problems in reconciling the interpretation of the UNODC (2005d:132) with the published article. The UNODC states: "The study showed an average consumption of 0.6 grams per day, and a consumption of, on average, 22 days per month. Average consumption per month was thus 14.9 grams of heroin (at street purity), which amounts to 179 grams per year. Applying the average purity of around 38 percent reported by forensic laboratories in the UK in 1997 (The Forensic Science Service, *Drug Abuse Trends,* various issues), average annual consumption would be 68 grams of pure heroin per problem drug user." The article, in fact, reports prior month quantity used by treatment modality and our estimate of the weighted average

monthly consumption of heroin (using procedures that might bias the figure upward) is 11.7 grams per month. At 38% purity, that is 4.45 grams per month, yielding 54 grams per annum. However, the data were collected in 1995, not 1997, so the purity may not be correct.

3. By comparison, in chapter 5, we estimate average annual consumption of almost 9 metric tons from 1996 to 2000 and about 8.2 metric tons from 2001 to 2003. The cross-period difference arises largely from a change in the UN's basis for calculating prevalence.

4. This estimate, which the ONDCP describes in the table notes as a projection, was simply an extrapolation of the 1998 figure on the assumption that little had changed. Although the series for the number of chronic users was stable for 1992 to 1998, that for occasional users fluctuated sharply, probably representing the small number of observations in the household survey on which it was based.

Appendix C

1. We define Central Asia as consisting of Kazakhstan, Kyrgyzstan, Tajikistan, Turkmenistan, and Uzbekistan. We address drug production and income for Afghanistan separately and elsewhere.

2. The data collection and analysis for this appendix was completed in 2004, under the auspices of a related project on drug markets and trafficking in Central Asia. We note some important changes in market conditions and cite a small number of relevant post-2004 publications, but we do not attempt to update our results more fully. Although a comprehensive update might be desirable, our analysis builds on a substantial informal data collection that was specific to the year 2000 and could not be replicated for a later year without considerable additional effort. Nevertheless, we believe that our results are still relevant today and, perhaps as important, we demonstrate a systematic approach for assessing the economic dimensions of opiate trafficking in the future.

3. Although not widely practiced, we note that the United Nations actively encourages inclusion of illegal goods and services in GDP (see OECD et al., 2002).

4. At the time of our data collection, 2001 was the most recent year for which sufficient data were available to support the analysis.

5. Indeed, more recent production data suggest that the boom year may have been a harbinger of things to come, specifically in terms of sustained high levels of production.

6. In contrast, in a more recent modeling effort, the UNODC (2005d:133) estimates the incomes—really the gross revenues—of retailers in "Central Asia and Transcaucasus" as $480 million in 2003, falling just outside the low end of our somewhat broader measure for 2000.

7. A $14 billion estimate also appears in regional press reports: "Today the drug business in Central Asia involves several million people and the annual turnover of this industry totals US $14 billion" (Manayev, 2000).

8. Although Central Asian countries have grown opium in the past, their cultivation has dwindled to minimal levels. The United Nations estimates that, since the late 1990s, 10 hectares or less of opium poppy are under cultivation, located primarily in Tajikistan (UNODCCP, 2002d:4; see also chapter 9, this volume). Prior to 1974, Kyrgyzstan was a major producer of licit opium (UNODCCP, 2002d:4).

9. Table 3.1 and figure 5.2 illustrate the trends in production for Afghanistan, Burma, and others.

10. This section relies heavily on Paoli (2001).

11. The prevalence rate reported by the UNODCCP (2002c:228) of 1.8% supports an estimate of about 2.2 million opiate users in the adult population; the prevalence rate of 0.9% reported the previous year by the UNODCCP (2001:231) supported a figure about half as large.

12. During the early stages of an epidemic there are many casual users who are just experimenting. During the course of an epidemic, many of these casual users will drop out; the remainder mostly use frequently. See Rydell and Everingham (1994) for an analysis of this with respect to cocaine in the United States.

13. By comparison, in chapter 5, we estimate more than half a million opiate users, on average, for 1996 to 2000 and more than a million for 2001 to 2003; the cross-period difference arises largely from a rapid increase in heroin use and addiction both within and across the two time periods.

14. The 30-metric-ton estimate is roughly consistent with the 2001 to 2003 estimate presented in chapter 5 and is substantially higher than the estimate for 1996 to 2000. As noted previously, the cross-period difference arises largely from a rapid increase in heroin use and addiction both within and across periods.

15. For a fuller discussion of the estimates and the issues surrounding them, see appendix B.

16. By comparison, in chapter 5, we estimate an average annual consumption of almost 9 metric tons for 1996 to 2000 and about 8.2 metric tons for 2001 to 2003. In this case, the cross-period difference arises largely from a change in the United Nations' basis for calculating prevalence.

17. Singleton, Murray, and Tinsley (2006:chapter 4) provide a more recent estimate of 8 metric tons for the United Kingdom for 2003. The 8-ton figure is roughly consistent with our chapter 5 estimates.

18. The EMCDDA (2002b:14–15) reports the estimated number of problem drug users for Norway and European Union nations, excluding Greece, from multiple sources for various years for 1995 to 2000. These are not specifically opiate data, but injecting drug use reportedly accounts for most problem drug use in many western European countries, and most users inject heroin. Estimates of problem drug use are all between 2 and 9 cases per 1,000 adults, age 15 to 64; estimates of injecting drug use, a subset of problem use, are generally between 2 and 5 cases per 1,000. The 1.5-million figure is intended as a high-end estimate of opiate use. We sum the largest estimate for each country for the most recent year available. The inclusion of non-opiate problem users in the data further supports the claim that the figure is high end. The implied prevalence rate for adults, age 15 to 64, would be almost 0.6%. The implied rate for the general population would be about 0.4%. By comparison, the flow model that underlies the consumption estimates in chapter 5 suggests an excess of 1 million users, but not fully 1.5 million (see World Bank [2002] for population data).

19. Using prevalence rates and population estimates from the UNODCCP (2002c) and World Bank (2002), respectively, we estimate there were about 45,000 opiate users in Greece in the late 1990s and another 30,000 in Switzerland in 2000. The United Nations reports prevalence rates of 0.5% for both Greece and Switzerland. Greece's reported rate is a "tentative estimate for the late 1990s (UNODCCP, 2002c:227–228)."

20. See World Bank (2002) for population data. Of the 125 million, which excludes Russia and the Ukraine, about 85 million are adults between the ages of 15 and 64. The half-million figure supports implied prevalence rate estimates in line with those of the European Union. The implied prevalence rate for adults, age 15 to 64, would be almost 0.6%; the implied rate for the general population would be about 0.4%. The flow model that underlies the chapter 5 consumption estimates—and makes use of United Nations-reported national prevalence rates—suggests roughly 300,000.

21. The EMCDDA (2002c:17–18) cites the 2001 CEEC national reports, with estimates from various years, as the source of the prevalence data; for Poland, the EMCDDA specifically notes the data are based on an "isolated study" conducted in 1996 to 1997, thus earning the disclaimer of "rather old" and of "limited reliability" despite their statistical underpinnings. As mentioned previously, the data refer to "problem drug use" in general, not opiate use specifically; however, the EMCDDA (2002c:19) claims: "The major problem drug in all candidate countries is heroin."

22. Latvia previously reported a very low rate (0.1%) to the United Nations for 2000. This is reflective of the uncertainty about these rates in nations with poorly developed indicator systems.

23. The figures were the most recent figures available at the time of this analysis, but the United Nations did not attribute them to a particular year.

24. The rate previously reported for Kazakhstan for 2000 was only 0.4%. The same rate was reported for Kyrgyzstan for the late 1990s (UNODCCP, 2002c:229).

25. In chapter 5 we assume an average 25% market share throughout 1996 to 2000 and 2001 to 2003, but our analysis suggests the likelihood of some growth in the share over the course of the periods.

26. Although the United Nations categorizes Turkey as a western European country, we exclude it from these calculations because it is much earlier in the shipping route and is more of a supplier than a component of the European market.

27. Our estimates of aggregate regional consumption are reasonably consistent with other, more recent estimates. The UNODC (2005d:133) reports total European consumption (West, East, and Central) of 164 metric ton in 2003 in comparison with our high-end estimate of 160 metric tons for Europe, Russia, and the Ukraine in 2000. The UNODC (2005d:133) also reports total Central Asian and Transcaucasus consumption of about 9 metric tons in comparison with our low-end estimate of 11 metric tons for Central Asia alone.

28. In an earlier version of this appendix, we began with a very rough estimate of Afghanistan's opiate income, as an anchor for the downstream estimates for Central Asia. We found that the drug trade's contribution to the Afghan economy was substantially lower in 2000 than during the postban era (see chapter 6 for recent estimates), likely reflecting the increased importance of the trade in the latter era.

29. For example, prices of opiates in successive stages of transit (e.g., at Afghanistan's export frontier and across the border in Tajikistan) reflect a combination of the cost of the opiates at the frontier and the value of the services provided in smuggling them into Tajikistan. The assignment of the value of the smuggling services is unclear. Ordinarily the value of these goods and services would be treated separately. The value of the goods would clearly count as an Afghan export, but the value of the services would be credited to one country or another depending on the residency of the provider.

30. In most instances, for a GDP-comparable income estimate, the first transaction in the importing country would serve as the cutoff point for attribution to

the exporting (e.g., Afghan) economy. Any economic activity after that point would generally be credited to the importer's (e.g., Tajikistan's) GDP, even if the opiates were handed off to another Afghan citizen. That citizen would be treated as either an employee of a foreign affiliate of an Afghan firm or an employee of a Tajik firm.

31. The three elements derive from the identity GDP = C + I + G + (X—M), where C is final consumption, I is investment, G is government purchases, X is exports, and M is imports.

32. The f.o.b. value includes the costs of transportation and insurance to bring the merchandise to the frontier of the exporting country or territory.

33. In the United States, the physical risks are from other dealers. In Central Asia, the police may be the principal source of such risks. The OECD et al. (2002:154) includes a discussion of whether bribes should be included in GDP, offering circumstance-specific suggestions. We include them here for conceptual and pragmatic reasons—they are folded into observed market prices.

34. Calculated as two thirds of Central Asia's total gross exports.

35. These differences are additional to differences in base year data selection. For example, the United Nations uses 2002 production estimates for Afghanistan with 2001 seizure and price estimates for neighboring countries. To the extent possible, we use 2000 estimates throughout.

Our estimates are even more consistent with the UNODC (2005d:133), which places regional retail income for Central Asia and Transcaucasus at about $480 million. The more recent United Nations estimate may be conceptually closer to ours in that it derives from an input/output table that imposes consistency on production, seizures, and consumption, but there appear to be substantial differences in underlying assumptions, such as those concerning consumption rates (see appendix B).

Appendix D

1. The FATA is divided into seven agencies—Khyber, Kurram, Orakzai, Mohmand, Bajaur, North Waziristan, and South Waziristan. There are also six small pockets of tribal areas known as *frontier regions*. These are transition areas between the FATA and the adjoining settled districts of the NWFP, and are jointly administered by the NWFP and the tribal agencies (Abbas, 2006).

2. This includes many born in Germany who cannot adopt German citizenship without losing their Turkish citizenship.

3. The PKK is a militant organization fighting for the creation of an independent Kurdish state in southeastern Turkey, where most of the population has Kurdish origin. Depending on the estimates, 28 to 40 million Kurds live in that part of Turkey and the neighboring northeastern Iraq, northeastern Syria, and northwestern Iran. According to journalistic accounts, more than 30,000 people have died since the late 1970s in the fight between the PKK and the Turkish army (Schlötzer, 2006).

4. More recent events also indicate corruption. In 1998, for example, the former chief of the narcotics bureau of the Istanbul police was accused of favoring some drug traffickers by destroying pieces of evidence or discontinuing investigations. After his demotion, the former narcotics policeman leveled similar accusations against the Istanbul police chief, the head of Turkey's security forces, and some of their staff and relatives. According to the *Turkish Daily News*, several politicians were also likely

involved in these schemes, but they were never formally incriminated (Aslaneli, 1998; see also Aslaneli, 1999). In 2004, the Turkish press reported that a former member of parliament and Kurdish clan leader had a gang of 25 people raid a prison in the southeastern city of Van to free his son who had been arrested for heroin trafficking (*Turkish Daily News,* 2004a, b).

5. There are up to 500,000 Kosovars and/or Albanians in Greece, 400,000 in Germany, 300,000 in Switzerland, 120,000 in Italy, and 60,000 in Austria, not to mention another 300,000 to 400,000 in North America. Criminal networks represent an extremely small part of this diaspora; however, exactly because of this, they can effectively conceal their illegal operations (Arlacchi, 2004:6–7; see also Barth et al., 1999, and Mai and Schander-Sievers, 2003).

6. A 2003 national survey estimated that Mexicans spend $1.6 billion on bribes a year—involving an estimated 100 million corrupt transactions—just to obtain public services (Jordan, 2004).

7. The ties between drug traffickers and law enforcement officers have been so tight since the 1960s that several well-known drug traffickers started their careers within the state apparatus. Miguel Angel Felix Gallardo, for example, who set up the Sinaloa cartel exporting large quantities of heroin in the United States during the 1970s and 1980s, was a former police officer (Lupsha, 1991; Astorga, 1996). Even today, many corrupt current or former police officers have second jobs or careers as hit men or bodyguards for drug kingpins (Golden, 2000; Pimentel, 2003:191; Thompson, 2005b).

8. Recent scandals in Mexico's high-security prisons (as well as the escape of one of the most prominent drug-trafficking leaders) show that the most powerful drug traffickers enjoy a very comfortable life there and are even able to run their illicit businesses and control their turf from jail, staging a shocking wave of drug-related killings in early 2005 (Sullivan and Jordan, 2005; Thompson and McKinley, 2005).

9. As mentioned in chapter 2, opium poppy was brought to Mexico during the late 19th century by Chinese immigrants, who began to cultivate it in the rugged Sierra Madre mountains, where it still grows today. From the 1930s onward, local Mexicans began to dominate the industry (Astorga, 1996).

References

Abbas, Hassan. 2006. "Profiles of Pakistan's Seven Tribal Agencies." *Terrorism Monitor* 4(20): 1–5. Online. Available at www.jamestown.org/terrorism/news/article.php?articleid=2370168. Accessed May 2007.

Abbas, Zaffar. 2004. "Pakistan's Undeclared War." *BBC News*. September 10. Online. Available at http://news.bbc.co.uk/1/hi/world/south_asia/3645114.stm. Accessed October 2007.

Abt Associates. 1999. *Estimating Heroin Availability*. Report prepared for the ONDCP. Online. Available at www.abtassociates.com/reports/5351.pdf. Accessed October 2007.

——. 2005. *Availability Estimates for Illegal Drugs in the United States through 2003: Cocaine, Heroin and Marijuana*. Unpublished report for the Drug Availability Steering Committee.

Acock Mary C. and Basil Acock. 2003. *Joint India-U.S. Licit Opium Poppy Survey (JLOPS) for 2003*. August.

Adler, Patricia A. 1985. *Wheeling and Dealing: An Ethnography of an Upper-Level Drug Dealing and Smuggling Community*. New York: Columbia University Press.

AFP, Agence France Presse. 2001. "Tajik Trade Representative Given 15-Year Sentence on Drug Charges." February 27.

——. 2004. "Curbing Rampant Afghan Opium Trade Will Take Karzai Years." December 5.

——. 2007. "Most Opium Now Processed inside Afghanistan: UN." June 25.

Ahmad, Diana L. 2007. *The Opium Debate and Chinese Exclusion Laws in the Nineteenth-Century American West*. Reno: University of Nevada Press.

Altsean-Burma, Alternative Asean Network on Burma. 2004. *A Failing Grade: Burma's Drug Eradication Efforts*. Bangkok: Altsean-Burma.

Alvarez, Elena H. 1995. "Economic Development, Restructuring and the Illicit Drug Sector in Bolivia and Peru: Current Policies." *Journal of Interamerican Studies and World Affairs* 37(3) Special Issue: Report on Neoliberal Restructuring: 125–149.

Anderson, Jon L. 2007. "The Taliban's Opium War." *The New Yorker* July 9. Online. Available at http://www.newyorker.com/reporting/2007/07/09/070709fa_fact_anderson. Accessed July 2007.

Anderson, John W. 1993. "Fortress Fit for King, or Trafficker: Accused Pakistani Drug Baron Flaunts Enclave Near Khyber Pass." *The Washington Post* April 29: A32.

Anderson, John W., and Kamran Khan. 1994. "Heroin Plan by Top Pakistanis Alleged: Former Prime Minister Says Drug Deals Were to Pay for Covert Military Operations." *The Washington Post* September 12: A13.

Anglin, M. Douglas, and Y. Yih-Ing Hser. 1990. "Treatment of Drug Abuse." In *Drugs and Crime*, ed. Michael Tonry and James Q. Wilson. Chicago: University of Chicago Press, pp. 393–460.

Arlacchi, Pino. 2004. *End of Mission Report: Fight against Corruption, Financial and Economic Crime.* November 5. Report prepared for the European Agency for Reconstruction. Mimeo.

Arlacchi, Pino, and Roger Lewis. 1990a. *Il mercato dell'eroina a Reggio Emilia e provincia.* Reggio Emilia: Provincia di Reggio Emilia.

——. 1990b. *Imprenditorialità illecita e droga: Il mercato dell'eroina a Verona.* Bologna: Il Mulino.

——. 1990c. "Droga e criminalità a Bologna." *Micromega* 4: 183–221.

Arsovska, Jana. 2006a. "Albanian Organized Crime Groups Evolve in Europe." *Jane's Intelligence Review* November: 1–5.

——. 2006b. "Albanian Organized Crime Groups in the Balkans: Symbiosis between Politics and Crime." *Jane's Intelligence Review* December.

Asad, Amir Zada, and Robert Harris. 2003. *The Politics and Economics of Drug Production on the Pakistan–Afghanistan Border.* Aldershot: Ashgate.

Ashouri, Mohammad and Mansour Rahmdel. 2003. *Final Report—Iran.* Report submitted for the project Modeling the World Heroin Market: Assessing the Consequences of Changes in Afghanistan Production. Tehran. Mimeo.

Asian Development Bank, United Nations Assistance Mission to Afghanistan, United Nations Development Programme, and the World Bank Group. 2004. *Securing Afghanistan's Future: Accomplishment and the Strategic Path Forward. A Government/International Agency Report.* March 17. Online. Available at http://www.adb.org/Documents/Reports/Afghanistan/securing-afghanistan-future-final.pdf. Accessed August 2005.

Aslaneli, Hakan. 1998. "Police Officers Are on Trial." *Turkish Daily News* December 19.

——. 1999. "Tantan Takes Control: New Interior Minister Intervenes in the Debate Over 'Good and Bad Police Officers.'" *Turkish Daily News* June 2.

Astorga, Luis. 1996. *El Siglo de las Drogas.* Mexico: Espasa Calpe.

Atasoy, Sevil. 2004. *The Opiate Trade in Turkey.* Report submitted for the project Modeling the World Heroin Market: Assessing the Consequences of Changes in Afghanistan Production. Istanbul. Mimeo.

Atha, Mathew, and Simon Davis. 2003. *UK Opiate Usage, Consumption, Attitudes and Prices: Combined Results of IDMU Surveys 1994–2002.* Online. Available at www.idmu.co.uk/opiates2003.htm. Accessed October 2007.

Atkin, Muriel. 1997. "Tajikistan: Reform, Reaction and Civil War." In *New States, New Politics: Building the Post-Soviet Nations*, ed. Ian Bremmer and Ray Taras. Cambridge: Cambridge University Press, pp. 603–634.

Bajun, Elena. 2003. ["Taste of Home: Who Stops Heroin Smuggling from Tajikistan?"] *Moskovskii komsomolets,* August 8. In Russian.

Ball, Desmond. 1999. *Burma and Drugs: The Regime's Complicity in the Global Drug Trade.* Working paper no. 336. Canberra: Strategic and Defence Studies Centre, Australian National University.

Banfield, Edward C. 1958. *The Moral Basis of a Backward Society.* Glencoe, Ill.: Free Press.

Barth, Ariane, Wolfram Bickerich, Maik Grossekathoefer, Peter Onneken, and Hans-Juergen Schlamp. 1999. "Sprache der Morde." *Der Spiegel* August 2: 42–46.

Baumler, Alan. 2000. "Opium Control Versus Opium Suppression: The Origins of the 1935 Six-Year Plan to Eliminate Opium and Drugs." In *Opium Regimes: China, Britain and Japan, 1839–1952,* ed. Timothy Brook and Bob T. Wakabayashi. Berkeley: University of California Press, pp. 270–292.

——. (ed.). 2001. *Modern China and Opium: A Reader.* Ann Arbor: University of Michigan Press.

Bayer, I., and Hamid Ghodse. 1999. "Evolution of International Drug Control, 1945–1995." *Bulletin on Narcotics* LI(1): 1–17.

BBC, British Broadcasting Corporation. 2001. *Unprepared South Russian Border Region Faces Genuine Migration Disaster.* November 15.

——. 2003. *Russian Guards Discover Heroin Cache on Tajik–Afghan Border.* October 25.

——. 2004. *Warrant Issued for Arrest of Tajik Drug Control Chief.* August 9.

——. 2006a. *Dozens Killed in Pakistan Clashes.* March 5.

——. 2006b. *Heroin Gang Chiefs Get 10 Years in Czech Prison.* February 20.

——. 2006c. *Wedding Guests Die in Mine Blast.* March 10.

——. 2007. *Profile: Kurbanguly Berdymukhamedov.* February 14. Online. Available at http://news.bbc.co.uk/2/hi/asia-pacific/6346185.stm. Accessed May 2007.

Beeching, Jack. 1975. *The Chinese Opium Wars.* London: Hutchinson.

Belair, Felix. 1971. "C. I. A. Identifies 21 Asian Opium Refineries." *The New York Times,* June 6: 2.

Bello, David A. 2005. *Opium and the Limits of Empire. Drug Prohibition in the Chinese Interior: 1729–1850.* Cambridge: Harvard University Asia Center.

Berridge, Virginia. 1984. "Drugs and Social Policy: The Establishment of Drug Control in Britain 1900–30." *British Journal of Addiction* 79: 17–29.

——. 1999. *Opium and the People: Opiate Use and Drug Control Policy in Nineteenth and Early-Twentieth Century England.* London: Free Association Books.

——. 2005. "'The British System' and Its History: Myth and Reality." In *Heroin Addiction and 'The British System': Understanding the Problem: Policy and the British System,* ed. John Strang and Michael Gossop. London: Routledge, pp. 7–16.

Bewley-Taylor, David R. 1999. *The United States and International Drug Control, 1909–1997.* London: Pinter.

Bhattacharaji, Romesh. 2007. *Case Study: India's experiences in licensing poppy cultivation for the production of essential medicines. Lessons for Afghanistan.* [London]: Senlis Council. Online. Available at http://www.senliscouncil.net/documents/india_case_study. Accessed December 2007.

BKA, Bundeskriminalamt. 2001. *Rauschgiftlagebericht 2009 Bundesrepublik Deutschland.* Wiesbaden: BKA.

——. 2002. *Rauschgiftlagebericht 2001 Bundesrepublik Deutschland.* Wiesbaden: BKA.

BKA, Bundeskriminalamt. 2005. *Bundeslagebild Rauschgift 2004 Bundesrepublik Deutschland*. Wiesbaden: BKA. Online. Available at www.bka.de/lageberichte/rg/2004/bundeslagebild_rg2004.pdf.

Blanchard, Christopher M. 2006. *Afghanistan: Narcotics and U.S. Policy*. CRS Report for Congress. Washington, D.C.: Congressional Research Service, The Library of Congress.

Block, Alan A. 1989. "European Drug Traffic and Traffickers between the Wars: The Policy of Suppression and Its Consequences." *Journal of Social History* 23(Winter): 315–337.

Boekhout Van Solinge, Tim. 2002. *The Swedish Drug Control System: An In-Depth Review and Analysis*. Piscataway, N.J.: Transaction.

Booth, Martin. 1998. *Opium: A History*. New York: St. Martin's Press.

Borisov, Timofei. 2001. ["Heroin was put inside cotton"]. *Rossiyskaya Gazeta* (Moscow), July 12. [In Russian].

Boudreaux, Richard. 2005. "Mexico's Master of Elusion: Since His Escape, Drug Cartel Chief Joaquin 'Shorty' Guzman Has Expanded His Empire, Waged War on Rivals and Become a Legend." *Los Angeles Times* July 5: A1.

Bourgois, Philippe. 1995. *In Search of Respect: Selling Crack in El Barrio*. Cambridge: Cambridge University Press.

Bovenkerk, Frank. 1995. *La Bella Bettien*. Amsterdam: Meulenhof.

Bovenkerk, Frank and Willemien Hogewind. 2003. *Hennepteelt in Nederland. Het probleem van de criminaliteit en haar bestrijding*, Zeist: Kerckebosch.

Bovenkerk, Frank, and Yücel Yesilgöz. 1998. *De Maffia van Turkije*. Amsterdam: Meulenhoff.

——. 2004. "The Turkish Mafia and the State." In *Organised Crime in Europe: Concepts, Patterns and Control Policies in the European Union and Beyond*, ed. Cyrille Fijnaut and Letizia Paoli. Dordrecht: Springer, pp. 585–602.

Boyum, David, and Peter Reuter. 2005. *An Analytic Assessment of U.S. Drug Policy*. Washington, D.C.: American Enterprise Institute.

Bramley-Harker, Edward. 2001. *Sizing the UK Market for Illicit Drugs*. RDS Report 74. London: Home Office Research and Development Statistics.

Braun, Norman, Bruno Nydegger Lory, Roger Berger, and Claudia Zahner. 2001. *Illegale Märkte für Heroin und Kokain*. Bern: Paul Haupt.

Bretteville-Jensen, Anne-Line. 2006. Drug Demand: Initiation, Continuation and Quitting. *De Economist* 154(4): 491–516.

Brook, Timothy, and Bob T. Wakabayashi (ed.). 2000. *Opium Regimes: China, Britain and Japan, 1839–1952*. Berkeley: University of California Press.

Bruun, Kettil, Lynn Pan, and Ingemar Rexed. 1975. *The Gentlemen's Club: International Control of Drugs and Alcohol*. Chicago: University of Chicago Press.

Buddenberg, Doris, and William A. Byrd (ed.). 2006. *Afghanistan's Drug Industry: Structure, Functioning, Dynamics and Implications for Counter-Narcotics Policy*. New York: UNODC and World Bank.

Burnett, Victoria. 2004. "Outlook Uncertain: Can Afghanistan Take the Next Step to Building a State?" *Financial Times* August 19.

Burns, John F. 1995. "Heroin Scourges Million Pakistanis." *The New York Times* April 5: A12.

Butler, William. 1997. *Criminal Code of the Russian Federation*. London: Simmonds and Hill.

Byrd, William A. and Doris Buddenberg. 2006. "Introduction and Overview." In *Afghanistan's Drug Industry: Structure, Functioning, Dynamics and Implications for Counter-Narcotics Policy,* ed. Doris Buddenberg and William A. Byrd. New York: UNODC and World Bank, pp. 1–24.

Byrd, William, and Olivier Jonglez. 2006. "Prices and Market Interactions in the Opium Economy." In *Afghanistan's Drug Industry: Structure, Functioning, Dynamics and Implications for Counter-Narcotics Policy,* ed. Doris Buddenberg and William A. Byrd. New York: UNODC and World Bank, pp. 119–154.

Carlson, Brian G. 2005. "Huseyin Baybasin: Europe's Pablo Escobar." *SAIS Review* 25(1), 69–70.

Carstairs, Catherine. 2005. "The Stages of the International Drug Control System." *Drug and Alcohol Review* 24(1): 57–65.

Caryl, Chrstian. 2001. "The New Silk Road of Death." *Newsweek* 113(12): 24–28.

Caulkins, Jonathan P. 2002. "Central Asia's Narcotics Industry: The New Golden Triangle." *Strategic Comments* 3(5).

——. 2007. The Need for Dynamic Drug Policy. *Addiction.* 102(1): 4–7.

Caulkins, Jonathan P., Doris Behrens, Claudia Knoll, Gernot Tragler, and Doris Zuba. 2004. "Markov Chain Modelling of Initiation and Demand: The Case of the US Cocaine Epidemic." *Health Management Sciences* 7: 319–329.

Caulkins, Jonathan P., and Peter Reuter. 2006. "Heroin Supply in the Long-Term and the Short-Term Perspectives: Comment on Wood et al." *Addiction* 101(5): 621–622.

CBN, Central Bureau of Narcotics. 2007. *Licit Cultivation.* Online. Available at http://cbn.nic.in/html/operationscbn.htm. Accessed June 2007.

Centlivres, Pierre, and Micheline Centlivres-Demont. 1998. "Tajikistan and Afghanistan: The Ethnic Groups on Either Side of the Border." In *Tajikistan: The Trials of Independence,* ed. Mohammad-Reza Djalili, Frédéric Grare, and Shirin Akiner. Richmond, Va.: Curzon, pp. 3–13.

——. 2000. "State, National Awareness and Levels of Identity in Afghanistan from Monarchy to Islamic State." *Central Asian Survey* 19: 419–428.

Chandra, Siddharth. 2000. "What the Numbers Really Tell Us about the Decline of the Opium Regie." *Indonesia* 70: 101–123.

Chao, Tzang Yawnghwe. 2005. "Shan State Politics: The Opium-Heroin Factor." In *Trouble in the Triangle: Opium and Conflict in Burma,* ed. Martin Jelsma, Tom Kramer, and Pietje Vervest. Chiang Mai: Silkworm, pp. 23–32.

Charles, Molly. 2001. "The Growth and Activities of Organized Crime in Bombay." *International Social Science Journal* 169: 359–368.

——. 2004. *Drug Trade Dynamics in India.* Report submitted for the project Modeling the World Heroin Market: Assessing the Consequences of Changes in Afghanistan Production. Mumbay. Mimeo. Online. Available at http://laniel.free.fr/INDEXES/PapersIndex/INDIAMOLLY/DRUGSDYNAMICSININDIA.htm. Accessed June 2006.

Charles, Molly, K. S. Nair, and Gabriel Britto. 1999. *Drug Culture in India: A Street Ethnographic Study of Heroin Addiction in Bombay.* New Delhi: Rawat.

Charles, Molly, K. S. Nair, A. A. Das, and Gabriel Britto. 2002. "Bombay Underworld: A Descriptive Account and Its Role in the Drug Trade." In *Globalisation, Drugs and Criminalisation: Final Research Report on Brazil, China, India and Mexico,* ed. Christian Geffray, Guilhem Fabre, and Michel Schiray. Paris: UNESCO, pp. 7–50. CD-ROM ed.

Charras, Igor. 1998. "L'Etat et les "stupéfiants": Archéologie d'une politique publique répressive." *Les cahiers de la sécurité intérieure* 32(deuxième trimestre): 7–28.

Chouvy, Pierre-Arnaud. 2002a. *Les territoires de l'opium: Conflits et trafics du Triangle d'Or et du Croissant d'Or.* Geneva: Olizane.

——. 2002b. "New Drug Trafficking Routes in Southeast Asia." *Jane's Intelligence Review* July 1: 32–34.

——. 2006a. "Afghan Opium: License to Kill." *Asia Times.* February 1. Online. Available at http://www.geopium.org/Chouvy-Asia_Times-1FEB2006-Licensing_ Afghanistans_Opium_Solution_or_Fallacy.html.

——. 2006b. *Le défi afghan de l'Opium.* Paris: Etudes.

CIA, Central Intelligence Agency. 2002. *The World Factbook.* Online. Available at https://www.cia.gov/library/publications/the-world-factbook/. Accessed June 2002.

——. 2006. *The World Factbook.* Online. Available at https://www.cia.gov/library/ publications/the-world-factbook/. Accessed June 2006.

——. 2007. *The World Factbook.* Online. Available at www.cia.gov/library/publications/ the-world-factbook/geos/ti.html. Accessed June 2007.

Clawson, Patrick, and Lee Rensellaer. 1996. *The Andean Cocaine Industry.* New York: St. Martin's Press.

CNP, Colombian National Police. 2004. *Balance de Aspersión de cultivos de amapola, 1994–2003.* January 6. Unpublished report.

Coghlan, Tom. 2004. "Up Close in Al-Qaeda Hunt." BBC News. October 13.

Cokgezen, Murat. 2004. "Corruption in Kyrgyzstan: The Facts, Causes and Consequences." *Central Asian Survey* 23(1): 79–94.

Coll, Steve. 1991. "Pakistan's Illicit Economies Affect BCCI: Bank Shaped by Environment of Corruption and Illegal Trade in Weapons, Drugs." *The Washington Post* September 1: A39.

Colombié, Thierry, Nacer Lalam, and Michel Schiray. 2000. *Drogue et techno: Les trafiquants de rave.* Paris: Stock.

——. 2001. *Les acteurs du grand banditisme français au sein des économies souterraines liées au trafic de drogues: Populations, organisations, practiques, mécanismes de contrôle des marchés et gestion des espaces de trafics régionaux et transfrontaliers.* Paris: IHESI.

Conroy, Mary Schaffer. 1990. "Abuse of Drugs Other Than Alcohol and Tobacco in the Soviet Union." *Soviet Studies* 42(3): 447–480.

Coomber, Ross. 2006. *Pusher Myths: Re-Situating the Drug Dealer.* London: Free Association Books.

Cornell, Syvante E. 2005. "Narcotics, Radicalism and Security in Central Asia: The Islamic Movement of Uzbekistan." *Terrorism and Political Violence,* 17 (4): 619–639.

Corpora, Christopher A. 2004. "The Untouchables: Former Yugoslavia's Clandestine Political Economy." *Problems of Post-Communism* 51(3): 61–68.

Costa, Antonio Maria. 2008. "*Making Drug Control 'Fit for Purpose': Building on the UNGASS Decade*" Statement of the Executive Director of the United Nations Office on Drugs and Crime to the 51st session of the Commission on Narcotic Drugs, Vienna, March 10. Mimeo.

Council of Economic Advisers. 2007. *Economic Report of the President.* Washington, DC: U.S. Government Printing Office, February. Online. Available at http://www. gpoaccess.gov/eop/2007/2007_erp.pdf. Accessed November 2007.

Council of Europe, Parliamentary Assembly, Committee on the Honouring of Obligations and Commitments by Member States of the Council of Europe. 2004.

Honouring of Obligations and Commitments by Albania. Doc. 10116, March 23. Online. Available at http://assembly.coe.int/Documents/WorkingDocs/Doc04/EDOC10116.htm. Accessed July 2004.

Courtwright, David T. 1982. *Dark Paradise: Opiate Addiction in America before 1940.* Cambridge: Harvard University Press.

———. 2001a. *Dark Paradise: A History of Opiate Addiction in America.* Cambridge: Harvard University Press.

———. 2001b. *Forces of Habit: Drugs and the Making of the Modern World.* Cambridge: Harvard University Press.

Courtwright, David, Herman Joseph, and Don Des Jarlais. 1989. *Addicts Who Survived: An Oral History of Narcotic Use in America 1923–1965.* Knoxville: University of Tennessee Press.

Couturier, Kelly. 1996. "Security Forces Allegedly Involved in Turkish Criminal Gang." *The Washington Post* November 27: A24.

———. 1998. "Report Ties Turkey to Assassins: Gunmen Allegedly Targeted Kurds." *The Washington Post* January 24: A17.

Cowell, Adrian. 2005. "Opium Anarchy in the Shan State of Burma." In *Trouble in the Triangle: Opium and Conflict in Burma*, ed. Martin Jelsma, Tom Kramer, and Pietje Vervest. Chiang Mai: Silkworm, pp. 1–22.

Crane, Barry, Rex Rivolo, and Gary Comfort. 1997. *An Empirical Examination of Counterdrug Interdiction Program Effectiveness.* Washington, D.C.: Institute of Defense Analyses.

CTK, Czech News Agency. 2003. "Tough Sentences Given to Foreigners for Smuggling 50 Kg of Heroin." July 11.

———. 2005. "Kosovo Drug Dealers Cooperate with Criminal Scene, Firms-Komorous." November 23.

Cultural Research Bureau. 2001. *Illicit Drug Market in Tehran.* Mimeo.

Dahlkamp, Jürgen, Susanne Köbl, and Georg Muscolo. 2003. "Bundeswher: Poppies, Rocks, Shards of Troubles." *Der Spiegel,* November 10.

DANE, Departamento Administrativo de Estadística, Dirección de Cuentas Nacionales. 2003. *Metodología y cálculo de las cuentas de producción y generación del ingreso para cultivos ilícitos.* Draft report. July. Bogotà: [DANE].

Dasgupta, Debarshi. 2007. "Pop Goes the Seed." *Outlook* June 18.

Davis, Anthony, and Bruce Hawke. 1998. "On the Road to Ruin: Narco-Dollars Lure Burmese Junta toward Heroin Dependency." *Jane's Intelligence Review* March: 26–31.

Day, Carolyn, Louisa Degenhardt, and Wayne Hall. 2006. "Documenting the Heroin Shortage in New South Wales." *Drug and Alcohol Review* 25(4): 297–305.

DCA, Drug Control Agency of Tajikistan. 2000. *The Dushanbe Illegal Drug Market.* Report submitted for the "UNDCP Global Study on Illicit Drug Markets." Mimeo.

———. 2002. *Assessment of the Drug Trafficking Situation in Central Asia.* Report on the results of the project Rapid Assessment of Drug Abuse in Central Asia. Dushanbe: [DCA].

———. 2004. [*Opiate Trade in Tajikistan.*] Report submitted for the project Modeling the World Heroin Market: Assessing the Consequences of Changes in Afghanistan Production. Mimeo. [In Russian].

DCSA. Direzione Centrale per i Servizi Antidroga. 2005. *Relazione Annuale.* Rome: DCSA.

De Angelis, Daniela, Matthew Hickman, and Shuying Yang. 2004. "Estimating Long-Term Trends in the Incidence and Prevalence of Opiate Use/Injecting Drug Use and the Number of Former Users: Back Calculation Methods and Opiate Overdose Deaths." *American Journal of Epidemiology* 160(10): 994–1004.

De Kort, Marcel, and Dirk J. Korf. 1992. "The Development of Drug Trade and Drug Control in The Netherlands: A Historical Perspective." *Crime, Law and Social Change* 17: 123–144.

de Liederkerke, Arnould. 2001. *La Belle Epoque de l'opium*. Paris: Editions de la Différence.

de Ridder, Michael. 2000. *Heroin: Vom Arzneimittel zur Droge*. Frankfurt: Campus.

De Wilde, Roeland. 2003. *Research Summary: The Formal and Informal Institutions of Legal Opium Production: Narcotics Law, Caste and Credit in Southern Rajasthan*. Mimeo.

DEA, Drug Enforcement Administration. 2000. *The Mexican Heroin Trade*. April. Washington, D.C.: Drug Enforcement Administration.

———. 2001. *Opium Poppy Cultivation and Heroin Processing in Southeast Asia*. March, DEA-20026. Washington, D.C.: Drug Enforcement Administration. Reprinted at http://www.shaps.hawaii.edu/drugs/dea20026/dea20026.html.

———. 2002a. *Drug Intelligence Brief: Burma Country Brief*. May. Washington, D.C.: Drug Enforcement Administration.

———. 2002b *Drug Intelligence Brief: India Country Brief*. May. Washington, D.C.: Drug Enforcement Administration.

———. 2002c. The Drug Trade in Colombia: A Threat Assessment. March.

———. 2003a. *Drug Intelligence Brief: Methamphetamine: The Current Threat In East Asia and the Pacific Rim*. September. Washington, D.C.: Drug Enforcement Administration.

———. 2003b. *Mexico: Country Profile for 2003*. November. Washington, D.C.: Drug Enforcement Administration.

———. 2006. *Authorized Sources of Narcotic Raw Materials*. Docket no. DEA-282P, *Federal Register* 71(192): 58569–58571. Online. Available at www.deadiversion.usdoj.gov/fed_regs/rules/2006/fr1004.htm. Accessed June 2007.

Degenhardt, Louisa, Carolyn Day, Wayne Hall, and Dave Bewley-Taylor. 2007. *The Australian 'Heroin Shortage' Six Years On: What, If Any, Are the Policy Implications?* Briefing paper 12. London: Beckley Foundation.

Degenhardt, Louisa, Peter Reuter, Linette Collins, and Wayne Hall. 2005. "Evaluating Factors Responsible for Australia's Heroin Shortage." *Addiction* 100: 459–469.

Der Spiegel. (2005). "Albanien: Eldorado für Heroin und Kokain." *Der Spiegel* July 18: 87.

Desroches, Frederick. 2005. *The Crime That Pays: Drug Trafficking and Organized Crime in Canada*. Toronto: Canadian Scholar's Press.

Dhawan, Anju. 1998. "Traditional Use." In *South Asia Drug Demand Reduction Report*, ed. UNDCP Regional Office for South Asia. New Delhi: UNDCP Regional Office for South Asia, pp. 49–52.

Dikötter, Frank, Lars Laarmann, and Zhou Xun. 2004. *Narcotics Culture: A History of Drugs in China*. Hong Kong: University of Chicago Press.

Dorabjee, Jimmy, and Luke Samson. 2000. "A Multi-Centre Rapid Assessment of Injecting Drug Use in India." *International Journal of Drug Policy* 11: 99–112.

Dorn, Nicholas, Michael Levi, and Leslie King. 2005. *Literature Review on Upper Level Drug Trafficking*. Home Office online report 22/05. Online. Available at http://www.homeoffice.gov.uk/rds/pdfs05/rdsolr2205.pdf. Accessed September 2007.

Dorn, Nicholas, Karim Murji, and Nigel South. 1992. *Traffickers: Drug Markets and Law Enforcement*. London: Routledge.

Dorn, Nicholas, Lutz Oette, and Simone White. 1998. "Drug Importation and the Bifurcation of Risk: Capitalization, Cut Outs and Organized Crime." *British Journal of Criminology* 38(4): 537–560.

Drug Availability Steering Group. 2002. *Drug Availability Estimates in the United States*. Online. Available at www.whitehousedrugpolicy.gov/publicationsavailability/pdf. Accessed October 2007.

Economist, The. 2005. "Kirgizstan: Not a Bed of Tulips." *The Economist* October 8.

Elitzak, Howard. 1999. *Food Cost Review: 1950–97*. Agricultural Economic Report no. (AER780). Washington, DC: Economic Research Service, U.S. Department of Agriculture. Online. Available at http://www.ers.usda.gov/Publications/AER780/. Accessed May 2005.

Embassy of the Republic of Turkey in Washington. DC. n.d. *PKK's Involvement in Drug Trafficking*. Online. Available at www.turkishembassy.org/governmentpolitics/ issueshrpkk.htm. Accessed December 2003.

EMCDDA, European Monitoring Centre on Drugs and Drug Addiction. 2002a. *Annual Report on the State of the Drugs Problem in the European Union and Norway*. Luxembourg: Office for Official Publications of the European Communities. Also online. Available at http://annualreport.emcdda.eu.int. Accessed June 2004.

——. 2002b. *Estimated Number of Problem Drug Users in EU Member States*. Luxembourg: Office for Official Publications of the European Communities. Online. Available at http://annualreport.emcdda.eu.int/pdfs/tab04-en.pdf. Accessed June 2005.

——. 2002c. *Report on the Drug Situation in Candidate CEECs*. Luxembourg: Office for Official Publications of the European Communities. Online. Available at http:// annualreport.emcdda.eu.int. Accessed June 2005.

——. 2006. *Annual Report 2006: The State of the Drugs Problem in Europe*. Luxembourg: Office for Official Publications of the European Communities. Online. Available at http://ar2006.emcdda.europa.eu/download/ar2006-en.pdf. Accessed June 2006.

——. 2007. *Annual Report 2007: The State of the Drugs Problem in Europe*. Luxembourg: Office for Official Publications of the European Communities. Online. Available at http://www.emcdda.europa.eu/html.cfm/index44682EN.html. Accessed March 2008.

Emerson, Tony. 1998. "Burma's Men of Gold." *Newsweek* April 20: 24–30.

Emmanuelli, Julien, and Jean-Claude Desenclos. 2005. "Harm Reduction Interventions, Behaviours and Associated Health Outcomes in France, 1996–2003." *Addiction* 100(11): 1690–1700.

Engvall, Johan. 2005. *Stability and Security in Tajikistan: Drug Trafficking as a Threat to National Security*. East European studies working paper no. 86. Uppsala: Uppsala University, Department of East European Studies.

Escobar Gaviria, Pablo. 2002. *Mi hermano Pablo*. Bogotá: Quintero editores.

European Parliament. 2007. Recommendation to the Council of 25 October 2007 on Production of Opium for Medical Purposes in Afghanistan, 2007/2125(INI). Online. Available at http://www.europarl.europa.eu/meetdocs/2004_2009/documents/re/ p6_ta-prov(2007)0485_/p6_ta-prov(2007)0485_en.pdf. Accessed September 2008.

Europol, 2003. *2003 European Union Organized Crime Report*. Luxembourg: Office for Official Publications of the European Communities.

——. 2004. *2004 European Union Organized Crime Report*. Luxembourg: Office for Official Publications of the European Communities. Also online. Available at http://www.europol.europa.eu/index.asp?page=publications&language=. Accessed October 2005.

———. 2005. *European Union Organized Crime Report*. Luxembourg: Office for Official Publications of the European Communities. Also online. Available at http://www. europol.europa.eu/index.asp?page=publications&language=. Accessed October 2006.

Farrell, Graham, and John Thorne. 2005. "Where Have All the Flowers Gone?: Evaluation of the Taliban Crackdown against Opium Poppy Cultivation in Afghanistan." *International Journal of Drug Policy* 16(2): 81–91.

FATF, Financial Action Task Force on Money Laundering. 2005. *Annual Report 2004–2005*. June 10. Online. Available at http://www.fatf-gafi.org/dataoecd/41/25/34988062. pdf. Accessed June 2006.

Fawthrop, Tom. 2005. "Business As Usual: Wa Drug Lords Dodge US Legal Action." *Irrawaddy Online Edition* April. Online. Available at http://www.irrawaddy.org/ archives.php. Accessed April 2006.

Felbab-Brown, Vanda. 2006. "Kicking the Opium Habit? Afghanistan's Drug Economy and Politics since the 1980s." *Conflict, Security and Development* 6(2): 127–149.

———. 2007a. *Opium Licensing in Afghanistan: Its Desirability and Feasibility*. Policy paper 1. Washington, D.C.: Brookings Institution.

———. 2007b. *The Conundrum of Drugs and Insurgency in Afghanistan*. Lecture given at the conference on Fighting Drugs and Building Peace, Open Society Institute, New York, May 14.

Feldafing Declaration. 2002. Online. Available at www.unodc.un.or.th/ad/feldafing/ paper.htm. Accessed May 2007.

Fijnaut, Cyrille, Frank Bovenkerk, Gerben Bruinsma, and Henk van de Bunt. 1998. *Organized Crime in the Netherlands*. The Hague: Kluwer Law International.

Fijnaut, Cyrille, and Letizia Paoli (ed.). 2004. *Organised Crime in Europe: Concepts, Patterns and Polices in the European Union and Beyond*. Berlin: Springer.

Financial Times Information. 2003b. "Tajik Police Make Record Heroin Seizure." February 19.

Finckenauer, James O., Joseph R. Fuentes, and George L. Ward. 2001. *Mexico and the United States: Neighbors Confront Drug Trafficking*. Online. Available at www.ojp. usdoj.gov/nij/international/trafficking_text.html. Accessed June 2006.

Forero, Juan. 2007a. "Colombian Officials Probe Uribe Allies in His Home State." *The Washington Post* April 16.

———. 2007b. "Traffickers Infiltrate Military in Colombia: Officers Provided Secret Information on U.S. Navy Ships." *The Washington Post* September 8.

Frantz, Douglas. 2002. "A Nation Challenged: Smuggling—Agents Seize Turkey's Largest Haul of Drugs, Said to Be from Afghanistan." *The New York Times* April 2: 12.

Ganguly, K. K., H. K. Sharma, and K. A. V. R. Krishnamachari. 1995. "An Ethnographic Account of Opium Consumers of Rajastan (India): Socio-Medical Perspective." *Addiction* 90(1): 9–12.

Giordano, Christian. 2002. "Balkanische Familienstrukturen und transnationale Migration." *Universitas Friburgensis* March 3: 19–21.

Glatzer, Bernt. 1999. "Is Afghanistan on the Brink of Ethnic and Tribal Disintegration?" In *Fundamentalism Reborn? Afghanistan and the Taliban*, ed. William Maley. London: Hurst, pp.166–181.

Gleason, Gregory. 2001. "Tajikistan Minister's Murder Points to Drug-Route Conflict." *Eurasia Insight* April 16.

Godze, Mert. 2001. "PKK Informant Tells of Gendarmerie Drugs Ring: 'We Transported Heroin in Helicopters.'" *Turkish Daily News* March 28.

Golden, Tim. 2000. "State Under Siege: A Special Report: War on Drugs Fails to Corral Mexican Gang." *The New York Times,* January 10: A1.

Goldstein, Paul J., Henry H. Brownstein, and Patrick J. Ryan. 1992. "Drug-Related Homicide in New York: 1984 and 1988." *Crime and Delinquency* 38(4): 459–476.

Gómez-Céspedes, Alejandra. 1999. "The Federal Law Enforcement Agencies: An Obstacle in the Fight against Organized Crime in Mexico." *Journal of Contemporary Criminal Justice* 15(4): 352–369.

Goodhand, Jonathan. 2005. "Frontiers and Wars: The Opium Economy in Afghanistan." *Journal of Agrarian Change* 5(2): 191–216.

Gooi, Kim. 1986. "Interview/Khun Sa: Just a Freedom Fighter." *Far Eastern Economic Review* February 20: 28–29.

Gossop, Michael, John Marsden, and Duncan Stewart. 1997. "National Treatment Outcome Research Study in the United Kingdom." *Psychology of Addictive Behaviors* 11(4): 324–337.

Goto-Shabata, Harumi. 2002. "The International Opium Conference of 1924–25 and Japan." *Modern Asian Studies* 36(4): 969–991.

Greenfield, Victoria A. 1991. *Bolivian Coca: A Perennial Leaf Crop Subject to Supply Reduction.* Ph.D. diss, University of California at Berkeley.

———. 1997. *Promoting Worker Rights in Developing Countries: U.S. Policies and Their Rationale.* Washington, D.C.: Congressional Budget Office.

Griffin, Michael. 2001. "Taliban's Grim Legacy: More Strife." *Los Angeles Times* December 23: 1.

———. 2003. *Reaping the Whirlwind. Afghanistan, Al Qa'ida and the Holy War.* London: Pluto Press.

Gruppo Abele. 2003. *Synthetic Drugs Trafficking in Three European Cities: Major Trends and the Involvement of Organised Crime.* Turin: Gipiangrafica.

Guevara, Rogelio. 2002. *Statement before House Committee on Government Reform.* December 12. Online. Available at www.usdoj.gov/dea/pubs/cngrtest/ct121202. html. Accessed July 2007.

Hall, Wayne, and Rosalie L. Pacula. 2003. *Cannabis Use and Dependence: Public Health and Public Policy.* Cambridge: Cambridge University Press.

Hammer, Joshua, with Llazar Semini. 2001. "The Gangsters' Paradise." *Newsweek* March 26: 21.

Hansen, Bradley. 2001. "Learning to Tax: The Political Economy of the Opium Trade in Iran, 1921–1941." *Journal of Economic History* 61(1): 95–113.

Haq, Ikramul. 1996. "Pak–Afghan Trade in Historical Perspective." *Asian Survey* 36(19): 945–963.

Harris, Paul. 2001. "Victorious Warlords Set to Open the Opium Floodgates." *Observer* November 25.

Hawke, Bruce. 1998. "Burma's Ceasefire in Danger of Unravelling." *Jane's Intelligence Review* November: 23–27.

———. 2004. "Burmese Banking: The Yangon Laundromat's Burnout Explained." *Irrawaddy* 12(4): 17–21.

HDPC, Human Development Promotion Center. 2002. *Human Development Report Albania 2002: Challenges of Local Governance and Regional Development.* Tirana: HDPC.

Heinzelmann, Steffen. 2006. "Flucht unter Feuerschutz: UN-Mission scheiterte kläglich." *Süddeutsche Zeitung* June 7: 2.

Hermann, Rainer. 2001. "Patronage, Pfruende, Paten: Die Tuerkei ist der orientalischen Despotie naeher als dem europaeischen Rechtsstaat." *Frankfurter Allgemeine Zeitung* January 23: 3.

Hess, Henner. 1973. *Mafia and Mafiosi: The Structure of Power*. Farnborough: Saxon House.

Hobbes, Thomas. [1881] 1968. *Leviathan*. Harmondsworth: Penguin.

Hough, Michael, and Mangai Natarajan (ed.). 2000. *Illegal Drug Markets: From Research to Policy*. Monsey, N.Y.: Criminal Justice Press.

HRW, Human Rights Watch. 2003. "'Killing You Is a Very Easy Thing For Us': Human Rights Abuses in Southeast Afghanistan." *Human Rights Watch Report* 15(5).

Hser, Yih-ing, Valerie Hoffman, Christine E. Grella, and M. Douglas Anglin. 2001. "A 33-Year Follow-up of Narcotics Addicts." *Archives of General Psychiatry* 58: 503–508.

Hughes, P. H., and O. Rieche. 1995. "Heroin Epidemics Revisited." *Epidemiological Reviews* 17(1): 66–73.

Hunt, Leon G., and Carl D. Chambers. 1976. *The Heroin Epidemics: A Study of Heroin Use in the United States, 1965–1975*. New York: Spectrum Books.

Hysi, Vasilika. 2004. "Organized Crime in Albania: The Ugly Side of Capitalism and Democracy." In *Organised Crime in Europe: Concepts, Patterns and Control Policies in the European Union and Beyond*, ed. Cyrille Fijnaut and Letizia Paoli. Dordrecht: Springer, pp. 537–562.

ICG, International Crisis Group. 2001a. *Central Asia: Drugs and Conflict*. ICG Asia report no. 25. November 26.

———. 2001b. *Fault Lines in the New Security Map*. ICG Asia report no. 20. July 4.

———. 2001c. *Tajikistan: An Uncertain Peace*. ICG Asia report no. 30. December 24.

———. 2003a. *Crack in the Marble. Turkmenistan's Failing Dictatorship*. Asia report no. 44. January 17.

———. 2004a. *Myanmar: Update on HIV/AIDS Policy*. Asia briefing. Yangoon/Brussels. December 16.

———. 2004b. *Tajikistan's Politics: Confrontation or Consolidation?* Asia briefing. Dushanbe/Brussels. May 19.

IMF, International Monetary Fund. 1993. *Balance of Payments Manual*. Washington, D.C.: IMF.

———. 2003. *Islamic State of Afghanistan: Rebuilding a Macroeconomic Framework for Reconstruction and Growth*. IMF country report no. 03/299. September. Washington, D.C.: IMF.

INCB, International Narcotics Control Board. 2005. *Narcotic Drugs: Estimated World Requirements for 2005—Statistics for 2003*. New York: United Nations.

———. 2008a. *Narcotic Drugs: Estimated World Requirements for 2008—Statistics for 2006*. New York: United Nations.

———. 2008b. *Report of the International Narcotics Control Board for 2007*. New York: United Nations. Also online. Available at http://www.incb.org/incb/annual_report.html. Accessed September 2008.

Institute of Forensic Sciences, Istanbul University. 2000. *Istanbul, Turkey*. Report submitted for the "UNDCP Global Study on Illicit Drug Markets." Mimeo.

Institute of Public Security, Chinese Ministry of Public Security. 2004. *An Empirical Study of the Heroin Market in China*. Report submitted for the project Modeling the World Heroin Market: Assessing the Consequences of Changes in Afghanistan Production. Beijing. Mimeo.

Institute of War and Peace Reporting 2004. "Tajikistan: Fall of Praetorian Guardsman." *Reporting Central Asia,* no. 306. August 10. Online. Available at http://www.iwpr. net/?p=rca&s=f&o=175176&apc_state=henirca2004. Accessed September 2007.

Inter-American Drug Abuse Control Commission. 2005. *Environmental and Human Health Assessment of the Aerial Spray Program for Coca and Poppy Control in Colombia.* Washington, DC: Organization of American States. Online. Available at www.cicad.oas.org/en/glifosateFinalReport.pdf. Accessed October 2007.

International Opium Commission. 1910. "Report of the International Opium Commission (Excerpts)." *British Medical Journal,* January 8: 93–97.

International Opium Convention. 1912. Signed at The Hague January 23. Online. Available at http://www.tc.columbia.edu/centers/cifas/drugsandsociety/background/ opiumconvention.html. Accessed September 2008.

International Strategic Studies Association. 2004. "Special Report: Report on Albanian Criminal–Terrorist Links Providing Key Intelligence for Olympics Security, 'War on Terror.'" *Defense & Foreign Affairs* XXII(24).

IOM, International Organisation for Migration. 2001. *Deceived Migrants from Tajikistan: A Study in Trafficking in Women and Children.* January.

Iskandarov K. 1998. "Influence of Afghan Crisis on the Situation in Tajikistan" (In Russian). *Centralnaja Asia y Kavkas,* 6.

ITAR-TASS News Agency. 2003 "Value of Heroin Seized Near Moscow Amounts to Five Million USD," 31 July.

Jacobs, Bruce A. 1999. *Dealing Crack: The Social World of Streetcorner Selling.* Boston: Northeastern University Press.

Jelsma, Martin. 2001. *Vicious Circle: The Chemical and Biological War on Drugs.* Amsterdam: TransNational Institute. Online. Available at www.tni.org/archives/ jelsma/viciouscircle-e.pdf. Accessed October 2007.

———. 2005a. "Learning Lessons from the Taliban Opium Ban." *International Journal of Drug Policy* 16(2): 98–103.

———. 2005b. *The UN Drug Control Debate: Current Dilemmas and Prospects for 2008.* Online. Available at www.tni.org/detail_page.phtml?page=archives_jelsma_ budapest. Accessed October 2007.

Jennings, John. 1997. *The Opium Empire: Japanese Imperialism and Drug Trafficking in Asia, 1895–1945.* Westport, Conn.: Praeger.

Jiménez-Lerma Juan Manuel, Miguel Landabaso, Loseba Iraurgi, Ricardo Calle, Juan Sanz, Miguel Gutiérrez-Fraile. 2002. "Nimodipine in Opiate Detoxification: A Controlled Trial." *Addiction* 97(7): 819–824.

Johnson, Bruce. 1975. "Understanding British Addiction Statistics." *UN Bulletin on Narcotics* 27(1): 49–66.

———. 2008. "The 'Flexible' Response of Cannabis Markets to Enforcement/Interdiction Policy: An International Review of Market Transformations and Elasticities." Paper presented at the Second Annual Conference of the International Society for the Study of Drug Policy. Lisbon, 4 April.

Johnson, Bruce D., Paul J. Goldstein, Edward Preble, James Schmeidler, Douglas S. Lipton, Barry Spunt, and Thomas Miller. 1985. *Taking Care of Business: The Economics of Crime by Heroin Abusers.* Lexington: Lexington Books.

Joint Kokang-Wa Humanitarian Need Assessment Team. 2003. *Replacing Opium in Kokang and Wa Special Regions, Shan State, Myanmar.* Online. Available at www.unodc.org/pdf/myanmar/replacing_opium_kogang_wa_regions.pdf. Accessed October 2007.

Jordan, Mary. 2004. "The Bribes That Bind Mexico—and Hold It Back." *The Washington Post* April 18: B01.

Kale, Prashan, Singh, Harbir, Perlmutter, Howard. 2000. "Learning and Protection of Proprietary Assets in Strategic Alliances: Building Relational Capital." *Strategic Management Journal* 21(3): 217–237.

Kamm, Henry. 1971. "Asians Doubt that U.S. Can Halt Heroin Flow." *The New York Times*, 11 August: 1.

Kamminga, Jorrit and Peter van Ham. 2006. "How to Beat the Opium Economy." *International Herald Tribune*, 1 December: 6.

Kaplan, David, and Alec Dubro. 2003. *Yakuza: Japan's Criminal Underworld*. Berkeley: University of California Press.

Katz, Michael L., and Harvey S. Rosen. 1994. *Microeconomics*, 2nd ed. Burr Ridge, Ill.: Irwin.

Kessler, Robert E. 1995. "Throwback to Gunga Din Days." *Newsday* December 19: A25.

Khamonov, Igor. 2005. *Opiate Trade in Tajikistan*. Report submitted for the project Modeling the World Heroin Market: Assessing the Consequences of Changes in Afghanistan Production. Mimeo.

Khan, Ahmed A. 2004. *Opiate Trade in Pakistan*. Report submitted for the project Modeling the World Heroin Market: Assessing the Consequences of Changes in Afghanistan Production. Mimeo.

Khan, Ahmed A., Syed S. H. Shah, Amir Z. Asad, S. Amjad, and S. Shahzad, 2000. *The Illicit Drug Market in Peshawar*. Report submitted for the "UNDCP Global Study on Illicit Drug Markets." Mimeo.

Khattak, Iqbal. 2003. *Increase in Poppy Cultivation in Pakistan in 2003*. June. Mimeo.

Kinzer, Stephen. 1998. "Turkish Inquiry Links Government Agents to Assassinations." *The New York Times* January 26: A3.

Kinzig, Jörg. 2004. *Die rechtliche Bewältigung von Erscheinungsformen organisierter Kriminalität*. Berlin: Duncker and Humblot.

Kleemans, Edward R., M. E. I. Brienen, Henk G. van de Bunt. 2002. *Georganiseerde criminaliteit in Nederland: Tweede rapportage op basis van de WODC-monitor* [Organized Crime in the Netherlands: Second Report Based upon the WODC-Monitor]. The Hague: WODC.

Kleemans, Edward R., E. A. I. M. van den Berg, Henk G. van de Bunt. 1998. *Georganiseerde criminaliteit in Nederland: Rapportage op basis van de WODC-monitor* [Organized Crime in the Netherlands: Report Based upon the WODC Monitor]. The Hague: WODC.

KLPD, Korps Landelijke Politiediensten [Netherlands Police Agency]. 2006. *Heroin: Subreport Crime Pattern Analysis 2005*. Driebergen: Korps Landelijke Politiediensten.

Klerks, Peter P. 2000. *Groot in de hasj: Theorie en praktijk van de georganiseerde criminaliteit* [Big in Hashish. Theory and Practice of Organized Crime] Antwerp: Kluwer Rechtswetenschappen.

Knox, Kathleen. 2004. "Tajikistan: Heroin Busts Tie Russian Military to Drug Trade." *Eurasia Insight* July 5.

Korf, Dirk, and Hans Verbraek. 1993. *Dealers and Dienders*. Amsterdam: Criminologisch Instituut Bonger.

Kozel, Nicholas J., and Edgar H. Adams. 1986. "Epidemiology of Drug Abuse: An Overview." *Science* 234(4779): 970–974.

Kramer, Heinz. 2000. *A Changing Turkey: The Challenge to Europe and the United States.* Washington, D.C.: Brookings Institution.

Kramer, Tom. 2005. "Ethnic Conflict and Dilemma for International Engagement." In *Trouble in the Triangle: Opium and Conflict in Burma,* ed. Martin Jelsma, Tom Kramer, and Pietje Vervest. Chiang Mai: Silkworm, pp. 33–60.

———. 2007. *The United Wa State Party: Narco-Army or Ethnic Nationalist Party?* Washington, DC: East-West Center Washington.

KT-NON, Kernteam Noord- en Oost-Nederland. 2002. *General Crime Pattern Analysis Turkey, 2000–2001.* Zwolle: Kernteam NON.

Kumar, Arun. 2002. *The Black Economy in India.* New Delhi: Penguin.

Laber, Jeri, and Barnett Rubin. 1988. *"A Nation Is Dying:" Afghanistan under the Soviets 1979–87.* Evanston, Ill.: Northwestern University Press.

Lalam, Nacer. 2004. *The French Heroin Market.* Report submitted for the project Modeling the World Heroin Market: Assessing the Consequences of Changes in Afghanistan Production. Paris. Mimeo.

Lamour, Catherine, and Michel R. Lamberti (pseud.). 1974. *The Second Opium War.* London: Allen Lane.

Landesco, John. [1929] 1968. *Illinois Crime Survey 1929: Part III.* [Reprinted as *Organized Crime in Chicago.*] Chicago: University of Chicago Press.

Lintner, Bertil. 1992. "Heroin and Highland Insurgency in the Golden Triangle." In *War on Drugs: Studies in the Failure of U.S. Narcotics Policy,* ed. Alfred McCoy and Alan A. Block. Boulder, Colo.: Westview Press, pp. 281–317.

———. 2000. *The Golden Triangle Opium Trade: An Overview.* March. Online. Available at www.asiapacificms.com/papers/pdf/gt_opium_trade.pdf. Accessed October 2007.

———. 2001. "Afghanistan Taliban Turns to Drugs." *Far Eastern Economic Review* October 11.

———. 2002. *Blood Brothers: The Criminal Underworld of Asia.* New York: Palgrave.

Liu, Melinda. 1989. "Burma's 'Money Tree.'" *Newsweek* May 15: 42–49.

Lowes, Peter D. 1966. *The Genesis of International Narcotics Control.* Geneva: Droz.

Lupsha, Peter A. 1992. "Drugs Lords and Narco-Corruption: The Players Change But the Game Continues." In *War on Drugs: Studies in the Failure of U.S. Narcotics Policy,* ed. Alfred W. McCoy and Alan A. Block. Boulder, Colo.: Westview, 177–196.

MacCallum, Elizabeth P. 1928. *Twenty Years of Persian Opium (1908–1928).* Opium Research Committee of the Foreign Policy Association. Reprinted in *Narcotic Addiction and American Foreign Policy,* ed. Grob Gerland. New York: Arno Press.

MacCoun, Robert J., and Peter Reuter. 2001. *Drug War Heresies: Learning from Other Vices, Times, and Places.* New York: Cambridge University Press.

Macdonald, David. 2005. "Blooming Flowers and False Prophets: The Dynamics of Opium Cultivation and Production in Afghanistan under the Taliban." *International Journal of Drug Policy* 16(2): 93–97.

Machmadiev, Haidar. 2003. "Die Agentur für Drogenkontrolle beim Präsident der Republik Tadschikistan." *Kriminalistk* 11: 662–664.

Madi, Maral. 2004. "Drug Trade in Kyrgyzstan: Structure, Implications and Countermeasures." *Central Asian Survey* 23(3–4): 249–273.

Mai, Nicola, and Stephanie Schander-Sievers. 2003. "Albanian Migration and New Transnationalisms." *Journal of Ethnic and Migration Studies* 29(6): 939–949.

Maingot, Anthony P. 2002. *Studying Corruption in Colombia.* Institute for National Strategic Studies of the National Defense University. Online. Available at www.ndu.edu/inss/books/books%20-%201999/Crisis%20What%20Crisis%20Eng%20 0ct%2099/cris7.html. Accessed July 2007.

Maitra, Ramtanu. 2005. "Follow the Drugs: US Shown the Way." *Asian Times* October 27.

Major Donors Mission. 2001. *The Impact of the Taliban Prohibition on Opium Poppy Cultivation in Afghanistan,* A mission report presented to the Major Donors countries of UNDCP, 25 May. Online. Available at http://www.davidmansfield.org/ all.php. Accessed June 2006.

Maley, William (ed.). 1998. *Fundamentalism Reborn? Afghanistan and the Taliban.* London: Hurst.

———. 2002. *The Afghanistan Wars.* New York: Palgrave.

Manayev, Kanai. 2000. "Narcotic Flood Threatens to Wash Away Central Asian Stability." *Times of Central Asia* December 30. Online. Available at www.mapinc. org/drugnews/v00/n1942/a07.html. Accessed October 2007.

Manderson, Desmond. 1987. *Proscription and Prescription: Commonwealth Government Opiate Policy 1905–1937.* National Campaign Against Drug Abuse, monograph series no. 2. Canberra: Australian Government Publishing Office.

Mansfield, David. 1999. "Alternative Development: The Modern Thrust of Supply Side Policy." *United Nations Bulletin on Narcotics* LI (1–2): 19–44.

———. 2001a. *An Analysis of Licit Opium Poppy Cultivation: India and Turkey.* Online. Available at http://www.davidmansfield.org/all.php. Accessed November 2006.

———. 2001b. *The Displacement of Opium Poppy Cultivation: A Shift in the Regional Threat?* Paper for the U.K. Foreign and Commonwealth Office Department of Drugs and International Crime. September. Online. Available at http://www. davidmansfield.org/all.php. Accessed November 2006.

———. 2002. *The Economic Superiority of Illicit Drug Production: Myth and Reality.* Paper presented at the International Conference on the Role of Alternative Development in Drug Control and Development Cooperation. January 7–12. Online. Available at http://www.davidmansfield.org/all.php. Accessed November 2006.

———. 2004a. *Coping Strategies, Accumulated Wealth and Shifting Markets: The Story of Opium Poppy Cultivation in Badakhshan 2000–2003.* Report prepared for the Aga Khan Development Network. Online. Available at http://www.davidmansfield.org/ all.php. Accessed November 2006.

———. 2004b. *What Is Driving Opium Poppy Cultivation? Decision Making Amongst Opium Poppy Cultivators in Afghanistan in the 2003/4 Growing Season.* Paper presented at the UNODC/ONDCP Second Technical Conference on Drug Control Research, July 19–21. Online. Available at http://www.davidmansfield.org/all.php. Accessed November 2006.

———. 2006. "Responding to the Challenge of Diversity in Opium Poppy Cultivation in Afghanistan." In *Afghanistan's Drug Industry: Structure, Functioning, Dynamics and Implications for Counter-Narcotics Policy,* ed. Doris Buddenberg and William A. Byrd. New York: UNODC and World Bank, pp. 47–76.

Mansfield, David, and Chris Martin. 2000. *Strategic Review: The Role of Central Asia as a Conduit for Illicit Drugs to Western Europe.* April. Mimeo.

Manski, Charles, John Pepper, and Carol Petrie. 2001. *Informing America's Drug Policy: What We Don't Know Can Hurt Us.* Washington, D.C.: National Academy Press.

Manski, Charles, John Pepper, and Yonette Thomas. 1999. *An Assessment of Two Cost-Effectiveness Studies of Cocaine Control Policy*. Washington, D.C.: National Academy Press.

Marat, Erica. 2006. "Impact of Drug Trade and Organized Crime on State Functioning in Kyrgyzstan and Tajikistan." *The China and Eurasia Forum Quarterly* 4(1): 93–112.

Martínez-Muñoz, Luis R. 2004. *Instrumentos de ordenamiento territorial y urbano*. Bogotá: Universidad Nacional de Colombia.

Matrix. 2007. *The Illicit Drug Trade in the United Kingdom*. Home Office Online Report 20/07. Online. Available at http://www.homeoffice.gov.uk/rds/pdfs07/rdsolr2007. pdf. Accessed February 2008.

Maung, Maung Oo. 2001. "Above It All." *Irrawaddy* 9(29): 10–11.

McAllister, William. 2000. *Drug Diplomacy in the Twentieth Century*. London: Routledge.

McCoy, Alfred W. 1991. *The Politics of Heroin: CIA Complicity in the Global Drug Trade*. Brooklyn, N.Y.: Lawrence Hill Books.

——. 1999. "Lord of Drug Lords: One Life as Lesson for U.S. Drug Policy." *Crime, Law and Social Change*: 30 (4): 301–331.

——. 2003. *The Politics of Heroin: CIA Complicity in the Global Drug Trade, Afghanistan, Southeast Asia, Central America, Colombia*. 2nd rev. ed. Chicago: Lawrence Hill Books.

McDermott, Roger N. 2002. *Border Security in Tajikistan: Countering the Narcotics Trade?* Conflict Studies Research Centre. K36. Online. Available at www.defac.ac.uk/colleges/csrc/document-listings/ca/ K36. Accessed November 2005.

McGuire, Nancy. 2002. *Combating Coca in Bolivia and Colombia: A New Perspective on the Forces that Drive Peasant Coca Farming*. Unpublished paper prepared for the Council for Emerging National Security Affairs. Online. Available at www.censa.net/publications/GT/Nancy_MG/Coca.pdf. Accessed July 2007.

Meyer, Kathryn, and Terry Parssinen. 1998. *Webs of Smoke: Smugglers, Warlords, Spies and the History of the International Drug Trade*. Lanham: Rowman and Littlefield.

Miller, Christian. 2002. "Rebels Push Colombia toward Anarchy." *Los Angeles Times* June 29: 1–1.

Milsom, Jeremy. 2005. "The Long Hard Road out of Drugs: The Case of the Wa." In *Trouble in the Triangle: Opium and Conflict in Burma*, ed. Martin Jelsma, Tom Kramer, and Pietje Vervest. Chiang Mai: Silkworm, pp. 61–94.

Ministerio del Interior y de Justicia, DNE. 2002. *La Lucha de Colombia contra las drogas ilícitas: Acciones y Resultados*. Bogotá: Ministerio del Interior y de Justicia.

Moore, Mark H. 1974. *The Effective Regulation of an Illicit Market in Heroin*. Lexington, Mass.: Lexington Books

Moreau, Ron, and Sami Yousafzai. 2003. *Afghanistan: A Deadly Habit*. Newsweek, 23 July. Online edition. Available at http://www.newsweek.com/id/57799?tid=relatedcl. Accessed October 2008.

Moskovskii komsomolets. 2000. ["Child Obliged to Swallow Heroin with Tea."] *Moskovskii komsomolets* July 27. [In Russian.]

Mudambi, Ram, and Chris Paul. 2003. "Domestic Drug Prohibition as a Source of Foreign Institutional Instability: An Analysis of the Multinational Extralegal Enterprises." *Journal of International Management*, 9 (3): 335–349.

Muench, Peter. 2004. "Wo die Panzer parken hinterm Hindukusch." *Süddeutsche Zeitung* October 1: 3.

Musto, David F. 1987. *The American Disease: Origins of Narcotics Control*. New York: Oxford University Press.

MVD, Ministry of the Interior of the Russian Federation. 2000. [*Drug Control and Crime Prevention in the Russian Federation: Organised Crime and Illicit Drug Trafficking in the Russian Federation*.] Moscow: Ministry of the Interior of the Russian Federation. [In Russian.]

National Drug Monitor. 2003. *Drug Situation in the Netherlands*. National report. Lisbon: European Monitoring Center on Drugs and Drug Abuse.

Naqvi, Zareen F. 1999. *Afghanistan–Pakistan Trade Relations*. Islamabad: World Bank.

Nazarov, Nustam. 2005. "Statement." In *First Task Force Coordination Meeting: Minutes, 2005*. Dushanbe, January 19.

NCB, Narcotics Control Bureau, India. 2001. *Annual Report 2000–2001*. Delhi: Narcotics Control Bureau.

——. 2002. *Annual Report 2001–2002*. Delhi: Narcotics Control Bureau.

——. 2003. *Narcotics Annual Report 2002*. Delhi: Narcotics Control Bureau.

——. 2004. *Narcotics Annual Report 2003*. Delhi: Narcotics Control Bureau.

NCIS, National Criminal Intelligence Service. 2005. *UK Threat Assessment: The Threat from Serious and Organised Crime 2004/05—2005/06*. London: NCIS.

Nepram, Binalakshmi. 2002. *South Asia's Fractured Frontier: Armed Conflict, Narcotics and Small Arms Proliferation in India's North East*. New Delhi: Mittal.

Nett, Jachen C. 2006. *Repression und Verhaltensanpassung in lokalen Heroin- und Kokainmärkten*. Bern: Haupt.

Newman, R. K. 1989. "India and the Anglo-Chinese Opium Agreements, 1907–1914." *Modern Asian Studies* 23: 525–560.

——. 1995. "Opium Smoking in Late Imperial China." *Modern Asian Studies* 29: 765–794.

Niazi, Tarique. 2006a. "Pakistan's Peace Deal with Taliban Militants." *Terrorism Monitor* 4(19): 4–7. Also online. Available at www.jamestown.org/terrorism/news/article.php?articleid=2370153. Accessed May 2007.

——. 2006b. "The Geostrategic Implications of the Baloch Insurgency." *Terrorism Monitor* 4(22): 8–11. Also online. Available at www.jamestown.org/terrorism/news/article.php?articleid=2370209. Accessed May 2007.

NNICC, National Narcotics Intelligence Consumers Committee. 1997. *The Supply of Illicit Drugs to the United States 1996*. Washington, D.C.: National Narcotics Intelligence Consumers Committee.

Nordland, Rod, with Juliette Terzieff, Roy Gutman, John Barry, Jasmina Mironski, and Zoran Cirjakovic. 2001. "Fire in the Mountains." *Newsweek* March 26. Online. Available at http://www.newsweek.com/id/80226. Accessed September 2004.

Nordt, Carlos, and Rudolf Stohler. 2006. "Incidence of Heroin Use in Zurich, Switzerland: A Treatment Case Register Analysis." *The Lancet* 367(9525): 1830–1834.

Nourzhanov, Kirill. 2005. "Saviours of the Nation or Robber Barons? Warlord Politics in Tajikistan." *Central Asian Survey* 24(2): 109–130.

Observatorio Español sobre Drogas. 2005. *Informe 2004: Situación y tendencias de los problemas de drogas en Espana*. Madrid: OED. Also online. Available at www.pnsd.msc.es/Categoria2/publica/pdf/oed-2004.pdf. Accessed October 2007.

OECD, Organization for Economic Co-operation and Development, et al. 2002. *Measuring the Non-Observed Economy: A Handbook*. Paris: OECD.

Office of Applied Studies. 2005. *National Survey on Drug Use and Health*. Online. Available at www.oas.samhsa.gov/NSDUH/2k4nsduh/2k4tabs/Sect4peTabs1t015. pdf. Accessed September 2007.

Olcott, Martha B., and Natalia Udalova. 2000. *Drug Trafficking on the Great Silk Route: The Security Environment in Central Asia*. Working paper no. 11. Washington, D.C.: Carnegie Endowment for International Peace.

Olsson, Börje, Caroline Adamsson-Wahren, and Siv Byqvist. 2001. *Det tunga narkotikamissbrukets omfattning i Sverige 1998*. MAX-projektet: delrapport 3, entralförbundet för alkohol- och narkotikaupplysning. Stockholm: CAN.

ONDCP, Office of National Drug Control Policy. 1994. *Heroin Users in New York, Chicago, and San Diego*. Washington, D.C.: ONDCP.

———. 1999. *What America's Users Spend on Illegal Drugs, 1988–1998*. Washington, D.C.: ONDCP.

———. 2001. *What America's Users Spend on Illegal Drugs, 1988–2000*. Washington, D.C.: ONDCP. Prepared for ONDCP, Office of Programs, Budget, Research and Evaluation under HHS contract no. 282–98–0006 by ABT Associates, Inc of Cambridge, Mass. Online. Available at www.whitehousedrugpolicy.gov/publications/pdf/american_ users_spend_2002.pdf. Accessed June 2003.

———. 2004. *The Price and Purity of Illicit Drugs: 1981 through the Second Quarter of 2003*. Washington, D.C.: Executive Office of the President.

———. 2007. *Current State of Drug Policy: Successes and Challenges*. Washington, D.C.: The White House.

Osmonaliev, Kairat. 2005. *Developing Counter-Narcotics Policy in Central Asia: Legal and Political Dimensions*. Silk Road paper. January. Online. Available at http://www. silkroadstudies.org/Silkroadpapers/Osmonaliev.pdf. Accessed September 2007.

Ovenden, Claudia, Wendy Loxley, and C. Mcdonald. 1995. *The West Australian Drug Market: Descriptions from Convicted Drug Dealers, 1992*. Perth: National Centre for Research into the Prevention of Drug Abuse, Curtin University of Technology.

Owen, David. 1934. *British Opium Policy in China and India*. New Haven, Conn.: Yale University Press.

Pain, Adam. 2006. "Opium Trading Systems in Helmand and Ghor Provinces." In *Afghanistan's Drug Industry: Structure, Functioning, Dynamics and Implications for Counter-Narcotics Policy*, ed. Doris Buddenberg and William A. Byrd. New York: UNODC and World Bank, pp. 77–116.

Pakyntein, Shri. 1958. "Opium Production Campaign in Assam 1." *United Nations Bulletin on Narcotics* 10(3): 12–14.

Paoli, Letizia. 2000. *Pilot Project to Describe and Analyse Local Drug Markets—First Phase Final Report: Illegal Drug Markets in Frankfurt and Milan*. Lisbon: EMCDDA.

———. 2001. *Illegal Drug Trade in Russia. Project commissioned by the United Nations Office for Drug Control and Crime Prevention*. Freiburg: Edition iuscrim.

———. 2002. "The Paradoxes of Organized Crime." *Crime, Law and Social Change* 37(1): 51–97.

———. 2003a. "The Invisible Hand of the Market: The Illegal Drugs Trade in Germany, Italy, and Russia." In *Criminal Finances and Organising Crime in Europe*, ed. Petrus C. van Duyne, Klaus van Lampe, and James L. Newell. Nijmegen: Wolf, pp. 19–40.

———. 2003b. *Mafia Brotherhoods. Organized Crime, Italian Style*. New York: Oxford University Press.

———. 2004. "The Illegal Drugs Market." *Journal of Modern Italian Studies* 9(2): 188–208.

Paoli, Letizia 2005. "The Ugly Side of Capitalism and Democracy: The Development of the Illegal Drug Market in Post-Soviet Russia." In *Ruling Russia: Crime, Law and Justice in Post-Soviet Russia*, ed. William A. Pridemore. Lanham, Md.: Rowman and Littlefield, pp. 183–202.

——. In press. "The Frankfurt Drug Market." In *Illegal Drug Markets in Four European Cities: A Comparison of Patterns and Policies*, ed. Letizia Paoli. Berlin: Duncker and Humblot.

Paoli, Letizia, and Cyrille Fijnaut. 2004a. "Comparative Synthesis of Part II." In *Organised Crime in Europe: Concepts, Patterns and Policies in the European Union and Beyond*, ed. Cyrille Fijnaut and Letizia Paoli. Dordrecht: Springer, pp. 603–623.

——. 2004b. "Introduction to Part I: The History of the Concept." In *Organised Crime in Europe: Concepts, Patterns and Policies in the European Union and Beyond*, ed. Cyrille Fijnaut and Letizia Paoli. Dordrecht: Springer, pp. 21–46.

Paoli, Letizia, and Peter Reuter. 2007. "Drug Trafficking and Ethnic Minorities in Western Europe." *European Journal of Criminology*, 5: 13–37.

Parker, Howard, Catherine Bury, Roy Egginton. 1998. *New Heroin Outbreaks Among Young People in England and Wales* Crime Detection and Prevention Series #92. London: Home Office. Also online. Available at http://www.homeoffice.gov.uk/rds/prgpdfs/fcdps92.pdf. Accessed September 2005.

Parsinnen, Terry. 1983. *Secret Passions, Secret Remedies: Narcotic Drugs in British Society, 1820–1930*. Philadelphia: Institute for Studies in Human Issues.

Pasotti, Marc. 1997. *Joint UNDCP/CICP Mission to Tajikistan: Rapport Provisoire.* November. Mimeo.

Peak, Maitland J. "Aaron." 2001. *Summary: Fact Finding Mission to Kazakhstan.* Open Society Institute, 2001. Online. Available at www.eurasianet.org/policy_forum/epf030101.shtml. Accessed October 2007.

Pearson, Geoffrey, and Dick Hobbs. 2001. *Middle Market Drug Distribution.* London: Home Office Research, Development and Statistics Directorate.

Perez-Gomez, Augusto. 2005. *Drug Consumption in Colombia, 1992–2003.* Unpublished paper.

Perras, Arne. 2006. "Für die einen Engel, für die anderen Teufel: Während die USA über die Islamisten geschockt sind, erhoffen sich viele Somalis von ihnen Frieden." *Süddeutsche Zeitung* June 7: 2.

Pimentel, Stanley. 2003. "Mexico's Legacy of Corruption." In *Menace to Society: Political Criminal Collaboration around the World*, ed. Roy Godson. New Brunswick: Transaction, pp. 175–197.

Pindyck, Robert S., and Daniel L. Rubinfeld. 2005. *Microeconomics*, 6th ed. Upper Saddle River, N.J.: Prentice Hall.

Ponce, Robert. 2002. *Rising Heroin Abuse in Central Asia Raises Threat of Public Health Crisis.* Online. Available at www.eurasianet.org/departments/insight/articles/eav032902a.shtml. Accessed October 2007.

Preble, Edward, and John J. Casey. 1969. "Taking Care of Business: The Heroin User's Life on the Street." *International Journal of the Addiction* 4: 1–24.

Pugh, Michael. 2004. "Rubbing Salt into War Wounds: Shadow Economies and Peacebuilding in Bosnia and Kosovo." *Problems of Post-Communism* 51(03): 53–60.

Pütter, Norbert. 1998. *Der OK-Komplex: Organisierte Kriminalität und ihre Folgen für die Polizei in Deutschland.* Münster: Westfälisches Dampfboot.

Radji, A. H. 1959. "Opium Control in Iran: A New Regime." *Bulletin on Narcotics* 11(1): 1–2.

Raisdana, Fariborz. 2004. *The Opiate Trade in Iran*. Report submitted for the project Modeling the World Heroin Market: Assessing the Consequences of Changes in Afghanistan Production. Tehran. Mimeo.

Raisdana, Fariborz, with the cooperation of Ahmad Gharavi Nakhjavani. 2002. "The Drug Market in Iran." *Annals of the American Academy of Social and Political Sciences* July: 149–166.

Ramirez, Maria Costanza. 1993. "El Cultivo de la Amapola en Colombia." Paper presented at the International Technical Seminar on Illicit Poppy Cultivation in Latin America, United Nations Drug Control Program, Bogota, May.

Ramírez, María Clemencia. 2001. *Entre el Estado y la guerrilla: Identidad yciudadanía en el movimiento de los camerinos cocaleros del Putumayo*. Bogotá: Instituto Colombiano de Antropología e Historia.

Rashid, Ahmed. 2001. *Taliban: The Story of Afghan Warlords*. New Haven, Conn.: Yale University Press.

Rebscher, Erich, and Werner Vahlenkamp. 1988. *Organisierte Kriminalität in der Bundesrepublik Deutschland: Bestandsaufnahme, Entwicklungstendenzen und Bekämpfung aus der Sicht der Polizeipraxis*. Wiesbaden: Bundeskriminalamt.

Rehm, Jurgen, Patrick Gshwend, Thomas Steffen, Felix Gutzwiller, Anja Dobler-Mikola, and Ambros Uchtenhagen. 2001. "Feasibility, Safety, and Efficacy of Injectable Heroin Prescription for Refractory Opioid Addicts: A Follow-up Study." *The Lancet* 358(9291): 1417–1423.

Reid, Gary, and Genevieve Costigan. 2002. *Revisiting "The Hidden Epidemic": A Situation Assessment of Drug Use in Asia in the Context of HIV/AIDS*. Fairfield: The Centre for Harm Reduction, The Burnet Institute, Australia.

REITOX (Germany). 2003. *Report to the EMCDDA by the REITOX National Focal Point: German Drug Situation 2002* Online. Available at http://www.emcdda.europa.eu/html.cfm/index34309EN.html. Accessed October 2008.

REITOX (Sweden). 2005. *2005 National Report to the EMCDDA by the REITOX National Focal Point*. Lisbon: Sweden EMCDDA.

Renard, Roland D. 1996. *The Burmese Connection: Illegal Drugs and the Making of the Golden Triangle*. Boulder, Colo.: Lynne Rienner.

———. 2001. *Opium Reduction in Thailand 1970–2000. A Thirty-Year Journey*. Bangkok: United Nations International Drug Control Programme Regional Centre for East Asia and the Pacific.

Reuter, Peter. 1983. *Disorganized Crime: The Economics of the Visible Hand*. Cambridge, Mass.: MIT Press.

———. 1985. *The Organization of Illegal Markets: An Economic Analysis*. Washington, D.C.: National Institute of Justice.

———. 1995. "The Decline of the American Mafia." *Public Interest* 120(Summer): 89–99.

———. 1998. "Book Review: World Drug Report." *Journal of Policy Analysis and Management* 17(4): 730–734.

———. 1999. "Drug Use Measures: What Are They Really Telling Us?" *National Institute of Justice Journal* April: 12–19.

———. 2006. Drug Control in Bolivia. School of Public Policy, University of Maryland. Mimeo.

Reuter, Peter and Jonathan P. Caulkins. 2004. "Illegal Lemons: Price Dispersion in the Cocaine and Heroin Markets." *UN Bulletin on Narcotics* LVI: 141–165.

Reuter, Peter, Gordon Crawford, and Jonathan Cave. 1988. *Sealing the Borders*. Santa Monica, Calif.: RAND.

Reuter, Peter, and Victoria Greenfield. 2001. "Measuring Global Drug Markets: How Good Are the Numbers and Why Should We Care about Them?" *World Economics* 2(4): 159–173.

Reuter, Peter, and John Haaga. 1989. *The Organization of High-Level Drug Markets: An Exploratory Study*. Santa Monica, Calif.: RAND.

Reuter, Peter, and Mark A. Kleiman. 1986. "Risks and Prices: An Economic Analysis of Drug Enforcement." In *Crime and Justice: An Annual Review of Research*, vol. 7, ed. Norval Morris and Michael Tonry. Chicago: University of Chicago Press.

Reuter, Peter, Robert MacCoun, and Patrick Murphy. 1990. *Money from Crime: A Study of the Economics of Drug Dealing in Washington, DC*. Santa Monica, Calif.: RAND.

Reuter, Peter, Emil Pain, with Victoria Greenfield. 2003. *The Effects of Drug Trafficking on Central Asia*. Mimeo.

Reuter, Peter, and Harold Pollack. 2006. "How Much Can Treatment Reduce National Drug Problems?" *Addiction* 101: 341–347.

Reuter, Peter, and David Ronfeldt. 1992. "Quest for Integrity. The Mexican–US Drug Issue in the 1980s." *Journal of Interamerican Studies and World Affairs* 24(3): 89–153.

Revista Semana. 1997. "Memorando Confidencial." *Revista Semana* no. 798. September 15.

RFE/RL, Radio Free Europe/Radio Liberty Transcaucasia and Central Asia Newsline. 2003. *Number of Tajik Workers Dying in Russia Is Reported to Be Rising*. July 22.

Richards, John F. 2002. "Opium and the British Indian Empire: The Royal Commission of 1895." *Modern Asian Studies* 36(May): 375–420.

Riley, K. Jack. 1996. *Snow Job: The War against International Cocaine Trafficking*. New Brunswick, N.J.: Transaction Publishers.

Risen, James. 2006. *State of War: The Secret History of the CIA and the Bush Administration*. New York: Free Press.

Robins, Philip. 2008. "Back from the Brink: Turkey's Ambivalent Approaches to the Hard Drugs Issue." *The Middle East Journal* (Fall): Forthcoming.

Roig-Franzia, Manuel. 2006. "In Mexican Drug War, a Desperate Measure: Limited Legalization Sharpens Focus on Traffickers Rather Than Users." *The Washington Post* April 30: A12.

Rossijskaja Gaseta. 2001. ["Tajik Attempts to Smuggle Heroin Apples into Russia."] *Rossijskaja Gaseta* August 2. In Russian.

Roston, Aram. 2002. "Central Asia's Heroin Problem." *The Nation* March 25.

Royce, Knut. 1993. "Country Run on Drugs: CIA Report Says Heroin Is Pakistan's 'Lifeblood.'" *Newsday* February 23: 6.

Rubin, Barnett R. 2000. "The Political Economy of War and Peace in Afghanistan." *World Development* 28(10): 1789–1803.

———. 2003. *The Fragmentation of Afghanistan: State Formation and Collapse in the International System*. Karachi: Oxford University Press.

———. 2004. *Road to Ruin: Afghanistan's Booming Opium Industry*. New York/ Washington, D.C.: Center on International Cooperation, Center for American Progress.

Rubin, Barnett R. and Jake Sherman. *Counter-Narcotics to Stabilize Afghanistan: The False Promise of Crop Eradication*. New York: Centre on International

Cooperation. February. Online. Available at http://www.cic.nyu.edu/afghanistan/docs/counternarcoticsfinal.pdf. Accessed April 2008.

Ruggiero, Vincenzo. 1992. *La roba: Economie e culture dell'eroina*. Parma: Pratiche editrice.

——. 2000. *Criminal Franchising: Albanian and Illicit Drugs in Italy*. Monsey: Criminal Justice Press.

Ruggiero, Vincenzo, and Nigel South. 1995. *Eurodrugs: Drug Use, Markets and Trafficking in Europe*. London: UCL Press.

Rush, James. 1985. "Opium in Java: A Sinister Friend." *Journal of Asian Studies* 44(3): 549–560.

——. 1991. *Opium to Java*. Ithaca, N.Y.: Cornell University Press.

Rydell, C. Peter, and Susan S. Everingham. 1994. *Controlling Cocaine*. Santa Monica, Calif.: RAND.

Safronov, Rustem. 2002. "Turkmenistan's Niyazov Implicated in Drug Smuggling." *Eurasia Insight* March 29.

Saleh, Jehan. 1956. "Iran Suppresses Opium Production." *Bulletin on Narcotics* 8(3): 1–2.

Samanta, Pranab Dhal. 2002. "Drugs on Our Doorstep." *The Hindu* April 7.

Scheerer, Sebastian. 1981. *Die Genese der Betäubungsmittelgesetze in der Bundesrepublik Deutschland und in den Niederlanden*. Göttingen: Otto Schwarz.

Scherer, Frederic M., and David Ross. 1990. *Industrial Market Structure and Economic Performance*. Boston: Houghton Mifflin.

Schlötzer, Christiane. 2006. Rätselhaft und rücksichtlos: Die PKK is schwer zu fassen. *Süddeustsche Zeitung* April 4: 2.

Schreier, Carsten. 2003. *Drogenszene, Bettelei und Stadtstreichertum im Deutschen Rechtsstaat aus präventiver Sicht*. Ph.D. diss. Humboldt Universität zu Berlin. Also online. Available at www.dissertation.de/FDP/3898256987.pdf. Accessed October 2007.

Senate of Canada Special Committee on Illegal Drugs. 2002. *Cannabis: Our Position for a Canadian Public Policy. Report of the Senate Special Committee on Illegal Drugs*. September. Online. Available at http://www.parl.gc.ca/common/Committee_SenRep.asp?Language=E&Parl=37&Ses=1&comm_id=85. Accessed April 2007.

Senlis Council. 2005. *Feasibility Study on Opium Licensing in Afghanistan for the Production of Morphine and Other Essential Medicines*. Online. Available at www.senliscouncil.net/documents/feasibility_study_conclusions_and_recommendations. Accessed October 2007.

Sharma, Kartikaija. 2000. "States Scam." *The Week* November 12.

Sharma, N. D. 1999. "Opium Factor in Mandsaur." *The Tribunal* September 9.

Shaw, Mark. 2006. "Drug Trafficking and the Development of Organized Crime in Post-Taliban Afghanistan." In *Afghanistan's Drug Industry: Structure, Functioning, Dynamics and Implications for Counter-Narcotics Policy*, ed. Doris Buddenberg and William A. Byrd. New York: UNODC and World Bank, pp. 189–214.

Shcherbakov, Sergei. 2000. *Identifying Challenges Associated with Evaluating Foreign Trade Transactions in Illegal Drug Trafficking*. Paper presented at the 13th meeting of the IMF Committee on Balance of Payments Statistics, Washington, D.C., October 23–27, BOPCOM-00/27.

Shirazi, Habibollah A. 1997. "Political Forces and Their Structures in Tajikistan." *Central Asian Survey* 16(4): 611–262.

Shvaryov, Aleksandr. 2004. ["'Grayhead' Falls From Grace."] *Vremya novostei* August 10: 1–2. In Russian.

Sieber, Ulrich, and Marion Bögel. 1993. *Logistik der Organisierten Kriminalität. Wirtschaftswissenschaftlicher Forschungsansatz und Pilotstudie zur internationalen Kfz-Verschiebung, zur Ausbeutung von Prostitution, zum Menschenhandel und zum illegalen Glücksspiel.* Wiesbaden: Bundeskriminalamt.

Simpson, David. 2002. "In Albania Politics, Are the Changes Skin-Deep?" *The New York Times* November 21: 4.

Singleton, Nicola, Rosemary Murray, and Louise Tinsley. 2006. *Measuring Different Aspects of Problem Drug Use: Methodological Developments.* Online publication 16/06. London: Home Office.

Smith, Martin. 1991. *Burma: Insurgency and the Politics of Ethnicity.* London: Zed.

Smolka, Michael, and Lutz G. Schmidt. 1999. "The Influence of Heroin Dose and Route of Administration on the Severity of the Opiate Withdrawal Syndrome." *Addiction* 94(8): 1191–1198.

SOCA, Serious Organised Crime Agency. 2006. *The United Kingdom Threat Assessment of Serious Organised Crime 2006/7.* Online. Available at http://www.soca.gov.uk/assessPublications/downloads/threat_assess_unclass_250706.pdf. Accessed November 2007.

Spapens, Toine. 2006. *Interactie tussen criminaliteit en opsporing: De gevolgen van opsporingsactiviteiten voor de organisatie en afscherming van xtc-productie en -handel in Nederland.* Antwerp: Intersentia.

Spapens Toine, Henk van de Bunt and Laura Rastovac. 2007. *De wereld achter de wietteelt.* The Hague: Boom Juridische Uitgevers.

Speaker, Susan L. 2001. "'The Struggle of Mankind against Its Deadliest Foe': Themes of Counter-Subversion in Anti-Narcotics Campaigns, 1920–1940." *Journal of Social History* 34(3): 591–610.

Spear, Brit. 2005. "The Early Years of Britain's Drug Situation in Practice: Up to the 1960s." In *Heroin Addiction and "The British System": Understanding the Problem: Policy and the British System,* ed. John Strang and Michael Gossop. London: Routledge, pp. 17–42.

Stares, Paul B. 1996. *Global Habit: The Drug Problem in a Borderless World.* Washington, D.C.: Brookings Institution.

Stiftung Zentrum für Türkeistudien. 2003. *The European Turks: Gross Domestic Product, Working Population, Entrepreneurs and Household Data.* Online. Available at www.tusiad.org.tr/haberler/basin/ab/9.pdf#search=%22european%20turks%22. Accessed October 2006.

Strang, John, and Michael Gossop. 2005. "Misreported and Misunderstood. The 'British System' of Drug Policy." In *Heroin Addiction and "The British System": Understanding the Problem: Policy and the British System,* ed. John Strang and Michael Gossop. London: Routledge, pp. 7–16.

Strang, John, Paul Griffiths, and Michael Gossop. 1997. "Heroin Smoking by 'Chasing the Dragon': Origins and History." *Addiction* 92(6): 673–683.

Strittmatter, Kai. 2004. "Ein Volk auf Entzug." *Süddeutsche Zeitung Magazin.* March 5: 4–13.

Sukhravardy, Nuritdin. 2002. "Heroin Customers: The Double Bottom of the Tajik Diplomacy." *CentrAsia* November 2.

Sullivan, Kevin. 2003. "Citing Corruption, Mexico Shuts Drug Unit: Military Raids Offices in 11 States; 200 Employees Being Questioned." *The Washington Post* January 21: A14.

Sullivan, Kevin, and Mary Jordan. 2005. "Prisoners Undercut Mexican Drug Crackdown: Lenient Penal Policies, Corruption Allow Cartel Leaders to Thrive Behind Bars." *The Washington Post* January 30: A23.

Sweet, Matthew. 2001. *Inventing the Victorians*. London: Faber & Faber.

Szalavitz, Maia. 2005. "Let A Thousand Licensed Poppies Bloom." *The New York Times* July 13: A21.

Taylor, Arnold H. 1969. *American Diplomacy and the Narcotics Traffic, 1900–1939: A Study in International Humanitarian Reforms*. Durham, NC: Duke University Press.

Theodore, Elizabeth, S. 2003. "Summers: The Musical Debuts." *Harvard Crimson* online edition, September 18. Online. Available at www.thecrimson.com/article. aspx?ref=348802. Accessed June 2007.

Thompson, Ginger. 2005a. "Corruption Hampers Mexican Police in Border Drug War." *The New York Times* July 5: A3.

———. 2005b. "Rival Drug Gangs Turn the Streets of Nuevo Laredo into a War Zone." *The New York Times* December 4: A6.

Thompson, Ginger, and James C. McKinley, Jr. 2005. "Mexico's Drug Cartels Wage Fierce Battle for Their Turf." *The New York Times* January 14: A3.

Thompson, Tony. 2002. "Heroin 'Emperor' Brings Terror to UK Streets: Tony Thompson Reports on a Turf War in the Capital and Reveals That Its Trail of Murder and Violence Leads back to the Jail Cell of a Turkish Drug Baron." *The Observer* November 17: 10.

Thoumi, Francisco E. 1995. *Political Economy and Illegal Drugs in Colombia*. Boulder, Colo.: Lynne Rienner.

———. 2003. *Illegal Drugs, Economy and Society in the Andes*. Washington, D.C.: Woodrow Wilson Center.

———. 2005. "Why the Taliban Poppy Ban Was Very Unlikely to Have Been Sustained after a Couple of Years." *International Journal of Drug Policy* 16(2): 108–109.

TI, Transparency International. 2005. *Transparency International Corruption Perception Index 2005*. Online. Available at http://www.transparency.org/policy_research/ surveys_indices/cpi/2005. Accessed April 2007.

Times of Central Asia. 2000. "Tajik Drug Business Grows into Industry." *Times of Central Asia* October 19.

———. 2002. "Former Deputy Defence Minister Charged with Drug Smuggling." *Times of Central Asia* June 14.

Titus, Paul. (ed.). 1996. *Marginality and Modernity: Ethnicity and Change in Post-Colonial Balochistan*. Karachi: Oxford University Press.

Tiwari, Deepak. 2000. "Opium Woman: Femida Berhamuddin Controls Her Uncle's Smuggling Operations." *The Week* September 17.

TNI, Transnational Institute, 2002. *A Failed Balance: Alternative Development and Eradication*. Debate paper no. 4. Amsterdam: Transnational Institute. Also online. Available at http://www.tni.org/detail_pub.phtml?know_id=126&username=guest@ tni.org&password=9999&publish=Y. Accessed March 2007.

———. 2005. *Downward Spiral: Banning Opium in Afghanistan and Burma*. Drugs & Conflict debate paper no. 12. Amsterdam: Transnational Institute. Also online. Available at http://www.tni.org/detail_pub.phtml?know_id=70&username=guest@ tni.org&password=9999&publish=Y. Accessed March 2007.

Torres, Edgar, and Armando Sarmiento. 1998. *Rehenes de la Mafia*. Bogotá: Intemedio.

Townsend, Jacob. 2006. "The Logistics of Opiate Trafficking in Tajikistan, Kyrgyzstan and Kazakhstan." *The China and Eurasia Forum* 69–92.

Tragler, Gernot, Jonathan P. Caulkins, and Gustav Feichtinger. 2001. "Optimal Dynamic Allocation of Treatment and Enforcement in Illicit Drug Control." *Operations Research* 49(3): 352–362.

Treerat, Nualnoi, Nopparit Ananapibut, and Surasak Thamno. 2004. *The Opiate Trade* in Thailand and Myanmar. Report submitted for the project Modeling the World Heroin Market: Assessing the Consequences of Changes in Afghanistan Production. Bangkok. Mimeo.

Tribunale di Milano. 1996. *Sentenza nella causa penale contro Dilek Mustekabi + 16,* Procedimento n. 4280/94. February 28.

Tribunale di Palermo, Ufficio Istruzione Processi Penali. 1985. *Ordinanza-sentenza di rinvio a giudizio nei confronti di Abbate Giovanni + 706.* November 8.

Trocki, Carl. 1999. *Opium, Empire and the Global Political Economy.* London: Routledge.

Tullis, Lamond. 1995. *Unintended Consequences: Illegal Drugs and Drug Policies in Nine Countries.* Boulder, Colo.: Lynne Rienner.

Turkish Daily News. 2000. "Turkish Press Scanner: Godfather Apprehended." *Turkish Daily News.* August 16.

——. 2004a. "Ex-Politician, Full-Time Suspect Strikes Again." *Turkish Daily News* July 22.

——. 2004b. "International Warrant Issued for Former Deputy." *Turkish Daily News* September 11.

——. 2005. "Drug Use by Young People on the Rise." *Turkish Daily News* April 21.

UN Security Council, United Nations Security Council. 2005. *Report of the Secretary-General on the United Nations Interim Administration Mission in Kosovo, S/2005/335.* May 25. Online. Available at http://daccessdds.un.org/doc/UNDOC/GEN/N05/339/18 /PDF/N0533918.pdf?OpenElement. Accessed October 2006.

UNAIDS. Joint United Nations Programme on HIV/AIDS. 2006. *2006 Report on the Global AIDS Epidemic.* Geneva: UNAIDS.

——. 2007. *07 AIDS Epidemic Update.* Geneva: UNAIDS.

UNDCP, United Nations International Drug Control Programme. 1994. *The Illicit Opiate Industry of Pakistan.* Islamabad: UNDCP.

——. 1997. *World Drug Report.* Oxford: Oxford University Press. Also online. Available at http://www.unodc.org/unodc/en/data-and-analysis/WDR.html. Accessed October 2005.

——. 1998a. *Strategic Study #1: Analysis of the Process of Expansion of Opium Poppy Cultivation to New Districts in Afghanistan.* Islamabad: UNDCP.

——. 1998b. *Strategic Study #2: The Dynamics of the Farmgate Opium Trade and the Coping Strategies of Opium Traders.* Islamabad: UNDCP.

——. 1999a. *Strategic Study #3: The Role of Opium as a Source of Informal Credit.* Islamabad: UNDCP.

——. 1999b. *Strategic Study #4: Access to Labour: The Role of Opium in the Livelihood Strategies of Itinerant Harvesters Working in Helmand Province, Afghanistan.* Islamabad: UNDCP.

——. 2001a. *Afghanistan Annual Opium Poppy Survey 2001.* Vienna: UNDCP.

——. 2001b. *Global Impact of the Ban on Opium Production in Afghanistan.* Vienna: UNDCP.

UNDCP ROSA, United Nations International Drug Control Program Regional Office for South Asia. 1998. *South Asia Drug Demand Reduction Report.* New Delhi: UNDCP Regional Office for South Asia.

UNDP, United Nations Development Programme. 2000. *Tajikistan Human and Development Report*. Dushanbe: UNDP. Also online. Available at hdr.undp.org/en/reports/nationalreports/europethecis/tajikistan/tajikistan_2000_en.pdf. Accessed June 2004.

———. 2002b. *Human Development Report 2001: Making New Technologies Work for Human Development*. New York: UNDP.

UNGASS, United Nations General Assembly Special Session. 1998. *Political Declaration of the General Assembly*. A/S-20/4. Online. Available at www.un.org/ga/20special/poldecla.htm. Accessed September 2007.

United Nations. 1949. "Opium Production throughout the World." *Bulletin on Narcotics* 1: 6–38.

———. 1972. *Single Convention on Narcotic Drugs, 1961 as amended by the 1972 Protocol Amending the Single Convention on Narcotic Drugs*. Online. Available at http://www.unodc.org/pdf/convention_1961_en.pdf. Accessed June 2008.

———. 1988. *Convention against the Illicit Traffic in Narcotic Drugs and Psychotropic Substances, 1988*. Online. Available at http://www.unodc.org/pdf/convention_1988_en.pdf. Accessed June 2008.

United Nations, Commission of the European Communities—Eurostat, International Monetary Fund, Organisation for Economic Co-operation and Development, World Bank, 1993. *System of National Accounts 1993*. Brussels/Luxembourg, New York, Paris, Washington, D.C. Online. Available at http://unstats.un.org/unsd/sna1993/toctop.asp. Accessed June 2003.

UNODC, United Nations Office on Drugs and Crime. 2001. *Afghanistan Annual Opium Poppy Survey 2001*. Online. Available at www.unodc.org/pdf/afg/report_2001–10–16_1.pdf.

———. 2002. *Strategic Programme Framework. UN Drug Control Activities in Myanmar*. October. Online. Available at http://www.unodc.org/pdf/myanmar/myanmar_country_profile_spf_2002.pdf. Accessed June 2006.

———. 2003a. *Lao's People Democratic Republic: Country Profile*.Bangkok: UNODC Regional Center for East Asia and the Pacific.

———. 2003b. *Myanmar: Opium Survey 2003*. June. Online. Available at http://www.unodc.org/pdf/publications/myanmar_opium_survey_2003.pdf. Accessed June 2006.

———. 2003c. *The Opium Economy in Afghanistan. An International Problem*. January. Online. Available at http://www.reliefweb.int/library/documents/2003/unodc-afg-31jan.pdf. Accessed June 2006.

———. 2004. *2004 World Drug Report*. Vienna: UNODC. Online. Available at http://www.unodc.org/unodc/en/data-and-analysis/WDR.html. Accessed June 2006.

———. 2005a. *KOWI Papers: Draft Umbrella Document*, May 25.

———. 2005b. *Summary Findings of Opium Trends in Afghanistan, 2005*. September 12. Online. Available at http://www.unodc.org/pdf/afg/2005SummaryFindingsOfOpiumTrendsAfghanistan.pdf. Accessed June 2006.

———. 2005c. *Thematic Evaluation of UNODC Alternative Development Activities*. Vienna: UNODC. Also online. Available at www.unodc.org/pdf/publications/Thematic_eval_AD_Nov05.pdf. Accessed October 2007.

———. 2005d. *World Drug Report*. Vienna: UNODC. Also online. Available at http://www.unodc.org/unodc/en/data-and-analysis/WDR.html. Accessed June 2006.

———. 2006. *World Drug Report*.Vienna: UNODC. Also online. Available at http://www.unodc.org/unodc/en/data-and-analysis/WDR.html. Accessed June 2007.

———. 2007a. *World Drug Report*. Vienna: UNODC. Also online. Available at http://www.unodc.org/unodc/en/data-and-analysis/WDR.html. Accessed August 2007.

UNDOC, United Nations Office on Drugs and Crime. 2007b. *2007 World Drug Report Seizures.* Online. Available at www.unodc.org/pdf/research/wdr07/seizures.pdf. Accessed August 2007.

——. 2008. *World Drug Report.* Vienna: UNODC. Also online. Available at http://www. unodc.org/unodc/en/data-and-analysis/WDR-2008.html. Accessed October 2008.

UNODC Afghanistan. 2003. *Community Drug Profile #5: An Assessment of Problem Drug Use in Kabul City.* July. Online. Available at http://www.unodc.org/pdf/afg/ report_2003–07–31_1.pdf. Accessed August 2004.

UNODC Country Office Colombia. 2003. *Colombia 2003, Country Profile.* Online. Available at http://www.unodc.org/pdf/colombia/Colombia Country Profile version final julio 2003. Accessed June 2004.

UNODC Russian Federation. 2005. *Illicit Drug Trends 2004.* August. Moscow: UNODC Russian Federation.

UNODC and Central Committee for Drug Abuse Control. 2004. *Myanmar Opium Survey 2004.* October. Vienna: UNODC. Also online. Available at http://www.unodc. org/unodc/en/crop-monitoring/previous-surveys.html. Accessed June 2006.

——. 2005. *Myanmar Opium Survey 2005.* November. Vienna: UNODC. Also online. Available at http://www.unodc.org/unodc/en/crop-monitoring/previous-surveys. html. Accessed June 2006.

UNODC and Government of Afghanistan, Counter Narcotics Directorate. 2003. *Afghanistan: Opium Survey 2003.* October. Vienna: UNODC. Also online. Available at http://www.unodc.org/unodc/en/crop-monitoring/previous-surveys.html. Accessed June 2006.

——. 2004. *Afghanistan: Farmers' Intentions Survey 2003–2004.* February. Vienna: UNODC. Also online. Available at http://www.unodc.org/unodc/en/crop-monitoring/ previous-surveys.html. Accessed June 2006.

——. 2005. *Afghanistan: Opium Rapid Assessment Survey.* March. Vienna: UNODC. Also online. Available at http://www.unodc.org/unodc/en/crop-monitoring/ previous-surveys.html. Accessed June 2006.

UNODC and Government of Afghanistan Ministry of Counter Narcotics. 2005. *Afghanistan Drug Use Survey 2005.* November. Online. Available at http://www. unodc.org/pdf/afg/2005AfghanistanDrugUseSurvey.pdf. Accessed January 2006.

UNODC and Ministry of Social Justice and Empowerment, Government of India. 2004. *The Extent, Pattern and Trends of Drug Abuse in India: National Survey.* New Delhi: Ministry of Social Justice and Empowerment, Government of India, and United Nations Office on Drugs and Crime Regional Office for South Asia.

UNODC, Central Committee for Drug Abuse Control, Lao National Commission for Drug Control and Supervision and Office of the Narcotics Control Board. 2007. *Opium Poppy Cultivation in South East Asia: Lao PDR, Myanmar, Thailand.* October. Also online. Available at http://www.unodc.org/pdf/research/icmp/south_ east_asia_report_2007_web.pdf. Accessed March 2008.

UNODC ROSA, United Nations Office on Drugs and Crime Regional Office for South Asia. 2003. *India Country Profile.* New Delhi: UNDCP Regional Office for South Asia.

UNODCCP, United Nations Office for Drug Control and Crime Prevention. *World Drug Report 2000.* Oxford: Oxford University Press. Also online. Available at http:// www.unodc.org/unodc/en/data-and-analysis/WDR.html. Accessed October 2005.

——. 2001. *Global Illicit Drug Trends.* New York: United Nations. Also online. Available at http://www.unodc.org/unodc/en/data-and-analysis/WDR.html. Accessed October 2005.

———. 2002a. *Country Profile Russian Federation*. Moscow: UNODCCP.

———. 2002b. *Drug Abuse in Pakistan: Results from the Year 2000 National Assessment Study*. New York: United Nations.

———. 2002c. *Global Illicit Drug Trends 2002*. New York: UNODCCP.

———. 2002d. *Illicit Drugs Situation in the Regions Neighbouring Afghanistan and the Response of ODCCP*. Vienna: UNODCCP.

UNODCCP Sub-Office in Tajikistan. 2000. *The Drug Trade in Afghanistan and Its Regional Implications: Trafficking Patterns along the Afghan Border with Tajikistan*. Vienna: UNODCCP-ROCA.

Uribe, Sergio. 1997. "Los cultivos ilícitos en Colombia." In *Drogas Ilícitas en Colombia: Su Impacto Económico, Político y Social*, ed. Francisco Thoumi, Sergio Uribe, Ricardo Rocha, Alejandro Reyes, Edgar A. Garzón, Andrés López, Juan G. Tokatlian, and Manuel Hernández. Bogotá: PNUD, Ministerio de la Justicia y del Derecho, Dirección Nacional de Estupefacientes, Editorial Ariel, pp. 35–136.

———. 2004. *Development of the Colombian Heroin Industry: 1990–2003*. Report submitted for the project Modeling the World Heroin Market: Assessing the Consequences of Changes in Afghanistan Production. Bogotá. Mimeo.

U.S. Census Bureau. 2006a. *Historical Estimates of World Population*. Online. Available at www.census.gov/ipc/www/worldhis.html. Accessed April 2007.

———. 2006b. *Total Midyear Population for the World: 1950–2050*. Online. Available at www.census.gov/ipc/www.worldpop.html. Accessed April 12, 2007.

U.S. Department of Agriculture, Economic Research Service. 2008. Data Sets: Commodity and Food Elasticities. Online. Available at www.ers.usda.gov/Data/Elasticities/. Accessed May 2008.

U.S. Department of Justice. 2005. *Eight High-Ranking Leaders of Southeast Asia's Largest Narcotics Trafficking Organization Indicted by a Federal Grand Jury in Brooklyn, New York*. Press release. Online. Available at www.usdoj.gov/usao/nye/pr/2005jan24.htm. Accessed June 2005.

U.S. Department of State, Bureau of International Narcotics and Law Enforcement Affairs. 1999. *International Narcotics Control Strategy Report 1998*. Washington, D.C.: Bureau of International Narcotics and Law Enforcement Affairs, U.S. Department of State. Also online. Available at http://www.state.gov/p/inl/rls/nrcrpt/. Accessed June 2005.

———. 2000. *International Narcotics Control Strategy Report 1999*. Washington, D.C.: Bureau of International Narcotics and Law Enforcement Affairs, U.S. Department of State. Also online. Available at http://www.state.gov/p/inl/rls/nrcrpt/. Accessed June 2005.

———. 2002. *International Narcotics Control Strategy Report, 2001*. Washington, D.C.: Bureau of International Narcotics and Law Enforcement Affairs, U.S. Department of State. Also online. Available at http://www.state.gov/p/inl/rls/nrcrpt/. Accessed June 2005.

———. 2003. *International Narcotics Control Strategy Report, 2002*. Washington, D.C.: Bureau of International Narcotics and Law Enforcement Affairs, U.S. Department of State. Also online. Available at http://www.state.gov/p/inl/rls/nrcrpt/. Accessed June 2005.

———. 2004. *International Narcotics Control Strategy Report, 2003*. Washington, D.C.: Bureau of International Narcotics and Law Enforcement Affairs, U.S. Department of State. Also online. Available at http://www.state.gov/p/inl/rls/nrcrpt/. Accessed June 2005.

———. 2005. *International Narcotics Control Strategy Report, 2005*. Washington, D.C.: Bureau of International Narcotics and Law Enforcement Affairs, U.S. Department of State. Also online. Available at http://www.state.gov/p/inl/rls/nrcrpt/. Accessed June 2005.

———. 2006. *International Narcotics Control Strategy Report, 2006*. Washington, D.C.: Bureau of International Narcotics and Law Enforcement Affairs, U.S. Department of State. Also online. Available at http://www.state.gov/p/inl/rls/nrcrpt/. Accessed June 2007.

———. 2007. *International Narcotics Control Strategy Report*. Washington, D.C.: Bureau of International Narcotics and Law Enforcement Affairs, U.S. Department of State. Also online. Available at http://www.state.gov/p/inl/rls/nrcrpt/. Accessed June 2007.

———. 2008. *International Narcotics Control Strategy Report, 2008*. Washington, DC: Bureau of International Narcotics and Law Enforcement Affairs, U.S. Department of State. Also online. Available at http://www.state.gov/p/inl/rls/nrcrpt/. Accessed June 2008.

U.S. Department of State, Office of the Coordinator for Counterterrorism. 2007. *Country Reports on Terrorism 2006*. Washington, DC: U.S. Department of State. Also online. Available at http://www.state.gov/s/ct/rls/crt/. Accessed March 2008.

U.S. Department of Treasury. 2003. *Fact Sheet: Dawood Ibrahim,* attached to press release "U.S. Designates Dawood Ibrahim as Terrorist Supporter: Indian Crime Lord Has Assisted Al Qaida and Supported Other Terrorists in India," JS 909. October 16.

U.S. House of Representatives, Select Committee on Narcotics Abuse and Control, 1977. *Opium Production, Narcotics Financing, and Trafficking in Southeast Asia*. 95th Congress, 1st Session. Washington, D.C.: U.S. Government Printing Office.

Van Duyne, Petrus C., and Michael Levi. 2005. *Drugs and Money: Managing the Drug Trade and Crime-Money in Europe*. London: Routledge.

Van Ours, Jan C. 1995. "The Price Elasticity of Hard Drugs: The Case of Opium in the Dutch East Indies, 1923–1938." *Journal of Political Economy* 103 (2): 261–279.

Vargas, Ricardo M. (ed.). 1995. *Drogas, Poder y Región en Colombia,* vols. 1 and 2. Bogotá: CINEP.

———. 2005. "Drugs and Armed Conflict in Colombia." In *Trouble in the Triangle: Opium and Conflict in Burma,* ed. Martin Jelsma, Tom Kramer, and Pietje Vervest. Chiang Mai: Silkworms Books, pp. 193–223.

Vargas, Ricardo M., and Jacqueline Barragán. 1995. "Amapola en Colombia: Economía ilegal, violencias e impacto regional." In *Drogas, Poder y Región en Colombia,* vol. 2, ed. Ricardo M. Vargas. Bogota: CINEP.

Vishinsky, K. 1998. *Analysis of the Spread of Psychotropic Substances in Russia and specifically Moscow*. Moscow: Scientific Research Institute of Narcology, Ministry of Health.

Wakabayashi, Bob T. 2000. "From Peril to Profit: Opium in the Late Edo and Meiji Eyes." In *Opium Regimes: China, Britain and Japan, 1839–1952,* ed. Timothy Brook and Bob T. Wakabayashi. Berkeley: University of California Press, pp. 55–77.

Walker, William O. III. 1991. *Opium and Foreign Policy: The Anglo-American Search for Order in Asia, 1912–1954*. Chapel Hill: University of North Carolina Press.

Wang, Yeh-Chien. 1967. "Tu Yueh-Sheng (1888–1951): A Tentative Political Biography." *The Journal of Asian Studies* 26(3): 433–455.

Ward, Christopher, and William Byrd. 2004. *Afghanistan's Opium Drug Economy.* World Bank South Asia Region PREM working paper series report no. SASPR-5. Washington, D.C.: World Bank.

Washington Post, The. 1978. "The Arrest of Jaime Herrera." October 23: A26.

Watson, Paul. 2005. "Afghanistan: A Harvest of Despair." *Los Angeles Times* May 29: A1.

Weatherburn, Don, Craig Jones, Karen Freeman, and Toni Makkai. 2003. "Supply Control and Harm Reduction: Lessons from the Australian Heroin 'Drought.'" *Addiction* 98: 83–91.

Weber, Max. 1969. *The Methodology of the Social Sciences.* Trans. and ed. Edward A. Shils. New York: Free Press.

Weiner, Matt. 2004. *An Afghan 'Narco-State?': Dynamics, Assessment and Security Implications of the Afghan Opium Industry.* Canberra: Strategic and Defence Studies Centre, Australian National University.

Weiner, Tim. 2002. "Mexican Drug Agent Crossed the Line Once Too Often." *The New York Times* February 18: A4.

Weintraub, Peter, and David Lawton. 1978. "Thailand's Drug Trade Tangle." *Far Eastern Economic Review* April 28: 23–27.

Weschke, Eugen, and Karla Heine-Heiß. 1990. *Organisierte Kriminalität als Netzstrukturkriminalität, Teil 1.* Berlin: Fachhochschule für Verwaltung und Rechtspflege.

Westerbaan, Nico. 2004. The View from the Hills: An Interview with Col. Yord Serk. *Irrawaddy* 12(2): 21.

Wetherall, Ben. 2005. "Tajik President Tightens Grip on Power, Opposition Leader Sentenced on Terror Charges." *World Markets Analysis* October 6.

WFP and JICA, World Food Program and Japanese International Cooperation Agency. 2003. *Rapid Need Assessment Mission to Poppy Growing Areas of Kokang and Wa (Myanmar), 20 November to 1 December.*

WHO, World Health Organization. 2002. *World Report on Violence and Health.* Geneva: World Health Organization.

Wise, David, and Thomas B. Ross. 1964. *The Invisible Government.* New York: Random House.

WODC, 2003. *European Sourcebook of Crime and Criminal Justice Statistics—2003.* The Hague: WODC:

Wood, Evan, Jo-Anne Stoltz, Kathy Li, Julio S. G. Monaner, and Thomas Kerr. 2006. "Changes in Canadian Heroin Supply Coinciding with the Australian Heroin Shortage." *Addiction* 101(5): 689–695.

World Bank. 2001. *Brief Overview of Afghanistan's Economy.* World Bank Watching Brief for Afghanistan, October.

——. 2002. *2002 World Development Indicators.* Washington, D.C.: The World Bank.

——. 2004a. *Tajikistan Country Brief 2003.* September. Online. Available at web18. worldbank.org/ECA/eca.nsf/ExtECADocbyUnid/9366132396040B1685256D80005 7B35E?Opendocument. Accessed November 2005.

——. 2004b. *World Development Indicators.* Washington, DC: The World Bank.

Wren, Christopher S. 1998. "Road to Riches Starts in the Golden Triangle." *The New York Times* May 11: 8.

Wright, A. E. 1958. "The Battle against Opium in Iran: A Record of Progress." *Bulletin on Narcotics* X: 8–11.

Zaitch, Damián. 2002. *Trafficking Cocaine: Colombian Drug Entrepreneurs in the Netherlands.* The Hague: Kluwer Law International.

Zaremba, Maciej. 2007. "Wir kamen, sahen und versagten." *Süddeutsche Zeitung Magazin* August 24: 16–25.

Zao Oo. 2003. Throwing Good Money after Bad: Banking Crisis in Burma. Burma Fund policy brief no. 3. Washington, D.C.: Burma Fund.

Zelitchenko, Alexander. 1999. "An Analysis of Drug Trafficking and Use within the Area of the International UN Project 'Osh Knot.'" *The Times of Central Asia* November 18.

———. 2004. *The Afghan Narco-Expansion of 1990.* Bishkek: Continent.

———. n.d. *Red Poppy Flowers of Issik-Kul Lake.* Unpublished document.

Zeller, Tom. 2002. "Of the People, By the Warlords." *The New York Times* November 24: 6.

Zheng, Yangwen. 2005. *The Social Life of Opium in China.* Cambridge: Cambridge University Press.

Zhou, Yongming. 1999. *Anti-Drug Crusades in Twentieth-Century China: Nationalism, Identity and State Building.* Lanham: Rowman and Littlefield.

———. 2000. "Nationalism, Identity and State Building: The Anti Drug Crusade in the People's Republic, 1949–1952." In *Opium Regimes: China, Britain and Japan, 1839–1952,* ed. Timothy Brook and Bob T. Wakabayashi. Berkeley: University of California Press, pp. 380–404.

Zviagelskaya, Irina. 1997. *The Tajik Conflict. Russian Center for Strategic Research and International Studies.* Online. Available at www.ca-c.org/dataeng/st_09_zvjag.shtml. Accessed November 2005.

Index

Page numbers followed by "f" denote figures; "t" denote tables; "n" denote notes